Reprints of Economic Classics

THE PRINCIPLES OF POLITICAL ECONOMY

THE PRINCIPLES OF POLITICAL ECONOMY

BY

HENRY VETHAKE

SECOND EDITION

[1844]

WITH AN ESSAY

HENRY VETHAKE
JACKSONIAN RICARDIAN

By Joseph Dorfman & Rexford G. Tugwell

REPRINTS OF ECONOMIC CLASSICS

AUGUSTUS M. KELLEY · PUBLISHERS

NEW YORK 1971

First Edition 1838

Second Edition 1844

(Philadelphia: J. W. Moore, *No. 138 Chestnut Street*, 1844)

Reprinted 1971 by

AUGUSTUS M. KELLEY · PUBLISHERS

REPRINTS OF ECONOMIC CLASSICS

New York New York 10001

ISBN 0 678 00301 7

LCN 66 21698

Printed in the United States of America
by Sentry Press, New York, N. Y. 10019

HENRY VETHAKE

HENRY VETHAKE

Jacksonian Ricardian *

The influence of David Ricardo on economic thought in the United States of the nineteenth century was enormous. It was felt not only by such native thinkers and teachers as John McVickar, but by most others as well. One of these others, of some importance in the higher learning, was Henry Vethake, who differed in many ways from McVickar but shared with him the Ricardian belief in laissez faire. McVickar was a Whig; Vethake was a Jackson-Van Buren Democrat; but both were free traders. McVickar was an ultra-respectable New York clergyman besides being a professor. Vethake was a professor, but instead of being a clergyman, was an administrator of varied experience in the academic world, his intellectual bent being for mathematics and physical science rather than theology; and, perhaps it should be noted, he was a Presbyterian, not an Episcopalian. Both departed from Ricardian doctrine in certain respects—the American environment had at least some effect—especially in conceptions of public policy.

Perhaps Vethake's admiration for Ricardo was enlarged by the English economist's success in business affairs; at least he spoke of him "as that distinguished political philosopher, statesman and *merchant* who began life with an inconsiderable capital and died worth several millions of dollars." [1] At any

[1] Vethake, "The Distinctive Provinces of the Political Philosopher and the Statesman," *The Merchants' Magazine and Commercial Review*, II (February, 1840), 109–10. Italics are in the original.

* Reprinted from *Early American Policy: Six Columbia Contributors* by Joseph Dorfman and Rexford G. Tugwell [1960] by permission of Columbia University Press.

rate he must be considered a follower of Ricardo, however striking certain of his departures from the received doctrine. Vethake differed in another way from McVickar. He was not of English but of Dutch Calvinist stock. His parents, who originally came from Germany, had been residents in British Guiana at the time of his birth and he had been brought to the United States as a child.[2] In 1804 he entered Columbia College, where his interest in mathematics and natural philosophy (physics) appeared. These were taught by John Kemp, who was also a teacher of geography. The range of subjects—within his major interest—was surprisingly wide; for example, the courses for seniors included the "General Properties of Mathematics; Laws of Motion, Mechanical Powers, Construction of Machines, Hydrostatics, Hydraulics, Pneumatics, Optics, Astronomy and Electricity." [3] He was graduated, eighth in the class of twenty-two, in 1808, and began the study of law. In 1811 he received an M. A. which, in accordance with prevalent practice and following English precedent, was granted as a matter of course three years after receipt of the B. A.[4] The death of Professor Kemp in 1812, after which the college was headed by the eminent Presbyterian minister John M. Mason, opened for Vethake an academic opportunity.[5]

[2] The year of Vethake's birth has heretofore been given as 1790 or 1792, but in the old family Dutch Bible (*Biblia dat is De gantsche H. Schrifture vervattende alle de canonyke boeken des Ouden en des Nieuwen Testaments*, [Haarlem: John Enschede, 1780], given by a descendant to the Columbia University Libraries, there is on the flyleaf, "Frederick Hendrik Vethake; is geborn d. 26 May 1791."

[3] Minutes of the Trustees, April 9, 1789.

[4] Columbia awarded Vethake an LL. D. degree in 1836.

[5] The college trustees ingeniously solved in Mason's case the problem of meeting the requirement of the pre-Revolutionary War grant by Trinity Church that the president be a communicant of the Episcopal church. They chose as president an Episcopalian, but created a more powerful office for Mason, that of provost. After Mason's resignation in 1816 on grounds of ill-health, the office was abolished.

Largely through Mason's efforts, the state legislature in 1814 gave Columbia the land which is now occupied largely by Rockefeller Center and which was then described as "within a few miles of the city." In 1819 the trustees secured the repeal of the provision made by the grant that the college

He was then only twenty-one years old, but he was given a one-year appointment, at a salary of $1,000, to teach the "mathematical and geographical course." [6] In the following year Robert Adrain of Queen's College (now Rutgers) who was one of the leading mathematicians of his day, was made professor of mathematics, and Vethake went to Adrain's old post at Queens. When the professor of classics resigned in 1815 to take a pastorate, Vethake taught his courses for a term. Financial difficulties soon forced the college to suspend activities.[7]

Fortunately for Vethake, the College of New Jersey was having some difficulty in maintaining discipline. In 1817 a

---

must move to the property within twelve years. They argued that the repeal would enable them to make the land productive towards the support of the college and "remedy the want of fellowships on the European plan, and . . . provision for poor and meritorious scholars." (Minutes of the Trustees, Jan. 2, 1817, Feb. 7, 1818.)

[6] Minutes of the Trustees, Aug. 1, 1812.

Vethake in his report of the year's work suggested that his chair should be divided into two—mathematics and natural philosophy, including geography—and be taught by separate professors. The relations between the two areas were close, yet "they are . . . in their nature very distinct and the powers and habits of mind which qualify for eminence in the one are very different in the other. There are very few whose minds are habitually exercised in the rigid and (if I may use the expression) unbending accuracy of mathematical science [who] possess much taste or satisfaction in the experimental investigation of nature's laws." An alternative division, he said, would be for one professor to teach pure mathematics and the parts of natural philosophy which were "least experimental, namely mechanics and astronomy" and another to teach experimental philosophy. This would include geography, hydrostatics, hydrodynamics, pneumatics, electricity, magnetism, galvanism, optics, "and the general outlines of chemistry, particularly the subject of heat." (Vethake's report is in the Columbia University Libraries.)

[7] Vethake's first salary at Queen's was $800 and a house. He received $100 extra for teaching the classics courses; and when the college suspended he was allowed to continue occupying his house. Information is from Rutgers University, Treasurer's Records.

Vethake always retained a warm feeling for the college and, after its permanent revival in 1825, publicly recalled how the trustees and the leading citizens had cordially welcomed him on his arrival and continued to treat him with "a kindliness, a hospitality, and a consideration, not to have been expected by one who had very limited claims to such attentions—attentions deserving of this public acknowledgment." (Vethake, *An Address before the Literary Societies of Rutgers College* [New Brunswick, N.J.: Mosher, 1854], p. 6.)

series of riots occurred, during which, "after fastening the doors of the Tutors and of sundry students, the rioters set fire to the outbuilding in the rear yard and began to ring the College bell, with shouts of fire and rebellion." [8] After the suppression of the riot, when the vice president heard that he "had been sharply criticized by certain trustees following his undignified antics during the riot, he handed in his resignation." Vethake was chosen to teach his courses as professor of mathematics and natural philosophy. In addition to introducing "fluxions"—differential calculus—at the college, he also began giving the seniors lectures on political economy in 1819.[9]

In 1821 an opportunity arose to improve his situation. Dickinson College, in Carlisle, Pennsylvania, after a few years of suspension, was being revived by a grant from the state legislature of $6,000 and, in addition, $2,000 a year for five years. Vethake's old Columbia chief, the Reverend John M. Mason was made principal; [10] and he offered Vethake the professorship of mathematics and natural philosophy.[11] From

[8] John Maclean, *History of the College of New Jersey*, II (Philadelphia: Lippincott, 1877), p. 167; Thomas Jefferson Wertenbaker, *Princeton: 1746–1896* (Princeton: Princeton Univ. Press, 1946), pp. 170–71.

[9] In 1819 Vethake's title became professor of mathematics and mechanical philosophy.

[10] Mason in his inaugural *Address* expressed concern over the lack of "subordination to authority." He said regretfully "that in all the departments of society, from the parental control to that of the government, this is held by our youth in too little esteem . . . Such a temper . . . militates alike against the very constitution of our nature—against the most express commandments of God and against those principles of action, which at all times and in every place, but from peculiar causes, in the present day and in our own country, are necessary to the order of society and the happiness of individuals." A resolution was passed by the trustees at the same time, resolving "that no student shall recite any speech embracing political or national subjects, which might have a tendency in any degree to excite party feelings." (*A Narrative of the Proceedings of the Board of Trustees of Dickinson College from 1821 to 1830* [Carlisle, Penn.: Board of Trustees, 1830], p. 5.)

[11] At a salary of $1,500 and residence. A first offer of $1,250 had been refused.

Besides Vethake, Mason appointed the Reverend Joseph Spencer, who also became the local Episcopal minister, as professor of languages (classics), the start he taught economics to the seniors.[12] The character of Vethake's economics at the time is indicated by the reference to the subject in an oration delivered before the college's two student societies. The speaker, after referring to Political Economy as "the philosophy of national interest and the science of wealth," declared that "the burden of its exposition is the complex harmonies of the association of men." Although in the older works it concerned itself primarily with controversies over the important matter of nomenclature, recent speculation concerned itself more with the no less important aspect of inferring principles "of sound prudential & lucrative policy. It is the associate of the moral science of government, and is emphatically the study for Republics, whose peculiar and consummate aim, & natural beauty, is to unite efficiency with economy, and to whom profuse experiments in finance cannot be allowed." [13]

Another and more direct indication can be got from a letter

---

and the Reverend Alexander McClelland of the Dutch Reformed Church as professor of belles lettres and history of the human mind. In consideration of the Synod of the German Reformed Church establishing its seminary at Carlisle, the principal of the seminary became professor of history and German literature—with house rent paid by Dickinson—and students of the seminary were gratuitously admitted to the lectures on moral philosophy and chemistry.

When Mason resigned on grounds of ill-health he was succeeded by another Presbyterian, the Reverend William Neill, who took charge of the "religious training of the young men in Natural Theology, the Evidences of Christianity, and . . . Bible instruction on the Sabbath." (*Autobiography of William Neill*, ed. J. H. Jones [Philadelphia: Presbyterian Board of Education, 1861], p. 50.)

[12] The trustees' minutes of Dickinson definitely recognized that Vethake was teaching political economy by 1826. In that year they authorized certain theological students being trained in Carlisle "To attend lectures *inter alia* in 'political economy,' " and "Resolved that to the professorship of Mr. Henry Vethake be added that in political economy." (Cited from letter of J. H. Morgan to E. R. A. Seligman in Seligman, "The Early Teaching of Economics in the United States," in *Economic Essays Contributed in Honor of John Bates Clark*, ed. Jacob H. Hollander [New York: Macmillan, 1927], p. 310.) His title became professor of mathematics, political economy, natural and experimental philosophy.

[13] Charles F. Mayer, *The Second Annual Oration, Delivered Before the Belles Lettres and Union Philosophical Societies of Dickinson College* (Carlisle, Penn.: privately printed at the Herald, 1827), p. 8.

from Vethake to Mathew Carey in 1825 asking for statistical information needed to determine the relative costs and benefits of turnpikes, railroads, and canals.

His pragmatic attitude was, for his time, unusual. He expressed little concern as to whether the construction was undertaken by the state, by private capital, or by a mixture; the question of most importance, so long as the costs would be covered by revenue, was which mode of transportation would be cheaper and bring the most pecuniary gain, including a rise in the most important business asset of the day, land. But the letter also illustrates the difficulties, of which McVickar was well aware, of determining the economic desirability of public works in the era of tremendous expansion of transportation.

Carlisle, January 26th, 1825

Sir:

A meeting of the citizens of Cumberland County a few days since was held in Carlisle to consider the propriety of petitioning the Legislature "that during the present session an act may be passed for the construction of a complete water communication for boats of burden between the Susquehannah and the Allegheny, at the expense of the state." The meeting was convened in consequence of a communication made by the acting committee of the "Pennsylvania Society for the Promotion of Internal Improvement" of which committee you are a member, to A. Carothers Esq. of this place. After this communication had been read, a committee, of whom I am one, was appointed to obtain information on the important subject of the proposed canal, and more especially as to its relation to the prosperity of our own county, when the meeting adjourned to the 9th of February. If you could conveniently furnish me before that date with information on the following points you will much oblige me.

1st. In what manner has the construction of the turnpike road from Philada. to Pittsburg and of the Cumberland road to Wheeling, affected the comparative prosperity of the counties more or less remote from Philada. and Baltimore. I wish more particularly to know if it be possible to procure any where a comparative contemporary view of the prices of land for a series of years, before and after the construction of the roads, along these lines of communication.

2dly. The like information respecting the state of New York before, during and after, the construction of the Erie and Champlain canals.

3dly. The comparative expense of the construction of canals and railroads, with a comparative view of the expense of transportation by each.

You must excuse my troubling you with this matter, but I am encouraged to do so by your zeal on the subject of internal improvement, and your readiness to labour for whatever you conceive for the advantage of our country.

I have the honour to be

Very respectfully,

Your obt. servt.

Mathew Carey, Esq. Henry Vethake

P.S. Will you be so good as to give me such information as you conveniently can as to the cost of the Pennsylvania turnpike from Philada. to Pittsburg. The amount of the tolls annually received, & the amount and value of merchandize annually transported.

H.V.[14]

Peace and quiet seem not to have blessed the college. The students are reported to have engaged in "repeated attacks on a Professor's room and rebellions were the order of the day. . . . There were endless restrictions but little liberty." The student disturbances and their handling gave rise to the "final explosion" in 1829. At that time the entire faculty, including the principal, resigned. As a historian of the college wrote: "The faculty members were at odds not only with one another, and probably uncertain about their tenure, but they were at odds with the Board of Trustees," which had taken complete charge of disciplinary matters.[15] The trustees the

[14] Letter is in Historical Society of Pennsylvania collection.

[15] J. H. Morgan, *Dickinson College: The History of One Hundred and Fifty Years, 1783–1933* (Carlisle, Penn.: Dickinson College, 1933), pp. 218, 222). The college was later reopened under Methodist auspices.

following year issued a lengthy statement of the case; this was summarized by a student's letter:

They place the conduct of Doct. Neill, H. Vethake and several of the resigned members of their board in a quite disagreeable point of view, and one which is in no possible way enviable. On the other hand it entirely clears the Presbyterian part of the board of the old charge of sectarianism. McClelland appears, through the whole, to have acted his part as a professor ought to have . . . done, although most outragiously persecuted by the other members of the faculty. It is strongly suspected by some that . . . [Vethake] intends relating the other side of the story and I, for my part, sincerely wish he may, for I think, and indeed am certain, that both he and the old Doctor have been seriously misrepresented." [16]

Vethake, not surprisingly, replied to the trustees' statement. When power was vested in the board, he said, it was inevitably seized with a "spirit of legislation"; frequent legislation would "very naturally create a necessity for more legislation," and at length it was "perpetually meddling with the details of college government so as to reduce the Faculty almost to the condition of mere executive officers." Since the faculty tended to become timid and unwilling to act without consulting the trustees, the number of trustees' meetings increased and so did delays and the inefficiency of operations. Worse, the faculty was without the bond of union, that necessary "esprit de corps," which existed where the faculty was not continually interfered with in its appropriate province.

The major source of the ills, he complained, was the lack of faculty representation. Consequently the board must often legislate in the dark or be guided by frequently inaccurate and prejudiced statements of one of its own members who might be supposed to be better informed on the matter at issue than the others. Also, the trustees made a mystery of their proceedings so far as the faculty was concerned, and thus impaired the

[16] C. C. Hames to H. B. Wright, Dec. 16, 1830. Wyoming Historical and Geological Society collection.

mutual confidence that should exist between them. The remedy was to allow a regular representation of the faculty, at least when the discipline or order of the college was involved.[17]

Vethake seems to have had a certain following. On his return from a visit in 1829–30 to the leading mathematicians and physicists in Prussia, one student wrote to another, "Have you heard . . . how he was welcomed by old and young, large and small, literary and unlearned?" [18]

Meanwhile the College of New Jersey was seeking Vethake's services. Just before he had gone abroad he had refused the offer of its professorship of mathematics, because he felt that the salary of $1,000 and a house was inadequate. On his return, in 1830, he accepted the professorship of natural philosophy at $1,200 and a house. Vethake's courses included history for the sophomores, natural philosophy for the juniors, and natural philosophy, astronomy, and political economy for the seniors. The seniors were so impressed with his course on political economy that at their request his first lecture in January, 1831, was published.[19]

In 1830 Vethake became active in the movement to establish a national university in New York City which would resemble the universities on the Continent. Columbia College was con-

[17] Vethake, *Reply to a "Narrative of the Proceedings of the Board of Trustees of Dickinson College from 1821 to 1830"* (Princeton, N.J.: privately printed, 1830).

[18] J. F. Latta to H. B. Wright, July 19, 1830. Wyoming Historical and Geological Society collection.

[19] Vethake, *An Introductory Lecture on Political Economy, delivered at Nassau Hall, January 31, 1831* (Princeton, N.J.: W. D'Hart, 1831). It was reprinted in the influential free trade organ *Banner of the Constitution*, II (March 9, 1831), 113–15.

The editor of the *Banner*, Condy Raguet, had praised Vethake's performance with the statement that "the reputation of the professor for deep erudition in the mathematics is extensive, and the influence of his name, in connection with the lecture cannot fail to produce an accession of strength and numbers to our [free trade] cause" (*ibid.*, p. 119). The Carlisle *Republican* in an editorial hailed the lecture as presenting "the orthodox system of the economists" founded by Smith and Ricardo (*ibid.*, March 23, 1831).

sidered by critics to be too closely allied to the Episcopal Church, especially the "high church" element, and too much devoted to the classics and the cultivation of "gentlemen." As John McVickar's son and biographer put it, "the closeness . . . and conservative character of her corporation, her high appreciation of classical training and her churchly origins, created enemies and at this time they all combined in the attempt to give her a secondary position, by establishing, in New York, a great university which should unite in itself all the literary and scientific bodies in the city." [20] The chief promoter of the new institution chartered in 1831 was a Columbia trustee, the Reverend James M. Mathews, pastor of the South Dutch Reformed Church, who became its first president with the title of chancellor. The University of the City of New York (later New York University) was, like the recently established University of London, organized as a joint stock corporation with shareholders each entitled to one vote for every $100 of capital stock in choosing a governing board. A $10,000 subscription entitled its purchaser to nominate a professor, subject to the approval of the administration. A somewhat novel feature of the new institution was an embryonic fellowship system, which allowed large subscribers to send a pupil without charge.[21] It was voted that no "one religious denomination should at any time have a majority on the governing board." Albert Gallatin was chosen president of the university council.[22]

A call had been issued to prominent figures in the academic

[20] W. A. McVickar, *The Life of the Reverend John McVickar* (New York: Hurd and Houghton, 1872), p. 122.

[21] *The Constitution and Statutes for the present Government of the University of the City of New York* (New York: Mercein, 1831), pp. 4–5. Vethake attempted to use this provision to enable one of his able College of New Jersey students "to meet the *additional* expense of going to the University (board included) instead of continuing at Princeton." (Letter from Vethake to James M. Mathews, April 16, 1832, in Historical Society of Pennsylvania collection.)

[22] *New York University, 1832:1932*, ed. Theodore F. Jones (New York: New York Univ. Press, 1933), p. 17.

world and in cultural and business affairs to meet in New York City in October, 1830, to give advice on policy for the proposed new university. This three-day Convention of Literary and Scientific Gentlemen was the most impressive assembly of leaders in education that had as yet been held in the United States. Vethake took part. In fact, his was the first main address; and he used it to say that the existing colleges were "for those only who have the wealth necessary to enable them to consume many years of their lives in the exclusive, or nearly the exclusive, occupation of learning two complicated and difficult languages, very imperfectly, in most cases, if at all." He went on to advocate abolition of the Bachelor of Arts degree and the substitution for it of the French practice of alternate degrees, one in literature, which would require Greek and Latin, and one in science, which would not require the two dead languages, but would demand that the student make "a certain progress in *some* of the sciences, as, for example, in mathematics and natural philosophy, or in chemistry and natural history." He suggested that for the class system which was responsible for student solidarity and consequent riots, there should be substituted a curriculum with elective features. If these changes were made, "sons of persons in moderate circumstances—of our farmers and mechanics"—would be induced to enter the colleges; this would uplift the moral tone of the higher institutions of learning. Gallatin expressed a similar view. He thought that the proposed university should be a graduate school and at the same time should "diffuse knowledge and render it more accessible to the community at large." [23]

[23] *Journal of the Proceedings of a Convention of Literary and Scientific Gentlemen* (New York: Jonathan Leavitt and G&C&H Carvill, 1831), pp. 23, 35, 40, 170.

In the course of pointing out the advantages of a great university in New York, George Bancroft, the eminent historian and Jacksonian leader said something of importance:

"On men of letters the great commercial city would exert a favorable

Others expressed the hope that the new institution would give particular attention to many important branches of knowledge to which professorships were almost unknown in American colleges, notably: history, political economy, geography, statistics, agriculture, the principles of legislation, comparative anatomy, and the fine arts.

Vethake, whose address had deeply impressed Mathews, served from the start as a chief aide to the chancellor in the planning of the curricula and the selection of the faculty. It was natural that he should be among the first to be offered a major post. Residence in a big city was a major inducement to Vethake; he expressed a willingness to teach either mathematics or natural philosophy. In conformity with his wishes he was originally to be appointed professor of mechanical philosophy and astronomy. But on second thought he found fault with the title, because its lack of sufficient definiteness made it subject to misapprehension. He informed the chancellor that he intended to teach the various branches of natural philosophy as commonly understood. These were "Statics, Dynamics, Hydrostatics, Hydrodynamics, Pneumatics, Acoustics, Heat, Electricity, including Galvanism, Magnetism, Optics, Astronomy; to which it may be added as a separate branch, Meteorology." But mechanical philosophy was usually restricted to what was called mechanics. This included "Statics, Dynamics, Hydrostatics, Hydrodynamics, Pneumatics," with the latter term embracing the remainder of natural philosophy except astronomy, under the designation of "physics." Consequently, except for its length, the title

influence. The habit of the place is industry; and the literary man, partaking of the general excitement, is led to form habits of profound application. So, too, the varied intercourse with men of all nations, stirs the stagnant pool of superstition and prejudice. The immense movements in business, the daily spectacle of crowds of sail from every quarter of the world, the frequent presence of minds, which have been developed in the most diffused pursuits, or ripened under every sky, gradually yet surely tend to promote intellectual freedom, and to do away that narrow mindedness which is the worst enemy of improvement" (pp. 51–52).

professor of mechanics, physics and astronomy would be satisfactory. The most desirable title would be the one used at London University, that of professor of natural philosophy and astronomy.

Vethake's concern over a precision in the title of his chair involved a much more constructive matter; namely the prevention of a rigid boundary between the fields of chemistry and physics—areas which only recently had been separated and which were both undergoing substantial changes. The matter of title, as he explained, was of no consequence, provided the professor of chemistry who, besides chemistry proper must necessarily give instruction also in heat, electricity, and galvanism, understood that he did not have the exclusive right of instruction in those branches, but that they were equally open to both professors; that is, the professor of chemistry could take up anything in natural philosophy that would make his course more efficient and interesting, and vice versa. Vethake pointed out that he would find himself quite crippled if he could not take up certain aspects of chemistry. Both professors and courses would gain substantially by this mutual borrowing. Students in natural philosophy would be incited to cultivate chemistry, and students in chemistry would find their interest stimulated in natural philosophy. The arrangement would work well at the new university, he predicted, because the prospective professor of chemistry, his friend and colleague at the College of New Jersey, John Torrey, as a man of "liberal views," was taking the same attitude.[24]

Before the title of his chair was definitely settled, however, the authorities found it difficult to fill the chair of mathematics. Vethake searched for an appropriate person; but as he ex-

[24] Letter of Vethake to Mathews, March 10, 1832, in Historical Society of Pennsylvania collection. Torrey's full title was professor of chemistry, mineralogy and botany. He became a famous botanist; Asa Gray was his student and collaborator.

plained to the chancellor, the task was hard, because pedantry was a characteristic failing of mathematicians. Furthermore, there was need to consider the candidate's "religious or moral *tone*." [25]

The result was that when the first professorial appointments were made in July, 1832, he became, at his own suggestion, professor of mathematics and astronomy.[26]

At the same time, Vethake urged that the social sciences be given an important role in the university. He called attention to the need of history, especially the philosophy of history. This, as he put it later, should be "of the kind which has given origin to some of the best histories in the German language, and to which in France, we owe the celebrated work of the eloquent and philosophic Guizot on the civilization of modern Europe." [27] At his suggestion, the authorities also appointed him lecturer on history, and he scheduled a course of public lectures on the French Revolution of 1789.

Vethake was naturally anxious that there be a department of political economy, but barriers to its achievement were more than the difficulty of obtaining sufficient funds. This was indicated by Vethake in his suggestion to the chancellor in August, 1832, that the one temporary exception to the rule that a candidate for the B.A. should be examined by all the professors should be in the case of political economy, for while the subject was to be taught by a "*professor* and not by a lecturer [still] on account of the relation of the subject to party politics, and the peculiar jealousy entertained regarding it by the majority of the community, I would by all

[25] Letter of Vethake to Mathews, February 3, 1832, in Historical Society of Pennsylvania collection.

[26] Letter of Vethake to Mathews, July 3, 1832, in New-York Historical Society collection.

His salary was $2,000 plus the fees from his public lectures. In 1833, "natural philosophy" was added to his teaching load and title.

[27] Vethake, "The Distinctive Provinces of the Political Philosopher and the Statesman," p. 117.

means *not* make that subject essential to the obtaining of a diploma. To do otherwise might make enemies most unnecessarily of some, who might be conciliated by the course suggested." [28]

Vethake was disappointed to find a month later in the announcement of the university's opening that political economy was among those departments that would not be started at present, but would be added shortly.[29] He was concerned that at least a lecture course should be given. He had been asked by the authorities even before the university formally opened to give a series of lectures on "politico-economical subjects." Vethake was glad to give them, but there was then one fly in the ointment. They could only be three or four instead of a full series of ten or twelve if the auditors, he said, were of both sexes. As he informed the authorities, "If *ladies* are expected to be present (which I hope will not be the case) I shall find it very difficult to treat the subject at all on account of the manner in which the theory of *population* is necessarily involved in it." [30]

The problem was solved eventually by having Vethake deliver the lectures in the winter of 1832–33 in the same hall that housed the university, but under the auspices of the New York Young Men's Society. His listeners—like the

[28] Letter of Vethake to Mathews, Aug. 2, 1832, in Historical Society of Pennsylvania collection. Vethake thought the B.A. should be temporarily retained because some able students might otherwise be attracted to the older institution.

[29] Vethake had expected that his friend and fellow Columbia alumnus William Beach Lawrence would be appointed to the professorship. He wrote to Mathews on September 2, 1832 that he had missed, in the chancellor's public announcement, the appointment of Lawrence. (The letter is in the Historical Society of Pennsylvania collection.)

Lawrence had delivered in December, 1831, two lectures on political economy under the auspices of the Mercantile Library Association of the City of New York, whose building, Clinton Hall, was the temporary home of the university. He is discussed in the following essay.

[30] Letter of Vethake to John Delafield, Nov. 15, 1831, in Historical Society of Pennsylvania collection.

seniors of the College of New Jersey—considered them "eloquent and profound" and caused the opening address to be printed.[31]

Soon, however, Vethake was involved in difficulties with the administration. That the university would have a stormy beginning had already been foreshadowed by Gallatin's severance of all connections with it before it actually opened in the fall of 1832. As one of his biographers has put it, Gallatin felt that "none of the goals he thought desirable had been adopted." [32] It had been in operation only a little more than a year when it was "convulsed" by a series of "explosions," involving the faculty and the chancellor. These culminated in the resignation of three of the five members of the regular faculty, including Vethake. They presented their case to the public in a pamphlet. It was their contention that the chancellor had acted as though the university was only an ordinary college and that he viewed its operations from the standpoint of their publicity value. They accused the university council of being "blinded by the fact that the university needed money and that Dr. Mathews was particularly valuable to them as a procurer of that indispensable commodity." [33]

A year later Vethake, so often in disagreement with other

[31] Vethake, *An Introductory Lecture on Political Economy delivered in Clinton Hall before the New York Young Men's Society, Dec. 21, 1832* (New York: Moore, 1833).

[32] Raymond Walters, Jr., *Albert Gallatin: Jeffersonian Financier and Diplomat* (New York: Macmillan, 1957), p. 351.

Walters has pointed out that the university "in the course of several decades, adopted Gallatin's principles of scientific and English instruction to serve the people of many stocks in the city, and of graduate training" (p. 351).

[33] Henry Vethake, John Mulligan, and John Torrey, *An Exposition of the Reasons for the Resignation of Some of the Professors in the University of the City of New York* (New York: Van Norden, 1833).

For an illuminating discussion of the early difficulties of the University see Richard J. Storr, *The Beginnings of Graduate Education in America* (Chicago: Univ. Chicago Press, 1953), pp. 33–43.

administrators, found himself faced with the same difficulties. He had in 1834 been appointed to the presidency of Washington College (now Washington and Lee University), where he also served as rector of the board of trustees and professor of mathematics and moral philosophy. He had obtained the post through some friends at the College of New Jersey.[34]

In his inaugural address, after noting that it was of primary importance that every student should receive religious instruction, he denounced the "rigid conservatism" of instruction and curricula in the colleges. He pointed out that "there are . . . many quack teachers, who . . . have no other guide but a routine to which they were accustomed when they themselves were pupils, or which they have borrowed with little or no alteration from other teachers who have preceded them." He deprecated the characteristic method of having students recite the precise contents of the textbook. This precluded, he said, any questioning, any curiosity, any "spirit of independence" among them. When a vacant professorship occurred in "metaphysical, ethical, and political science it was not surprising that a multitude of candidates presented themselves. And, were we to judge simply from the number and very limited qualifications of the candidates, we would conclude that moral or political philosophy instead of being fitted to exercise to the utmost the powers of the human intellect, is a mere bundle of truisms, obvious to the comprehension of the dullest and most unlettered of men." He noted that "the sciences [both moral and physical] are of course intended to be taught as extensively as the time appropriated to them by the student will admit." He showed

[34] The salary was $1,000 and a house, plus an equal share with the two professors of the tuition fee of thirty dollars a year per student. He was told frankly that the stipend was not as high as at some institutions, "but considering the cheapness of living here, the salubrity of our climate, and some other advantages, the salary will we hope be deemed not inadequate." (Letter from committee to Vethake, Dec. 4, 1834, in Washington and Lee University, Treasurer's Office.)

his respect for economics by referring to it as the "modern science of political economy." [35]

Vethake did little teaching in the moral sciences. As a colleague, the Reverend Henry Ruffner, noted, "very few of the students were sufficiently advanced to study them." Ruffner thought his mathematics teaching was done with much ability, but that he showed some strong peculiarities. At examination he was heard to ask one astonishing question: "If 20 turkeys cost 50 cents apiece, what would be the cost of a hogshead of tobacco?"

Ruffner's son has left an excellent portrait of Vethake during this period. "He was a man of dignified appearance and manners, reserved yet cordial. He was perhaps six feet in height, with somewhat heavy features, round in body and limb without being fleshy." He seemed to be "disconnected from surrounding objects" and given to exercising "his reflective rather than his perceptive faculties. He showed in his teaching that besides a little dry humor now and then he was capable of profound and long sustained trains of thought. This he showed in another way. Chess was the gentleman's game in Lexington." The leading player admitted that Dr. Vethake not only went far beyond him, "but he introduced a style of playing that had not been known here previously, to-wit, the excogitation of a complete campaign down to the checkmate as soon as three or four opening moves had been made." [36]

Vethake soon again had difficulties over discipline. In 1836 a student who had been suspended assaulted him. As he lay prostrate, the professor of chemistry came to his rescue with a pair of tongs. The student summoned a party of his friends

[35] Vethake, *An Address Delivered at His Inauguration, as President of Washington College, Lexington, Virginia, February 21st, 1835* (Lexington, Va.: Baldwin, 1835).

[36] W. H. Ruffner, "The History of Washington College, 1830–1848," in Washington and Lee University, *Historical Papers*, No. 6 (May, 1904), pp. 26–27.

and attempted to waylay the rescuer. The participants were taken to court.

After this experience Vethake began looking for another position. It was necessary. He was recently married. While he was away on a trip in the northwest to see what there might be in the way of lands for speculation, he received notice of his appointment at the University of Pennsylvania as professor of mathematics.[37] There he became known, in the words of the future president, James A. Buchanan, as "one of the most learned, respectable and esteemed citizens of Pennsylvania." [38] In 1846 he was made vice-provost and eight years later provost of the university. In 1855 he exchanged the professorship of mathematics for that of intellectual and moral philosophy.[39]

[37] University of Pennsylvania, Minutes of the Trustees, August 23, 1836. (The minutes are in the secretary's office.) His salary was $2,300.

The chair of mathematics included "Algebra, Geometry, Plane and Spherical, Trigonometry with applications to Surveying, Navigation, etc., General Theory of Equations, Analytical Geometry including Conic Sections. Differential and Integral Calculus [and] Analytical Mechanics."

Vethake had declined the professorship of natural philosophy at Pennsylvania in 1828. (Letter of Vethake to Nicholas Biddle, August 24, 1828, in University of Pennsylvania collection, Office of the Archivist. Biddle was chairman of the Committee of the Trustees that was reorganizing the staff.)

[38] Notation by James A. Buchanan, dated April 27, 1848, on letter from Henry Vethake, dated April 22, to General Henderson, in the Historical Society of Pennsylvania collection.

[39] While provost, Vethake taught seven hours a week, spending four hours with the seniors, and three hours with the juniors. In his major course, the textbooks were *Elements of Mental Philosophy*, by the professor of mental and moral philosophy of Bowdoin College, Thomas C. Upham, and *The Elements of Moral Science*, by Francis Wayland, president of Brown University and author of the most popular treatise on economics, *The Elements of Political Economy*. Vethake used William Paley's *Natural Theology* and *Evidences of Christianity* in his courses on religion. Beginning in 1852, Vethake also lectured on the Constitution of the United States and used as the textbook Mordecai McKinney's *United States Constitutional Manual* (1845); 2d ed., titled *Our Government* (1856).

During his first year as professor of intellectual and moral philosophy, Vethake also taught history via Georg Weber's *Outlines of Universal History* (translation by Francis Bowen of Harvard) and logic from Archbishop Whately's *Elements of Logic;* but on October 9, 1855, the trustees decided that the professor of English language and literature should teach these subjects.

From the beginning of his tenure at Pennsylvania, Vethake lectured on political economy, but it was not until 1854 that the discipline was recognized as a part of the fixed curriculum and subject to examination.[40] The trustees on March 20, 1855, accepted the report of its committee on alterations of the Collegiate Department, which recommended among other things that political economy be a part of a provost's duties. The minutes of the board of trustees, of October 2, specifically speak of "Lectures on Political Economy every Wednesday at the fourth hour." In the minutes of February 5, 1856, political economy acquired more dignity. It was the regular subject for the seniors, and the provost's *The Principles of Political Economy* (1838; 2d edition, 1844), was specified as a text. This, like the manuals prepared by McVickar, followed in general the British classical school, but was more comprehensive and systematic, so much so that one college acquaintance was led to say that it was "better suited to interest political economists than college students." [41]

Vethake insisted that he did not treat political economy as being a "science only of hypothetical description," without any "necessary connection with . . . public affairs." The science included "the laws which regulate the production, distribution, and consumption of wealth"; in order to ascertain what course individuals and government should pursue or avoid in disposing of the wealth under their control, so as to maximize the happiness of mankind.

Vethake in his published introductory lectures had already elaborated on methodological issues. In his New York lecture, following a Newtonian model, he explained that to achieve

[40] Printed circular letter, University of Pennsylvania, Department of Arts and Letters, Dec. 13, 1854, addressed to Committee to Attend the Examination. Copy in minutes of the faculty, in the office of the archivist, University of Pennsylvania.

[41] W. H. Ruffner, "The History of Washington College, 1830–1848," p. 25.

a perfect theory in science, "we should know first all the causes which actually conspire to produce the phenomena to be explained," and second, "we should be able to determine accurately the effect produced by each separate and independent cause." Thereby prediction was possible. But the sciences centering in the human mind generally lack the necessary exact information and must often deal with probabilities, sometimes slight ones.

He cited three barriers to the progress of political economy even though its practitioners might possess an unquenchable love of truth: (1) the influence of their feelings and motivations in diverting them from properly estimating the relative importance of the manifold considerations involved in the phenomena; (2) the "undue weight attached by the mind to arguments that from the circumstance in which the individual is placed, are more frequently the object of attention than others, perhaps of equal comparative moment"; (3) the vagueness and ambiguity of language used in discussing the subject, which often led to confused and circular speculations.

Despite its limitations, continued Vethake, political economy contained the promise inherent in every science of a cumulative development. "Those limits which at one period task the power of the strongest minds for their discussion constitute in a subsequent age the inheritance of all, and come to be regarded . . . as so many elementary steps to a further advance, . . ."

In his published lecture at the College of New Jersey especially he had sought to overcome the suspicions directed against this new science and to show its usefulness to clergymen, lawyers, merchants, legislators, and statesmen. He recognized and countered several familiar criticisms: that political economists did not agree on the fundamental terms; that the study was new, metaphysical, and abstract; that its adepts were theorists with little practical sense; and that its conclusions conflicted with the precepts of religion, in particular with "respect to pauperism and its relief."

He felt it necessary to meet the argument that political economists were unnecessary since "nations have prospered from the beginning of time to the present" without their assistance, and that anyway their conclusions ran contrary to the wisdom of the ages. His answer was this:

> Now as regards the setting up of his [the political economist's] conclusions in opposition to the wisdom of the ages, everyone who has ever been guilty of expressing an original thought has done the same thing, and it is only by such "setting up" that there has been . . . an improvement in the condition of mankind, physical, social, moral or political.

He argued further that since other changes that were continually occurring were acknowledged to be beneficial,

> why should the changes proposed by the political economist alone be considered injurious to society? And without any mention of nations which, instead of advancing in prosperity without the aid of political economy, have declined without the like aid, are we to take for granted *a priori* that because a society enjoys a certain degree of prosperity, the counsels of the political economist would have no influence to augment that prosperity? The causes that conspire to produce the actual condition of a people, are manifold, some of them operating advantageously, and others disadvantageously. Will not, then, the science that comprehends within its scope the discovery of these causes, together with the means of giving additional activity to the former description of them, and of removing or weakening the energy of the latter, have a natural tendency in favor of the public welfare? . . . National prosperity, as the expression is generally employed, is perfectly consistent with a vast amount of misery. The condition of the great majority of the people, for example, in many European countries, which no one hesitates to denominate prosperous, cries aloud for improvement; and such improvement . . . is one of the principal objects of political economy.

He felt the need of empirical research throughout the economic world and made a contribution by editing an American version of McCulloch's *Dictionary, Practical, Theoretical and Historical, of Commerce and Commercial Navigation* (1839). His preface stated that "there is, generally speaking, an extreme difficulty in the United States of procuring statistical information, which may be depended on for its accuracy."

Vethake's *Principles of Political Economy* began with a comprehensive discussion of the theory of value. His sophisticated analysis of the mechanics of supply and demand in the determination of the exchange value of a commodity has a modern ring. He defined the supply of a commodity as

> the quantity of it which comes into the possession of the sellers and is offered by them for sale, during a given portion of time. This must be distinguished from the amount or stock of it [the commodity] which the sellers may think it for their advantage to keep on hand, in order to atttract purchasers to their respective stores or warehouses. . . . The demand is to be estimated by the number of offers to purchase made in a given time, at any given rate, and when more offers are made to purchase a commodity at its existing price than before, the demand is said to have increased, while the contrary will take place when the number of similar offers is diminished.

He pointed out that "in like manner, the demand for money is correctly said to become greater when people generally are more disposed than they previously were to retain it in their possession for future use." He examined in succession "the different modes in which variations in the relation between the supply of, and the demand for, commodities, can influence their prices." In the case of demand for a commodity remaining the same, but supply becoming more abundant, sellers must lower the price to avoid an accumulation of stock, which would be so much "dead and unprofitable capital." Many previous purchasers would buy larger quantities; and some who had refrained from buying would now become purchasers. The price would cease to fall when the "quantity disposed of is just equal to the supply."

If supply is reduced, while demand remains the same, "the interest of sellers will prompt them to raise its price, until in consequence of the corresponding diminution of the amount of sales, the quantity disposed of will . . . be just equal to the diminished supply."

In the case of the supply remaining the same, with increased demand, Vethake pointed out that

> we can suppose that an increase of demand to arise, either from a change in the fashions of the day, or from some new use to which the article in question is capable of being applied. But whatever the occasion of it may be, the sellers will be induced to raise prices; for by doing so, while they make greater profits, they can at the same time, dispose of the whole supply.

Last, he explained that a "diminution of demand" would obviously produce an effect directly opposite to that resulting from an increase of demand.

He also noted that prices were affected not only by actual

> variations in the rates of supply and demand but also by every expectation of the imminence of such variations at some future time. . . . Every expected future change in the rate of supply or demand will have an influence on present prices, so much the less in proportion to the *remoteness of the expectation*. . . . The degree, too, of that influence will depend, in some measure, on the *nature of the commodity*.

Notable was the inclusion of a chapter on "Effects of Monopolies on Prices." [42]

[42] Vethake did not make explicit use of mathematical economics; but he was a mathematician and was well acquainted with the works of men who were prominent in the development of that area. His library contained, e.g., Cournot, *Traité élementaire de la theorie des fonctions* and Charles Ellet, *Essay on the Laws of Trade*. Evidencing Vethake's interests in economics beyond the familiar standard authors was his possession of such

There was a sharp questioning of the doctrine, identified with Ricardo, that the price of a commodity was in proportion to the "amount of *labour* necessary from first to last to produce it." Since the theory was a "favorite one with some political economists of the highest order" it was worthy of examination, but it seemed to Vethake that no significant practical consequences depended upon its validity. The other element determining price, besides the quantity of labor in producing a commodity, was the "time that elapses from the application of the several portions of labour until the production of it is in its complete state." He conceded, however, that the prices of goods were more frequently lowered by a reduction of the quantity of labor necessary for their production, or

> what is the same thing, by a given quantity of labor having been rendered more productive, than by a diminution of the time required in production. Improvements of the latter description we know from experience to be confined within comparatively very narrow limits; while, on the other hand, improvements of a labor-saving nature have been introduced more especially in our own age, with extraordinary rapidity, and to a prodigious extent. Hence I would not object to the language of those writers who, when speaking generally, regard all improvements in the arts as resulting from a greater productiveness of labor.

Vethake most strongly and systematically attacked the view of the British classical economists, that only the labor directly applied to the production of material commodities should be classified as productive; in fact, he did this so

books as Karl H. Rau, *Finanzwissenschaft;* Simonde de Sismondi, *Nouveaux principes d'économie politique,* P. J. Proudhon, *Système des contradictions économiques, ou philosophie de la misère;* H. D. Macleod, *The Theory and Practice of Banking;* Thomas Hodgskin, *Popular Political Economy.* (*Catalogue of the Valuable Private Library of Henry Vethake to be sold at Auction . . . February 26, 1872, and following day by Bangs, Merwin & Co., New York, Charles C. Shelley, Printer.*)

For an interesting, recent account of Rau, see Z. Clark Dickinson, "The Library and Works of Karl Heinrich Rau," *Zeitschrift für die Staatswissenschaft,* Band 114, Heft 4 (1958), pp. 577–93.

forcefully that one of his former Dickinson students, the prominent minister the Reverend George W. Bethune, exclaimed in a public address at Pennsylvania: "God bless him for rescuing the physician, the jurist, the divine, the man of letters, and the man of science, out of the same category with jugglers and opera dancers, where previous economists had placed us as unproductive consumers." [43]

Vethake agreed that there could be "unproductive *consumption*" in the sense of wealth not designed for use as capital, but there could be no unproductive labor except when more labor than necessary was used to produce a particular good or when more of a commodity was produced than was required by "the comparative wants of the community." Whether the product be material or immaterial, the labor is productive, for the "*ultimate* product" of both is "*agreeable sensations*" of consumption. He thought that if the political economist succeeded in banishing from popular language such phrases as "the productive classes and the unproductive classes" the result would be a great political and moral advantage; it would be the most effective way of preventing "the 'workmen' . . . from esteeming themselves to be the only *useful* portion of a society."

He believed that "free competition between employers and employed" was an essential element of that "natural course of things" which was most beneficial to the interest of both rich and poor. Accordingly, he held the customary view that "trades' unions" were an "unmixed evil." At best they could succeed only temporarily, since their success would retard the rate of capital accumulation and this would be "accompanied by a less rapid increase of population and a diminution of the rate of wages." Similarly, Vethake gravely doubted that the adult laborer would benefit from a legis-

[43] *An Address Before the Philomathean Society of the University of Pennsylvania* (Philadelphia: John C. Clark, 1840), p. 24.

lative reduction of the work day. The leisure time to which he was not accustomed might "contribute to deteriorate instead of improving his condition, by being spent as often in dissipation and vice, as in the business of acquiring knowledge or exercising his mental faculties."

In the question of relief to the unemployed Vethake held views that were somewhat in advance of dominant opinion. These he had originally expressed in an essay which was designed to show the usefulness of political economy to the ministry.[44] He had begun with a radical thesis. "Improvements in machinery, and in the various arts of life," he said, "seem everywhere—under differing forms of government, and different modes of administration—to have been chiefly instrumental in improving the condition of the already more privileged and prosperous classes of society." But this situation was neither the exclusive consequence of vicious political institutions, nor the inevitable lot of humanity. The explanation lay in moral causes: the lack of foresight, thrift, and prudence, which resulted in an undue increase of population. Here, following Malthus, and casting the inquiry into mathematical form, he began with "Let us now suppose the population to be on the increase." The answer was to retard the increase by "all *proper* means," that is, the measures taken should voluntary. But Vethake differed from Malthus in favoring public poor relief.

There are those . . . who have been led to proscribe, as it were the wretchedness around them, and to look upon him who is reduced to beggary, very much in the light of one whose employment is to prepare the way for the reduction of many others . . . to the same wretched condition with themselves, and who should

[44] "An Essay on the Moral Relations of Political Economy" in Presbyterian Church in the United States, Board of Education, *Annual 1835*, ed. John Breckenridge (Philadelphia: privately printed, 1835), pp. 117, 143. Breckenridge, who was also recording secretary of the board, had been a student of Vethake at the College of New Jersey.

be dismissed without ceremony on that account, as *hostis humani generis.*

However, it was necessary to help those who "from infirmities, old age, or extreme youth, are unable to gain a livelihood, and such of the able-bodied labourers as having been thrown out of employment, cannot readily find employment again." He granted that such aid weakened the motive for the accumulation of wealth, but in the choice of evils people could not "put aside the sympathies of their nature or the precepts of the Bible."

For the involuntarily unemployed, Vethake proposed that work be provided in workhouses, or in their own homes, every such person to receive "less than the ordinary rate of wages, or what amounts to the same thing, . . . being systematically rendered less comfortable than . . . the independent labourer."

Vethake was among the first American economists to discuss systematically the economic effects of immigration. Immigrants of superior intelligence, or skill in any of the arts, or any superior qualifications were, he granted, a national gain. Other immigrant labor would not be a national benefit, if it did not bring capital sufficient for the employment of labor to an equal extent with the labor which it added to the existing working force, for the rate of wages would fall.

Speaking of government aid to religion, Vethake asserted that religion was the one great exception to the doctrine that what was, generally speaking, the duty of an individual in reference to the national welfare was also the duty of the government. "We are unanimous in thinking that the cause of religion is impaired . . . by an alliance with men in power, and that an entire equality of privileges on the part of the different religious sects [is best adapted] . . . to turn them from vain speculations and fruitless controversies with each other to the exercise of a practical piety."

It was different with education. Legislative appropriations for the common schools were proper in order that children might be prepared to become useful citizens, and public money should also be given to colleges and universities. Opponents of public aid for higher education, he pointed out, contended that since colleges were places for the education of the rich, the rich should bear the entire cost. There was a ready remedy: increase the public contribution to the institutions of higher learning. This would enable them to provide training at comparatively small expense. Since the public contribution would make possible a greater number of highly educated people, a taste for knowledge would be more surely and rapidly transmitted through the successive gradations of society. The resulting rise in the character of the laborer would increase his command over luxuries and necessaries. Similarly, there ought to be public support for science, literature, and the fine arts, and especially for the "useful arts" (which he felt was a misnomer since the "fine arts" were equally useful).

The ultimate justification for government aid for these "intellectual products" was that people could not estimate as accurately their relative advantages as they could material products, and if they had to depend on a "pre-existing demand," mankind would advance very slowly, if at all.

Government regulations to prevent persons not properly qualified from belonging to any of the learned professions, or from engaging in any other employment, should gradually disappear. They were based on the supposition that a "considerable portion of the community are not sufficiently well informed to be able to form a proper judgment concerning the qualifications of the professional man, or other *labourers*, for whose services he may be disposed to apply." Vethake predicted that, with the diffusion of knowledge, first one, and then another, of these restraints could be removed to the public advantage.

A class of government interferences with men's liberty of action was fortunately on its way out. This included government inspection of the quality of certain goods and the restriction of transactions in certain commodities to particular times and places. These annoyances to both buyer and seller were unaccompanied by compensatory advantages, and served merely to supply the occasion of "creating a number of offices for partisans or creatures of the administration."

But Vethake approved state regulation of railroad (and also canal) rates. Such enterprises were either legal or *de facto* monopolies. An existing railroad could prevent the rise of a competitor by virtue of its possession of the field. Should news of its extraordinary profits lead capitalists to consider promoting a competing enterprise, the old company could often postpone or even prevent its construction, by temporarily lowering the rates. The railroads should be built by private individuals or companies, under legislative authority; the rates should be fixed by government at a level that on the one hand would not raise undue obstacles to the "progress of improvement, and, on the other, secure the country the benefit of an interested agency in the superintendence of that progress, without making too great a sacrifice to the grasping spirit of monopoly"; but at the end of a given period the public should acquire the property at "original cost, or at any other stipulated price."

He felt that the law on the subject should be as general as possible in order to provide the maximum degree of impartiality toward every individual and every district of a country, both as to benefits rendered and as to damages to property inevitably suffered. He suggested that a "tribunal" should be established to decide on the expediency of proposed roads or canals. The commission would be guided by principles formulated by the legislature with the objective of determining how far the public good, viewed on the most extensive scale, justified an interference with private property without prior consent of the owner.

In the case of the post office, Vethake made a modification. After warning that a government should never view it as a source of revenue, he added: "I might, perhaps, with propriety, go even farther, and maintain the expediency, in so far as newspapers and periodicals are concerned, of making some *sacrifice* to promote by their circulation the diffusion of knowledge, political and literary, among the great body of a people."

Vethake devoted much more space to taxation than was customary. He thought that in principle much could be said for the view that the first source of taxation should be rent "wherever this may be paid, be it in agriculture, manufactures, or commerce; or I may say simply a tax upon the rent of *land;* considering land . . . as the representative of all the situations or sites in which there is a return of rent, to the proprietor, over and above the ordinary profits of the capital invested by him." Before any other taxes were levied, according to this principle, this source should be fully exhausted. Such a tax, he pointed out, was justified on the Ricardian doctrine that rent was conferred "*gratuitously* on the owners of the land" and that the owners could almost always calculate upon obtaining a continually increasing revenue with the country's growth in wealth and population, "and all the while without any sacrifice on their part." But there were insuperable objections, also Ricardian, to be made on grounds of both practice and equity. It was impossible to distinguish in practice between rent and profits (which included interest), especially in agriculture. Second, such a practice would be equitable only if it had been enforced in a country from its original settlement, for then every person who at any time possessed the land would know that it would now yield greater return than the ordinary profit of the capital he invested in it.

But in the actual state of things the case is very different. The possession of lands of a country has been passing, it may be for many centuries, with more or less frequency, from individual to individual, every new purchaser having as entire a reliance on the secure enjoyment of the produce, or advantages generally to be derived from it, as he could possibly have in the possession of any other kind of property. Hence . . . it would be quite as unjust, and therefore inexpedient, to tax exclusively or in an extraordinary degree the owners of the soil, as it would be to tax exclusively or in an extraordinary degree any other class of the community.

Vethake expressed qualified sympathy for an inheritance tax, but more enthusiasm for a tax on collateral inheritance. The best tax would be a uniform direct tax on property. Next would be an income tax, but this was less desirable than a property tax because the incomes of individuals could not be estimated as accurately as their property "or the amount of what they are at any time worth." Such a tax on every man's property in the same proportion "would be a refinement on the doctrines of free trade. It would be proclaiming to the world that the government is in no case instituted for the purpose of discriminating between the different classes of society, according as they are rich or as they are poor; and that where the public good requires a certain amount of the wealth produced to be taken by the government, every portion of it should be affected exactly in the same way as if the productiveness of labor were proportionally diminished." He was aware of the view that the tax should be progressive rather than proportional; for example, that "a man owning property to the value of $100 is less able to bear the loss of a dollar than another worth $100,000 is able to bear the loss of $1,000; and that to tax them proportionally is therefore in fact to do injustice to the former." But he thought that the advantage of a proportional property tax in reducing much of the jealousy between the rich and the poor overbalanced any "temporary inconvenience." In fact, a progressive tax would be inexpedient and unjust: for government to take from the wealthy more than their proportional share meant that government would be sitting in judgment on the distribution of wealth, and determining at pleasure how much of it should belong to the rich and poor. Vethake, like Jefferson, contended that governments "travel out of their province" and invade the right of property when they interfere with the distribution of wealth. Taxation of the wealthy, that is, depriving them of their property, should be done only "when it can be shown to be ultimately advantageous to the rich themselves, to an extent more than equivalent to the loss incurred by them in the first instance." On this basis, interestingly enough, he thought that a case might be made for factory legislation for children. As the "general principles of taxation," Vethake laid down that "the amount of taxation should be as small as is possible, consistent with a due regard to the interests for the protection and promotion of which governments are instituted. . . . The next general principle . . . is that, other circumstances being the same, it is desirable the taxes imposed should be so distributed as to give occasion to as few transfers of capital as possible. . . . Another principle, closely connected with the preceding, is, *caeteris paribus*, that an old tax is preferable to a new one. . . ."

"A tax which will have the effect of lowering the profits received in a branch of industry where the circulating predominates over the fixed portion of the capital invested, is preferable to one which will diminish the profits of capital where this is in a greater degree fixed than circulating. The truth of this proposition follows necessarily from the greater facility, generally speaking, of transferring circulating than fixed capital. Taxes should be imposed rather on a commodity which is prepared for *final* consumption than upon one which is in any degree the material on which labour is still further exerted; rather also upon such objects as cannot easily, on account of their possessing a great value in proportion to their bulk, or for any other reason, be subtracted from the operation of the taxes; and they should be imposed with a view to readiness and economy of collection." [45]

Vethake's views on a public debt were, like McVickar's, hardly the standard Ricardian views. He complained that the supposed evil of a public debt was the subject of as much vague and unnecessary declamation as any other important point of the science: "The evil is often very much exaggerated, while it is sometimes entirely misconceived." The amount of damage depended on the degree to which the borrowed money was unproductively expended. So far as the proceeds were properly expended, as for "national defense or other purposes of public utility," the expenditure was a national good, just as was an individual's debt which enabled him to reap a gain in excess of the inconvenience of paying interest.

To redeem the national debt would not remedy the unproductive expenditure of any portion of the borrowed

[45] Vethake's specific proposals in taxation accorded with those of free traders in general, and were well expressed in the article on "Political Economy" appearing in the opening issue (January, 1833) of the famous New York literary organ, *The Knickerbocker*. The writer offered three alternative methods of providing revenue for the federal government. First, it could be done through the proceeds from the public lands which had been ceded by older states for the support of the federal government. The writer suggested that those lands with "better husbandry may be sold or farmed out," so as to obtain at all times sufficient revenue. The other possibilities were "direct taxation bearing on all the products of industry throughout the country," or a ten percent ad valorem duty on all imports.

The editor stated that "we shall be happy, in the existing curiosity upon the subject of political economy, to contribute all in our power toward arriving at sound principles, by inviting those skilled in 'The New Science,' to unfold their different views in our pages."

money. If the holders of the debt are residents, as in the case of a domestically held debt, redemption would

be equivalent simply to a transfer of the amount of the debt from the pockets of the community in general to those of the creditors; the community, on the other hand, being relieved, in time to come, from the payment of the interest. But to possess a given portion of wealth and to pay the interest upon it, is here manifestly the same thing, in reference to the country regarded as a whole, as to part with that wealth and to be relieved from the payment of the interest.

The only economic gain from redemption of the public debt was merely the avoidance of the cost involved in collecting taxes for interest payments. He granted the moral effect of repayment in confirming the public credit, and the impression it produced on other nations of the magnitude of the national resources.

On the tariff, at that time so important an issue, Vethake had been politically active, especially as a delegate to the great Free Trade Convention of 1831 in Philadelphia, in urging a reduction of duties.[46] He was in principle a free trader, but he recognized a number of temporary exceptions or modifications. The relevant ones in the circumstances of an agricultural country, especially one continually spreading itself over a vast wilderness, were: (1) The introduction of manufactures, even at the immediate national sacrifice implied by tariff duties or bounties, would, by furnishing a greater diversity of occupations, be favorable to the development by the people of greater intellectual and therefore ultimately of greater physical powers. Every individual could then more readily find an occupation adapted to his talents;

[46] Albert Gallatin, who was chairman of the Free Trade Convention, prepared its *Memorial* (1832) to Congress. It proposed that the duties be so reduced as to leave, after the extinguishment of the public debt, only "that amount of revenue which may be necessary to meet the ordinary exigencies of the Government." The average rate, it was held, should be under twenty percent.

and "inventions" in the various arts would be made more rapidly, because "opportunity would be afforded of comparing together, a greater number of the processes actually employed in them"; (2) The population of a country might be diffused over too great an area, when compared with its numbers, and thus be subject to a considerable moral disadvantage. "A greater proportion of the people must then be almost necessarily destitute of the means of education as well as the services of religion, or must possess them to a diminished extent."

There were offsets to these advantages. They were presented with some novel Ricardian twists, going beyond the tariff itself.

> Although . . . every occupation is equally advantageous on the average, to both the capitalists and the labourers concerned—and therefore to the country in general, *insofar as the capitalists and labourers are capable of appreciating the various circumstances of advantage or disadvantage connected with it,*—it is likewise true that men are apt in most cases to exaggerate the prospects of advantage, and to do the reverse of this in reference to those of disadvantage. . . . At every period of life, we perceive individuals speculating in lotteries, in the stocks, and in property of every description, on the same principle; even with a full knowledge of the chances of success being against them, everyone looks with a more or less sanguine expectation to a prosperous result.

Thus capital and labor, relatively speaking, were drawn more to occupations in which the value of the products fluctuated most. In other words, occupations producing luxuries would be more crowded than those producing necessities; manufactures consequently would be more attractive than agriculture.

Another closely related disadvantage of manufacturing was the "sudden declension" to which many of its branches were subject, because of the "diminution of demand"—a reduction that might arise from a change in fashions. This frequently threw a large number of laborers out of employment, who would be forced at least for a time to be content with a reduced standard of living. The lowering of their ideas of a competent livelihood might tend to lead to a permanently degraded condition. This reenforced the arguments for not encouraging manufactures by legislation, before the arrival of "the natural period of their introduction."

Economists were agreed, he said, that the national welfare required that industries called into existence by war, should be given protection, if necessary, in peace time, as long as the threat of war was serious. It would be expedient, he argued, for government to impose a tariff for "the purpose of giving greater stability to the employment of capital." After considering the future prospects of the country in the light of past experiences, and surveying existing international relations, he thought that a tariff of five to ten percent would be reasonable.

Moderate protectionists felt that these views provided a common ground from which both the protectionists and the free traders might start. As the reviewer in the protectionist *North American Review* explained, Vethake

> is in favor of duties . . . sufficient to give stability to the national industry, so that it may not be alternately established and taken up on the succession of war and peace; and he thinks that if a discrimination is made in laying duties, it ought to be made so as to favor the production of articles necessary for national defense.[47]

Both *The North American Review* and the free-trade *New York Review* criticized his acceptance of the Malthusian doctrine of population as not appropriate to America's present condition, but their major criticism was directed to his monetary views.

Vethake agreed in general with the exponents of laissez

[47] "Vethake's Political Economy," *The North American Review*, XLVII (July, 1838), 248.

faire in holding that banks, by their power to expand and control currency, were the chief source of panics and depressions. When the circulating medium was expanded beyond its ordinary amount, "or average or usual state," the merchants not only could punctually pay their debts, but would also be prompt to make new purchases. Relying on the continuance of this state of things, they would extend their credit farther than they were accustomed to do. If the expansion should go on for a time they would be enabled by the corresponding rise of prices to make large profits; "and speculations generally, by whomsoever made and of whatever kind, will eventuate successfully." But reaction was inevitable. In the absence of other causes, the mere increase in the circulating medium would soon bring a contraction; for the rise in prices would result in larger imports and reduced exports; specie would be demanded from the banks to meet the balance, and the banks would be forced to curtail discounts. Money would become less abundant, and therefore more difficult to obtain. But merchants, especially, must obtain funds to meet contracts or suffer the penalty "attached to a failure." Some might be able to meet their engagements by paying high interest for loans, but many others would become bankrupt. "Those individuals who have been relying upon the receipt of the money due to them by others, and who have failed to receive such payment, will in their turn, very frequently, be prevented, in consequence, from paying with puntuality what they themselves owe. The distress . . . will thus be extended through the various ramifications of society, and will be everywhere more or less intensely felt, according to the magnitude of the *disturbance* to which the currency of the country has been subject."

After pointing out that the evils of a contraction of the

currency considerably overbalanced the "advantages or seeming advantages" of the previous expansion, he commented, "I must not forget to add the diminished production which must ensue from the greater number of persons who, at every period of this kind, are thrown out of employment altogether, or are only partially employed."

Whereas in the contraction the wage earners suffered from unemployment, in the expansion they suffered from the lag of wages. "A customary rate of wages, comes, indeed, to be paid in every place and in every employment; which, *because it is a customary rate*, is only slowly alterable."

On monetary policy however, Vethake took a "Jacksonian" position or, more precisely, a modification of the position of Jackson's heir and successor, Martin Van Buren. Like McVickar, he held that there should be only one issuer of paper money, so as to prevent monetary panics—"periodical convulsions"—but, unlike McVickar, he proposed that this power be entrusted not to a privately controlled national bank or national banking system, but to the general government. It would issue non-interest-bearing treasury notes or drafts to the public creditors who would have the option of receiving "hard money" or notes, and the notes would be receivable in payment of taxes.

Until these reforms were achieved, Vethake held, the usury laws should not be completely repealed. He agreed that since there should be "a free trade in money as in . . . every other commodity," all usury laws in principle should be eliminated, but he opposed "absolute repeal, so long as a limited number of banking institutions exist in a country, possessing peculiar privileges, and capable of combining together to diminish unexpectedly the quantity of money in circulation"; that is, the laws should be continued "until the power of regulating the currency of the society by means of an issue of paper money shall be taken from the banks and unrestricted competition shall also be permitted in the business of lending money."

The New York Review complained that, since his monetary scheme was an open approbation of President Van Buren's proposed substitute for private banks of issue, it was a "foul stain" on his economics and constituted "plotting a death blow to political economy." [48]

[48] "Vethake's Political Economy," *The New York Review,* III (July, 1838), 236.

President Van Buren's proposal, which became law as the Sub-Treasury or Independent Treasury System, provided that the government would pay out and receive only "hard" money and only at the Treasury and other places set up as sub-treasuries.

Vethake's scheme was based on that of Secretary of the Treasury Levi Woodbury in 1837. Woodbury based his views on the proposition that "the spirit of the Constitution and the first principles of political economy," require that a paper currency should always be equivalent to specie.

"While chartered and used solely for local purposes, the regulation and control of [banks] are supposed to belong exclusively to the States. But their organization as well as responsibilities and an early reform in both, became questions of great importance to the Treasury when connected with them, as heretofore, in the capacity of either public depositories or the sources of a portion of the currency received for public dues. . . . A wide departure has been made from the original principle of having its issues of paper rest on a foundation . . . of specie alone, and that used in deposite chiefly for commercial objects. [When] the paper issued rests, like mere bills of exchange, almost exclusively on credit, and that credit not always guarded in the best practicable methods, such a currency . . . must become exposed to many of the vicissitudes of commerce, forfeit most of its original character as the actual representative of money and lose its security in a considerable degree as a circulating medium for the use of either the community or the Government. Under such circumstances, that calamity . . . will often ensue which happened during the last spring [of a panic and suspension of specie payments]."

But there was a need of a sound paper currency for large payments, distant remittances, exchange, traveling, and especially in places where gold did not circulate. To achieve it, Congress should authorize the Treasury to issue non-interest bearing certificates "payable in specie to bearer or order as well as being receivable for all public dues." These would be paid to the public creditor when he preferred them and sufficient specie was in the Treasury. "This kind of paper would be very convenient in form, and would differ little from the drafts now in use in the banks, except being drawn on a known specie fund, and expressing on the face not only this, but their being receivable in the first instance for all public dues. It would possess the highest credit attainable in society." The other main provision of Woodbury's scheme brought it close to Ricardo's plan: The Treasury

The North American Review denounced Vethake's modified sub-treasury scheme as being simply government paper money. Nothing in economics, declared the reviewer, had been better settled than that such things must be avoided, but he did add an interesting qualification—"so long as the medium can be maintained any other way." [49]

Vethake acquired a certain disillusionment about the possibility of achieving salutary reform. He voiced it thus:

Unfortunately for the interests of the community, the questions relating to our circulating medium have been for a long period involved in the contentions of party politics, and so it would seem that they are likely to continue; a most unpropitious condition of things to obtain a proper degree of public attention to the principles on which our circulating medium should be most safely, as well as most steadily, constituted.[50]

But as for political economy as a science, he never lost his conviction of its usefulness. In a lecture before the Mercantile

would invest any considerable temporary surplus or "unexpected excesses" in "safe state stocks [there were no federal securities then] at the market rate," and consequently they could be easily liquidated to meet requisitions when required. (Woodbury, "Report on the Finances," September and December 1837, reprinted in *Reports of the Secretary of the Treasury*, IV [Washington: Rivers, 1851], pp. 9, 25–26, 102–3, 106–7.)

[49] The reviewer approved of Vethake's support of poor laws, but found many serious errors and contradictions in addition to the fatal one on the currency. These included: "regulation of government cannot create capital, but only divert it from one course to another; that the capital of a country is a fixed quality; that the value of the circulating medium, whether greater or less in quantity, and whatever in kind, always bears a certain proportion to the whole capital of the country; that population has a natural tendency to increase more rapidly than food and clothing; that banks can *expand*, that is, *augment* circulating medium at pleasure, though Mr. Vethake says, not indefinitely, that facility of credit is identical with augmentation of the amount of currency, that one employment is as worthwhile to the country as another; that there is a *natural* period for introducing the useful arts into a community."

The reviewer, in amplifying his view that government regulation could increase capital, declared that "not only legislative acts but the judicial administration of the laws, the invention of a useful machine, and a thousand other influences that work through the community, *create* capital by increasing or giving greater effect to industry."

[50] *Encyclopaedia Americana*, vol. XIV, ed. Henry Vethake (Philadelphia: Lea and Blanchard, 1846), p. 615.

Library Company of Philadelphia (1839),[51] he complained that the colleges neglected its study just as they did other social sciences so essential for "the political education of their pupils" who, in many instances, were destined to become the nation's statesmen. And even when these subjects were taught, there was "a timidity in the discussion of disputed points, lest offense should be given to any considerable part of the public." This rendered the instruction uninteresting and futile. The remedy he suggested was that a college appoint two lecturers of political economy, "one of them maintaining and defending the received doctrines of the science, and the other impugning them." If the critic should be so hostile to the received doctrines as to object to being called a political economist, he might be titled "lecturer on statistics or any other title he might prefer." The student or his parent would decide which set of lectures the student should attend, but Vethake hoped that he would desire both. Such a procedure would be better for the cause of truth, the best interests of society, and the exercise of the students' intellectual faculties. It would provide a far more valuable education than that of making them the "passive recipients of the contents of whole libraries, filled with the records of other men's thoughts." [52]

Fifteen years later Vethake again complained that political economy had not been given its rightful place of at least second to "the wider spread of Christianity" as an agent of progress. Because of certain prejudices, it was "*tabooed*" alto-

[51] The Mercantile Library Company of Philadelphia, like the Mercantile Library Association of the City of New York, was an early business school. The audience was composed largely of merchants' clerks.

[52] Vethake, "The Distinctive Provinces of the Political Philosopher and the Statesman," p. 111.

A few colleges zealously pushed political economy. At Brown University, for example, a prize, the Jackson Premium, was awarded in the subject (letter of Francis Wayland to William E. Tolman, July 28, 1849, in Brown University Library collection). Tolman was awarded the prize that year for his "disputation" bearing the title *Libertas*.

gether even in some of the colleges of the United States. Yet it dealt with problems "upon the proper solution of which not the welfare merely, but the stability of society" depended. It aimed, he said, "at advancing no faster than consists with a maintenance of the rights of property . . . and urges a change only after public opinion is fully prepared for its introduction." [53]

He did somewhat change his idea of a university with the passing years. He stood for the old order of the dominance of the Greek and Latin classics in a national controversy that began in 1852. Leading scientists including Alexander D. Bache, Louis Agassiz, James D. Dana, and Benjamin Peirce, in 1851, saw a possibility of setting up a true graduate school in Albany, New York, that would be like the continental universities, notably Berlin. This caused considerable excitement among administrators of the established colleges, and they appointed committees to look into ways of meeting the threat. At Pennsylvania, one of the trustees, the Protestant Episcopal Bishop, Alonzo Potter, who had formerly been vice president and professor of mathematics and natural theology and of moral philosophy and political economy at Union College, strongly supported advanced studies.[54] He declared that "no *city* college in this country has yet reached any considerable magnitude." He thought the University of Pennsylvania should engage in graduate work and thereby be in a position to extend the curriculum. Students should be given an opportunity to pursue their studies further than

[53] Vethake, *An Address before the Literary Societies of Rutgers College*, pp. 17–18.

[54] Potter published a popular manual, *Political Economy* (New York: Harper, 1840). The book was largely a reprint of one by the British economist and member of parliament G. Poulett Scrope, *Principles of Political Economy* (London: Longman, Rees, Orme, Brown, Green, & Longman, 1833). For a detailed study of both works see M. J. L. O'Connor, *Origins of Academic Economics in the United States* (New York: Columbia Univ. Press, 1944), pp. 204–13.

they were able to do at present at any college. More attention should be given to American history, the sciences, and the mechanical arts. There should be freedom in choosing studies and free competition in teaching. Prize scholarships and fellowships should be established.[55]

Most of these statements seem to echo Vethake's former views; but now he defended the established scheme of things: "At twenty-five, an age when according to . . . the new plan . . . students might be supposed to be in attendance . . . there are few who have not an expectation of being heads of families, living in comfort and even luxury." And comparisons with German universities were irrelevant. Scientific subjects, for example (which were being stressed by the supporters of the university), were neither popular nor considered important in the German universities. He had found, for example, at the University of Berlin in 1829–30 that out of 2,000 students only twenty took differential and integral calculus with Öhm, and that Encke had only five persons in physical astronomy. Gauss had informed him at Göttingen, which had 1,700 students, that he had only one student in physical astronomy, and that for some years there had been no demand for his tickets.[56] The few students attending the faculty of philosophy, as distinct from the professional faculties of law, medicine, and divinity, were chiefly persons preparing for careers in teaching, civil service, and diplomacy, that is, persons for whom there were no equivalents in the United States. In the United States hardly anyone deliberately

[55] Printed letter from Alonzo Potter to Joseph R. Ingersoll, July 8, 1852; copy in the University of Pennsylvania Library.

[56] The German professor received a substantial salary and also the fees paid by the auditors for his course. Francis Lieber, who advocated a similar system at Columbia in 1859, asserted, "All German professors, indeed all European professors, receive salary and the fees. Law professors such as Mittermaier, make at times 20,000 guilders a year by their lectures. The more they make the more the governments are pleased, because it shows the flourishing state of the respective university." (Letter of Lieber to S. B. Ruggles, Aug. 31, 1859, in Lieber papers, Library of Congress.)

chose to teach, except under financial pressure and then only as a temporary expedient. As for holding government offices, either by appointment or election, no American "in his sane mind, would . . . set about systematically to make a special preparation for filling them." Fitness was not the basis for government appointments; and victory of the opposite party or the operation of rotation in one's own party might mean loss of a job.[57] Furthermore, the scheme, with its free tuition and more than one professor in a subject, would require a "fund which we may despair of seeing in our day collected and applied to the support of any single college or university."

Four years later Vethake had become so conservative in this matter that he felt free higher education would be the first step toward the "very brink of the worst species of socialism." [58]

He did, however, remain sufficiently true to the spirit of free inquiry to oppose the old view that textbooks should be subjected to a "preliminary" censorship by college authorities. "Which textbooks should be used, ought, I think, to be left very much to the professor," he wrote to a committee of trustees of his alma mater in 1857. Similarly he would leave complete freedom to the instructor as to the modes and means of instruction in his special department. The authorities should only "prescribe to each professor, the general subject and the extent of his course." [59]

Years of strife and loneliness took their toll. Professor Ruffner's son saw Vethake in 1851 in the chess room of the Athenaeum in Philadelphia, "sitting taciturn and wrapt, as if he had never done anything else, and never meant to do anything else, but play a dead game of chess." [60] He had a

[57] Printed letter from Henry Vethake to William M. Meredith, Nov. 27, 1852; copy in University of Pennsylvania Library.

[58] Vethake, *An Address before the Literary Societies of Rutgers College*, p. 22.

[59] Vethake, "Communication, Feb. 27, 1857," in *Statements, Opinions, and Testimony Taken by the Committee of Inquiry Appointed by the Trustees of Columbia College* (New York: Amerman, 1857)

[60] W. H. Ruffner, "The History of Washington College, 1830–1848," p. 28.

difficult course to follow as head of the University of Pennsylvania.[61]

There were controversies not only with trustees, as in the past, but also with faculty members. At times it seemed that some of the trustees were hardly tactful with him. For example, in 1852 there was a move to establish a school of mines, completely separate from the college proper, in the university for training in engineering and allied disciplines and with a bachelor of science degree. Vethake contended first of all that such a development would be prejudicial to the efficiency and prospects of success of the newly established scientific department in the college, for it would entice a good number of able young men who otherwise would be glad of the opportunity to be in the scientific department. There was little reason why they could not take mathematics in the college rather than have their own instructor. Finally, it seemed strange to him that while he was professor of mathematics, the instruction in pure mathematics in the proposed school should be given by the present professor of natural philosophy in the college.[62] As he pointed out, he approved of the objective, but he thought that it could be accomplished without setting up a completely independent school.

As provost, Vethake found fellow faculty members somewhat too individualistic. The one major defect in the organization of the university, he thought, was the provost had too little power. In a *Letter . . . on the Subject of the Duties of the Provost* (1859), he told the trustees that

> Too little importance is attached to the office of the Provost. Although regarded very generally by the trustees, the public, and

[61] H. M. Lippincott, *The University of Pennsylvania* (Philadelphia: Lippincott, 1918), p. 101.

[62] Letter of Vethake to Messrs. J. R. Ingersoll, G. M. Wharton, & T. Wagner, late members of a committee of the Board of Trustees of the University of Pennsylvania, April 30, 1852, in Historical Society of Pennsylvania collection.

the parents and guardians of the students as mainly responsible for the proper management of the institution, he has only an equal vote on the Faculty with every other member. He may be continually, and for years, outvoted on the measures of discipline or of a different nature, proposed by him; and worse than this, all action of the Faculty may be arrested, where there is an even number of members, as is the case at present, by a steady vote of three to three, four to four, etc. The Professors too, who are thus, so to speak, successively triumphing over the Provost will very naturally, be led to treat him with an ever diminishing respect, while the students will do the like, becoming aware of his being unsupported by a majority of the Faculty. To me it seems to be essential for the prosperity of the Literary Department of the University that at least when the Faculty, including the Provost, shall be divided on a question, this shall be decided by another and casting vote of the Provost,—any action being for the most part better than none. But I may mention also, that in nearly all our colleges, especially in those which have flourished most—Harvard, Yale, Princeton, [Union College in] Schenectady, Columbia College in the city of New York, etc. etc., it has been judged expedient to give greater importance and weight to the President or Provost by making him a member of the Board of Trustees. And it may be proper to mention that, in all the institutions just referred to, excepting only Columbia College, the President is *ex-officio* (in the absence of the Governor of the State) the President also of the Board of Trustees. In the Columbia College, he is not necessarily the presiding officer, but simply a member of the board. He is, however, clothed with a veto power on the proceedings of the Faculty.

As in other matters, Vethake's request was in fact a very modest one.

Beyond these difficulties involving more or less personal matters were those broad controversial issues that hardly made Vethake's path a smooth one. With other institutions attempting to become the peers of the leading universities of Europe, the university was bound to appear somewhat behind the times. The failure of those experiments might justify Vethake's view that the time was not ripe for the great venture,[63] but it hardly eliminated the contentiousness that characterized the growth of the colleges of the day. Furthermore, the fact that he was an ardent free trader and prognosticator of the demise of the protective tariff or, as he called it, the "restrictive system," in the leading protectionist state, would certainly have surcharged the atmosphere.[64] But there must have been some satisfaction when he retired, in knowing that among the would-be successors who were seriously considered was George W. Bethune, who had implored the Dickinson students to

> make yourselves thoroughly acquainted with Political Economy, which, despite the abuse that has been heaped upon it, as mere theory, cold, abstract, and uncertain, aims next to Christianity itself for the happiness of mankind. Lay fast hold of the laws God himself has given to the commerce and products of nations, and which like his other laws, can never be violated without a consequence of penalty. And then, stand fast as freemen, as patriots, as men of science and truth, and demonstrate the interests of the people to the American mind and heart.[65]

In 1859 Vethake resigned as provost. He was made emeritus professor of moral philosophy and given an honorarium of

[63] For example, Columbia valiantly started a postgraduate program in 1858, but it soon had to be suspended, for, as one lecturer commiserated with another: "My dear Fellow-Lecturer to many benches and few hearers, had we not better turn Buddhists at once and lecture, in deep meditation to ourselves, on ourselves, and by ourselves?" (Francis Lieber to George Perkins Marsh, Jan. 12, 1859, in David Lowenthal, *George Perkins Marsh* [New York: Columbia Univ. Press, 1958], p. 196).

Vethake explained that he was willing to go somewhat beyond the "existing demand," but if there was practically no demand there was little sense in starting an advanced program.

[64] Vethake's successor, the Reverend Daniel R. Goodwin, used as a text, the moderate protectionist treatise of Francis Bowen of Harvard, *The Principles of Political Economy* (1856).

[65] Bethune, *The Duties of an Educated Man: An Oration Before the Literary Societies of Dickinson College* (Philadelphia: Lippincott, 1843), p. 39. In his *Plea for Study*, delivered before the literary societies of Yale in 1845, Bethune gave a little clearer statement: "That most philanthropic science, Political Economy, which next to the Gospel, whose legitimate offspring it is, will do more than anything else for the elevation and fraternization of our race."

$1,250, and a fund was collected for the painting of his portrait.[66]

After leaving teaching at Pennsylvania in 1860, he accepted the professorship of higher mathematics at the Polytechnic College of the State of Pennsylvania.[67] He died in Philadelphia on December 16, 1866.

Vethake's economic philosophy was well summed up in the hope that through the spread of the science of political economy not only would the masses be taught contentment, but the rich, instead of proceeding on the principles of a "rigid conservatism to oppose every reform would become anxious for the introduction of reforms fast enough to prevent any supposed necessity or pretext for revolutionary action on the part of the multitude." More specifically, he explicitly spoke for the sober mercantile mind of the Jacksonian as the ideal. This he summed up in urging the merchant to follow the maxim of Ricardo, "to be content with small profits upon their goods," and thereby receive the "double advantage of at once acquiring wealth and of earning the approbation of their customers." [68] This tied up with his general belief that

[66] University of Pennsylvania, Minutes of the Trustees, April 5, May 3, 1859.

[67] This school, which was chartered in 1853, "enabled companies engaged in works of improvement to obtain technicians," and thus, as its *Announcement* of 1860 stated, had "become an important agent in the skillful and economical development of the vast resources of the continent, and in the elevation of the industrial professions to the true rank in the scale of human employments."

It was the first American institution offering a curriculum leading to a degree in mining engineering. It appears to have disappeared in the 1890s.

[68] Vethake, "The Distinctive Provinces of the Political Philosopher and the Statesman," pp. 109–10.

As Joshua Bates of Baring Brothers commented to Francis Wayland not long afterward, in the United States there was "a higher *average* of intellectual power, of education, of wealth, of comfort, of temperance, and of religion, than in any other country, and this would soon be apparent could you prevail upon people to look on a dishonest man as a rogue and avoid dealing with him." The big problem was to reason the "trading community" out of the idea that they could gain great wealth quickly by

the system of laissez faire would achieve a society where there would not be as now "even in the most progressive communities, the wealthy . . . few, and the many poor," but a sufficiently numerous group of people in any neighborhood who were "not a great deal more wealthy" than the poorer class, for under these circumstances the poor would be stimulated to better their condition.

---

sharp, speculative practice. "The variation in the amount of currency is one chief cause of the uncertainty, and too often failure of success in commercial professions. If you could fix the amount of Bank notes that can be issued as Sir Robert Peel is about to do here, much misery could be saved." (Letter of Bates to Wayland, May 18, 1844, in Brown University Library.)

THE

PRINCIPLES

OF

POLITICAL ECONOMY.

BY

HENRY VETHAKE, LL.D.

ONE OF THE PROFESSORS IN THE UNIVERSITY OF PENNSYLVANIA; A MEMBER OF THE AMERICAN PHILOSOPHICAL SOCIETY; ETC.

Second Edition.

PHILADELPHIA:
J. W. MOORE,—NO. 138, CHESTNUT STREET.

1844.

TO

THE NUMEROUS YOUNG MEN

WHO,

AT DIFFERENT PERIODS DURING THE LAST SIXTEEN YEARS,

HAVE ATTENDED

HIS LECTURES ON POLITICAL ECONOMY,

The following Treatise,

EMBRACING THE SUBSTANCE OF THOSE LECTURES,

TOGETHER WITH

SUCH ADDITIONS AND ALTERATIONS

AS HAVE BEEN SUGGESTED BY HIS LATEST REFLECTIONS,

IS INSCRIBED

BY THEIR FRIEND,

THE AUTHOR.

ERRATA.

Page 79,—4th line from the bottom, for "rise" read "fall;" and 3d line from the bottom, for "fall" read "rise."

110,—1st line from the top, omit the words "those circumstances which constitute."

126,—12th line from the top, for "them" read "these."

127,—Last line on the page, for "positions" read "propositions."

133,—13th line from the bottom, after "of" read "a."

167,—16th line from the top, for "provided" read "especially if."

170,—8th line from the top, insert, after the word "importation," the words "or production."

222,—17th line from the top, in place of the words "in order to lend it" read "to be lent."

251,—2d line from the bottom, for "manner" read "matter."

288,—5th line from the bottom, for "1832" read "1833."

306,—13th line from the top, for "philanthrophist" read "philanthropist."

371,—8th line from the bottom, for "visits" read "visit."

376,—10th and 14th lines from the bottom, for "tithes" read "the tithe."

395,—15th line from the top, after the word "government" insert "to be consumed by it unproductively."

TO THE NUMEROUS YOUNG MEN WHO, AT DIFFERENT PERIODS DURING THE LAST SIXTEEN YEARS, HAVE ATTENDED HIS LECTURES ON POLITICAL ECONOMY,

The following Treatise,

EMBRACING THE SUBSTANCE OF THOSE LECTURES, TOGETHER WITH SUCH ADDITIONS AND ALTERATIONS AS HAVE BEEN SUGGESTED BY HIS LATEST REFLECTIONS, IS

INSCRIBED

BY THEIR FRIEND,

THE AUTHOR.

CORRECTIONS.

Page 28—6th line from the bottom, for "transference" read "transfer."
110—1st line from the top, omit the words, "those circumstances which constitute."
126—12th line from the top, for "them" read "these."
127—last line on the page, for "positions" read "propositions."
133—13th line from the bottom, after "of" read "a."
159—15th line from the top, for "thing" read "things."
167—16th line from the top, for "provided" read "especially if."
170—8th line from the top, insert after the word "importation" the words "or production."
222—17th line from the top, in place of the words "in order to lend it" read "to be lent."
251—2d line from the bottom, for "manner" read "matter.
288—5th line from the bottom, for "1832" read "1833."
306—13th line from the top, for "philanthrophist" read "philanthropist."
332—14th line from the bottom, for "will" read "shall."
334—5th line from the bottom, for "economist" read "economists."
371—8th line from the bottom, for "visits" read "visit."
376—10th and 14th lines from the bottom, for "tithes" read "the tithe."
395—15th line from the top, after the word "government" insert, "to be consumed by it unproductively."

PREFACE.

THE following treatise is a systematic exposition of the principles of political economy. Avoiding almost all reference to other writers whose opinions differ from his own, and avoiding also any direct notice of the controversies which have been agitated by the many distinguished men who have successively occupied the path of investigation in which he has ventured to follow them, the author has aimed to arrange the various topics comprehended in his general subject in as logical an order as is practicable, and in a manner the best adapted for the instruction of the student.

The difficulty, however, of accomplishing the objects aimed at has been realised by him to too great an extent, for him to suppose for a moment that he has succeeded in doing more, than approach somewhat nearer to their accomplishment than he would have done, but for the efforts which he has repeatedly made during the delivery of his lectures, in a period of not less than fifteen years. Much of this difficulty, it may be observed, arises from the circumstance of there being scarcely any one topic, in the whole range of the science of political economy, which has not relations less or more numerous with almost every other. Writers on the subject who make a rule to themselves to treat of every topic in succession under a separate head, never formally returning to it the second time, labour for this reason under a great disadvantage. The author has not hesitated to sacrifice every consideration, in respect to arrangement, to that of being enabled to advance from the beginning to the end of his treatise without taking any proposition for granted, the truth of which he had not previously endeavoured to establish.

He has, besides, in no case made use of any technical term, without first defining it with as much exactness as was in his power, or without defining it immediately afterwards.

And it may be proper to state that, to adapt what he has written still farther to the purposes of instruction, he has divided it into a great number of *short* chapters; thus affording frequent resting places, whence the student can look back and survey the ground over which he has advanced.

But while his work is offered to the colleges, and other higher seminaries of education in our country, as a text-book of instruction on the subject of which it treats, he is desirous of having it understood at the outset, that it is neither a compilation from the works of others, nor a mere elementary treatise. It is hoped that the *political economist* will find in it enough of novelty, and of novelty that is consistent with truth, for him not to regret the time which he may have bestowed on its perusal.

Among those parts of the present treatise which the author himself is disposed to regard as most worthy of attention, is first, the manner in which the whole subject is introduced; the definitions not being arbitrarily given, but, on the contrary, being simply the assignment of names to classes of objects. The classification itself, too, is always founded on the nature of things; and the names are assigned as much as possible in accordance with common usage.

In the next place, the *bold* innovation has been attempted of comprehending as well immaterial or intellectual products as those which are material, not only under the definition of wealth, but likewise of capital. What are the advantages of doing so, need not be here stated. The author will now only remark that the simultaneous extension in this manner of the terms wealth and capital he considers to be of no slight importance, to enable the reader to take a proper view of the whole ground which it is proposed to explore; and that, perhaps contrary to first appearances, our language in reference to both capital and wealth will become thereby more accordant with the ordinary modes of speech, than would otherwise be the case. Should the reader, after having advanced through the fourth chapter of the first book, hesitate to yield his assent to the propriety of the definitions in question, he is earnestly requested, when he shall have finished the perusal of the *sixth* chapter of the same book, to reperuse the preceding fourth chapter. If his doubts of that propriety shall then not have been removed, so confident of it is the author, that he would still be disposed to say to him what D'Alembert is reported to have said to a young aspirant after knowledge, who, in despite of all the explications which that distinguished mathematician could give him of the *metaphysics* of the *calculus,* was obstinate in disbelieving their validity; to wit, to go on with the study of the subject, and faith will in the end infallibly come.

The author would direct the reader's attention particularly to the manner in which the theories of rent and of population have been explained and modified,—theories which lie at the foundation of all that follows, and without a due understanding of which, what follows will appear altogether confused and unintelligible. Those theories are now presented in the same form as that in which they have been delivered in the author's courses of political economy, beginning so long since as the year 1822. His views too, as they appear in the present treatise, relating to population, in connexion especially with the subject of pauperism, were published in one of our American annuals, in 1834.*

It may also be mentioned that political economy is not regarded in the present treatise as a science only of a hypothetical description, and as having no necessary connexion with the administration of public affairs, or with the transactions of private life. So far from this, one great object which the author has had in view, has been to point out its application to both of these; and to the *moral relations* of the science,— relations which, in his opinion, confer upon it its principal importance,—he has given a peculiar prominence.

* "The Annual of the Board of Education," edited by the Rev. John Breckinridge, D. D.

Every effort, moreover, has been made to exhibit the doctrines of political economy in as concise a form as is consistent with perspicuity, in reference to the convenience as well of the student, as of such persons as may already be acquainted with the existing state of the science. The former would, very probably, be repelled from the study of a much larger treatise; and the latter would be quite as likely as any other class of persons, to look upon a great book as a great evil.

The conciseness just mentioned, together with the complicated nature of the subject,—every topic which it embraces having numerous relations to almost every other, as has been already stated,—would have rendered it impossible for each separate chapter of the work to have been so written as to be wholly intelligible to one who had not systematically perused the preceding chapters. While the author, then, will not be guilty of the affectation or weakness of deprecating criticism, he asks of every individual who wishes to deal fairly with him, or with his subject, not to commence the perusal of this volume at the middle or end, but to commence at the beginning of it.

With these remarks, the present treatise on political economy is respectfully submitted to the public.

Philadelphia, Feb. 1st, 1838.

TABLE OF CONTENTS.

BOOK FIRST.

BOOK SECOND.

On the tendency of rents, profits, and wages, to rise or fall in the progress of society;—together with the laws which determine the numbers of a people.

BOOK THIRD.

The theories of money, and of banking.

BOOK FOURTH.

On the productiveness in the same degree of the different branches of industry ; and on the interference with the natural distribution among them of labour and capital.

BOOK FIFTH.

On the interference of individuals and of governments with the natural order of things, founded on other grounds than the unequal productiveness of the different branches of industry.

THE PRINCIPLES OF POLITICAL ECONOMY.

BOOK FIRST.

DEFINITIONS OF TERMS; AND THE THEORY OF VALUE.

CHAPTER I.

DEFINITIONS OF UTILITY AND WEALTH—OBJECT OF POLITICAL ECONOMY.

If we look around us, we shall perceive that society is so constituted, that, while only a small portion of mankind are placed by Providence in circumstances of such affluence as to render them disinclined to make any exertions, whether bodily or mental, to enlarge their means of enjoyment, most persons are engaged in producing, either what is to be directly appropriated to satisfy their own desires, or, more frequently, what is destined, by being exchanged for the products of the labour of others, to minister to the enjoyment of their fellow-men. In other words, most men are producers of *utility*, in the sense in which this word is understood in political economy. For, leaving to the moralist the decision of the question whether many objects of man's pursuit may not in reality be injurious to him, and whether he be not often making a sacrifice of higher, but future, gratification, or even sometimes subjecting himself to future suffering, that he may administer to himself perhaps a small amount only of present enjoyment, the political economist regards every thing as useful which is capable of satisfying, in any degree whatever, any of man's *actual* wants and desires. Thus spirituous liquors are said to be possessed of utility, because they are of a nature to be objects of men's desire; which desire they evince, and afford a measure of, by the sacrifices they are willing to make in order to obtain them; and this utility is ascribed to those articles, notwithstanding that their use may, in most cases, be justly condemned, and the philanthropist, and the christian, may feel it a duty to make every proper exertion to repress the inconveniences, or mischiefs, they occasion.

But I wish not to be misunderstood. I do not mean to insinuate, or to admit, that the political economist, because he employs the word utility in reference to man as he is, and not as he ought to be, and because the *immediate* object he has in view is not the moral improvement of the species, adopts a low standard of morals, or is indifferent to such improvement. As well might the votary of any one department of science be fairly chargeable with necessarily undervaluing, and taking no interest in the progress of, any other; and the pursuits of the astronomer or chemist be condemned as vicious in their tendency, because, in observing the phenomena, and investigating the laws, of *material* nature, they take no cognizance of the categories of right and wrong. So far indeed, I may remark, is the science of political economy from leading to conclusions adverse to the bests interests of mankind, and so far is it from even turning the attention of individuals, or of governments, entirely from moral to physical considerations, and teaching them to advance the happiness of society by measures wholly unconnected with morality, that I hope to make it appear to the conviction of my readers, as a legitimate deduction from the principles of the science, that there is no more efficient method of promoting the *physical* well-being of a people than to diffuse among them, as extensively as possible, the blessings of religion, of morals, and of education. It may likewise be added, that no branch of human knowledge exhibits to us more beautiful illustrations of the consistency of all truth, and of that unity of design which pervades the various provinces of creation.

No person, after having become acquainted with the elements of our subject, will fail to perceive the desirableness, if not the necessity, of having some word to designate the idea intended to be conveyed by the term utility, as I have defined it; and if any inconveniences should result from the same term being occasionally employed in another acceptation, this will only be one of many instances of a similar kind, which are continually occurring out of the domain of the exact sciences, and which require from the student, as an essential condition to the acquisition of real knowledge, a certain perspicacity in readily perceiving the different shades of meaning of which the same forms of language admit. Whenever also an idea is considered as of sufficient importance to require it to be designated by a single term, almost the only practicable method of proceeding, in fixing upon the proper word for the purpose intended, is to select such an one as is already employed to denote some idea bearing an analogy to that which is to be expressed; for to coin an entirely new word may be regarded as wholly out of the question. The closer, too, the analogy, the better, as less violence is then done to existing usage. Now in the instance under consideration, the term utility is certainly employed very much in accordance with the meaning attached to it in common language. We speak of a bad use of an object, as well as of a good use of it; and we speak of the utility of weapons, both of offence and defence, although, if men were prevented, by the non-existence of those of the former description, from injuring one another, a considerable addition would be implied to the sum of human happiness. It seems to me, then, that it cannot reasonably be denied that the political economists are fully justified in the use they make of the term utility; while it may be allowed, that they are also called upon to be cautious how they confound this use of it with its more dignified acceptation, when it refers, not to the gratification alone of his present desires, but to man's happiness in reference to the whole of his future career.

Of the various objects which are possessed of utility, there are a few distinguished from the rest, by one of these two peculiarities; that they are either not susceptible of being appropriated,—or are supplied to us gratuitously in such abundance by the liberality of nature, that no one is willing to bestow his labour, or what amounts to the same thing, the products of his labour, for the purpose of procuring them. The air we breathe, the light and heat of the sun, and, very generally, the water we drink, are examples of this class. All other objects having utility, besides these, are comprehended under the general denomination of *wealth.*

Since the very small number of things useful which do not constitute any portion of wealth are, from their very nature, never the products of human labour, to produce and to consume wealth are entirely synonymous with the production and consumption of utility.

And the province of political economy may now be stated to be, to determine the laws which regulate the production, distribution, and consumption, of wealth; with the practical object in view of ascertaining the course to be pursued, or avoided, by individuals, and by governments, in the disposal of the wealth under their control, so as to promote, in as great a degree as possible, the happiness of mankind.

CHAPTER II.

RELATION OF UTILITY TO WEALTH ILLUSTRATED—DEFINITIONS OF LABOUR, VALUE, &c.

From the definitions given in the preceding chapter, it follows that utility and wealth are not indicative of two independent classes of things, but that the one class is comprehensive of the other. All wealth is useful. On the other hand, whatever is useful is not necessarily a portion of wealth.

That which is incapable of being appropriated, or is supplied to us without limit, can have no claim to be styled wealth, however great the degree of its utility may be. Hence a case may be supposed seemingly paradoxical. Let the supply of a certain article of wealth, bread for example, be indefinitely augmented. Like atmospheric air, it will constitute no portion of wealth. By increasing the wealth of the community then,—we have diminished it. This seems certainly much like a contradiction in terms. Yet the difficulty is of very easy explanation. In the two cases, before and after the indefinite augmentation of the stock of bread, this article has merely a different place in our classification. In the former case, it is classed under the head of wealth; in the latter, it is ranked with the few useful objects which have been excluded from our definition of that term.

If we now make a contrary supposition, such as that water has become scarce in a beseiged town, where it was before so readily and abundantly procurable as to be had gratuitously, the consequence will plainly be that it must henceforth be regarded as wealth; and the enemy may, therefore, by simply cutting off the supply of water, have increased the wealth of those whom he has been making every exertion to distress. Here likewise, it must be hardly necessary to remark, the seeming contradiction arises from the removal of the article in question from one of our classes to the other. And when this is distinctly perceived by the reader, any suppositions of the kind which may be made will form no objection with him to the propriety of our definitions.

Again, according to our definition of wealth, it will be proper to say of a man who has only a sixpence in the world, that he is possessed of wealth. The expression may perhaps, to some ears, sound not a little singular; and it will be because we frequently employ the word wealth in a *relative* acceptation, as implying a more than usual amount of the various objects which I have stated it to comprehend. This, however, ought not for a moment to cast any doubt on the propriety of the definition of it above given. There are two points to be considered in the business of defining. The one has reference to our classifications or arrangements: the other to the name by which a class of ideas or objects is to be designated, after it is once formed. The former is generally the more important of the two; although the latter is very far from being unimportant. We must first examine whether a certain number of objects possess common properties which are fitted to render them interesting as a class, in their relations to science or the ordinary purposes of life, so as to require to be frequently spoken of together; and this point being determined in the affirmative, nothing remains, as has been already mentioned, than to apply, to designate the class, that word which has been hitherto used in an acceptation the most analogous. In the instance under consideration, there can be no question of the importance as a class of the objects I have denominated wealth: the only dispute must be as to its name, respecting which I shall say more as I advance in my subject. At present, I shall merely observe that the definition of wealth which I have adopted can be shewn to be improper in only one or other of two ways; first, by pointing out some other word whose ordinary meaning is more analogous than is that of wealth to what this is intended to denote; or, secondly, by showing that, however desirable it may be to bestow some name upon the class of objects which I call wealth, the word wealth should, nevertheless, be reserved to designate another class of objects, still more analogous in its nature to what that word signifies in ordinary usage. He who is unprepared to do either of these has, as yet, no right to object to the use I make of the word; even though it should partake occasionally of that ambiguity which is so frequently the result of the poverty of language.

When, however, in a certain context, the word wealth has been so exclusively used in a relative sense as to render it singular to apply it *absolutely*, and this application of it can be readily avoided, it seems to me that it would be well to adhere to the established usage in the case. The phrase, *a man of wealth*, is an instance of this sort. But where usage is not so decided as here, it would, perhaps, be better to avoid the ambiguous expression altogether, if it can be done without awkwardness.

The adjective *wealthy* is always employed in a relative acceptation.

By the wealth of a community or nation, is meant all the wealth which is possessed by the persons composing it, either in their individual or corporate capacities.

I have already had occasion to use the word *labour;* and, in doing so, it was scarcely possible for my meaning to have been misunderstood. Still it may be as well for me to define it with as much precision as I can, with a view to avoid all future misunderstanding. Labour then, — it is of human labour alone of which I speak,—is *exertion* of body or mind, and exertion of a painful or at least disagreeable nature, which, of course, one only consents to make with the prospect of receiving, sooner or latter, an adequate compensation.

There is, consequently, much muscular action, and voluntary muscular action too, that is not labour. It would be unpleasant for us *not* to exert our bodily or muscular powers in a certain degree. Indeed the *pain* of absolute and continued repose would be intolerable. So likewise with respect to the mind. All thought is not intellectual labour: only that thought is *laborious* which implies continued study.

If labour be thus defined, we may conceive of the occasional existence of wealth without its having been produced by labour. Of this nature is the game obtained in the exercise of the pleasures of the chase, the fruit that is plucked by the traveller from a bush growing wild by the way side, or a precious stone unexpectedly picked up by him who is engaged in exploring the solitary places of the earth, in search of objects of a different description. Wealth of this kind bears, however, a very inconsiderable proportion to that which labour produces. The errour would therefore have been an insignificant one, at least practically speaking, had wealth been defined to consist of "the products of labour;" or, to express myself in equivalent terms, when we say that those products constitute all that we mean by wealth, we shall be asserting what is very nearly coincident with the definition of it already adopted,—so nearly coincident with it as to justify me, when I hereafter speak of wealth, in regarding it generally as identical with the products of labour.

Although I have comprehended the utility which is the product of intellectual, equally with that which is the product of bodily labour, under the denomination of wealth, it will be perceived that I exclude the labour by which wealth is produced from being thus denominated. But it may be said that men are ever to be found who are willing to exchange what they have procured by means of their own labour, and, in general, a portion of what they possess, for the labour of others, and that, on this account, labour ought itself to find a place in the inventory of wealth. Not so, however; because the only reason why labour has any exchangeable value is its productiveness. When wages are paid to the labourer, what is in reality purchased are the *services* rendered by him, or, in other words, the products of his labour. So too, where the institution of slavery exists, the price of the slave must be viewed as a payment in part for what his labour is expected to produce; his maintenance constituting the remaining part of that payment. To class labour, therefore, with the products of labour, under the same name, would not only be to confound together cause and effect, but would also be estimating the latter twice. It is true that no practical errour would result from thus in every case doubling the amount of existing wealth, because the same proportion would still continue between the wealth of one country and that of another, as well as between the wealth of a country at any one period of time and its wealth at any other period. But notwithstanding this, the advantages of not denominating labour wealth, and of applying this term only to the products of labour, will, I think, be found to be far from inconsiderable, in reference both to the precision of our classifications, and the simplicity of our language, in political economy.

Every species of wealth is occasionally exchanged by its owner for other portions of it, the possession of which is preferred by him at the time of making the exchange; and what is ordinarily given in exchange for any product, at a given time and place, or in the same *market*, is called its *exchangeable valüe.* Thus if three hats were ordinarily exchanged for a coat, it would be equally proper to say, that the exchangeable value of a coat was three hats, and that the exchangeable value of a hat was the third part of a coat. The same of any other portions of wealth, whether material or immaterial. And so too of labour, although labour be not included, excepting metaphorically, under the designation of wealth.

Value has sometimes been distinguished into exchangeable

value or value in exchange, and value *in use.* But as value in use is altogether synonymous with utility, the employment of it may be dispensed with. When I speak of value, I shall, accordingly, always mean exchangeable value.

Whatever is offered in the market for any thing else is denominated a *commodity.* Every species of wealth is, therefore, a commodity. And labour is one also.

From the definitions of the terms, we may infer that the exchangeable value of any commodity may be expressed in as many different forms of speech as there are other commodities for which it is ordinarily exchanged. As all wealth is, however, most frequently exchanged for money, it becomes desirable to have some word to designate the exchangeable value of a commodity when estimated in money; and this is what is meant by the term *price.*

It must be obvious that wealth may be defined, in perfect consistency with the definition of it originally given, to consist of every thing, material or immaterial, *having exchangeable value;* with the exception alone, as in the case of that definition, of human labour, when this is understood strictly as applying to labour itself, and not to the services or products of labour. And it may perhaps appear to some of my readers that the last mentioned definition would be the simpler, and therefore to be preferred, of the two. For the possession of utility, the capacity of appropriation, and the existence of a commodity in limited quantity, it substitutes the single condition of having exchangeable value. I have, nevertheless, *based* the present treatise on the former definition, as the more philosophical one; since the only reason why an object has exchangeable value, is because of its being possessed of utility, because it can be appropriated, and because its supply is not unlimited.

CHAPTER III.

NATURE OF MONEY—THE PRECIOUS METALS CONSTITUTE THE MONEY OF THE WORLD.

Money is that commodity which is most frequently exchanged for every other.

I might, with perhaps sufficient propriety, content myself, for the present, with this very general statement of the nature of money. But as many of the false theories that prevail concerning it are founded on misapprehensions of its true nature, it may not be altogether inexpedient to say something more, at once, on the subject.

The attention of my readers may be called to the fact, that the precious metals—gold and silver—constitute the money of the world; although in peculiar states of society, and in certain secluded districts, a variety of other commodities may have been employed as the medium of exchange; for example, cattle among nations of shepherds, certain ornamental shells among some very rude tribes, salt in Abyssinia, and iron among the Lacedæmonians of the age of Lycurgus. In calling gold and silver the money of the world, it is possible that I may seem to have overlooked the copper money, and the paper money, in circulation. The former, however, is used only for purchases of small value; and the whole amount of it is but an inconsiderable portion of the circulating medium. It may be observed with respect to the latter, that, in most cases, the reason of its constituting a portion of that medium is, that it is the record, and the evidence, of an obligation to pay on demand, or at a future day, a certain value estimated in the precious metals. It is also worthy of remark, that the payments made, or moneys transmitted, from one country to another, consist almost exclusively of these metals.

Not only would the quantity of copper money in circulation be wholly inadequate for such a purpose, but the expense of its transportation would put *this* out of the question; and as to paper money, it maintains, generally speaking, its full credit, and therefore value, only in the country where it is issued, and where it is convertible into *specie*, which will, of course, be sent abroad in preference to it.

And it may not be here out of place for me to answer the inquiry, which must naturally present itself, how it has happened, that gold and silver have obtained a preference over all other commodities, as the general medium of exchange. This will be very readily understood, if we first look at the inconveniences to which society, as it is at present constituted, would be subjected, were there no circulating medium,—and at the manner in which men would naturally proceed in order to supply that deficiency. Take the case of the baker, and suppose him to be desirous of procuring butcher's meat. He goes, accordingly, with his loaves, to the butcher, who may very possibly already be sufficiently supplied with bread; and he may therefore be obliged to go to another, and another, before he is able to accomplish his object. So likewise may the case be in reference to other commodities, and other tradesmen. Every individual will, however, gradually learn of what articles the persons with whom he deals are most frequently in need, and will be desirous to have a supply of them in his own possession, to facilitate by this means the making of his purchases. Instead of exchanging directly the products of his industry for what he intends to consume, he will procure with a portion of them, in the first instance, what may thus serve him as a medium of exchange. In this manner too, we can perceive without difficulty that, where there are one or two commodities, whose properties render them better fitted than any others to constitute such a medium, they will be gradually adopted for that purpose. Now the precious metals have properties of the kind adverted to in a very striking degree. These are, *first*, their durability: they do not deteriorate in quantity, or quality, by being kept on hand. *Secondly*, they possess a great value in a small bulk, which enables them to be kept, and to be transported from place to place, at little comparative expense. *Thirdly*, their exchangeable value, or the amount of other commodities which they can purchase, does not vary as rapidly as that of most others (I am now merely stating facts, without attempting to account for them). *Fourthly*, they can always be procured in the same degree of fineness, or alloyed with exactly the same proportion of baser metal; which, I may remark, is done to make them less soft than in their pure state, and consequently less subject to wear. *Fifthly*, they admit of being divided into small portions, of the same weight as well as fineness; so that purchases of all degrees of magnitude may be conveniently made with them. *Sixthly*, that weight and fineness can be certified by stamping upon those portions certain marks or figures not easily effaceable, or, in other words, by *coining* them. The more attentively any one will compare the degree in which gold and silver possess these properties with that in which they belong to all other things, the more will he be satisfied of their peculiar adaptation to constitute a medium of exchange.

The motives which would lead, in the manner that has been explained, to the use of the precious metals as a medium for exchanging all other commodities, on the hypothesis of society being constituted as it is with the exception of the non-existence of such a medium, it must be evident, cannot be otherwise than influential in producing a like result where-ever, and whensoever, the divisions of labour begin to be introduced. We find, accordingly, the fact to have been so in the earliest periods of the history of our race; as is authentically attested in the Scriptures of the Old Testament. We read, for example, in the 13th chapter of Genesis, of Abraham, that he was "rich in cattle, in silver, and in gold." And again, in the 23d chapter of the same book, his purchase is recorded of the field of Machpelah, as a burial place for Sarah his wife, for four hundred shekels of silver, *current money with the merchant.*

From what has now been said concerning money, its true nature, as well as the relation which it bears to every other portion of wealth, will, I hope, be sufficiently understood, to enable the reader to follow my reasonings, untrammeled by any preconceived and unfounded notions with respect to it. And I shall therefore proceed with the business of classification and definition.

CHAPTER IV.

DEFINITIONS OF CAPITAL, OF THE WAGES OF LABOUR, AND OF THE ACCUMULATON OF WEALTH—IMMATERIAL AS WELL AS MATERIAL PRODUCTS THE SUBJECTS OF ACCUMULATION.

WHATEVER may be the wealth of any individual, there are only two ways in which he can dispose of it, with a view to his own advantage. He may appropriate it either to the gratification of his present, or of his future wants. In the latter case, he is said to *save* a portion of his wealth. This again can be done, first, by retaining it in his possession, and, in the mean time, not applying it to any use; and secondly, by employing it in setting persons to work, who, while they consume it, are at the same time engaged in producing new wealth, or, in the language of political economists, are engaged in the *reproduction* of wealth,—in the reproduction of it, too, with a *profit.**

* The *lending* to another of a portion of one's income is not a mode of appropriating it distinct from the two which have been mentioned; for the wealth so disposed of must necessarily be appropriated by the *borrower* in one or other of those two modes.

There is scarcely any thing which, when reserved for future consumption in the first of these two methods, does not deteriorate, and eventually perish. Where man thus forbears the work of destruction, time, or rather the constant action of natural causes, takes it up, and sooner or later brings the most durable things to decay. Gold and silver are, for this reason, almost the only commodities any one ever thinks of keeping in his possession for more than a short period of time unemployed. And as almost the only motive for doing this (which every one knows is denominated *hoarding*,) is an impression of the insecurity of property, very few people will have recourse to it in a civilised community, where the arbitrary will and rapacity of the governors, and the license of evil-disposed individuals, are effectually held in check by the dominion of the laws. To save will therefore, in the great majority of instances, be identical with the appropriation of wealth to the purpose of again producing wealth. When it is so appropriated, it is styled *capital;* which is hence a class of objects separated from, and comprehended in, the more general class of wealth; and just as, while every portion of wealth is possessed of utility, every thing useful does not constitute a portion of wealth, so all capital is necessarily wealth, while much of wealth has no claim to be denominated capital.

Before proceeding any farther, the reader should endeavour to render himself familiar with the above statement respecting the nature of what is saved and appropriated as capital. He should continually bear in mind that it is destined to be consumed equally with the wealth which is not saved. The former of these, too, may be, and very frequently is, *more rapidly* consumed than the latter. In illustration of this, compare the food and clothing of the labourer, with the mansion, and the furniture of various kinds, ornamental as well as useful, with which it has been provided, of his employer. Indeed, the being saved or not being saved, the being employed as capital or not being employed as capital, has no relation whatever to slowness or rapidity of consumption, but simply to the circumstance of the wealth in question being, or not being, appropriated to the *reproduction* of wealth.

The only consistent meaning which the political economist can attach to the *accumulation* of wealth is its increase through the instrumentality of increased savings. Wealth will, consequently, accumulate in proportion to the rate at which, at any particular time, capital is accumulating. Here, in order to guard against misapprehension, I may remark that, *in different countries, and at different periods in the same country*, equal increments of wealth may not correspond with equal increments of capital; for capital, like labour, is not always, and everywhere, in the same degree productive.

From what precedes, the reader, I hope, will distinctly perceive that immaterial products, in the same manner precisely as material products, can be saved and made to constitute a portion of capital; and *that they therefore admit of accumulation in the proper sense of this term.* When I pay wages to any workman whom I employ, what I really pay him, that is his *real wages*, will be rightly estimated by the amount of the various necessaries and luxuries of life which I shall have enabled him to obtain. I might have made a very different disposition of those necessaries and luxuries: and they may be truly said to have constituted a portion of my property or wealth. The circumstance that the *specific* commodities disposed of by me were never in my *immediate* possession is of no moment in this respect. It suffices that they were under my control; the evidence of which is to be found in the power I have exerted in causing their transference from one individual to another. Now the real wages of the labourer, as the term has just been explained, are in no case confined exclusively to material products. Even in the most degraded communities, there is scarcely any one of the labouring *poor*, who does not consume occasionally what is immaterial. Of this nature, obviously, is the protection which he receives from the government and laws under which he lives, and the advice given by a physician to his family in periods of sickness. Other illustrations, too, will readily occur to the reader. In so far as he pays for any such immaterial products with the money which I have given him, will they constitute a portion of his wages, that is a portion of *my* savings or capital. And as capital, and therefore wealth, are always accumulated by means of augmented savings, it is manifest that immaterial are, equally with material products, the subjects of accumulation.

But it may be said that the impossibility of immaterial products being accumulated is the necessary consequence of their being consumed in the act of production; because this circumstance puts forever out of the question the existence of any excess of production over consumption.

To this objection I reply, that the amount of the wealth which exists at any time unconsumed,—and this is unquestionably the measure of the excess of *previous* production over consumption,—has no fixed relation to the command which the community possesses over the necessaries and luxuries of life, or, in other words, to the only purpose to which the objectors themselves will admit the accumulation of wealth to be subservient. This is manifest in respect to all such necessaries or luxuries as are of an immaterial nature. But the proposition can be shewn to be equally true when we confine our view to material wealth. Just in proportion as any object is more rapidly consumed, will it yield a greater gratification to its possessor in a given portion of time,—all other circumstances, of course, remaining the same. If we suppose the period of its consumption to be diminished one-half, the gratification derived from it in a given time must, therefore, be doubled. The *whole* amount of gratification, that is of necessaries or luxuries enjoyed, will consequently continue unaltered. So likewise if the diminution of the period of consumption be in any other ratio. Any diminution of the kind, however, necessarily implies that the excess of previous production over consumption has become less than it was before. Hence the existence of such excess, in any degree, has no essential connexion with human happiness, and ought not to constitute a criterion of the existence of wealth. Besides, whoever adopts this criterion cannot, in my opinion, without inconsistency avoid regarding the durability of an object, irrespective of any other consideration, as a measure of the wealth which is embodied in it, or with which it is identical; so that, for example, a certain quantity of hardware, instead of constituting only an equal portion of wealth with corn of the same exchangeable value, ought to be estimated, merely because it is in its nature more durable, as of greater amount than the latter,—an estimate which few or none will hesitate to reject at once, as an absurdity.

I have said that by the accumulation of wealth is meant its increase through the instrumentality of increased savings, or of an increase in the capital of the community. This account of the nature of accumulation implies, it may not be superfluous to add here, although perhaps sufficiently obvious from what has been above-mentioned, that, when wealth is accumulated, a greater amount of it is *consumed*, as well as produced, in a given time; for if such were not the case, there would be no augmentation whatever of the advantages derived from wealth; and its augmented production would be a piece of pure folly.

That the amount of accumulated wealth is not to be measured by the excess of previous production over consumption, but by the amount of wealth which is *produced and consumed in a given time*,—and that immaterial products are susceptible of accumulation in the very same manner as material ones,—are propositions which I have taken some pains to establish, and to impress upon the reader's mind. And I have done so, both on account of their novelty, and of their importance, as I think, to a comprehensive and fully satisfactory view of the science of political economy. One or two writers may have had occasionally a glimpse of the latter; yet none, so far as I know, even of those who have applied the term wealth to immaterial as well as to material products, have sufficiently realised the possibility of immaterial products being accumulated, to induce them to embrace these under the denomination of capital; without doing which, the extension of the definition of *wealth* will be found to be merely a barren generality. The former of the two propositions I believe to be so entirely new, that it would be impracticable to point out a passage in the writings of any political economist, indicative of the remotest suspicion on his part of its truth. These propositions are intimately related to each other; since, as must be evident, if the excess of previous production over consumption is a correct measure of the wealth accumulated, to predicate accumulation in respect to that which is consumed in the very act of being produced, —that is of immaterial products,—would be a direct contradiction. In what degree, if in any, the possibility of such accumulation is important, the reader will be able to decide for himself in the sequel.*

* The possibility of accumulating immaterial products, and of their constituting a portion of capital, seem to me to be points of so much importance to a comprehensive and adequate view of the science of political economy, that I may be permitted in this note to restate the argument of the text in a concise form.

No other test of the *increase* of wealth can possibly exist, whether it be material or immaterial, than that a greater quantity of it is produced and consumed in a given time than before. But since nothing more is intended by the *accumulation* of wealth than the increase of it, it will manifestly be proper to speak of the accumulation of immaterial products.

Again, what is saved and appropriated as capital is not of necessity consumed slower than any other portion of wealth; it is merely consumed by a different class of persons. We have here therefore no reason why capital should not be composed, like that portion of wealth which is not capital, in part of the products which are immaterial, as well as of those which are material. And as, in almost every instance, the *real* wages of the labourer,—which wages, when advanced to

CHAPTER V.

CONSTITUENT ELEMENTS OF CAPITAL—PRODUCTIVE AND UNPRODUCTIVE CONSUMPTION—DISTINCTION OF CAPITAL INTO FIXED AND CIRCULATING.

CAPITAL consists, *first*, of the wages of labour.* *Secondly*, of those *instruments* and *constructions* of all kinds which assist the labourer in the production of wealth. *Thirdly*, of the materials, in different stages of preparation, on which his labour is exerted. *Fourthly*, of that amount of the finished commodity which it may be thought expedient by the owner of capital, or *capitalist*, as he is called, to keep on hand before selling it. And *lastly*, of the money appropriated to the circulation of the various other constituent portions of capital.

The wages of labour might seem, at first view, to comprise a part at least of the money mentioned under the last head, on

him by his employer, are a portion of the latter's capital,—consist, in a certain degree, of immaterial products, it will follow that immaterial products may be made to constitute a portion of capital.

Perhaps, too, the analogy which has been pointed out between material and immaterial products will be more clearly apprehended by the reader, if he analyse the mode in which the former of these administers to the gratification of our desires, and compare it with that in which we derive gratification from the latter. He will not be surprised at the closeness of the analogy in question, when he perceives, as he will not fail to perceive, that, in both cases alike, the *ultimate* product is simply—*agreeable sensations.* The entire utility of the house in which we dwell, for example, arises from its adaptation to produce a series of such sensations in our minds, just as the products of the painter or the musician are adapted to do.

* If any portion of the labourer's wages be not *advanced* to him by his employer, but be received by him only after the process of production is completed, he will then receive, besides his wages, profits upon them for the time their payment has been postponed; in other words, he may himself be regarded as a capitalist, whose capital has been invested together with that of his employer.

account of those wages being ordinarily paid in money. This is, however, not the case. We must be careful not to confound the real wages of the labourer with his money wages. The latter, as has been before stated, are only instrumental in procuring the former. The labourer, who receives money for his services, exchanges it again for the necessaries and comforts of life, both of a material and immaterial nature, which he is enabled by means of it to obtain; and the money is only transitorily in his possession.

With respect to the last of the subdivisions of capital which I have mentioned, it may very possibly be objected, that it is not of a sufficiently distinctive character; because the very same money that is employed to circulate the constituent portions of capital is also the medium for exchanging every thing else. This is a circumstance, nevertheless, of no importance; for it is undeniable that a certain *proportion* of the exchanges made, and, of course, of the money employed in making them, has a relation to capital; and it is this proportion, or amount, of money, which is meant to be classed under that denomination. It may also, perhaps, seem singular to some of my readers, that only a portion of the circulating medium should be styled capital. The singularity arises from the fact that *large* sums of money are commonly so designated, in consequence of this being the form in which the capitalist usually *realises* his property before he makes his *investments,* and from the capacity, and consequent liability, of all money to be employed with a view to reproduction. But in as much as the progress of an individual or nation in wealth is dependent, not on the amount of his property that is liable to be employed as capital, but on what is actually so employed, we want a term for the latter, and not for the former. Now capital is the term that has been selected for this purpose; and there can be no reasonable objection to it, until a better shall be offered as a substitute.

It might, possibly, be made a question whether "that

amount of the finished commodity which it may be expedient for the capitalist to keep on hand before selling it" is with propriety styled capital. That it is so styled in the actual business of life, must be notorious to every one. Such, for instance, is, to a very considerable extent, the capital of the merchant. In every case, too, where we speak of the profits of capital, we mean, not only the profits on the wealth which is alone apparently employed in production, but likewise on all that portion of it which is thus kept on hand. And as both these portions do, in reality, always yield profits in proportion to the amount of each, may they not be said to be equally productive, and to be equally entitled to have the term capital applied to them? Farther light will, however, be shed upon this point, when I shall have treated of the determination of the prices of commodities by the cost of producing them.

Whatever is consumed as capital is said to be *productively consumed;* and what is otherwise consumed is said to be *unproductively consumed*. Thus the wages of the labourers whom I employ are a part of my productive consumption. On the other hand, my own food and clothing belong to my unproductive consumption.

A labourer may dispose of his wages, just as his employer may do of his wealth, in two different ways. He may make an immediate appropriation of them for the supply of his wants, or he may save and employ them as capital: in other words, he may consume them either unproductively or productively. Hence it follows, that the same wealth which constitutes the productive consumption of the employer of labour, may constitute also the productive or unproductive consumption of the labourer.

Capital is either *fixed* or *circulating*. Fixed and circulating are here relative terms; by fixed capital being meant that capital which is less rapidly, and by circulating capital that which is more rapidly consumed. When we have reference to the capital employed in the same branch of industry, it is customary to designate those specific portions of it which are *wholly* consumed in the act of production as circulating, and those portions which only suffer *wear and tear* as fixed capital. The fixed capital in one employment may, consequently, be consumed more rapidly than the circulating is in another.

CHAPTER VI.

DISTINCTION BETWEEN THE LABOUR WHICH IS PRODUCTIVE AND THAT WHICH IS UNPRODUCTIVE—WHY IT MAY BE DISPENSED WITH.

The writers on political economy who restrict wealth to matter are very naturally led to lay much stress on the distinction of *labour*, as productive and unproductive. According to them, the labour applied to the production of material commodities is alone productive; that which is applied to the production of immaterial commodities being regarded as unproductive. All persons engaged in agriculture, manufactures, or commerce, are therefore *productive labourers;* and magistrates, lawyers, physicians, teachers, poets, philosophers, clergymen,—as also players, opera-dancers, jugglers, and mountebanks,—are *unproductive labourers.*

It is not denied that an unproductive may often have a far greater influence in advancing the wealth of a country than a productive labourer; that the labours of a Watt or a Fulton, for instance, were in this respect equivalent to those of many thousands who have owed to them the very existence of their several occupations. Notwithstanding this, however, the consistency of the distinction in question is maintained on the ground of the one class of labourers being engaged in *directly* producing wealth, while the other class are only *indirectly* instrumental in its production,—a ground which is, without doubt, perfectly tenable, if immaterial products be excluded from the definition of wealth.

If now we suppose the *relation* of capital to wealth to be the same as that which I have stated in the preceding pages, it will be the productive labourers alone who are employed by capital; and, in order to determine whether any individual be a productive or unproductive labourer, we need only inquire whether he be, or be not, employed by capital.

But the political economists, on whose views I am now remarking, do not invariably regard as capital the wealth which is appropriated "to the purpose of again producing wealth." When, under any circumstances, the wealth produced is altogether unproductively consumed, it is obvious that no permanent addition is made to the wealth of the community. It follows that if we class the producers of the wealth thus consumed with the unproductive labourers, and therefore refuse to denominate the wealth by which they are employed capital, no errour will ensue in reference to the progress of national wealth; and it is in reference to this progress alone, that the distinction under consideration will be asserted by any one to be of any the least consequence. Although menial servants are in many cases occupied in adding utility to matter, the writers of whom I am speaking style them unproductive. No one who employs them does so with the object in view of becoming thereby richer: all that they produce is unproductively consumed; and their wages constitute, on this account, no portion of their employer's capital.*

So long as wealth is restricted in its signification to matter,

* That no one who employs menial servants does so with the object in view of becoming thereby richer, is a remark only generally true. A cook, for example, in a public hotel, is directly engaged in adding to his employer's wealth. According, therefore, to those political economists who adopt the distinction now under consideration, he must in this case be ranked with the productive labourers.

the distinction which has just been explained, between productive and unproductive labour (to repeat what I have already said) will be found to be always perfectly consistent with itself;—the numerous instances of apparent inconsistency that have been charged upon it, by different writers, being all of them founded on a misapprehension of the meaning attached to it by those who have adopted it. Its expediency is, however, a very different question. This depends entirely on the manner in which wealth and capital have been previously defined. If these terms have been applied exclusively to material objects, and if they have been so applied on account of the peculiar importance of such objects in their relation to the science of political economy, it will certainly become equally important to distinguish carefully between the producers of wealth, and all those who are engaged in producing what, however useful it may be, is not wealth. On the other hand, if wealth and capital are made to comprehend as well immaterial objects as material ones, every species of labour which is productive of utility, whether this utility be first, so to speak, embodied in matter, or not, will be productive, and the distinction in question will be made to disappear altogether. There will, at least, be no unproductive labour excepting when more labour than is necessary is employed to produce a particular commodity, or when more of it is produced than is required by the comparative wants of the community. I may remark that, when this is the case, while a certain portion of the *labour* employed is unproductive, every *labourer* will, nevertheless, be productive in a certain degree; for if he be in *no* degree productive, he will scarcely have any claim to the designation of a labourer.

Care must be had not to connect together too closely the distinctions of productive and unproductive labour, and of productive and unproductive *consumption*, so as to suppose that the rejection of the former will necessarily lead to the rejection also of the latter. This, on the contrary, being identical with the distinction between the wealth which is appropriated as capital and the wealth which is not so appropriated, will have its importance in no wise diminished.

Now if labour of every *kind* is productive, the labour of menial servants is productive. They are therefore employed by capital; or, in other words, their wages constitute a portion of their employer's capital. But to express ourselves thus is, it may be said, to set at defiance the established usage of language. Not more so, however, than those writers do who distinguish labour into productive and unproductive. The mode in which they contrive to render their use of the word capital consistent with ordinary usage has been already stated; and, by refusing to make any distinction, in respect to productiveness, between the different kinds of labour, I am not at all hindered from proceeding, if I so choose, in the same manner. On account of the whole of what menial servants produce, whether it be material or immaterial, being consumed unproductively, their wages may be omitted from among the constituent portions of capital, without affecting in the least the correctness of our conclusions concerning the progress of the capitalist or nation in wealth, or even the phraseology in which those conclusions are expressed. The reader may therefore if he pleases, understand me, in what is to follow, as making this slight modification of my definition of capital.

It may here be mentioned that a practical and *moral* advantage cannot fail to result from getting rid of the distinction between the productive and unproductive labourers. Mankind, instead of being separated into two classes having occupations essentially differing, and liable on this account to an interference with each other's interests, will come to be regarded as constituting one and the same great family. The political economist, by continually associating together in his investigations every species of manual or bodily labour with that of the most refined and exalted *intellect,* cannot fail to dignify the former in his estimation; while he will, on the other hand, contribute most effectually to remove from intellectual labour the *stigma* which is ordinarily implied by designating it as unproductive. If he shall succeed in banishing from the *popular* language such phrases as "the productive classes" and "the unproductive classes," he will have done more to prevent the "workmen" of a country from esteeming themselves to be the only *useful* portion of society, than he could possibly do by reminding his readers, every time he writes the word unproductive, that his object in applying it to any individual is not to pronounce him to be unproductive of utility, but of *material* objects having utility,—not to pronounce him to be a mere consumer of the products of the labour of others, but simply to be not employed by capital, although perhaps employed in continually conferring the most extensive benefits on his fellow-men. The definitions of technical terms, which do not accord with their popular acceptation, are very apt to be forgotten even by those who have paid some attention to the science to which those terms relate; and hence it is no uncommon thing to see the popular acceptation usurp the place of the technical, even in professedly scientific treatises.

Here I shall suspend, for the present, my remarks on capital and its relations, and shall likewise bring to a close the business of *mere* classification and definition.

CHAPTER VII.

INFLUENCE OF SUPPLY AND DEMAND IN DETERMINING THE EXCHANGEABLE VALUE OF A COMMODITY.

I HAVE already mentioned the fact of every species of wealth being the subject of frequent exchanges, and that the exchangeable value of a commodity might be regarded as a criterion of the existence of wealth. One of the topics, therefore, which naturally present themselves early for inquiry to the political economist is,—what the circumstances are that determined the *degree* of the exchangeable value of different commodities, or why the exchangeable value of any thing is just what it is, and no other. I proceed to the discussion of this topic.

Of the three conditions on which the existence of exchangeable value was stated to depend, the capacity of being appropriated is of an absolute and invariable character, whilst the other two, viz. the possession of utility, and a limited supply, admit of coexisting in all possible degrees; and the relation which these bear to each other, in reference to any two commodities, must consequently determine the degree of their exchangeable values, when they are compared together. Now, other circumstances remaining the same, in proportion to the utility of any object will be the desire to obtain it, and more of other things will be offered in exchange for it. Exchangeable value may, therefore, be regarded as determined, in every instance, by the relation which the *supply* of a commodity has to the *demand* for it.

Before, however, attempting to trace the manner in which this determination takes place, it is important to render the ideas attached to the terms supply and demand as distinct as possible, and to clear them of such ambiguities as might lead to errour or obscurity in our reasonings. I shall likewise premise that, since commodities are for the most part exchanged for money, the attention of the reader will be directed, in the first place, to the laws which regulate their *prices;* when it will be easy to infer those which apply to every case of exchangeable value.

By the supply of a commodity is to be understood the quantity of it which comes into the possession of the sellers, and is offered by them for sale, during a given portion of time; and we must carefully distinguish, in the case of *material* commodities, between the supply of a commodity as thus defined, and that amount or *stock* of it which the sellers may think it for their advantage to keep on hand, in order to attract purchasers to their respective stores or warehouses,—by ensuring to them the opportunity of at all times procuring, on application, whatever they may stand in need of, or by presenting for their selection a larger assortment of goods. The stock on hand among the sellers, and which they offer for sale, so far from having any *direct* proportion to the supply, is generally less as the latter is augmented, and greater as that is diminished; for it is plain that every seller will be more disposed to keep on hand a commodity, according as he has a less expectation of being shortly supplied with it, and so *vice versâ;* and nothing is easier than for the sellers to augment or diminish the stock on hand, in the one case by the raising, and in the other by the lowering, of prices.

By demand is not meant to be implied simply the desire of possessing. To this scarcely any limits can be assigned. Every one acquainted with the use of a commodity has necessarily the desire to possess it. But the desire to possess it, unless accompanied by an offer of money, or something else, in exchange for it, can obviously produce no effect whatever on its exchangeable value; because such a desire can in no way influence the sellers to part with it more or less readily. The demand with which we are concerned is to be estimated by the number of offers to purchase made in a given time, *at any given rate :* and where more offers are made to purchase a commodity at its existing price than before, the demand is said to have increased; while the contrary will take place, when the number of similar offers is diminished.

Let us now examine in succession the different modes in which variations in the relation between the supply of, and the demand for, commodities can influence their prices. And let our examination, in the first instance, have reference to *material* commodities.

1. The demand for a commodity remaining the same, let the supply become more abundant. If then its price were not to rise, the stock on the hands of the sellers would accumulate, without producing any counterbalancing advantage. It would be so much dead and unprofitable capital. To avoid such a state of things, and dispose of the additional supply, there is no other remedy for the sellers to have recourse to, but to lower the price of the commodity. Many of those persons who were purchasers before, will now purchase in larger quantity; and some, who were willing, rather than pay its former price, to dispense altogether with the article in question, will now become purchasers. Its price will only cease to fall, when the quantity disposed of is just equal to the supply.

2. If we now suppose the supply of a commodity to be diminished, while, as under the preceding supposition, the demand continues the same, it is clear that the interest of the sellers will prompt them to raise its price, until, in consequence of the corresponding diminution of the amount of sales, the quantity disposed of will not exceed, but be just equal to the diminished supply.

3. The supply remaining the same, let the demand be increased. Let the persons who before purchased a certain article now purchase a greater quantity of it; and let others who before did not purchase it at all now become purchasers. We can suppose such an increase of demand to arise, either

from a change in the fashion of the day, or from some new use to which the article in question is capable of being applied. But whatever the occasion of it may be, the sellers will be induced to raise prices; for by so doing, while they make greater profits, they can at the same time dispose of the whole supply.

4. A diminution of demand will, it must be obvious, produce effects directly opposite to those resulting from an increase of demand. The sellers will lower prices, until the purchases made shall be sufficient in amount to take off the supply.

5. The prices of things are affected, not only by actual variations in the rates of supply and demand, but likewise by every expectation of the occurrence of such variations at a future time. An expectation of an extraordinary future supply will operate to lower present prices in a two-fold manner; by directly influencing the minds of the sellers,— and by its influence on the sellers, through its operation on the minds of the buyers. First, the sellers, aware that the expected increase of supply, when it shall have actually occurred, will have the effect of lowering prices, will be anxious to make a greater number of present sales, and to diminish the stock they have on hand; for which reason they will at once sell cheaper. But, secondly, the buyers equally aware with the sellers of the expected increase of supply, will be induced to postpone their purchases to a certain extent. In other words, they will make a less present demand. And in this way too, it will be apparent from what has been said already, the sellers will be led to reduce their prices.

6. An expected diminution of supply must, of course, produce the opposite effect. The sellers will be disposed to raise prices, that they may reserve a larger stock of goods; and the buyers will make a greater present demand; which,

again, will be an additional inducement to the sellers to sell dearer.

7. An expected increase of demand will be a motive to the sellers at once to raise prices, thereby to retain a greater stock of goods on hand; and it will have a tendency to multiply the present number of buyers, and, in this way likewise, to raise prices.

8. An expected diminution of demand will have the contrary effect of lowering prices. The sellers will have a motive to diminish the stock they have at present on hand; while, in expectation of a fall of prices, the buyers will be inclined to postpone their purchases, and will thus, by making a less present demand, offer an additional motive to the sellers to dispose of their commodities at a lower rate.

It is scarcely necessary to remark that more than one of the causes which have been mentioned, of the variation of the prices of commodities, may be operative at the same time; when, of course, the effect actually produced will be complicated of the effects which they are calculated to produce if they act separately; and it is obviously very possible, that the causes in operation to vary prices might so neutralise each other's action, as to retain those prices at nearly an uniform rate.

Every expected future change in the rate of the supply or demand will have an influence on present prices, so much the less in proportion to *the remoteness of the expectation.* The truth of this cannot but be apparent from what has been stated.

The degree, too, of that influence will depend, in some measure, on *the nature of the commodity,* in relation to which the increase or diminution of supply or demand is expected. For example, if an article be of a perishable nature, an expected future diminution of supply or increase of demand, cannot be as strong an inducement to the sellers to raise its price, and to keep a large quantity of it on hand, as if it were more durable. An expectation of a diminished supply of oranges, three months hence, would produce little or no impression on their present prices: the fruiterers must, at all events, sell the whole of their stock within a time less than that specified, or consent to suffer a total loss by the perishing of the oranges. On the other hand, an expected diminution, at the end of the three months, in the supply of hardware or corn, which can be *stored* in the mean while without loss, would have a marked effect on the price of the article. Again, the willingness, or *power*, of any individual to postpone his purchases, will depend on the degree in which he stands in need of what is proposed to be purchased. If it be to him a necessary of life, he must procure it immediately; but if it be a mere luxury, he may contrive to do without it. Now if there exist an expectation of an increased supply of, or a diminished demand for it at a future day, it has been shewn that its price will fall partly in consequence of the diminution of present demand; which diminution, being itself the result of the disposition of the buyers to postpone purchasing, it follows that, according as an article is less an object of necessity, and more an object of luxury, its price will be affected by the expectation of an extraordinary supply, or of a decrease of demand, at a future day.

CHAPTER VIII.

THE SAME SUBJECT CONTINUED.

In prosecuting the inquiry into the circumstances, or causes, which occasion a variation in the prices of commodities, it has been impliedly supposed, that the money for which they are exchanged is in no respect whatever subjected to change. But money is itself a commodity, and therefore liable to the same changes in respect to supply and demand as all others. And in comparing it with any other which is supposed to undergo no changes of the kind, it must be obvious that we may reason concerning its exchangeable value, just as we did concerning prices. An alteration of the exchangeable value of money is, however, identical with an alteration in the price of the article with which it is compared. Hence the price of commodities will vary, not only on account of a change, present or expected, in the rate of their supply or demand, but likewise on account of any similar change in reference to the money for which they are bought or sold.

This last conclusion may be reached by an argument, although substantially the same, in a different form. When the demand for money increases, every thing else remaining unchanged, it is implied that the desire to possess money, rather than other things, is greater than before. Less money will therefore be offered in exchange for *all* other commodities; that is, there will be a general fall of prices. The contrary effect will be produced, it is plain, by a diminution in the demand for money. Any augmentation of the supply of money will, of course, be followed by a greater number of purchases, and any diminution of such supply by a less number of purchases. In the one of the cases just mentioned, there will, therefore, be a general fall of prices; and, in the other, a general rise of prices will take place. The prices of commodities will consequently vary, as before stated, as well on account of any previous alteration in the supply of or demand for money, as of such an alteration in respect to the commodities themselves.

The effect, moreover, on prices, of the supply of money, or the demand for it, becoming greater or less, is to cause them to rise or fall *in the same proportion*. So long as the necessities and desires of men remain unaltered, will the money *actually circulating* be applied to the procuring of the very same commodities. If the circulating medium be doubled, the price of *every thing* will be doubled; and the like in whatever other ratio that medium may be supposed to have increased; or in whatever ratio it be supposed to have diminished. The exchangeable values of commodities, other than money, when these are compared with each other, will hence remain unaffected by any supposed alteration in the supply of or demand for money; and we may, therefore, reason correctly concerning their exchangeable values universally, by assuming the supply of and demand for money to remain unaltered. But, when this is the case, it has been shewn that the price of every commodity will vary with every alteration in the present or expected rates of its supply or demand. We are hence entitled to conclude that, when any two commodities, other than money, are compared together,—and this even when their exchange takes place through the intervention of money,—their exchangeable values will depend on the degree of the supply and demand of *both*, in reference to the present and likewise to the future.

Again, since the exchangeable value of money, when estimated in reference to any other commodity, is dependent entirely on the quantity of money for which this is exchanged, so that, when the price of the commodity is reduced in any proportion, the exchangeable value of money, thus estimated, will be *augmented* in the very same proportion, it follows that money will have its value in exchange determined precisely like that of every other commodity, viz. both by the relation existing between supply and demand in respect to itself, and in respect to the commodity for which it is exchanged.

I have now, I hope, explained in an unexceptionable manner, and perhaps with more than sufficient fulness, the operation of the principles of supply and demand in determining the exchangeable values of *material* commodities. The question still remains,—on what principles are the exchangeable values of *immaterial* or *intellectual* products determined? And also on what principles is that of labour, or are the *wages* of labour determined? In reference to immaterial products, I may remark that there is no part of the foregoing reasoning which is not quite as applicable to them as to those that are material, excepting the circumstance of there being nothing in relation to the former analogous to the "stock on hand" among the sellers, of which mention has been made when treating of the exchangeable values of the latter. But my reasoning, it will be recollected, did not in any way assume that stock to be of a particular magnitude; and the conclusions to which I was led must, therefore, be equally true, however *small* that stock may be supposed to be. And it would be quite logical to infer their truth even in the case of that stock, to use the language of mathematicians, being diminished indefinitely; which is the case with all immaterial commodities. They are consumed in the very act of being produced, and cannot, it is manifest, remain even for an instant "on hand."

But since they are not embodied in any intervening object, they may, very clearly, be resolved into the compensation or wages of intellectual labour; and the investigation of the theory of exchangeable value may, independently of what has just been stated, be completed by pointing out the causes which regulate wages. These too, it can easily be shewn, are determined, at any particular time, on the principles of supply and demand.

For this purpose, let us suppose in the *first* place, while the demand for labour remains the same, the supply of it to increase. The same amount of what is appropriated by the capitalists for wages will now have to be divided among a greater number of persons. The wages of each must, therefore, be diminished. *Secondly,* it is obvious that the contrary effect will follow a diminution of the supply of labour. *Thirdly,* let the amount of labour applied continue the same, and the demand for labour increase. Such a demand necessarily implies that a greater amount of wages is distributed among the same number of persons: of course, the share or wages of each will be greater than before. And *fourthly,* the contrary effect to this will plainly be produced by a diminished demand. This reasoning in regard to the exchangeable value, or wages, of labour, I need hardly say, is applicable to labour of every sort, bodily or mental,—however rude or refined.

The prices, or exchangeable values, of all things, including labour, are determined then, in every instance, by the relation subsisting between supply and demand.

CHAPTER IX.

NATURAL AS DISTINGUISHED FROM MARKET PRICES—NATURAL WAGES.

If prices were ever fluctuating, without regard to any fixed law, no other account could be given of them than that they are determined by the relation subsisting between supply and demand; and our analysis in respect to them would necessarily be here at an end. But wherever any constancy can be observed amidst the changes observed, there we may be assured that such a law exists, and is a legitimate subject for our investigation. Now any one who will carefully compare, for a sufficient length of time, the prices of a particular article, in any market, will find that, in a few cases only excepted, there is such a thing as a *mean* or *average* price, which may be regarded as invariable, while the actual or *market* prices seem, as it were, to oscillate about them, and to have a constant tendency to approach and to become equal to them. On what circumstances do these average prices depend? Or, which is the same thing, why is the price, at any period, of an article, what it is on the average, and neither more nor less? The inquiry is one, not only more recondite than that in which we have been lately engaged concerning market prices, but also more intimately connected with the most important deductions of our science. I must, therefore, ask the particular attention of the reader, while I pursue it.

It naturally subdivides itself into two separate inquiries; the one relating to the price or wages of *labour;* the other to the prices of the different constituent portions of *wealth.* I might, indeed, say here of *material* wealth, because, as it will be recollected I stated in the preceding chapter, the price or compensation for *intellectual* or *immaterial* products is resolvable into the wages of labour.

Let us first enter upon the inquiry respecting wages. It is obvious that, if the circumstances under which the labour of man is exerted were in other respects the same, wages will be every where always in proportion to the *quantity* of labour; in other words, the wages of labour will be the same in all employments. For if they were not so, labour would be transferred from those employments where lower wages were paid to others in which the remuneration of labour was higher; and the rising generation, in seeking for themselves, or parents, in seeking for their children, the most advantageous employments, will prefer such as yield the highest wages. In this manner, by diminishing in some employments, and increasing in others, the supply of labour, an equality of wages would be ultimately established; though with more or less rapidity, according to the greater or less analogy existing between the occupations from which and those to which the the transfer of labour is made, and the consequent facility or difficulty of making such transfer.

The wages of labour are however, in reality, exceedingly unequal. Compare, for example, the wages of a common day-labourer with those of the professional man, or with those of the artist. Hence we may infer that there *are* other circumstances, besides the quantity of labour applied, which have an influence on the amount of wages received in different occupations. These may be all classed under the two following heads.

1. The agreeableness, or disagreeableness, of an occupation. This includes such considerations as the following: the hardness or easiness of the work to be done; its being cleanly or filthy; its requiring a greater or less degree of exposure; its being healthy or the reverse; its being more or less steady; the probability or improbability of success in it;

its capability of being exercised *at home* or not; the degree of honour or disgrace attached to it. It will at once be perceived that considerations of this nature will combine with the amount of wages to be received, so to regulate the supply of labour in every occupation, as to establish an equality, not of wages, but of advantages and disadvantages *generally*, comprehending of course, under these terms, a higher or lower rate of wages, as an element, though one element only.

2. When different employments exact from the labourer peculiar endowments, natural or acquired. We have a case of this kind where any employment requires especial trustworthiness. The supply of labourers will obviously be limited in such a manner, as to establish on that account a higher rate of wages. Of this nature, likewise, are those employments, in which a preparatory and expensive education or training is necessary; in which case, the supply of labour will be so regulated as to determine a rate of wages sufficient to compensate, in addition to the labour actually applied, the expense laid out in qualifying the labourer for his occupation. His wages must be high enough to replace, on the *average*, the sum expended in his preparatory education, with the usual profits. So, at least, they would be, did not the hope of success in his profession or calling in life occasionally operate on the youthful mind with somewhat greater force than the apprehension of failure.

The circumstances which have been enumerated, while they cause a very great diversity to subsist in the amount of wages received in different employments, will also cause wages in each of them to *tend* continually to a certain rate, which, when attained, offers no inducement for a transfer of labour to or from it. These average wages, about which the market rates of wages are ever oscillating within certain limits, may be designated as *natural* or *necessary* wages; natural, because the market rates of wages have a tendency to coincide with them; and necessary, because they must be at least *so high*, in order to ensure the continued production of any commodity, in the usual quantity. And when, so to speak, an equilibrium takes place with respect to wages, by the contemporaneous establishment of their natural rates in all the various employments of industry, the rates of wages may be said to become *equalised*; although the expression may not be such as is altogether desirable, and is accurate only in reference to *all* the circumstances of advantage or of disadvantage, accompanying the application of a given quantity of labour.

CHAPTER X.

THE SUBJECT OF NATURAL WAGES CONTINUED.

There might perhaps in some occupations seem, at first view, to be no uniform *natural* rate of wages, on account of the compensation which is paid to different individuals for their work or services, during equal portions of time, being occasionally different. This is owing to the capacity, or skill, of all persons not being the same. He who does twice or thrice as much work *of the same sort*, in the same time, disposes in reality of twice or thrice the quantity of labour; the exchangeable value, or wages, of which will, therefore, be compensated in both cases alike. The wages of *labour* will be at a certain fixed rate in each occupation; while the daily, weekly, or monthly wages of the *labourer* may admit of a certain degree of diversity. Where, however, the work done is not such as all persons engaged in the same general employment are able to perform, the case will be similar to that already considered of *different* occupations, which require from the labourer different endowments, natural or acquired; and the effects on wages must necessarily be the same.

All that has hitherto been said on the present branch of our subject has been founded on the suppositions, *first,* that every individual, in seeking for employment, is actuated exclusively by interested motives,—and *secondly,* that full scope is given to the operation of the principles of supply and demand. Where either of these suppositions does not hold good, wages may be permanently above or below their natural rate. It may not be uninteresting to specify a case or two. One, and sometimes a very striking one, of the absence of interested motives in the regulation of wages, is presented by the christian missionary, who, not applying his ministrations where there is the most *demand* for them, using the word in its politico-economical acceptation, is often content with comparatively a slender portion of the comforts of life, or perhaps even exposes himself to peril and privation among remote and savage nations, for the sake of promoting the highest interests of his fellow-men. Those guilds or corporations of trades, statutes of apprenticeship, and other regulations of the kind, the offspring of the dark and middle ages in Europe, whose effect is to limit the supply of labourers, afford examples of cases in which wages may be artificially maintained at a rate higher than their natural rate. The salaries of public officers, also, have sometimes little or no immediate connexion with the principles of supply and demand. This arises from the dispensers of offices undertaking, in most cases very properly, to judge of the qualifications of applicants or candidates to fill them with advantage to the public, and of the amount of the salaries which it is fitting to pay. If an appointment to office involved simply a contract for the performance of certain duties, individuals could often be found willing to perform them for a small pecuniary compensation, or even no compensation at all. Indeed, some of the most important might actually command a considerable price in the market. How many persons, and very incompetent persons too, would be willing, for instance, to bid very high for the presidency of the United States, if, as happened to the throne of the Roman Empire, it were to be put up for sale at public auction!

Again, all that precedes has a relation to occupations pursued in the same place or district. But wages may, in different parts of a country, be at very different rates in the very same occupations. Besides the expense, in a greater or less degree, connected with every change of residence—an expense which the great majority of labourers may be very ill able to afford—man is, in general, on other accounts not readily to be moved from place to place. When he consents to the adoption of such a step, he must likewise make up his mind to a rupture of the ties of kindred and of friendship, and to do violence to the thousand associations which bind the heart of every one to the place of his birth, or the home of his youth,—to go, if his destination be a remote one, to perhaps an uncongenial climate, and a different system of manners and customs. Similar observations will apply to emigration from any country to a foreign one, and with still greater force; for the emigrant will, for the most part, have to encounter the inconvenience of a still greater diversity in the condition of society, together with those arising from a difference of language, and will, at all events, become subjected to another government, not always administered on better principles than his own; with which it may even come occasionally into hostile collision. The considerations, some or all them, which have been mentioned, do, in fact, produce a permanent difference in the rates of wages in different countries, and in different parts of the same country, by preventing as rapid and as extensive a transfer of labour, from where wages are lower to where they are higher, as would otherwise take place.

I shall conclude, for the present, my remarks on wages, by deriving from the doctrine of their equalisation in different employments the practical consequence, that although, if *every* individual were to be entirely indifferent in the choice of an occupation, such equalisation could not take place, and wages would vary according to no fixed law, the question of the choice of a profession or trade is still one of less importance and difficulty, and ought to be one of less doubt and hesitation, than is very commonly supposed; and a particular individual will incur but little hazard of committing any great mistake in his choice, if he follow the bent of his inclinations, and select that occupation for which he has, most probably, the greatest aptitude. Since all occupations in the same region of country are, on the average, every circumstance considered, equally advantageous, he may rest assured that if, at a particular period, there should be in one place an over-supply of any species of labour, there will, it is extremely probable, be contemporaneously an under-supply of the same species of labour in some *other* place, and that the over-supply in question can be only temporary. It is often very remarkable, also, how rapidly an under-supply of labour sometimes ceases to exist, and is even converted into the contrary state of things, by an influx of labourers from where the supply is more abundant,—each labourer being apt to forget that every other may be operated on, to induce a change of his residence, in the same manner as himself.

CHAPTER XI.

NATURAL PRICES—GENERAL RATE OF PROFITS—TRANSFER OF CAPITAL.

I PROCEED to the second head of inquiry in respect to *average* prices, viz. the circumstances which determine the average prices of commodities other than labour. If we suppose capital to be applied in every branch of industry under similar circumstances of advantage or of disadvantage, *profits excepted*, it will necessarily follow that these must also have a tendency every where to equality; for if they were at any time unequal, the interests of the capitalists would obviously lead them to transfer their capitals from the less to the more profitable employments; and this again, by diminishing the supply, and therefore *raising* prices in the former,—and increasing it in the latter, and therefore *lowering* prices,—would tend to the establishment of a *general rate* of profits. The market prices of commodities will, of course, continually fluctuate about those prices which determine that rate of profits, and will likewise always have a tendency to an equality with them. These average prices, as in the analogous case of wages, are denominated *natural* or *necessary* prices; natural, because market prices naturally tend to a coincidence with them; and necessary, because prices at least as high are necessary to secure the continued production of a commodity in the usual quantity. The deviations of market from natural prices may be greater, and endure for a longer time, according to the difficulty of transferring capital from the employments yielding a lower to those which yield a higher rate of profit.

The possibility has been taken for granted of transferring capital from one employment to another. In this nothing was assumed beyond what every one knows to be a fact. As, however, the *mode* in which such transfer is effected is a matter of some importance in its bearing on many practical questions, it may be worth while to endeavour to give precision to our ideas respecting it. It must be manifest, in the first place, that capital may sometimes be very readily transferred from one *analogous* employment to another. A steam engine, for example, employed in one manufacture, may, very possibly, be quite as well fitted for a different one. Indeed, there is a certain portion of capital which is almost equally suited for *every* employment: such, I mean, as the food and clothing of many classes of workmen. These, it is obvious, may be very nearly the same in very different occupations, and admit, consequently, of a ready transfer from one to any other. Again, though there are certain *specific* portions of capital which are absolutely *intransferable* from the purposes to which they are appropriated to certain others having little or no analogy with them, as, for instance, the ship from commerce to agriculture,—yet capital, estimating its amount by its exchangeable value, may, even in such cases, be said with propriety to be, to a certain extent, *gradually* transferable. How so? it may be asked. Does not this seem like a contradiction in terms? This is the explanation. The motive for *desiring* to transfer capital can here be no other than a difference in the rate of profits. Now if a specific portion of any one's capital be absolutely intransferable, that desire, it is plain, can only be productive of its proper effect by the transfer of the remaining portion of it; but this will not at once take place, and the portion of capital first mentioned be abandoned, unless a greater *amount*, and not simply a higher *rate*, of profits shall be received than before. The transfer in question will, therefore, be gradually effected by omitting, where it can conveniently be done, to repair the wear and tear of the old and intransferable portions of capital, and by not substituting new machinery or other instruments of production in their place, when those in use become dilapidated or unserviceable. By such a process alone, may the *navigating* capital of a nation, for example, be at all transferred from the ocean to the land.

It is usual to speak of the *losses* incurred by every transfer of capital from one employment to another. This is, however, an inaccuracy. The transfer is made, in order that the *whole* amount of profits received shall be augmented; and, no matter how much capital may have been abandoned in the transfer of the remainder, this remainder, because a greater amount of profits is now received than before, will have a greater exchangeable value than the entire capital had; and hence, so far from there having been any *real* loss of capital, the portion of it abandoned will have been more than compensated. If, indeed, the capitalist had been induced to transfer his capital, because profits, in the former application of it, had fallen below the general rate, he would have incurred a loss *before* any transfer had taken place; which, so far from giving occasion to any *additional* loss, is had recourse to for the purpose of preventing such a result.

Although the distinction between capital as more or less readily transferable is not identical, as must have been already perceived, with that of circulating and fixed capital, they will nevertheless be found, in the majority of instances, to approach very near to each other. Hence it is that, in reference *generally* to the transfer of capital, it is quite customary to speak of fixed capital as being of course transferred with difficulty; and the reverse with respect to circulating capital.

Perhaps it may be thought by some that, in order to demonstrate the law of the general equalisation of profits, it is unnecessary to establish the possibility, and still less so to exhibit the manner, of transferring capital from one employment to another; and that an equality of profits would ultimately, though in many cases slowly, be produced by the continual application of the *accumulating* capital to the most profitable employments. But, not to mention that, in a stationary or declining country, there is no such thing as an accumulation of its capital, speaking of this as a whole, an attentive consideration of the subject will enable my readers to perceive that, if capital be in fact accumulating, or, which is the same thing, be increasing, it must do so in *all* or *nearly all* employments, and that an addition must, in consequence, be making simultaneously, as well to the comparatively intransferable portions of the capital of a country, as to those that are transferable,—to fixed and circulating capital alike. We may therefore conclude, that to invest any portion of the accumulating capital, so as to yield the greatest profits, implies in every case a transfer of capital, excepting only when the newly existing capital is *already* most profitably applied,—and implies too a transfer of *fixed* capital. The only exception to *this*, and it is a very rare one indeed, being when the *less* profitable employments might happen to have circulating capital alone applied to them.

Before proceeding farther, it may be proper to mention that, in my reasoning on the subject of natural prices, I have taken for granted the possibility of producing every commodity in a greater or less quantity, at pleasure. Now this is not *always* true. There are a few things which, from their very nature, do not admit of reproduction at will; and of whose exchangeable value no other account can be rendered than that it is determined on the principles of supply and demand. They have a market price, but no natural price. "Some rare statues and pictures, scarce books and coins, wines of a peculiar quality which can be made only from grapes grown on a particular soil, and of which there is a very limited quantity, are all of this description."

CHAPTER XII.

SUBJECT OF NATURAL PRICES CONTINUED—THE ORDINARY RATES OF PROFITS—DETERMINATION OF THE PRICES OF COMMODITIES BY THE COST OF PRODUCING THEM.

In establishing the existence of a general rate of profits, and the existence likewise of certain natural or necessary prices, which, when paid for any commodity, will yield the capitalist that rate of profits, and to which market prices have a constant tendency to conform, it will be recollected that a perfect similarity was assumed as regards every circumstance of advantage or disadvantage in the application of capital to different employments, excepting only the rate of profits to be received. Now if those circumstances be supposed to vary in different employments, as they in reality do to a certain extent, though in general to an extent that is inconsiderable when compared to the variations in the similar circumstances which have an influence on the rate of wages, it is evident that they will so modify the distribution of capital, as to reduce the rate of profits in each employment so much below the general or average rate, as may counterbalance the possession by the capitalist of any peculiar advantages in other respects,—and to raise it on the contrary supposition. Advantages of the kind adverted to were conferred on *agricultural* capital in the different countries of Europe by the feudal system, which associated, not only nobility, but also peculiar privileges and power, with the possession of large landed estates. And even in our own country, where the spirit of civil and religious liberty has, from its first settlement by Europeans to the present time, watchfully guarded against the introduction of institutions partaking in any degree of feudality, the right of *suffrage* has been in certain cases confined by the constitutions of some of the states to freeholders; thus granting a peculiar, though perhaps a comparatively slight, advantage to the owner of *real* property. Independently, however, of any peculiarity in the organisation of government, or the institutions of society, the possession of real property,—of houses and land,—in consequence of their visible and permanent character operating on the minds of men, makes a stronger impression of riches than an equal amount of *personal* property would do. Their owner gains more of that consideration and influence in society which is every where, in a greater or less degree, acquired by the possessors of great wealth, and will, consequently, be induced to content himself with a diminished rate of profits.

The inequality existing, at the same period of time, in the profits of capital among different nations, having a constant and extensive intercourse with each other, is to be accounted for on the same principles. If an inhabitant of any one country could, by transferring his capital to another, augment his profits,—and the remark is equally applicable, only in a less degree, to the transfer of capital from one province to another of the same country,—he might, nevertheless, be disinclined to take such a step, through an unwillingness to be separated from his property, and to entrust it to foreign management and foreign legislation; and the difficulties in the way of his emigrating with his property,—difficulties which have been already stated,—are far from being at all times easily overcome.

But although, in consequence of the different circumstances of advantage or disadvantage in which capital is applied, profits will not tend to an *absolute* equality in all employments, even in the same district of country, it is plain that they will have a tendency to be at such a rate in each, as will offer no motive for transferring capital from one employment to another; and that rate will, of course, be the *ordinary* rate of profits. When, too, the ordinary rates subsist at the same time in all employments, profits, as in the analogous case concerning wages, may be said to be *equalised.* With respect to natural prices, they will have the same relation to the various ordinary rates, that they were shewn to have to the *general* rate, of profits; and their relation to the market prices of commodities will also be the same as before.

I may here derive a like practical lesson concerning the *channel* into which capital can, at a given time and place, be most profitably directed, as I did in reference to the choice of an occupation, when I treated of the equalisation of wages. There is room, no doubt, for the exercise of that sagacity which is the characteristic of the expert man of business, in the disposition to be made of capital; but it is still true that, let an individual dispose of his capital in any employment as he will, he cannot expect to make *eventually* more than the ordinary profits. Those investments of capital, indeed, which seem often to promise most are very apt to be less profitable than others. Just as, when any market is supposed to be understocked with labour, *there* labourers will congregate from other quarters, and will, in consequence, bring about frequently a contrary state of things; so, with the exception of a few who may succeed in getting the *start* of all others, the capitalists, who embark in speculations on account of an impression generally diffused of their being more than ordinarily profitable, are precisely those who are most likely to be losers instead of gainers. Every one acts very much as if others had not the same motives with himself to do as he is doing. And so much capital comes to be invested as to glut the market with its products, and to cause prices to fall, and sometimes to fall ruinously low to the producers. Instances of the kind can scarcely fail to occur upon the unexpected opening of ports of commerce; and also on the granting by governments of peculiar encouragement or privileges to any one branch of industry over others.

It may now be mentioned that, where the price of any thing

is just sufficient, *besides replacing the capital consumed in its production, to yield the ordinary profits to the capitalist,* it is said to repay *the cost of producing it.* Hence *natural prices* are determined by the cost of production. And since *market prices* are ever fluctuating within certain limits about natural prices, and tend continually to an equality with them, the cost of production may be correctly said to regulate prices *universally,* market as well as natural.

CHAPTER XIII.

EFFECTS OF MONOPOLIES ON PRICES.

THE two important laws which have been deduced, of the equalisation of profits in the different branches of industry, and of the determination of the prices of commodities by the cost of producing them, do not apply to the case of a *monopoly.*

Let us suppose the exclusive privilege of producing a particular article to be bestowed on an individual, or a number of individuals associated together and acting in concert. In the first instance, let it likewise be supposed that the capital at their disposal is *not* sufficiently large to enable them to supply the market with the commodity which they produce, in sufficient abundance to cause it to be sold as low as its natural price. The consequence is manifest, that they will receive more than the ordinary profits.

The supposition is, however, hardly admissible that they will not in all cases, while they make more than the ordinary profits, have it in their power to borrow, or otherwise to procure, an additional capital, if they should deem it expedient to do so. Let us then assume, in the next place, that the monopolists find no limit to their power of producing, in a deficiency of capital. The exertion of this power will be now limited only by the interest of the producers. They will *understock* the market; because, by so doing, they will receive more than the ordinary profits; while, at the same time, these profits will be yielded to them by the capital which they may invest in any of the *unmonopolised* branches of industry.

If, in this state of things, capital be transferred from the monopoly to other employments, two effects of an opposite description must result: the profits of the portion transferred will be diminished; and those of the remainder will be augmented. The former will yield only the ordinary profits; and the profits of the latter will be augmented in consequence of the rise of prices resulting from the diminution in the supply of the monopolised commodity. These two effects cannot be always equal to, and neutralise, each other; for, if so, when the whole monopoly capital is transferred, its profits ought not to be less than before. But it is evident that they will then be lessened, because they will be just equal to the ordinary profits.

Nor can any one of the two effects produced be, in this manner, uniformly greater than the other, so that profits shall be *continually* lessened; because, if this were the case, when capital is transferred in the contrary direction, from other employments to that which is monopolised, the excess of the actual above the ordinary profits ought, on the other hand, to become continually greater and greater. But this also does not, and cannot, correspond with the fact. As soon as the transfer is sufficient to cause the market price of the monopolised commodity to fall so low as its natural price, the whole capital of the monopolists will yield profits no higher than at the ordinary rate; and a further transfer will diminish still more the amount of profits received.

We are, hence, entitled to conclude that there is a certain amount of capital which can be most advantageously, on the whole, invested in the production of any monopolised commodity,—an amount *less* than what would naturally be invested in its production, if all persons were at liberty to engage in it, —yielding more than the ordinary rate of profits, and maintaining prices at a higher level than they would *naturally* be at.

The height to which it is for the advantage of the monopolists to raise prices and profits, by diminishing the supply, varies with the nature of the commodity they produce. It needs no formal proof to be convinced that they will be disposed to raise them higher, according as this commodity approaches more nearly to the character of a necessary of life. What, however, is not so obvious, although experience makes it equally certain, is that the profits of capital, very frequently, even where luxuries are the objects of production, increase in a much greater ratio than the supply is diminished. This is strikingly exemplified by the following instance, out of many that might be adduced from the history of monopoly. The Dutch East India Company, when, through a miscalculation of the demands of the market, they had imported into Holland too large a quantity of *spices*, found it for their interest to consign a certain portion to the flames, rather than offer the whole for sale; the value received for the remainder more then compensating the company for what was burned.

If, instead of the exclusive privilege of producing a commodity being granted to any individual, or company of individuals, they have the exclusive power to produce it *in a particular manner*, this manner being the most advantageous or economical one, either in consequence of the possession by them of some secret in the arts, or of their having a *patent* right to the sole use of new and improved methods of production, or otherwise, the effects in regard to prices and profits will clearly be the same as in the case of their possessing an entire monopoly,—with this exception, the reason of which is obvious, that they could not raise prices, and of course their profits, at least for any length of time, higher than to the rate which would enable other capitalists to make the ordinary profits in the accustomed modes of producing.

It may be proper to mention here, as partaking in a degree of the nature of a monopoly, the advantage which those parties have in any market who *first* engage in an employment. There are always extraordinary expenses at the outset in every new undertaking; while some time must necessarily elapse before the customers of the producers already established can be induced to deal with the competitors of the latter on equally favourable terms. The existing producers may, moreover, often exclude any apprehended competition by temporarily lowering their prices, and indemnifying themselves for the temporary loss by raising prices when competition has ceased to be threatened. Such a course can, however, be practised with effect only in markets which are very limited in their nature, and more especially in respect to commodities which, in other and neighbouring markets, may be sold at a lower price, without offering a motive sufficient for their being *imported*, on account of the expense of transportation.

A large capitalist has similar advantages too over smaller capitalists, in addition to the greater economy with which his capital is susceptible in many cases of being managed. He can *afford* to receive a diminished rate of profits for a time, for the sake of excluding competition.

CHAPTER XIV.

OF RENT.

Many branches of industry do not yield the same rate of profits to all the different portions of capital invested in them. This is always the case when the *situations* adapted to the investment of capital are not all equally favourable to production. A very striking instance of the kind is furnished by agriculture, both on account of the very great diversity in the quality of the land, and the very different degrees of facility with which its produce can be conveyed to market. And a similar remark, differing only in the *extent* of its application, may be made in reference to the mines, to the fisheries, to such manufactures as are produced in circumstances more or less favourable, as, for example, such as are produced through the instrumentality of water power, and even in reference to trade, for, in every town or village, there are certain situations which are regarded, and in reality are, the best *stands* for business,—where the largest profits are made. In all such cases, it is the capital *last applied* which yields a rate of profits in correspondence, or equilibrium, with the ordinary rate of profits in other employments generally; since if it yielded less, it would, of course, have been otherwise invested, and if it yielded more, a greater amount of capital would have been invested together with it in the same branch of production, so as, by augmenting the supply of the commodity produced, to make this supply more abundant, prices consequently lower, and thus to cause profits to fall to the ordinary rate.

The last applied portion of capital may, in general, be supposed to be applied *under the most unfavourable circumstances.* Take, for instance, the case of the *land.* As society advances, additional capital will be applied, both to the land already cultivated, and for the purpose of taking new land into cultivation. When it is applied to the former, every one at all acquainted with the nature of the soil will at once acknowledge the impossibility of the produce increasing proportionally: the application of a double capital will not be followed by a double crop. On the other hand, when new land is taken into cultivation, the returns to the capital applied to it cannot be as large as those to the capital before applied to *older* land, or the new would before have had the preference. This was before passed by, either because it was of inferior fertility, or less favourably situated with respect to a market. A similar mode of reasoning, too, will apply, with a very slight modification, not in any degree affecting its force, to all the other instances enumerated, of employments yielding unequal profits to the different portions of capital applied to them.

An exception of which the proposition admits,—that the last applied capital is, at the same time, that which is applied under the most disadvantageous circumstances,—is where *mistakes* in judgment occur on the part of individuals when investing their capital. Another is when the *situations* or *sites* where capital was before applied have, since such application, deteriorated, and where, on account of the difficulty of transferring the capital already applied, this continues for a time invested as heretofore, though with profits below the ordinary rate. With these exceptions, and they are exceptions of comparatively little practical consequence, always implied, we may consider the proposition to be established.

Now the natural price of any commodity has been shewn to be that price which, after replacing the capital consumed in producing it, will yield to the capitalists the ordinary profits. It follows, therefore, from what has been stated that the *cost of production*, which determines the price of a commodity, is the cost of producing it with the capital last applied, or with the capital applied under the most disadvantageous circumstances in which the commodity in question is actually produced.

Political economists have found it expedient to separate from the profits received in any employment that portion by which they may exceed in amount those yielded to the capital invested most disadvantageously in the same employment, and have designated such excess by the name of *rent.* All land, consequently, yields rent, excepting the land just *taking* into cultivation; and so too does every portion of capital which is applied to the land before cultivated, with the exception only of what is the last applied. And having separated from profits every thing beyond the ordinary rate, under the denomination of rent, we are again entitled to say, that the ordinary rate of profits is yielded by every portion of capital,—the case of a monopoly only excepted;—and that profits are, therefore, *equalised* throughout all the various branches of industry.

Inasmuch, also, as the prices of commodities are determined by the cost of producing them by means of that portion of capital which yields simply the ordinary profits, without enabling the capitalist to pay any rent, it is a necessary consequence, that *the amount of rent paid by other capitalists has no concern in the determination of prices:* and I may remark that this is a point of great importance to be remembered.

CHAPTER XV.

THE SUBJECT OF RENT CONTINUED—DISTRIBUTION OF THE WEALTH PRODUCED, AMONG THE DIFFERENT CLASSES OF LANDLORDS, CAPITALISTS, AND LABOURERS.

The receivers of rent are usually classed together by political economists, under the denomination of *landlords.* It is, in fact, the proprietor of the land in cultivation (and an analogous remark may be made in every case of the payment of rent) who will receive the rent paid, after deducting from the *net* produce of the land the ordinary profits of the capital invested on it. This is obvious if he be likewise the owner of the capital so invested. And if he farm out his land to another, the latter will pay for his lease the ordinary profits of the capital invested on the land by the former, together with the rent. If *more* than this were paid, the farmer would not have a sufficient motive for taking the lease; for he will not receive, in addition to the wages of his labour, the ordinary profits of the capital he may himself employ. The farmer will not pay *less* than the amount stated, because he would then make more than the ordinary profits; and others would, of course, be found willing to make a higher offer for the lease to the landlord. So that, at all events, the landlord, or proprietor of the land, receives the rent: and it is worthy of notice that he does so, not as a compensation for any expenditure incurred by him upon the land in bringing it into cultivation, or subsequently improving it,—on all these he receives *profits,*—but as a compensation for the use of the *natural* powers of the soil.

Rent, as it is commonly understood, is not to be confounded with the acceptation of this term in political economy. When one person pays to another a certain sum, say 500 dollars per annum, for the lease of a farm, this sum is usually called its rent; whereas, according to the definition which I have given of the term rent, it is very possible that only a small part of the sum just mentioned is entitled to be so denominated; and the remainder may, therefore, constitute the profits of the capital invested on the land.

It may be difficult, and frequently even impossible, to distinguish accurately in a particular case between what is rent and what is profits. But the difficulty is not greater than is often that of distinguishing between profits and wages. Some tradesmen, apothecaries for example, are supposed by most persons to make more than the ordinary profits; when, in reality, the greater part of what is so styled is, properly speaking, the wages of the labour employed. Such occasional practical difficulties or inconveniences, in the application of the distinctions in question, will not be found to detract from their utility, or from the soundness of the conclusions to which we shall be led.

Here it will not be uninteresting, or unimportant, to note the manner in which the products of labour are distributed among the three different classes, of landlords or proprietors, —capitalists,—and labourers. Since it may be assumed that there is nothing produced without the use or aid of *some* capital, or advances made by the capitalists to the labourers in their employ, it is manifest that the whole produce of labour comes, in the first place, into the hands of the capitalists. They then distribute to the landlords their share of it, and also pay to the labourers, not any share of it to which the latter are entitled, but their wages, or compensation *in advance* for their labour, which is to be applied anew in the business of production.

Each of these classes may of course, on receiving their portion of the wealth produced, exchange it for money, or for any other commodities which they prefer to have in their possession; and the possession of any specific portion of what is produced, or the right of possessing it, may thus be transferred from individual to individual many times before it is actually consumed,—and consumed either productively, or unproductively.

I may remark too that, notwithstanding political economists speak of the *separate* classes of landlords, capitalists, and labourers, the same person may unite in himself the characters of landlord, of capitalist, and of labourer, or of any two of them. This, however, no more invalidates the propriety of such a classification than that a physician, happening occasionally to be versed in theological learning, should render it inexpedient to draw any line of distinction between theology and medical science.

Instances are continually presented of capitalists who labour themselves in superintending the application of their capital to production. The farmer, who is the owner of the land which he cultivates, is manifestly at once both landlord and capitalist. And this, it is equally manifest, will not prevent him from being at the same time engaged in *labouring*, if he so choose.

The land which pays rent will have a greater exchangeable value than the capital which has been invested upon it. Suppose this capital to amount to $10,000; and let the rate of profits be 10 per cent. Now if we assume the rent of the land to be $200, it will follow that the farmer who *leases* it will have to pay to the landlord $1200 per annum,—without taking into consideration what he would have to pay, in order to replace the wear and tear of the capital invested. The value of the land will therefore amount to a capital yielding $1200 profit, that is, on the suppositions which have been made, to a capital of 12,000 dollars.

But if we regard the capital invested in the land, viz. $10,000, as the product of labour, in accordance with that definition of wealth which makes it to consist in "the products of labour," would it be equally proper, it may here be asked, to regard as such the remaining $2000? Or ought not this portion of wealth to be viewed rather as having been produced independently of any *direct* application of labour, and in consequence merely of the existence of a right of property in land? If so, we shall have presented to us such an extensive exception to the proposition that wealth consists of the products of labour, as to preclude us from identifying it at any time with those products. To the question just put, I answer, however, in the negative. A moment's reflection will enable the reader to perceive that rent differs in no respect in its relation to labour from any other portion of the wealth produced, excepting that it has been produced under comparatively more advantageous circumstances,—circumstances, nevertheless, precisely the same in kind with those in which what remains to the farmer, after paying his rent, is produced. No one will deny this *remainder* to be the product of labour: and, therefore, no one can consistently deny rent to be likewise the product of labour.

CHAPTER XVI.

THE DIFFERENT MODES IN WHICH THE COST OF PRODUCTION, AND THEREFORE PRICES, MAY BE MADE TO VARY.

To return, for a short time, to the subject of prices. They have been shewn, it will be recollected, to depend, in the case of every commodity, on the cost of producing it, *by means of that portion of capital which pays no rent.* And it will also be recollected that, when the price at which any commodity is sold is just such as to replace the capital consumed in producing it, and to yield to the capitalist the ordinary profits, it is said to repay the cost of production. It is interesting to trace the different modes in which this cost, and consequently, the price of the commodity as dependent upon it (I speak of course of natural price) can be made to vary. I shall state the variations in question, with their causes, in reference to a consequent *fall* of prices; and the causes which are calculated to produce a change of an opposite description, will afterwards be manifest to every one.

But before I do this, I shall remark that where a number of causes either act together, or are capable of doing so, the only mode in which a satisfactory theory can be deduced, is to trace the consequences resulting from the action of each cause separately, abstracting from all consideration whatever of the others; and when that action is understood, we shall likewise know what the effects actually to be produced will be, when two or more of them act together. It may not be wholly unnecessary, too, to caution the reader, not merely in reference to what is immediately to follow, but likewise throughout the present treatise, lest he should too hastily generalise the inferences drawn when the operation of a single cause alone has been considered, and apply them inadvertently under every diversity of circumstances.

The cost of production may be separated into the two following elements; the capital consumed in producing a commodity, and the ordinary profits on the *whole* of the capital employed. Hence prices will fall, either when the capital consumed, or when the amount of profits received, is diminished.

Let us, however, analyse somewhat more in detail the circumstances which lead to a fall of prices. They will fall, *first*, when, every thing else remaining unchanged, the amount of capital employed is less than it was before. When this takes place, it is plain that prices must fall, as well because of the diminished amount of capital consumed, as on account of the profits of the capitalist being necessarily reduced exactly in proportion to the diminution of the capital employed.

Secondly, the same effect will be the consequence of a substitution of *fixed* for *circulating* capital. The latter was defined to be composed of every specific portion of capital which was wholly consumed in the act or process of production,—and the former to consist of those specific portions of capital which are only subjected, during the production of a commodity, to wear and tear. The substitution of fixed for circulating capital, therefore, necessarily implies a diminished consumption of capital, and a consequent fall of prices. To put this in the *most* striking point of view, let us compare the two extreme cases of a commodity produced altogether by means of circulating capital, and of another produced by capital *absolutely* fixed. And for the sake of greater precision, let us estimate the capital employed at a particular value, say $10,000, with the rate of profits at 10 per cent. In the first mentioned case, what is produced will be sold for $11,000; and in the last mentioned, for only $1000; these being the sums which will, in the two cases respectively, repay the cost of production. The price of it will also obviously range from $1000 to $11,000, according to the greater or less degree of the *fixedness* of the capital, by the aid of which it is produced.

Thirdly, the time may be diminished during which a given amount of capital is employed in production. When this occurs prices will fall, in consequence of the diminution of the profits required to be paid.

Fourthly, prices will fall from any previous reduction of wages; for since wages constitute a portion of capital, such reduction will be tantamount to the requiring of the employment, in the production of any particular article, of less capital than before;—and the proportion of circulating to fixed capital will likewise have become less.

And *lastly*, if we suppose the *rate* of profits to be diminished, the amount of profits to be received in any case will also be diminished; and, for this reason, agreeably to what has been stated, prices must be lowered.

More than one of the causes which are thus capable of effecting a fall of price may act at the same time, or may cooperate with some of the opposite causes, the tendency of which is to *raise* prices,—with this exception, that, so long as all other circumstances remain the same, (including of course among these circumstances, the productiveness of labour,) a general fall of wages is inconsistent with a contemporary general fall of profits; nor is it then possible for wages and profits to rise together. On the contrary, as wages fall profits must necessarily rise, and vice versâ.

This will be apparent if we look, for a moment, at a particular case or two. Let the capital of an individual be assumed to consist of $5000 in the form of wages, and of $5000 of a different description,—profits being 10 per cent. The whole profits received will, therefore, amount to $1000. Now let wages fall 5 per cent. The consequence will be, that, to employ the same labour as before, and to produce the very same commodities, a capital of only $9750 will be required, only $4750 having to be paid for wages, instead of $5000. There is also $250 less of capital consumed to be replaced; and this amount of what is produced will hence be added to the clear profits, and will raise them from $1000 to $1250; so that what is taken from wages is necessarily transferred to profits.—Again, let wages amount to $4000, and every other species of capital employed to $6000. When wages fall 5 per cent, the requisite capital to be employed will be diminished, as in the previous case, on account of the diminution of the whole amount of wages to be paid. That capital will now be only $9,800, instead of $10,000; and profits will amount to $1200, instead of $1000. In comparing together the two cases we have been considering, the augmentation of profits resulting from the same proportional fall of wages will appear to be not only unequal, it being in the one $250, and in the other $200, but such as to render the *rate* of profit different, in reference to the amount of capital employed: $1250 profit on $9750 is obviously at a higher rate than $1200 on $9800. And, speaking generally, the new rate of profits will be lower according as less labour is put in motion by a given capital. But such a state of things cannot continue: a transfer of capital from the less to the more profitable employments will take place, until the rate of profits in all shall be equalised. But the ordinary profits in all must then, it is clear, be greater than they were before the supposed fall of wages.

So much in respect to the effects of a *fall* of wages on profits. And it may be shewn, in a similar manner, *mutatis mutandis*, that a rise of wages and a fall of profits will likewise accompany each other.

This rise of wages, or of the rate of profits, while the other at the same time falls, will affect the prices of commodities very differently, according to the degree in which wages or profits enter into the cost of production. And it will, in general, be true, that prices will suffer proportionally *more* alteration from a given change in the rate of wages, and *less* alteration from the corresponding change in the rate of profits, where the circulating predominates over the fixed portion of the capital employed. As these two effects are always in opposite directions, it is also plain that the prices of some commodities will rise, while others at the same time fall; and their exchangeable values, when compared with one another, will be made to vary.

In all that has been above said concerning the manner in which the cost of production, and *prices* in consequence, may be made to vary, the value of money has been tacitly assumed to remain unaltered. If any change should, however, take place in the mean time in respect to that value, so that a given sum of money should become more or less efficient in procuring the necessaries and luxuries of life, this will in no degree affect the correctness of our conclusions; since any such change, as has been before explained, will itself raise or lower the prices of all things in the very same proportion.

The necessary connexion, on the supposition of no simultaneous augmentation of the productiveness of labour, of a fall of wages with a rise of profits, as well as the rise of prices which would sometimes be consequent upon a fall in the rate of wages, being once distinctly understood, the inconsistency will be apparent of attributing, as some persons are apt to do, the low prices of British goods, when compared with the same description of goods of American manufacture, chiefly to the low rate of wages in Great Britain, instead of attributing them to the comparative lowness of wages and profits, *taken together*. Were it possible, indeed, to raise the wages of labour at once in that country, by the interference of the government, or in any other manner, in as much as this could only be accomplished at the expense of profits, it will follow from what has been stated, that the prices of all those commodities which are the products chiefly of fixed capitals, instead of rising in value, would be sold at a still cheaper rate; and Great Britain would, in consequence, be enabled to export them abroad with a still greater probability than before of their being preferred to the similar products of other nations in the market of the world. I may add here that, since most of the British goods which are imported into the United States are, in fact, the products in a very considerable degree of fixed capitals, a rise, and not, as is very commonly supposed, a fall of wages in Great Britain, would cooperate with a protecting tariff, in the encouragement of our manufactures.

CHAPTER XVII.

THE PRICE, OR EXCHANGEABLE VALUE, OF ANY THING CANNOT BE REGARDED AS DETERMINED IN EVERY INSTANCE BY THE QUANTITY OF LABOUR APPLIED, FROM FIRST TO LAST, IN PRODUCING IT.

I SHALL conclude what I have to say on the subject of prices, and exchangeable values generally, by an inquiry as to the correctness of a theory, which is a favourite one with some political economists of the highest order; although no practical consequences of any moment depend upon its being true or not.

The writers to whom I allude have attempted to shew that the price of a commodity is always in proportion to the amount of *labour* necessary, from first to last, to produce it; but, in my opinion, have attempted to do so unsuccessfully. Indeed, the fact of the occurrence of a single instance of an augmentation of price without the instrumentality of human labour,—the only species of labour with which we are here concerned,—seems to me to be quite sufficient to evince the fallacy of the theory in question. Such an instance is afforded by wines that improve from the mere effects of age. The merchant who keeps them on hand must, of course, expect to receive the ordinary profits of capital; and the price of the wine will be augmented by the amount of those profits. If we now suppose that, by means of some contrivance or other, and without increasing the *first cost* of the wine to the merchant, the same improvement in its quality as before could be effected in half the time, it is clear, on the principles already explained, that the price of such wine must necessarily fall, so as to exceed its original cost only by the profits upon it for the time thus diminished; and we would then, consequently, have the price of an article *lowered*, notwithstanding the same quantity of labour, neither more nor less, had been applied to its production.

But the instance I have adduced is not a solitary one of the kind: others, though perhaps not quite so striking, are presented to us in the various arts of life, whenever improvements take place of a nature to enable a given quantity of labour to be productive of a commodity *in a shorter period of time after it is applied* than before. Let us look for a moment at the art of *tanning*. It is here impossible for human labour, no matter what amount of it may be exerted, to complete the process of production in less than a certain period. The reason is that the materials to which that labour is applied must, in different stages of the process, be subjected to the slow and separate operation of the powers of nature, using this expression in contradistinction to the powers exerted by man in the application of his labour. Under these circumstances, it must be evident that the price of *leather* can be made to fall in either of two ways,—by lessening the amount of labour required, from first to last, to produce it, and consequently of the wages to be paid, or by abridging the time which elapses from the applying of any portion of the labour employed till the last act of production be performed. I mean this, it needs hardly be mentioned, on the supposition of the rates of wages and profits remaining unaltered. Should the time just mentioned be diminished, while the labour required continues the same, the instance under consideration will be perfectly analogous to that of the wines before spoken of: in both instances alike, prices will have been affected by the diminution of the profits to be paid. And they will, in fact, never be determined exclusively by the amount of the labour exerted, except in the scarcely supposable case of a commodity being produced by it without any advances whatever on the part of the capitalist.

There is then another element of price besides the quantity

of labour employed, from first to last, in producing a commodity, to wit, the time that elapses from the application of the several portions of labour until the production of it in its complete state. But it has been objected that although labour has power to *produce*, it is impossible to understand how such a power can be predicated in reference to time, which is not a real entity, but merely a *mode* of existence. No such power is, however, intended to be ascribed to it. Human labour, and *natural agents*, are the only powers concerned in the business of production. The former of these, it may be observed, is incapable of exerting itself without the co-operation of the latter; and it is, therefore, impracticable, in any case whatever of such co-operation, to point out how much is man's workmanship, and how much nature's. It would be wrong to regard that time, which has been stated to have an influence on prices, to be in any manner indicative of the degree in which natural agents co-operate with man. Nor is this a matter of any the least moment in relation to our present inquiry: so long as a certain time must necessarily intervene between the application of any portion of labour and the completion of a commodity, just for so long a time must profits be realised on the wages advanced, and will the consequent effect be produced on prices, whether the materials to which the labour is applied be operated on, in the mean time, by natural agents, so as to augment their utility, or whether they continue in the same, or be even brought into a worse, condition. The amount, for example, expended in building the foundation and walls of a house, will be entitled to quite as much of profits, and will have an influence on its value when it is completed, equally great, as if, instead of their remaining nearly in an unaltered state while awaiting, so to speak, the completion of the interior structure, they had had their utility augmented, in a ten-fold degree, by the operation of natural agents.

When the time, of which I have been speaking, is

said to determine a certain amount of profits on the capital expended in the employment of labour, or, what is at present the same thing, on the wages of labour, those profits are not to be understood as being in *exact* proportion to the time. It is evident that this is never the case with the profits of capital. Whatever may be the amount of profits on a given portion of it for a year, if received at the expiration of that period, *somewhat less than half as much* will be the proper remuneration for its use during six months; for such remuneration may then itself be employed productively. The case is entirely similar to that of the interest of money, with respect to which every one knows, that a half per cent. at the end of every month is preferable to six per cent. at the end of a year. This view of the relation of profits, and consequently of prices, to the time during which capital is employed, before a return is made to it, is entirely inconsistent with the supposition, that those who deny the exclusive influence on prices of the quantity of labour applied, from first to last, in the production of a commodity, ascribe to mere time a certain occult or mysterious power, which, from its very nature, it cannot possibly possess. If they in reality did so, it is very obvious that they would also maintain, for they would be driven to maintain, that such power is always exerted in proportion *exactly* to the time which is supposed to exert it; since every effect is always proportional to its cause.

It may, nevertheless, be conceded that the prices of commodities are much more frequently lowered by the diminution of the quantity of labour which is requisite for producing them, or, what is the same thing, by a given quantity of labour having been rendered more productive, than by a diminution of the time required in production. Improvements of the latter description we know from experience to be confined within comparatively very narrow limits; while, on the other hand, improvements of a labour-saving nature have been introduced, more especially in our own age, with extraordinary rapidity, and to a prodigious extent. Hence I would not object to the language of those writers who, *when speaking generally*, regard all improvements in the arts as if they resulted from a greater productiveness of labour; and indeed, I would not hesitate myself, after the remarks which have been now made, to do the like, merely, however, in order to avoid the necessity of employing a multiplicity of words.

BOOK SECOND.

ON THE TENDENCY OF RENTS, PROFITS, AND WAGES, TO RISE OR FALL IN THE PROGRESS OF SOCIETY;—TOGETHER WITH THE LAWS WHICH DETERMINE THE NUMBERS OF A PEOPLE.

CHAPTER I.

EFFECTS OF THE DIMINISHING RETURNS FROM THE LAND UPON THE EXCHANGEABLE VALUE OF THE DIFFERENT PRODUCTS OF INDUSTRY, AND UPON RENTS,—OBJECTIONS TO THE THEORY OF RENT REFUTED.

In the preceding book, I have defined, with as much precision as was in my power, the principal technical terms of political economy. I have also, as I flatter myself explained distinctly the nature of price and of exchangeable value, as determined by the cost of production; together with the manner in which they will be necessarily subjected to change, in consequence of any of the previous changes of which that cost is susceptible.

These are points of so much importance as to lie at the foundation of a proper understanding of every branch of our general subject; and we are now prepared to enter with advantage into an examination of the laws that, in the progress of society, determine the rates of the increase of population and of the accumulation of wealth, and that regulate the *proportions* in which the products of industry are distributed among the different classes of landlords, capitalists, and labourers. In prosecuting this object, I shall begin by supposing the various causes which have a tendency to produce an alteration in the condition of society in any country, and, of course, the effects actually produced by them, to continue the same in every respect as at present; with the exception of the changes which may result, either directly *from an increase of the population*, or in consequence of the necessary operation of such increase, in giving occasion to a greater or less intensity of action on the part of other causes of change. And the inquiry at once presenting itself for consideration is:—Are there, in fact, any circumstances in the nature of things which, on the supposition I have made, will necessarily affect the productive powers of labour, for the better or the worse, or will induce a rise or fall of rents, profits, or wages?

Such a circumstance is to be found in the nature of the land, and its limited extent. The different portions of it are not of the same degree of fertility, nor equally favourably situated with respect to a market; and the returns yielded, on the application to the same land of equal successive portions of capital and labour, will be continually diminishing. Hence, as has been already shewn, the origin, and the inequality, of rents; hence also, it is quite obvious that an increased population will be unable to produce *proportionally* as much as before.

What has just been said, in reference to the diminishing returns from the land in agriculture, the reader will perceive is equally applicable in reference to the mines, the fisheries, and, in short, to all employments where rents are paid. And I am desirous that this applicability of my argument will hereafter be borne in mind in all similar cases, without any farther mention being made of it. By thus being enabled to consider the *land* as the representative of a class, I shall have it in my power to express myself more simply, and more concisely.

Another consequence, resulting from the diminishing returns from the land, is that the exchangeable value of agricultural products will rise in comparison with that of manufactured ones; for the cost of producing the former will now be comparatively greater than that of producing the latter. That such will be the fact will appear from the consideration that there is no reason why a given capital, constituted in the same manner, and employed during the same time, should not be as efficient to produce the same quantity in manufactures as formerly, except the increased cost of the *agricultural* raw material to which the labour of the artisan is applied.

As additional capital and labour are applied to the land, rents will, from the cause the effects of which we are now tracing, be continually rising. The proprietors of the land will receive a larger and a larger share of the produce of the soil. To make this as clear as I can, let all the land of a country be supposed to consist of say *ten* different kinds, in relation to the circumstances which would invite to its being taken into cultivation; having regard as well to favourableness of situation with respect to a market, as to fertility. Now so long as the best land, No. 1, alone is taken into cultivation, there will be no rent; the whole net produce will be profits. But as soon as the next quality, No. 2, is cultivated, rent will begin upon No. 1; and it will amount to the difference of the produce of the two kinds of land. No. 2 will yield the capitalist the ordinary profits: No. 1 will, besides those profits, pay rent. When capital is invested on No. 3, rent will begin on No. 2, and will amount to the excess of the net produce derived from it above that derived from No. 3. The rent paid by No. 1 will now, it is manifest, again rise, so as to be equal to the excess of its produce over that of No. 3, instead of the excess of it over that of No. 2. And so on when numbers 4, 5, 6, &c. are taken into cultivation. The same mode of exposition may be applied to the successive investments of capital on the land already cultivated; numbers 1, 2, 3, &c. denoting the equal portions of capital invested (because thus successively invested) under continually more and more disadvantageous circumstances. It must be likewise evident that our reasoning will not be the less accurate, if, instead of ten, we suppose the number of our classes to be any other than ten, or even to be multiplied indefinitely, so as to accord with the real state of the facts, when scarcely any two portions of land are precisely in the same circumstances of fertility or situation. The proposition advanced may, therefore, be considered as established, in so far as the rent of land is to be estimated by the share of its produce which goes to the landlord. But since, as has been explained, the exchangeable value of a given portion of that produce will have been augmented, rents will rise on this account also. The owners of the land will, therefore, have a larger share of the *whole* produce of labour; and their condition will be a continually improving one.

I have so much confidence in the *force* of the statement just given of the theory of rent, that I might, I think, safely neglect all consideration of the objections which have been made to it. I shall, however, notice two of them; and they are the only ones I have met with exhibiting the slightest shade of plausibility.

It is, in the first place, said, that there is no land any where to be found, for which, when leased by its owner to any individual, the latter does not pay rent. There are, for instance, barren tracts in the highlands of Scotland which are incapable of compensating the *labour* applied to them, and which, nevertheless, constitute no exception to this general remark. But it may be replied, that it is only in appearance they do not. When any considerable tract is leased, it may very well happen that certain portions of it are entirely worthless, and pay in reality no rent, although they seem to do so because of their being comprehended within land of a superior quality. Again, in every instance in which the objection under consideration has been urged, it will be found that rent is paid for land on which, however comparatively unproductive, some labour has been previously bestowed, or, in other words, on which some capital has been invested; and what is paid may, therefore, be no more than the profits of such capital. Lastly, we might safely grant to the objector, without any risk of thereby affecting practically the correctness of the theory in question, that no proprietor of land will have any motive to let another individual occupy it gratuitously, and that the motive to lease it will only arise when it can afford to pay rent. Instead of saying that all land pays rent excepting the last taken into cultivation, we shall have to say that all land yields rent, including that which is last taken into cultivation, which, however, yields the smallest rent possible, or at most a very trifling rent.

In the second place, it is asserted, and correctly asserted, that, according to those political economists who adopt the theory of rent as I have explained it, were the fertility of the land to be every where augmented, rents would fall; because it would not be necessary to cultivate land of as inferior quality as before; and because the exchangeable value too of agricultural products would become less, determined as this is by the cost of production under the most disadvantageous circumstances in which production actually takes place. It is then argued that if, on the contrary, we suppose the land to diminish in fertility, it will necessarily follow that rents will continually rise; and, consequently, they will be at their highest rate when the diminution of fertility shall have reached its ultimate limit, to wit, that of absolute barrenness. Is not this, it may be asked, a demonstration *ex absurdo* of the fallacy of "the theory of rent?" I answer, no. What the theory maintains is that, *the general rate of fertility being given,* rents will, in the progress of society, be continually rising, the proprietors of the land having a larger and a yet larger amount of the whole of its produce, and having, too, on account of its ever increasing exchangeable value, a larger and larger command over the whole produce of labour. If we now compare the land, when its general fertility is at a certain rate, with the same land when its fertility is different, the proposition which has just been stated will, it is obvious, be consistently modified so as to allot to the proprietors of the land, not in all cases an ever increasing *amount* of its produce or of the whole produce of labour, but simply a larger *proportional share* of what is, in fact, produced. There is no absurdity in supposing rent, thus understood, to be the highest at the nearest approach to the condition of perfect barrenness on the part of the land: a certain proportional share of a thimble-full of a commodity may be in any degree larger than a *smaller* share of millions of bushels.

CHAPTER II.

FARTHER EFFECTS OF THE DIMINISHING RETURNS FROM THE LAND ON THE EXCHANGEABLE VALUES OF COMMODITIES, ON THE SUM OF PROFITS AND WAGES, ON PROFITS, AND ON THE INCREASE OF POPULATION AND WEALTH.

To proceed with the consequences necessarily resulting from a supposed increase of population, under the circumstances in which man is placed on earth, of being obliged to apply his labour to the land ever more and more disadvantageously.

Since the *whole amount* of wealth produced is less than it

would otherwise have been, and since also, notwithstanding the diminution of that amount, a larger portion is separated from it for rent, it follows that the capitalists will receive a less *proportion* than they did before, or which is the same thing, the rate of profits will be reduced, and will remain thus reduced, unless the reduction should be counteracted in part, or wholly, by a contemporary fall of wages; which, my readers will not have forgotten, is equivalent to a rise of profits.

If we suppose wages and profits to fall in the same proportion, such an alteration in their rates, it may be worthy of mention, will have no effect to alter the exchangeable values of commodities. But agreeably to the principles already explained, should profits have fallen in a greater degree than wages, the exchangeable values of all commodities which are the products chiefly of fixed capitals will fall, when compared with the exchangeable values of those which are produced where the predominant portion of the capital employed is circulating. The contrary likewise will, of course, take place, if the fall of wages be the greater of the two.

But our object, at present, being to trace the consequences resulting from an increase of the population of a country, while we, at the same time, suppose the action of all other causes to remain unaltered, excepting only in so far as they may have their intensity augmented or diminished by the supposed increase of population,—and this with a view to the simplifying, as much as possible, of our investigations,—let us, with the same view, also suppose the entire diminution of the *sum* of profits and wages, consequent, as has been explained, upon the application of additional capital and labour to the land, to affect profits exclusively, and wages to remain at the same rate.

Although my reasoning will proceed on the supposition just made, it will be easy afterwards to modify the conclusions arrived at, according as the diminution of the sum of profits and wages is supposed to affect both profits and wages, or *wages* exclusively. Indeed, such a modification of them will be so very easily accomplished, that the reader may be left to accomplish it for himself.

My first proposition now will be, that a less rapid accumulation of capital will take place than before;—a proposition the truth of which might, perhaps, seem at first to be sufficiently manifest from the mere fact of the sum total of production being now comparatively less than it was, and from its consequence, that every individual of the community will, *on the average*, have a less income, and will thus be disposed to *save* less. What is produced is, however, now somewhat differently distributed. The landlords get not only a larger proportional share of the whole produce, but a greater *quantity* of it than they were before entitled to; and the capitalists suffer the *whole loss* incurred in a diminished rate of profits. Will this new distribution of the products of labour be favourable or unfavourable to saving? It will be unfavourable; more especially so where rights of primogeniture, entails, or any other politieal or legal arrangements, have the effect of forming, and keeping together, large landed estates. No persons are, in general, less apt to employ or consume their incomes productively than the very wealthy proprietors of such estates; and, on the other hand, no class of persons are so much disposed to accumulate property as the capitalists. Such accumulation will not, therefore, be promoted by a transfer of a part of their incomes from them to the landlords. And again, the lower the *rate* of profits the less inducement is there to save. To illustrate this, take two cases differing widely from each other: that of a person having at his disposal $2000, when the rate of profits is 100 per cent. per annum; and of another with the same sum, when the rate of profits is only one per cent. per annum. Now what motive will the persons supposed have respectively to save a certain portion of their income, say $500? An equal amount of present gratification must be foregone by both ; while, in return, the one will be enabled at the expiration of a year, instead of $500, the value of the gratification he might have enjoyed, to command a sum of only five dollars more,—and the other will receive altogether as much as $1000. I need not say which of them has the stronger motive to save. And the inference to be drawn from the comparison of other cases, approaching more nearly in their circumstances to each other, will only be different in degree.

Again, if wages continue always the same, population and capital will advance together at an equal rate. This is manifest, because population, under the supposition made, must necessarily increase at the same rate with that portion of capital which consists of wages; and this last rate is again in proportion to that of the accumulation of the whole amount of capital. Hence too, since the accumulation of capital has been shewn to be continually retarded in consequence of the effects necessarily resulting from the diminishing returns to capital and labour, when equal portions of them are successively applied to the land, it follows that population and wealth will be ever augmenting at a slower, and yet slower rate.

The following consequences have now been deduced: that, in the progress of society, *from the very nature of the land,* the whole amount of wealth produced will be *proportionally* diminished, that is proportionally to the amount of labour applied; the exchangeable value of agricultural products will rise in reference to all other products; and rents will be continually rising, and therefore continually inducing, by their rise, a corresponding rise in the value of the land ;—also, that when wages are supposed to continue the same, profits will fall; there will be a less rapid accumulation of capital; and the rate at which population and wealth increase must, in consequence, be continually retarded.

CHAPTER III.

EFFECTS, IN AN OPPOSITE DIRECTION, OF THE PROGRESS OF HUMAN INVENTION.

The consequences which have been deduced are, however, modified, and in certain cases altogether counteracted, by the effects resulting from the development of the powers of human invention, in their application to the various arts of life. The labour of man is thus rendered more efficient to produce; and the effects of the diminishing returns from the land on the whole amount produced may in this manner, it is evident, be either partially or entirely counteracted, or be even more than counteracted, according to the degree of the augmented efficiency of labour.

In the following remarks I shall assume, it may be here mentioned, that, wherever the contrary is not expressly stated, the degree of industry exerted by a community continues always the same,—and that the proportion which the members of it who do not labour at all bears to those who do continues likewise unaltered. If then, to use the language of mathematicians, these quantities, thus at first assumed to be *constant*, be supposed to become at any time afterwards *variable quantities*, the consequences on the amount of wealth produced, and on the *progress* of national wealth, will, it is manifest, be entirely similar to those resulting from the augmented or diminished productiveness of labour, as the case may be; and such variation in the circumstances before supposed to remain unaltered, it will be perceived, will in no wise affect the correctness of the conclusions which I am about to deduce. These circumstances are, indeed, only very slowly alterable; and, for this reason, the favourable effects which may occasionally result from a variation of them are quite inconsiderable, when compared with those which are consequent upon the progress of human invention in the arts.

The removal, too, of any of those *restrictions* which have, in every nation, more or less trammelled the industry of the people, and prevented it from being as productive as it would otherwise have been, will also be followed by effects perfectly analogous to those resulting from improvements made in any of the modes or processes of production. And hence, when the progress of human invention is asserted to be the antagonist principle to the necessarily diminishing returns of the land, on the application to it of successive equal portions of labour and capital, that progress should be understood, as comprehending the class of improvements which has just been mentioned.

If improvements in all the arts were to take place *at the same rate*, they would obviously have no effect to alter the exchangeable values of things; and that rise in the value of agricultural products, and corresponding fall, when compared with these, in that of manufactured ones, which were before shewn to result from the necessity of having recourse to inferior soils, would not at all be affected. But if we suppose, in accordance, very generally so at least, with the real state of things, that improvements are introduced in less rapid succession, and to a less extent, in agriculture than in the other arts, we shall have an additional reason why the cost of production in the former should continually become relatively greater, and the exchangeable value of agricultural produce should be always on the rise.

With respect to rents, the effect of *agricultural* improvements will be to cause them to fall; for the land which is cultivated, in consequence, under the most unfavourable circumstances, needs not be as inferior as that which would be otherwise so cultivated; and we may, indeed, *conceive* the improvement to be so great as to cause land of the first quality alone to be cultivated, when no rent at all would be paid. But besides this, the effect of agricultural improvements is to diminish the cost of producing in agriculture, and therefore to lower the exchangeable value of what is produced. Not only will the landlords get a smaller portion of the products of the land; but they will be able to exchange that portion for less of the necessaries and luxuries of life than before.

Improvements in any of the arts, *other than agriculture*, will cause rents to rise. This will be effected in the following manner. If we suppose, at first, no additional capital and labour to be applied to the land, there will be an extraordinary demand for agricultural products, more especially for the agricultural raw material to be used in manufactures, which will of course raise their exchangeable value, and by thus making it worth while to take new land into cultivation, cause a transfer of capital from other employments to agriculture. Rents must then rise; worse lands being then cultivated, and the exchangeable value of agricultural products becoming, of course, at the same time greater, in comparison with other commodities. It needs scarcely be added that from the very first, therefore, these effects will take place by means of the application of the accumulating capital in the proper proportion to every department of production, including agriculture.

That so long as wages continue at the same rate,—a supposition I have been continually making,—agricultural improvements will tend to produce a *rise of profits*, is the necessary consequence of the whole amount of production being augmented, while, at the same time, rents are made to fall.

On the same supposition again of a permanent rate of wages, improvements in any of the other arts, *by augmenting the amount produced*, will have a favourable operation on profits. But while this is the case, they will likewise tend, *by raising rents*, to diminish profits. Now which of these tendencies will have the greater efficiency? Will profits, in reality, rise or fall? This question does not, in my opinion, admit of a general answer; for the degree in which rents will rise must necessarily depend on the greater or less *rapidity* with which the returns from the land diminish, on the application to it of successive equal portions of capital. This diminution may be supposed to take place so rapidly that rents shall absorb a greater amount than the additional production; when it follows, of course, that profits will fall. It may, on the other hand, go on at a rate sufficiently slow to admit of profits rising simultaneously with rents. The one, as well as the other, of these results may, very possibly, in fact occur in different countries, or at different times in the same country; although I am disposed to think the latter of the two to do so much more frequently, and in *new* countries almost always so.

Improvements in the arts, *by augmenting the amount of wealth produced*, will likewise manifestly induce a more rapid accumulation of capital. But as every rise of rents, to which they may give occasion, will produce, as has been shewn, a distribution of wealth in a certain degree unfavourable to saving, the rate of accumulation will, on this account, be prevented from being as rapid as it would otherwise be. The rate of increase, too, of the population being determined, when wages are supposed to continue always the same, by that of the accumulation of capital, whatever causes have a tendency to accelerate the latter must likewise tend to accelerate the former.

On a review of the sometimes agreeing, and sometimes disagreeing results to which we have been led, in relation to the varying amount and distribution of the wealth produced, I think there can be no hesitation to infer that, *all things considered*, rents will, in the progress of society, be continually rising; that it is possible for profits to rise or fall; and that, if the same rate of wages be always paid, capital and population may increase together at the same accelerated rate, or at the same retarded rate. These conclusions will hardly be called in question, even by those who may possibly find a difficulty in *at once* admitting the correctness of one or two of my propositions, relating to the manner in which wealth is at different times distributed. And indeed, although it is sufficiently interesting to trace the progressive distribution of wealth, most of the *great practical questions* which look to the principles of political economy for their solution, and on the proper solution of which consequences of much moment to the well-being of society may be dependent, require nothing more, in reference to the conclusions just stated, than an assent to the possibility of capital and population, while they augment *together*, to do so with different degrees of rapidity; a proposition which may be surely regarded, if any proposition can be so regarded, as quite undeniable by the dullest, as well as by the most acute objector.

It may here be mentioned that the continual rise of rents, which has been theoretically deduced, accords with the results of actual experience; for the exchangeable value of land being always in proportion to the rent which it yields, together with the profits of the capital invested on it, a continual rise of rents implies necessarily a corresponding progressive augmentation of that value; and *this* is well known to be the general fact. It is the expectation, too, of such a rise in the value of land, as has already been mentioned, that often enables it to command a price in the market quite disproportionate to the value of what it produces, and that sometimes confers upon it a value when it is as yet altogether unproductive.

CHAPTER IV.

INTIMATE CONNEXION OF THE SUBJECTS OF WAGES AND POPULATION —CHECKS TO POPULATION.

ASSUMING the rate of wages to remain unchanged, we have inquired into the variations to which, in the progress of society, rents and profits will be subjected. But the receivers of wages are far more numerous than the classes who live on rents and profits, and indeed constitute the main body of every community. Moreover, the poorer classes of society are, for the most part, of this description of persons. And the happiness of a people, as regards the degree in which it is determined by the necessaries and luxuries of life they can command, will depend much more on high or low wages being paid, than on the comparative rate of profits, or on the amount of rents received by the landlords. Accordingly, the great practical object of the political economist is not so much to promote the interests of the wealthy, by any attempt to enlarge the sources of their incomes, as to investigate, and to put into execution, the measures best adapted to give the poor man the highest remuneration for his labour that may be practicable, and to elevate him to as high a rank in the scale of society as the laws of nature, aided, and not trammelled, in their beneficial tendencies, by the co-operation of individuals and of governments, will permit.

The important question, therefore, now presents itself for inquiry:—What are the circumstances which regulate the rate of wages? And I do not mean here their comparative rates in different occupations: of these I have already treated with sufficient fulness. I mean the actual amount of the necessaries and luxuries of life which, in each respectively, any one is enabled to procure in exchange for his labour or services.

In reply to the question which has been put, I may, in the first place, remind the reader that wages have been shewn to be determined, in every case, on the principles of supply and demand,—by the relation, that is, subsisting between the supply of labour and the demand for it: and as the supply of labour, all other circumstances remaining the same, is in proportion to the number of labourers, and this again in proportion to the amount of the whole population; while, on the other hand, the demand for labour is measured by that portion of the capital of a country which consists of wages, and which, again, is proportional to the whole amount of that capital;—it will follow, that the rate of wages is dependent on the relation which the capital of a country bears to the numbers of the people. So long as this relation continues the same, wages will remain unaltered. If the population remain stationary, wages will rise or fall according as capital increases or decreases. And as an increase or decrease of capital can, in that case, (the same quantity of labour being always applied) only, it is evident, take place with an advance or decline in the arts, wages will then rise or fall with every such advance or decline. If, on the other hand, we suppose the amount of capital not to alter, the number of people will determine the rate of wages: in fact, the very same amount of wages will have to be divided among a greater number of persons.

Hence it appears that the laws which regulate the increase of population must first be investigated, before the subject of wages can be fully understood; or, in consequence of their intimate connexion, it would, perhaps, be more proper to say that both subjects should be investigated together. To this investigation I shall now accordingly proceed.

I set out with the remark that the checks to the increase of population may manifestly be classed under the two heads of the *preventive,* and the *positive* checks: the former prevent the birth of human beings; the latter destroy them after they have been brought into existence. Of the former description, are late marriages, and vicious practices of various kinds not at all necessary to be here enumerated. Every cause of mortality, such as disease, pestilence, wars, infanticide, are of the latter description. It is obvious that we may conceive these checks to operate in so great a degree, as either to keep the population of any region or district of country stationary, or even to cause it to retrogade;—or, on the contrary, we may conceive them to operate in a degree *insufficient* to prevent altogether its increase. Indeed, any *one* of the enumerated checks, whether preventive or positive, may be conceived to act with an energy adequate to the production of either of the two former effects; and, *a fortiori,* to all of them co-operating together, with the exception of the comparative lateness of marriage, the same results may be attributed;—so that, were every individual to marry on attaining the age of maturity, and the *whole power* of population to be thus called into activity, this would fail to supply, or to do more than supply, the places of those who were cut off. In reality, however, the checks to population very seldom operate with an energy like this. In a few peculiarly unhealthy spots, and during the actual prevalence of pestilence or war, such may happen to be the case. Nevertheless, it may be laid down as a general law, established by observation, that population has the power to keep itself stationary, or even to advance, without the necessity of exerting the whole procreative force of the community. We find many nations, too, *rapidly* augmenting in numbers, while every individual composing them is far from marrying, as soon as he has reached the age of maturity. How many persons, for example, are there not in this predicament in the United States, where the numbers of the people can be shewn, after making every allowance for immigration, to have doubled themselves in a period so short as twenty-five years,—and where, at the present time, no one will deny that, independently of the accession which it is receiving from abroad, population is doing much more than sustain itself! Whatever other causes may be, therefore, in operation to retard the progress of population, we are entitled to regard the delay of marriage, and, as a necessary consequence, the number of those who never marry at all, as among the causes which are, in every country, conspiring to produce that effect. This proposition may, very possibly, appear to the reader so obviously true, as, for the moment, to subject me to the imputation of being exceedingly common-place. But there are some subjects which have been so involved and obscured by controversy, that it is advisable, when treating of them, to run some hazard of incurring such an imputation, rather than fail of being perfectly understood. Of this nature is the subject of population. And indeed, the truth of the very proposition of which I am speaking has been boldly, although, in my opinion, very absurdly, denied by one writer at least of reputation in our own country. His words are, that "the mass of the people in all countries, and at all periods, have married, and always will marry, upon their arrival at maturity."

The question now presents itself:—Why the delay, of which I have spoken, as to marriage? Or, in other words, why do not all men marry as early as the physical constitution of their nature will permit? The most prominent reason that can be given, for their not doing so, is the difficulty of procuring the means of support; and by the means of support I not only mean the food which is necessary for the sustaining of life, but likewise all the various *necessaries* and *luxuries* which each individual is desirous of acquiring,—so desirous of acquiring, that, rather than forego doing so, he prefers the *postponement* of marriage. Population may, then, be said to be *checked* by the difficulty of procuring the means of *support*.

When these become any where more abundant, population augments with a greater rapidity; and where they become less abundant, the contrary will take place. This law is *most strikingly* illustrated in the case of the great mass of the receivers of wages, or, to use the ordinary language on the subject, in the case of the "working classes." When wages experience, from whatever cause, a sudden rise, that is when the labourers unexpectedly come to possess, in a greater quantity than before, the necessaries and luxuries of life, it is uniformly found that the number of marriages is increased. A very sensible influence on their number is exerted by an extraordinarily fruitful season, or by one which is in an extraordinary degree unfruitful; as is to be inferred from the actual registers of marriages kept in different parts of England. When also in East Prussia, in the year 1711, a pestilence swept off, as it is said, one third of the inhabitants, and when wages rose, in consequence, considerably above their usual level, the number of marriages was prodigiously increased in the following year. In a tract of country where their annual number had been 6000, it was doubled. It is not, therefore, at all surprising, that no effects of the pestilence should have been remarked after a few years, and that the Prussian population should so soon, as writers state, have appeared to have *restored* itself. It is worth noting too, that all this marrying, and giving in marriage, took place under the peculiarly unpropitious circumstances of the gloom and mourning in which almost the whole community were involved, on account of the deaths of relatives and friends,—circumstances calculated, of course, to render the remarkable result still more remarkable.

Now it must be manifest, from the known constitution of human nature, that the effects which have been shewn to result from an alteration in the existing rate of wages are likewise to be attributed to every variation in the accustomed *incomes* of individuals, from whatsoever sources those incomes may be derived; nor is there any reason why those effects should be limited to the cases when incomes or wages are *small.* When rents or profits increase, the landlords and capitalists will be influenced exactly in the same way as the labourers are by a rise of wages; and whatever may be the condition of the different classes of society, whether they be rich or poor, enlightened or the reverse, any improvement in their worldly circumstances will invariably operate as a stimulus to marriage. Not, indeed, in the same degree. That proportionate increase of his income which would constitute a motive strong enough to induce the marriage of every uneducated labourer might, very probably, not be adequate to influence the determination of many among the wealthy. For few or none among the labouring poor remain unmarried through choice. It is the difficulty of procuring the means of support alone which restrains their inclinations. On the other hand, according as the minds of men are cultivated and refined by education, or the circle of their enjoyment is extended, not only does the sexual passion become less dominant, and is more readily counteracted by other desires and passions, but individuals will be found who, notwithstanding any supposable accession to their wealth, would still continue to live a life of celibacy, through an excess of that fastidiousness of taste and of feeling, and that strength of acquired habits, which are inseparable concomitants of education and refinement.

If we make the contrary supposition of a general *diminution* of income, the consequent *decrease* in the number of marriages will, of course, as in the former case, extend to all classes of people, and also in a greater degree to the poor than to the rich.

From this view of the subject, it might be imagined that the effects, which have been stated to result from a *rise* of wages, should sometimes be counteracted, and entirely neutralised, by the opposite effects of a contemporaneous fall of rents or profits,—especially of the latter. Yet inasmuch as the proportion of those who gain their livelihood by the receipt of wages, in exchange for services rendered by them, is vastly greater than the number of those who live by rents or profits; and as the great majority of the receivers of wages are precisely those members of the community who are most readily induced to marry by any improvement in their circumstances; and moreover, since, *in the progress of society*, it will frequently, if not generally, be found that profits and wages rise or fall *together*;—we see how it is that every rise of wages, *unaccompanied by a corresponding improvement in the habits of the people*, is in fact always productive of an increased number of marriages, and why every fall of wages has invariably the opposite effect.

CHAPTER V.

THE SUBJECT OF POPULATION CONTINUED.

The proposition which I have been endeavouring to establish, and which I hope I have succeeded in establishing to the satisfaction of the reader, is that "population is every where checked by the difficulty of procuring the means of support." This, however, is a very different proposition from that which asserts population to be checked by the difficulty of procuring the means of *subsistence*. Both of them cannot at the same time be true, unless subsistence be used synonymously with the means of support, as applying to the whole revenue or income of individuals, whether this be valued at 100 or 10,000 dollars per annum. But this sense of the word, notwithstanding it is in some measure countenanced by the authority of Dr. Johnson, in his dictionary, appears to me to be entirely at variance with the common use of language.

If subsistence be understood to comprehend the food, clothing, shelter, and, in short, whatever is indispensable to the preservation of human life in its rudest and most degraded condition, it may be confidently affirmed that the difficulty of procuring the means of subsistence is no where the immediate or actual check to population. No people have ever existed, even the most rude, who have not, in some measure lived in the enjoyment of what, relative to a mere subsistence, may be denominated luxury: and the mass of the population in all civilised countries are, in general, far enough removed from the limits prescribed by a hard and *savage* necessity.

But if the difficulty of procuring the means of subsistence, as the term is just now supposed to be used,—and, perhaps, this is the proper mode of using it,—be not an immediate check to population, can it be regarded as an *ultimate* check? Does it present a limit beyond which population cannot be conceived to increase; a limit which, when reached, will render it necessary that the numbers of mankind should be kept down, either by a diminution of the number of marriages and births, or by the aggravated devastations of disease? The answer to this question will depend entirely upon the comparative productiveness of labour in the different stages of the progress of society. If, when the number of labourers is doubled, the products of their labour will also be doubled, it is plain that no limits whatever can be assigned to the increase of population. So if labour should become comparatively more and more productive. But on the other hand, if the powers of production should not keep pace with the multiplication of the number of labourers, population could not increase at all, unless we at the same time suppose the share of its products received by each individual to be less than before: and population, on this supposition, and on this supposition only, may continually approximate to the limits of a mere subsistence.

The effect of the portion of the community who before lived on rents or profits also becoming labourers, or of the community generally becoming more industrious, would no doubt be to retard the deteriorating process which has been mentioned; but it must be likewise evident that the causes of this retardation of the evil would be wholly inadequate to prevent it altogether.

Mr. Malthus however, and most other political economists, restrict the meaning of the term subsistence to *food* merely. In this acceptation of it, it is even more obvious than in the preceding that the difficulty of procuring the means of subsistence is not, in general, an immediate check to the increase of population. Indeed it is never so, excepting in the comparatively very rare case of actual famine. Nor can it be the ultimate check to that increase; for, as has been already explained, long before the whole labour of the community could be applied to the exclusive production of food, or, what amounts to the same thing, to the exclusive production of those commodities in exchange for which they obtain food, population would have become stationary.

But enough, for the present, in respect to erroneous opinions, or in respect to objectionable modes of expressing correct ones. Let us now proceed with the deduction of such consequences as flow legitimately from the law which has been established,—that population is every where checked by the difficulty of procuring the means of support. First, since when those means become at any time more abundant, that is whenever the checking or counteracting *force* is in any degree removed, population begins immediately to increase with more rapidity than it did, we can make no hesitation to assent to the following propositions,—that population is ever *pressing* on the means of support,—and that population has a *tendency* to increase more rapidly than the means of support. These two propositions are, in fact, only different modes of expressing that from which I have asserted them to be obviously deducible.

Yet it is proper to mention that there are writers who have

objected to the ascribing to population a tendency to increase more rapidly than the means of *subsistence ;* pronouncing the term tendency to be one of such ambiguity as to be very properly discarded altogether from our present subject; and denying, too, the propriety of speaking of any thing as having a tendency to advance more rapidly than another in a particular direction, when they, in truth, advance together. Now as the very same objections are capable of being made to the asserted tendency of population to increase more rapidly than, or beyond, the means of *support;* and as the term tendency is a convenient one, which cannot easily be got rid of in reference to the subject of population, without the use of much and frequent circumlocution; I shall remark, in justification of its being employed in the manner in question, that it is so employed in perfect analogy to the use made of the term tendency in mechanical philosophy, which is the source whence it has been borrowed. When a *force* has been prevented in any manner from producing its proper effect of motion in a particular direction, the body on which it acts is still said to have a tendency to move as if not thus prevented from moving. The mechanician, for example, speaks of the tendency of a heavy body, placed on a table or horizontal plane, to descend in the direction .of gravity, though, in reality, its motion is wholly prevented by the resistance of the plane. So again, a body, placed in one of the scales of a balance, is very properly said to *tend* towards the earth, even when in equilibrium with an equal weight in the opposite scale; and this tendency is experimentally shewn to exist, in the only way in which it can be made to appear, to wit, by removing or weakening the counteracting force,—when the body actually falls to the ground. In morals also, we continually compare the influence of *motives* on the mind with the action of mechanical causes on matter. We speak familiarly of the tendency of a motive to produce its appropriate effect on the conduct; and this when the actual determination of the mind, through the operation of other motives, is directly the contrary. And in the case under consideration, which has led to these remarks, it should be recollected that the sexual passion, and the desire to marry, are not extinguished in the breasts of that portion of the community who continue to live in a state of celibacy, but are only counteracted by the opposite motive of a desire for the enjoyment, in a greater degree, of the various conveniences and luxuries of life. If these become at any time more abundant, or, in other words, if adequate means for the support of a family are more easily procurable, a greater number of marriages will take place, and the previous existence of the tendency of population to increase, faster than the means of support can be provided, will immediately become manifest. Hence, likewise, it appears that this tendency is always in exact proportion to the force of the check which is presented by the difficulty of procuring the means of support; and consequently, that it is greatest, not when population increases *most rapidly*, but, on the contrary, when this increase is the *slowest*. It will, of course, also be true, that, when population is actually making the most rapid progress, the tendency in question will be the least.

This tendency I shall hereafter designate as *the principle of population*, in conformity with the general usage of the writers on political economy, when they speak of it in reference to the difficulty of procuring the means of *subsistence;* and we shall at any time be enabled to form something like an estimate of this tendency, or of the energy with which this principle is acting at any particular time and place, by comparing the actual rate at which the population is increasing with the rate at which it would increase, were there no difficulty whatever in procuring the means of support. Of course, the last mentioned rate cannot be ascertained with absolute precision; but it is easy to approach to it, by assuming it to be at least as rapid as the rate at which the population has actually increased in some one country, or region of country, situated in average circumstances of mortality, and of those circumstances which constitute the various other checks to the progress of population, the delay of marriage only excepted. Since, therefore, population has actually doubled itself, from its own resources, in the United States of America,—which is probably about as fair a field for observation on the subject as could be desired,—in so short a period of time as twenty five years, we may conclude that it has *generally* the power of doubling itself in that period of time; and we see, consequently, how great must be the tendency of population to increase beyond the means of support in countries where it is actually stationary, or even declining; or, in other words, we see how actively the principle of population would exert itself, if the checks to its exertion were to be suddenly removed.

CHAPTER VI.

THE SAME SUBJECT CONTINUED—HABITS OF THE COMMUNITY IN RELATION TO MARRIAGE—HOW THOSE HABITS ARE TO BE IMPROVED.

The principle of population being once established, it will follow that the average, necessary, or natural rate of wages in any country must remain always the same, *so long as the habits of the people generally in relation to marriage continue the same;* for every rise of wages which may occur under these circumstances, from whatever cause originating, will lead to a more rapid augmentation of the population; and this again will require, and be accompanied by, the pushing of cultivation on inferior soils, and, in general, under more disadvantageous circumstance than would otherwise be the case; which, in its turn, as has already been explained, will diminish the amount of *proportional* production, and thus, as has likewise been explained, reduce wages, and reduce them too to their former level. It is unnecessary to trace the process by means of which a similar return to the former and accustomed rate of wages will be brought about, if wages, instead of having risen, be supposed to have fallen. My readers cannot avoid perceiving that it is one perfectly analogous to that which has just been described, only occurring in an opposite direction.

Now all this, it will be borne in mind, is on the supposition of no alteration taking place in the habits of the people, in respect to marriage. But these habits have been intimated to be, and they are notoriously (though at all times only slowly alterable) very different in different countries, and in the same country at different periods. That rate of wages, for instance, which would determine the marriage of every inhabitant in Ireland, would be regarded by a large proportion of Englishmen as inadequate for the support of a family; and, in the United States, would by many of the labouring poor be pronounced to be insufficient for a single individual.

Let the alteration in respect to the habits of the community be such as to determine, all other circumstances remaining the same, a diminution in the number of marriages; in other words, let these, in general, take place at a less early period of life than heretofore. The consequence will be that the increase of population will be retarded; recourse will not so soon be had to inferior soils; the total proportional amount of production will be greater than it would otherwise have been; and wages will rise. They must, too, continue at this higher rate so long as the habits of the people do not again change.

It is plain that every thing will occur in a contrary order, if we suppose those habits to vary in an opposite direction. The progress of population will *then* be accelerated; land will consequently be cultivated under more disadvantageous circumstances than would otherwise be the case; the sum of what is produced will be lessened proportionately to the numbers of the people; and wages will be permanently depressed.

We may, therefore, lay it down as a general proposition,—and it is, perhaps, the most important proposition in the whole science of political economy,—that, in every country, and in every period, the rate of wages is determined by the *habits* of the people, as this term has been applied by me in the present chapter.

It becomes of the utmost moment to inquire into the various causes which are capable of affecting those habits, in order that we may know how they may be *improved*, and a larger command of the necessaries and luxuries of life secured to the great mass of the community. Now there are obviously only two ways of doing this: *first*, by multiplying the wants, and thereby stimulating the desires of the people generally, for every enjoyment of life that is not of an injurious or immoral tendency; for, in proportion to the multiplication of the sources whence enjoyment may be derived, will the enjoyment derived from any one of them be in our estimation of comparatively less importance, and comparatively less an object of desire. By thus imbuing the people with a taste for enjoyment other than that resulting from the gratification of the sexual passion, they will, *naturally* and *voluntarily*, be led to retard the average period of marriage, and to check, by so doing, the too rapid increase of population. The *second* way in which the same result can be produced is by inculcating habits of *foresight*,—increasing in this manner the disposition of individuals to have regard to their power of obtaining the comforts of life in the *future*, as well as at the present,—a disposition leading them to make a still larger provision before marrying, or at least to see their way clearer before them in the world before doing so than would otherwise be the case.

I have said that these were the only ways of checking the too rapid increase of population. It would have been more proper to have said that these were the only ways in which it was expedient, or just, to attempt to apply such a check. All *compulsory* abstinence from marriage is unquestionably to be deprecated. Not to speak of the immoral consequences of every measure of the kind, an extreme degree of *odium* will unavoidably attach to it, on account of its partial operation on the poorer classes of the community. Those who would thus be prevented from marrying would be sufferers without any counterbalancing advantage on their part, and might reasonably require the rich to partake with them in the sacrifice to be made for the general good of the next generation. Such a measure would, indeed, be equivalent to a violation of the rights of *property;* for when a portion of a person's property is taken from him, the consequence is that his enjoyment of the necessaries and luxuries of life must become proportionally contracted; and a diminution of enjoyment will equally take place among the poor, when the *luxury* of marriage is reserved in any degree for the richer classes.

No account is moreover, in my opinion, to be made of any effect which can be produced on the minds of the labouring poor, in inducing them to delay the period of marriage, by indoctrinating them in the correct principles of political economy. To attempt this by such means would be wholly useless. Unless those desires which constitute the motives of action on the part of the poor man be in some degree *modified,* so as to induce him to do willingly, or by preference, what it is wished that he *should do,* no mere theoretical conviction of the happiness of the community being promoted, by the retardation of the average period of marriage, will render him willing to sacrifice for the general good what he deems to be promotive of his own happiness. And to deliver, as some political economists have seriously and philanthropically proposed, *popular* lectures from time to time on the importance to the general welfare, of every individual looking well before he marries to the length of his purse and the prospect he may have of obtaining a livelihood for himself and family, may be characterised as not merely useless, but absolutely ridiculous.

Nothing of this kind, the reader will bear in mind, has been recommended in the present treatise. I say to no man "do not marry." My dependence for accomplishing the proposed object, viz. the retarding of the too rapid increase of population, rests on the simple operation on the minds of men of the *moral* causes which have been mentioned in the present chapter. Let individuals, and let governments, do every thing in their power to enlarge the desires of the great body of the people, and to promote among them the growth of habits of foresight. And if the object in view shall be, not compulsorily, but voluntarily, accomplished by these means, no class of persons will have reason to complain.

It may here be proper to notice an objection which has been urged, and been urged with an air of much triumph, against the consistency of the recommendations which have just been made. While the poor man is told that he ought to cultivate as *extensive* a taste, so to speak, for *enjoyment* as possible, and ought not to be satisfied with consuming only a comparatively inconsiderable amount of the luxuries of life,—he is at the same time told, that he ought not to consume what he has in his power to consume, but to save a portion of it, and that the more he saves the better; and this is asserted to be a contradiction in terms. This objection is, however, founded on a very superficial view of the subject. It is surely quite possible for an individual to have an enlarged desire for luxuries, and at the same time to be more solicitous than he was wont to be to have it in his power to consume them at a *future* period. Habits of foresight do not imply on his part a disposition to be content with a diminished consumption, but simply that he has been led to prefer a different distribution of his consumption than heretofore;—that he has become more anxious to secure to himself and family a *continuance* of their present rate of enjoyment. So far, I may add, from there being any ground for the alleged inconsistency, it will generally be found that when the desire for present enjoyment is extended, that for future, when compared with present enjoyment, will be also extended.

CHAPTER VII.

MEANS OF ENLARGING THE DESIRES OF MEN, AND OF INCULCATING UPON THEM HABITS OF FORESIGHT—INFLUENCE OF MORAL CAUSES IN DETERMINING THE COMMAND OF THE COMMUNITY OVER THE NECESSARIES AND LUXURIES OF LIFE.

Now what are the means of enlarging the desires of men? And what is the most effectual mode of inculcating habits of foresight on the great mass of the community?

We may, in the first place, look to education, using this term in its most extensive meaning, for a satisfactory answer to these questions. This is sufficiently evident not to require me to enter into any details of illustration. Just in proportion as men are made acquainted with the properties of things, and their understandings become expanded, will they be apt to be dissatisfied with a contracted range of enjoyment. And habits of foresight will be the necessary result of the general diffusion of education, intellectual, moral, and religious. The intellectual man lives not only in the present, but likewise in the past and in the future,—and in the past, in so far as it is conceived to be an index of the future. He whose actions are continually guided by the consideration of *duty*, cannot but be much occupied in tracing their remoter effects. Who, likewise, will more probably be possessed of an habitual foresight in the affairs of life, than the individual whose attention is much and systematically diverted from the contemplation of the fleeting present to that of the eternal future?

But, secondly, individuals and governments should do every thing in their power to promote the progress of improvement in the arts, and, what has been stated to be tantamount to such improvement, to effect as entire a removal as is practicable of the various restrictions upon man's liberty of applying his labour and capital as he may deem to be most conducive to his own interests,—restrictions which, notwithstanding the lights of political economy, are still in a greater or less degree existent in every country. A greater productiveness of labour will then ensue, and will operate advantageously, by its tendency to enlarge the desires of the community for enjoyment. This result will be brought about in the following manner. The first effect, as has already been very fully explained,—will be a corresponding increase in the amount of wealth produced. Wages will then rise; and a stimulus will, in consequence, be applied to population. As this becomes more numerous, and more numerous too than it would otherwise have been, the necessity will sooner occur of having recourse to inferior soils and to less advantageous circumstances in respect to cultivation; and wages would hence gradually fall to their former level, *were the habits of the community in relation to marriage to continue unchanged.* But these habits would not continue unchanged. The great body of the people, having for a time become accustomed to the enjoyment of a greater amount than before of the conveniences and luxuries of life, will not readily relapse into their former condition. They will, rather than subject themselves to the risk of doing so, consent to the postponement of marriage for a short time; and their condition generally will, accordingly, be somewhat elevated. Every improvement in the arts has, therefore, a tendency to produce two distinct effects; first, to increase the numbers of a people, and secondly, to enlarge their command, on the average, over the various enjoyments which are the products of human labour. I may likewise observe, that these two effects do not keep pace with each other; but while the one takes place in a greater degree, the other must necessarily do so in a less degree.

It can scarcely be necessary to remark that, where improvements are continually making, the effect, unless counterbalanced by the action of other and opposing causes, will be a *gradually* augmenting rate of wages. Another remark, the correctness of which is not quite so obvious, but which will be perceived by the reader on a little reflexion to be true, is that, when population is actually increasing with great rapidity, or, in other words, when it is, comparatively speaking, unchecked, it will be much easier, by retarding the average period of marriage, to prevent its *too rapid* increase, than when that period is already late, and when, of course, the population is only slowly increasing.

To the two modes which have been mentioned of improving the condition of a people may be added, in the third place, all the institutions and contrivances of various kinds, such, for example, as savings' banks and benefit societies, that are calculated to promote habits of foresight, and that are not, commonly and strictly speaking, comprehended among the means of education; as also the abolition of all such institutions, and the repeal of all such laws, as tend to encourage habits of improvidence without any compensating advantage,—at least to as great an extent, and as speedily, as is consistent with humanity, and with a fidelity to the subsisting *vested* claims of the poor.

And I may mention, in the fourth place, the expediency, with a view to the improvement of the general condition of a people, of extending to the poorer and less educated portion of them a direct influence on the operations of the government, *as soon as they are sufficiently enlightened for such influence to be entrusted to them, with safety to their own and their country's permanent interests.* Where a representative government has been instituted, the extension of the right of suffrage will contribute much to elevate the general character of the citizens, by directing their thoughts to matters of a higher and more enduring importance than the petty concerns of their immediate neighbourhoods or of their every day life. Conscious of his weight in the community of which he is a member, each voter will necessarily possess a certain self-respect, which will render him less disposed to aim at sensual gratification as the principal object for which he was brought into existence, and less disposed to take any step that is likely to depress his condition in society. The very exercise, too, of the right of suffrage by any one will, from what has just been stated, obviously tend to qualify him more and more for the *proper* exercise of it.

Here if the question be asked,—by what criterion shall we determine the *safety* of any proposed extension of the right of suffrage? I reply that the question, although having an intimate relation to the science of political economy, does not lie properly within its domain, and is therefore one to which I may, with propriety, decline giving an answer. It will be sufficient for me, at present, to make the now common-place remark, that the right of which I am speaking can be advantageously extended exactly in proportion as a community is a religious, moral, and intelligent community; and to remark also that a people who are so extravagant in their expectations of the benefits to be derived from mere political change, as to expect from it any *sudden* and *extraordinary* elevation in the condition of the labouring and poorer classes of society, or who conceive that the only reason why many are poor is that a few are rich, are but ill prepared for performing the functions of self-government. A people of this description will be very apt on coming to the possession of power in a state, especially on coming into possession of it suddenly, to advance from change to change, and from revolution to revolution, until no government excepting one of the strongest and most despotic kind will be able to maintain itself amidst the universal disregard of every thing established, or be able to protect the community from being overwhelmed by the horrors of anarchy.

The student of political economy who has advanced thus far in the present treatise cannot fail, it seems to me, to perceive the enlarged views which this science opens upon the condition and prospects of mankind. By the importance which it attaches to the influence of moral causes on the physical condition, so to speak, of society, it must at once assume a high rank in his estimation among the sciences; and he will not hesitate to hail the general diffusion of its doctrines, as not the least important means of contributing to the advancement of the best interests of his fellow-men. It must likewise be now apparent,—to repeat the language already used in the outset of this work,—"that no branch of human knowledge exhibits to us more beautiful illustrations of the consistency of all truth." What, indeed, can be more striking in this point of view, as well as more gratifying to the philanthropist and the christian, than the *fact*, so unequivocally *demonstrated* by the political economist, that "there is no more efficient mode," to repeat again my own language, "of promoting the physical well-being of a people, than to diffuse among them, as extensively as possible, the blessings of religion, of morals, and of education!" And I think that I shall hardly be contradicted by any of my readers who have carefully read and understood the contents of the preceding pages, when I assert that the general diffusion of religion, of morals, and of education, would be *decidedly the most efficient mode* of ensuring to the community at large, as extensive a command, as is at all practicable, over the various necessaries and luxuries of life,—a proposition, of course, still more remarkable than the one just before mentioned.

CHAPTER VIII.

AN INCREASE OF POPULATION NOT A CRITERION OF NATIONAL PROSPERITY—EMIGRATION FROM, AND IMMIGRATION INTO, A COUNTRY—IMPORTANCE OF CAPITAL AUGMENTING AT AN UNIFORM OR ACCELERATED RATE.

It must be evident, from what precedes, that to assume the fact of an increase of the population of a country to be a certain criterion of its prosperity, as some are disposed to do, would be to commit an egregious errour. Where the capital of the country has not been increased in a corresponding ratio, or more than a corresponding ratio, the wages of labour must necessarily have fallen, and the condition of the mass of the community have become comparatively degraded.

However desirable, in the ruder states of society, may be the acquisition of numbers, with a view to the common defence, even at such an expense as has just been mentioned, this is very far from being the case in a more advanced period of civilisation, and especially among the more civilised nations of our own age. Power depends now in a much greater degree on intelligence and wealth than on mere animal energy; and that people, who permit themselves to approximate in their condition to the limits of a mere subsistence, are prepared most effectually for subjugation to the will of either a domestic or foreign master.

Emigration is by many relied upon as an infallible means of curing the evils of a redundancy of population. But it is quite obvious, from the theory which has been expounded, that no benefit will accrue to a country from the emigrating of a portion of its inhabitants, if the expenses they incur in doing so, together with the property they may take with them, shall exceed the amount of capital which would suffice to employ and support them at home;—excepting only the benefit to be derived from the remaining capital of the country being applied under somewhat more advantageous circumstances, because applied to the *land* under less *disadvantageous* circumstances than it would otherwise have been. This benefit, too, would be experienced in only a slight degree,—*with any probable amount of emigration*,—on account of the difficulty of transferring capital from agriculture to other employments. And we may easily conceive the expenses of emigration, together with the capital removed by the emigrants, to be more than enough to counterbalance any supposable benefits to be conferred on their fellow-countrymen.

If we, however, assume the contrary of this to take place, the benefit conferred will manifest itself in a general rise of wages. The very same effects precisely will then ensue as in the case of a rise of wages consequent upon an augmentation of capital; and which effects, having been already sufficiently explained, I shall not repeat.

It is not denied that instances may sometimes occur of evils resulting to a country from emigration, wholly independent of any immediate and corresponding diminution of its wealth. It may suffer a loss, and a very considerable loss, from the general emigration of its more intelligent, skilful, or industrious citizens, whose places can only be very slowly supplied. Of this nature, for example, were the consequences to France of the revocation, by Louis XIV., of the edict of Nantes. But measures of this character have fortunately but seldom been enacted, even by the most despotic and tyrannical governments; and, in an age of advancing intelligence, the possibility of their occurrence is scarcely to be admitted as in any manner modifying our conclusions on the subject of emigration.

With respect to *immigration* into a country, on the supposition of the immigrants being possessed of superior intelligence, skill in any of the arts, or superior qualifications of any description whatever, they will be a gain to their adopted country. If this supposition do not hold good, the advantages to be derived from them, (I am referring, as I have been all along doing in the present chapter, to the advantages exclusive of the increase of population, which increase, other circumstances being the same, is unquestionably a national benefit) will depend, generally speaking, on the amount of capital which they may bring with them. If such capital be insufficient for the employment of labour, to an equal extent with the labour which they have added to that already employed in the country, it is plain that the effect of the immigration in question will be to induce a lower rate of wages; and this, however temporary its continuance may be on account of the diminished action of the principle of population, is of course to be regarded as a national evil.

An exception to the conclusions just deduced is presented in the case of foreign labourers with little or no property, who, on arriving in such a country as the United States, do not enter into competition with the natives in the more thickly settled parts of it, but, proceeding to the borders of the cultivated territory, unite their efforts there with those of others who are engaged in extending the dominion of civilised man over the wilderness. In such circumstances it is quite possible, as is well known, that their labour may add to, instead of subtracting from, the power of their neighbours to obtain the necessaries and luxuries of life, or, what is the same thing, may augment, rather than diminish, the rate of wages.

Another exception to the conclusions which have been deduced in relation to the advantages or disadvantages resulting to a country from immigration into it from foreign countries, arises where the immigrants consist in a greater proportion than common of able-bodied men. Even though they should be entirely destitute of property on their arrival, it is manifest that they may, quite possibly, more than compensate, by the greater proportional production which will ensue, for the support which they must in the first instance derive from the capital of the country at the expense of the labourers already employed in it.

It may be mentioned, that the *loss* to any country, thus resulting from the *emigration* of a disproportinate number of able-bodied men, is in every respect similar to the gain to be derived by the country to which they emigrate.

And to avoid being misapprehended by any of my readers, it is proper for me to state distinctly, that I am far from denying that a greater amount of *human happiness* may, in almost every instance, have been produced by the emigration of a number of the inhabitants of one country to another. Even when the emigrants are wholly without property, the advantages which they will enjoy may more than counterbalance the inconveniences occasioned by them to the population generally of their adopted country. Nor do I mean to call in question the expediency, under certain regulations, of opening the door to emigrants from abroad, by extending to them the rights of citizenship, or conferring upon them privileges of a more contracted nature before they become citizens. Indeed, to discuss this topic at all would be to travel wholly beyond the limits of a treatise on political economy.

The benefits derived by a nation from a rapid augmentation of its capital have been fully explained. I will now mention further that it is in a high degree desirable, however rapidly capital may be augmenting, that the *rate* of its augmentation should not be a diminishing one. Suppose the capital of a district of country to have had ten per cent. added to its amount in a certain time. Now if we likewise suppose the habits of the people in respect to marriage to remain the same, wages will have remained unaltered, and the population will have augmented by one-tenth. But if, in the next equal period of time, the capital of the district in question shall not have become greater in the same proportion,—if it shall have augmented by one-ninth only, instead of one-tenth,—it is plain that population cannot augment as fast as it did before, unless we suppose a deterioration of the condition and habits of the people; and it must also be plain, that the *moral appliances* requisite to prevent such deterioration, will have to become continually more and more efficient, according as the rate of the augmentation of capital is diminished. Now as the habits of a community in respect to marriage are only slowly, and with difficulty, alterable, it follows, that this rate should be rendered, if possible, an increasing, or at least an uniform one. The evils, indeed, which are consequent upon a diminishing rate of the augmentation of capital may be such as to be uncompensated for by the beneficial effects of a comparatively large augmentation of it in a given period of time; and it would be far better to sacrifice something of this, if, by so doing, that rate could be rendered an uniform, or more than an uniform rate.

CHAPTER IX.

EFFECTS OF CHEAP OR DEAR FOOD ON THE NUMBERS AND CONDITION OF A PEOPLE—AND EFFECTS, ON THEIR NUMBERS, OF AN EXTRAORDINARY MORTALITY, OF IMPROVEMENTS IN MEDICINE, AND OF THE MONASTIC INSTITUTIONS.

It has been before stated that a greater degree of industry, on the part of the labourers of a country generally, is equivalent in its effects to those resulting from a greater productiveness of labour. That in some of the most civilised nations no improvement of the kind of any moment is to be expected, or even desired, will be apparent, if we bear in mind the number of hours in the day during which their *operatives* are already kept employed. There are other nations, however, in which the state of things in this respect is very different. Where the necessary wants of men are comparatively few, and where *education* has not exerted its power of creating in them new desires, they will not readily forego the *pleasures of indolence.* For illustrations of this position, we may look at the habits in relation to industry of the uncultivated tribes of the more temperate climates of the earth, and especially of those tribes which dwell in the regions of perpetual summer. These scarcely need either shelter or clothing, and are satisfied with a scanty portion only of food: their enjoyments, other than what may be obtained *gratuitously* from the hand of nature, are exceedingly limited; and they, accordingly, are seldom excited to any extraordinary exertions of industry.

In every country too, where the necessaries of life are cheap, and the luxuries of life dear, the motive to industry, (all other circumstances, of course, being supposed to be the same) will be very considerably less with the mass of the population, than where luxuries are cheap and necessaries dear; and the former state of things will be found to be decidedly the preferable one of the two. As an illustration of this position, let us assume that, in a certain country, the labourer can, by working nine hours in the day, obtain what constitute to him the necessaries of life, and that he can procure a certain amount of luxuries by working one hour in the day more; and let us also assume that, in some other country, the case is exactly reversed,—that the same amount of necessaries are to be had by means of one hour's work, and the same luxuries by means of nine hours' work. The reader cannot fail to perceive, without any argument on my part, how much greater probability there is of the indolence, —I may say the *natural* indolence,—of the labourer, getting the better of his desire for the enjoyment of luxuries, in the latter case than in the former.

The introduction of the potato into Ireland, as the principal article of food, has no doubt had a *tendency*, as every other *improvement* in the arts of life would have had, to augment the population of that country, and to raise the wages of labour. That the former of these two effects has actually occurred there, is known to every one: but that the wages of labour continue to be extremely *low* is equally well known. What, then, have been the causes which have prevented their rise? It would be irrelevant to undertake to answer this question fully; and I shall merely remark, that *one* of those causes has, very probably, been the cheap food of the people, —cheap when compared with the prices of what are esteemed by them to be luxuries,—rendering them less disposed than they would otherwise be to obtain them. On account of this contraction of their desires for luxuries, while the industry of the people may not have been impaired to the same extent as it would have been in a warmer and more *relaxing* climate, the effect, in accordance with the theory of population which has been expounded in the present book, has been an *extraordinary* multiplication of the numbers of the people; and that amount of labour, which, had such multiplication not taken place, would have sufficed to procure for the workman a certain portion of the luxuries as well as necessaries of life, is now scarcely adequate to supply him with what is absolutely necessary to enable him to exist.

Among the apparent anomalies which admit of an easy explication, when the theory of population is once understood, is the greater prosperity often exhibited by a comparatively barren country than by one blessed with very superior advantages of situation and soil. This ceases to be a mystery which is only to be wondered at, as soon as we are prepared to acknowledge the immense influence of moral causes in determining the command of the mass of a community over the various enjoyments, material as well as immaterial, of life.

It is now also easy to understand the more *remote* effects, on the numbers of a people, of an extraordinary mortality, or of an increased rate of mortality. The first effect will, plainly, be to augment the wages of labour; the whole amount of wages will be distributed among a less number of persons. But even when these *specific* wages are consumed, it will still be true that the rate of wages will be higher than they were prior to the supposed mortality; for the labour of the community will now be more productive than heretofore, it being applied under less disadvantageous circumstances. This state of things, however, will not continue. The principle of population will act with an increased energy, and wages will in consequence fall; but they will not fall to their former level precisely, on account of the enlarged desires of the people for enjoyments, arising from their consumption for a time of the various products of labour in greater quantity than before. In short, every thing will take place in the same manner as I have described in the perfectly analogous case, of a rise of wages resulting from any extraordinary augmentation in the capital of a country.

The instance of East Prussia, in the beginning of the last century, has already been adduced, as illustrative of the energy with which the principle of population will act, when disease, by thinning the ranks of a people, has raised the wages of labour. I may here observe that the same instance, as also many others of a similar kind occurring in other parts of the world, have been frequently referred to as affording evidence to establish the propositions,—that disease, war, and every other supposable *positive* check to population, are in reality no checks at all, unless they act so extensively as to render it impossible for the whole power of population, when brought into activity, to restore the numbers of a people,—and that most of the countries of Europe are now quite as populous as they would have been if, instead of being frequently engaged in bloody wars with each other, they had maintained among themselves for centuries the most peaceable relations. In proof also of these positions, the very great increase of the population both of Great Britain and of France, during the wars of the French Revolution, has been cited. But surely this is pushing the consequences of the theory of population too far, or rather mistaking the proper consequences of that theory. Even though we should suppose no interval of time to occur between the death of an individual and the supplying of his place by the birth of another individual,—it must be manifest that the quantity of wealth produced will not be as great as before. Many years must elapse before the infant just born will be able to perform the work of the deceased labourer. But again, more persons must be born than have died, in order that they shall be equally numerous with the latter when they shall have arrived at the same age. Hence, while a diminished production is taking place, there will be also an increased consumption; and wealth, and therefore population, will not augment as rapidly as they would otherwise do. This, however, is not all. In every war, at least every war which might have been avoided, there is a great unproductive consumption, that is a diminution of capital, or a diminution, under the most favourable circumstances, of the rate at which capital is increasing; and this implies, as has been shewn, a diminished population.

Improvements in medicine, which protract the lives of the existing generation of men, produce effects, it is evident, exactly the reverse of those resulting from wars or any of the other causes of an extraordinary mortality. The number of marriages and births will be lessened, but not to the same extent as the number of lives preserved.

The theory of population points out the true mode in which the numbers of mankind were affected by the monastic institutions of Europe, and of the other quarters of the world. After what has been stated, the reader cannot fail to perceive that the *celibacy* of the monks had no effect whatever on those numbers. By omitting to marry, they only made room for a greater number of marriages among the community at large. But in so far as they contributed, by their mode of life, to a diminished production of wealth, the effect in question will, without doubt, have also been produced; since, other circumstances being the same, population and wealth always augment together. In this respect, however, the case of the monks is not a peculiar one. Whether any individual of the community contributes, or does not contribute, to the progress of national wealth, depends of course on the amount of wealth produced by him, when compared with what he consumes unproductively. Were the monks, then, productive labourers? To what extent was their labour productive? And what was the comparative amount of their consumption? According to the answers which may be given to these questions, will they be pronounced to have retarded, or accelerated, the progress of population. It is obvious, too, that those answers will differ according to the estimate which we may form of the utility, or inutility, of the services rendered by them to their fellow-men.

Many more illustrations of the action of the principle of population might here be given. Those already adduced will, however, suffice for the present; and others will occur as we proceed, when we shall have first discussed some one or two topics not yet treated of, or only touched upon, to which they have relation.

BOOK THIRD.

THE THEORIES OF MONEY, AND OF BANKING.

CHAPTER I.

ON THE COMPARATIVE VALUE OF GOLD AND SILVER MONEY, IN DIFFERENT COUNTRIES, AND AT DIFFERENT TIMES IN THE SAME COUNTRY.

I SHALL now resume the consideration of the subject of money,—a subject, not only of great practical importance, but one likewise concerning which there are as many erroneous notions prevalent, among even the more thinking portion of the community, as perhaps concerning any other in the whole range of political economy. This science, too, presents for discussion scarcely any subject, of much moment, which does not require, in order to be *thoroughly* understood, that correct opinions in relation to money should be first entertained.

And in what is to follow, I shall pursue the method adopted in the preceding part of this work, of supposing among a multitude of changes, all equally liable to take place, only a single one in fact to occur,—and of tracing the various other changes which must then necessarily ensue. By thus examining the effects produced by the separate action of the different causes of change, we shall be enabled afterwards to estimate correctly the effects that any number of them, acting conjointly, are calculated to produce.

Let the following suppositions be made ;—that the circulating medium, throughout the world, consists wholly of the precious metals, gold and silver; that the supply of this medium, as well as of all other commodities, in relation to the demand existing for them, is such as to render the price of every thing the same in every country; and also, that all things, including money, can be transported from place to place without any expense whatever. On these suppositions, which, as I proceed, will be varied, and rendered more conformable to the real state of the facts, let us inquire what the consequences will be if the supply of money become at any time greater, in some one place or country, than it has hitherto been.

The first effect will, plainly, be a local rise of prices. A motive will thus be offered for importing commodities, other than money, from other parts of the world, and paying for them in money,—and for sending money abroad, rather than those other commodities which were before exported in exchange for the usual imports. This interchange will, of course, continue, until, by increasing at home the supply of commodities other than money, and diminishing that of gold and silver, and by diminishing the supply abroad of commodities in general, and increasing that of gold and silver, the prices of things shall again become every where the same. As, however, the supply of money in the market of the world will, obviously, have become greater than it was before, prices will every where have become somewhat higher; or, which is the same thing, the value of the precious metals will have fallen.

Here the question presents itself:—will this state of things be a lasting one? It will not; for the capital applied to the producing of gold and silver will no longer yield the usual profits. Less capital will, in consequence, be applied to the working of the mines; the supply of those metals will not be sufficiently great to compensate for the consumption to which the portion of them in use as money, or for other purposes, is subjected; and their value must again rise, and prices fall. When these shall have fallen to their former level, it is manifest that the motive for employing a less amount of capital in mining will cease to exist, and every thing will return to the state in which it was before the supposed augmentation of the supply of money.

In shewing, as I have done, the effect resulting from an increase of the money which circulates to be, first a local, and next a general rise of prices, and, last of all, a complete return to the state of things in respect to money and prices originally existing, I have said nothing concerning the length of the period during which the whole series of changes is performed. At present, what I wish my readers particularly to note is the result that is *ultimately* produced.

Effects opposite to those just mentioned must necessarily ensue, when the supply of money in any country is supposed to have diminished, instead of having increased. What those opposite effects will be, the reader can easily trace for himself.

Whatever deviations, then, may occur, either in excess or deficiency, from the ordinary rate of supply of the precious metals, the consequent rise or fall of prices can only be temporary; and the average value of money will now, it is plain, be determined, like that of every other commodity, by the cost of production.

Hence, I may remark, the comparative values of gold and silver will be determined by the cost of producing them respectively. While, too, it is only because the cost of production, in reference to both these metals, has been diminished since the discovery of America, that their value is now much less than it was before that event; so it is only because the cost of producing gold is about sixteen times as much as that of producing silver, that the former is sixteen times as valuable as the latter.

As money is, indeed, only that commodity which is most frequently exchanged for every other, the determination of its value by the cost of producing it needed not to have been specially deduced. I might have safely taken for granted that none of my readers would hesitate to apply to it the established principles concerning the exchangeable values of commodities in general. The reason why I have not done this has been, simply, that I might the more strongly inculcate a point of so much importance, as the proposition in question will be perceived in the sequel truly to be.

The conclusions which I have arrived at in the present chapter have been founded on a number of suppositions; one of which is that money is synonymous with gold and silver. Let us inquire whether those conclusions will have to be in any manner modified, if the supposition just stated be not admitted; and that it cannot be admitted, consistently with the actual condition of things, is a matter of notoriety.

In the first place, let money consist, not of gold and silver merely, but of gold and silver *coin*, that is of pieces of those metals having certain marks stamped upon them, to certify that they are of given weight and fineness. By whom, or by whose authority, the money is coined, would be of no more importance, for our present purpose, than is its form, or the particular manner in which it is divided and subdivided, did not governments (who have every where undertaken to be the exclusive coiners of money) sometimes consent to coin gold and silver gratuitously,—exchanging for *bullion* an equal quantity of *specie*;—a measure which I need not say would never be adopted by any individual, or association of individuals less numerous than the nation of which they are members. When the business of coining money is thus performed by government gratuitously, or, speaking more correctly, at the national expense, it is evident that, in the case of an increased supply of money occurring, there is no reason why specie, rather than bullion, should be sent out of the country to pay for the extraordinary amount of importation, which I have shewn would necessarily take place, excepting that the former has impressed upon it a certificate of its weight and fineness, on which a great reliance can be put. This circumstance, however, will cause it to be sent abroad, while the bullion is retained at home; and the series of consequences ensuing will be just such as were deduced on the supposition of there being no difference whatever between specie and bullion.

But if the bullion in the country be not exported, its price, equally with that of every other commodity, money excepted, will be enhanced; which is the same thing as to say, that a given quantity of gold or silver is worth more when uncoined than when it is coined. The coin will therefore not only be exported from the country, but a portion of it will be melted down and converted into bullion. It is manifest that these two processes will be going on, and will cease, simultaneously; so that to suppose the money of the world to be augmented in any degree, will imply that its whole stock of gold and silver is augmented in the very same degree. Hence also, the same conclusions may be drawn, as when the circulating medium was supposed to consist of the precious metals, without reference to their being coined.

CHAPTER II.

THE SAME SUBJECT CONTINUED.

If a government, instead of exchanging coined money for an equal quantity of gold and silver in the form of bullion, should make a charge for coining,—a charge which is denominated technically by the term *seignorage*,—the only difference in the series of changes which I have traced above will be, that the process of melting down the coin and converting it into bullion, preparatory to its being used in the arts, will not commence until the supposed depreciation of money shall have proceeded so far as to reduce its value to that of an equal quantity of bullion. But whether any portion of the coin be converted into bullion, or not, no extraordinary increase in the supply of it can take place without being followed by a partial exportation of it to foreign countries; or, in other words, by the diffusing of the extraordinary supply throughout the market of the world; and consequently, by the diminished production of gold and silver, until the former state of things, in respect to the value of money, be entirely restored.

When money was regarded as consisting of uncoined gold and silver, and after the consequences had been deduced of a supposed augmented supply of it, I made the obvious remark that precisely the contrary consequences would flow from a *diminished* supply of it. It must be now equally obvious that exactly a similar remark may be made in reference to such a supposition, whatever may be the relation which money or specie bears to the precious metals when these have not been coined. And, as before, I will not enumerate those consequences, because they cannot fail to be suggested to the mind of the reader without my doing so.

Coined money will, on the average, have an advantage in exchange over bullion, exactly in proportion to the confidence which is generally reposed in the accuracy of what the stamp upon it is intended to certify, to wit, that it has a certain weight, and is alloyed in a certain fixed proportion with baser metal. This certificate, by enabling the coin to pass current without being assayed and weighed, dispenses with a certain amount of inconvenience and labour, on the part of him who receives it in payment for other commodities. It will, therefore, be preferred in the market to bullion, other circumstances being the same, that is, it will have a greater exchangeable value; and were the business of coining left free to every one who chose to engage in it, and were it then practicable (which would, evidently, not be the case) so to regulate it as to secure the entire confidence of the community in its being always faithfully performed, the excess of the exchangeable value of money over that of bullion would be determined by the cost or expense of coinage.

And it would not be in the power of government, by charging a higher seignorage than is sufficient to compensate the inconvenience and trouble above mentioned, to add any thing to the value of the coin. In order the better to perceive this impossibility, let us look at a particular case. Suppose ten dollars to be the value of an *eagle;* comprising in that value, not only the value of the gold contained in the eagle, but also the compensation in question. Now let the government not rest satisfied with receiving only ten dollars for the eagle, when it is issued from its mint, but endeavour to obtain an additional value for it, by means of an augmented seignorage. Let it, for instance, declare the eagle to be worth eleven, instead of ten dollars. What will be the consequence? Will the piece of money, whose nominal value has thus been arbitrarily raised a dollar, have its real value in exchange raised to the same extent? Certainly not. No one will be willing to give any more for it than is sufficient to procure in the market an equal quantity of gold bullion, together with the cost or expense of assaying and weighing.

Hence it is plain that the possessors of the precious metals will not have a sufficient inducement to bring them to the mint of government to be coined; and the coining of money would be altogether out of the question, excepting where the government is itself a producer of gold or silver,—or where it exacts a certain portion of the produce of the mines from those whom it permits to work them,—or where it obtains them in payment of taxes.

In as much, likewise, as a higher seignorage than is sufficient to repay the expense of coinage will have no effect on the real prices of things, or, in other words, on the quantity of gold or silver for which they will exchange, we may conclude that such a measure will have no tendency either to accelerate, or retard, that exportation or importation of money in payment for commodities, imported or exported, as the case may be, by means of which the equable diffusion of the circulating medium of the world is effected.

The supply of money has been supposed, under certain circumstances, to vary. Let us now suppose the *demand* for money to become in some one country either greater or less, while the supply of it continues unaltered; and, first, let the demand for it be diminished. This supposition, the reader will perceive, is equivalent to that of an augmented supply; for it implies a greater willingness than before, on the part of the holders of money, to dispose of it in exchange for other commodities. It is true that the actual quantity of money will not have been increased by the occurrence of a less demand for it than before; but its efficiency, as a medium of exchange, will have increased exactly in proportion as its circulation is quickened. When, for example, the rapidity of circulation is doubled, an hundred dollars will perform the same number of exchanges which two hundred did before, and the very same consequences must follow as if the circulating medium had been doubled in quantity; and so too, in whatever other ratio that rapidity may be supposed to have become augmented. Should the demand for money be greater, instead of less than it was, it will, of course, circulate more slowly, and the series of consequences ensuing will, manifestly, be the same as results from a diminution in the supply of money.

If we suppose the supply or demand in respect to any commodity, different from money, to vary, every one knows that its price will suffer alteration. There may be either a rise or fall of price. When a rise takes place, an importation from abroad of the commodity will follow, which will be paid for in money (all other circumstances, including the price of every thing else, remaining unchanged); and the importation of it, and payment for it, will go on together, until by diminishing the supply of it, and increasing that of money at home, and by increasing the supply of it, and diminishing that of money abroad, its price will be again every where the same. The like equalisation of prices throughout the world, it can be shewn, will take place, in case they should have *fallen* below their usual rate.

Whether, then, the relations of supply and demand, which ordinarily subsist in any country, are disturbed by an alteration in the supply of, or demand for money, or whether those relations are disturbed by an alteration in the supply of or demand for any thing else, such disturbance will more or less rapidly cease; and an entire equality in the prices of all things will be every where eventually re-established. Since, however, such disturbances will be continually occurring, this equality of prices will seldom, in fact, be found to subsist, and prices, in the various regions of the globe, will be continually oscillating, within certain limits, about the *equated* rates, if I may use this expression,—having all the while a tendency to become equal to them.

We have now arrived at the conclusion, that so long as the money of the world consists exclusively of gold and silver, whether in bullion or coined, and whether any seignorage be charged or not by the government for coining it,—and so long, too, as we take no account of the cost of transportation,—the prices of things will every where tend to an equality. Those prices, moreover, will have a tendency to be at such a rate as just to repay the cost of production,—on the one hand, to the producer of the precious metals,—and, on the other, to the producers of the different commodities for which they are exchanged. In other words, just so much of any commodity will, on the average, be sold for a given sum of money, as is equal to it in cost.

CHAPTER III.

THE SAME SUBJECT CONTINUED.

Let us now remove the supposition of the transportation of commodities being effected without expense. It is evident that their prices will then not tend to a *perfect* equality throughout the various countries of the world,—and that the price of any article may differ permanently in one country from what it is in another, by the expense of transporting from one to the other the article concerned, as well as the money for which it is exchanged. The reader will also, on a moment's reflection, perceive that the expense of transportation, using this term most comprehensively, is the *only* reason why the prices of things would not be, in reality, every where the same,—so long, at least, as the commerce between nations is entirely free from all legislative restrictions.

I may here mention, that there is nothing in the deviation of the prices of things from an entire and universal equality, induced by the expense of transportation, to prevent those prices from being determined, in the *several* countries of the world, by the cost of producing the precious metals, in the manner heretofore explained.

In respect to copper money, to the extent in which it performs the functions which, if it did not exist, would be performed by gold or silver money, will the effects of its use be manifestly equivalent to those resulting from the circulation it thus displaces. It is scarcely necessary for me to remark, that the existence of such a circulation as that now adverted to can in no wise modify the conclusions already arrived at in respect to the general equalisation of prices, and to their determination in every country by the cost of production, both in respect to money and the commodities purchased by it. And by the general equalisation of prices, I, of course, now mean their equalisation within the limits prescribed by the expense of transportation.

Before inquiring into the effects of the introduction of paper money, I will make a remark or two having relation to the matters treated in the preceding chapter, chiefly for the purpose of guarding against the possibility of my meaning being misapprehended.

I remark, in the first place, that the argument which has been adduced to prove the impossibility of augmenting the exchangeable value of the money of a country by means of the exacting, on the part of the government, of a higher seignorage than is adequate to compensate the toil and trouble of assaying and weighing, is equally applicable to *every* attempt to add to the exchangeable value of the money put into circulation, by assigning to it a greater value nominally, or, what amounts to the same thing, by causing money to be coined of the same nominal value as before, but containing a diminished amount of the precious metals.

In the next place, it may be proper for me to meet an objection which may perhaps be made to the position I have assumed to be an obvious one,—that a diminished demand for money implies an augmented rapidity in the rate of its circulation, and, on the other hand, that an augmented demand for it implies a diminished rate of circulation. Some persons might be disposed to maintain the opposite of this to be true. They might, and it must be acknowledged with some appearance of plausibility, argue, for example, that a man never makes a greater demand for money than when he is anxious to obtain it in order to fulfil the pecuniary engagements into which he may have entered, and when he is, consequently, the least disposed to retain it in his possession after he has obtained it; so that it is precisely, they might go on to say, when the demand for money is the *greatest*, that it circulates most rapidly. So too, the circulation of it takes place at the slowest rate, precisely when the demand for it is the least. To all this, however, I reply, that if we take this anxiety of the members of a community to obtain money to be evidence of their demand for it being great, we ought, consistently, to regard their anxiety to *part* with it in payment of their debts, as an evidence of their demand for it being small; and as these two anxieties, from the nature of the case, are equal to one another, we will be left without any means whatever of determining the extent of the demand actually existing at the time for money. But I have employed the term demand, in reference to money, in a sense different from that which has just been considered, and in one perfectly analogous to its ordinary acceptation when we speak of commodities other than money. When the demand for broadcloth, for instance, is said to be greater than it has hitherto been, a greater desire than before must necessarily exist for the possession of broadcloth, to be used or consumed, sooner or later, by its owner. It is in consequence of the existence of such a demand as this, that the merchant who deals in the article will be more desirous than he has heretofore been to purchase it, as well as to sell it to his customers, and that he will thus add his demand to that already existing. In like manner, the demand for money is correctly said to have become greater, when people generally are more disposed than they previously were to retain it in their possession for future use. Here again the analogy is complete, in this respect,—that, on account of the prevailing desire to keep more money in possession or reserve for future use, the merchants will likewise make a greater demand for for it by declining to supply themselves as extensively as they did before, with other commodities.

Another remark which I have to make is, that when in the preceding chapter I spoke of prices being dependent, in the several countries of the world, on the cost of producing the precious metals, I had reference, as well to the countries whose stock of those metals was procured from abroad, as to countries where they were extracted from the earth by mining, or by means of any other process. When the source from which a commodity is supplied to us is a foreign one, every dollar's value imported implies the exportation of a certain value to pay for it. Now if the exports be the product of the capital and labour of the country whence they are sent abroad, the imports may surely be regarded in the same light. The former are, in fact, only instruments for procuring the latter; and the labour and capital applied to the producing of the former are truly applied to the first stages in the production of the latter,—the remaining stages of their production being the act of transporting both exports and imports to their respective places of destination. Hence it is that we may speak, with entire propriety, of the cost to us of producing the precious metals, even though not a particle of them should be of domestic origin.

CHAPTER IV.

EFFECTS OF THE USE OF PAPER MONEY.

To simplify as much as possible the subject of paper money, let us, at first, suppose all money of the kind to have the well known form of *bank notes.* Also for the sake of simplication, let us suppose a particular case; — that the metallic money in circulation in some one country, or region of country,—say the state of Pennsylvania,—is equivalent to a specie circulation of a million of dollars, and that no paper money has as yet been introduced. In this condition of things, banks are established, which add to the circulating medium one hundred thousand dollars in notes representing specie, that is payable by the issuers to the holders of them in specie on demand. And, again for the sake of simplication, let it be supposed that this addition to the money previously in circulation is uniformly diffused over the state; so that every man having before $100 shall come to possess $110, and that every man having $1000 shall possess $1100,—and so on in like proportion. There must, evidently, be a general rise of prices; just as if the augmentation of the circulating medium had consisted of specie, instead of paper. What before sold for ten dollars will be sold for eleven. An extraordinary importation of commodities, other than money, and exportation of money, in payment for these, will ensue. The $100,000, added to the circulation of the state of Pennsylvania, will, in this manner, become an addition to the circulating medium of the world, and will be so diffused among the different nations composing it, as to cause an equal rise of prices in all of them;—or, in other words, the increase of the money of each country will be proportional to the quantity of money which it previously possessed. As before explained, in reference to the case when nothing but specie was supposed to circulate,—there will now too be a diminished production of the precious metals, until prices fall to their former level, and are again just such as to repay the cost of production to all the parties concerned.

I have said, until prices fall to their former level. Here there is a *slight* inaccuracy. While, if the addition which was made to the circulating medium had consisted of specie, the quantity of gold and silver required to supply the wear of the coin, as well as for other purposes, would, after prices had fallen to their original rates, be what it was before,—such will not be the case when the circulation is augmented by an issue of paper money. Indeed, were the prices of things then to subside to their former level, it is plain that, although the former amount of gold and silver made use of in the arts will be again made use of in them, the amount required in repairing the wear of the coin will be less than before, on account of the diminution of the quantity of the coin in circulation. On the whole, therefore, those metals will not need to be produced in as great abundance as previous to the issue of the paper which caused the temporary rise of prices. Hence too, they could not be produced as abundantly without depreciating in value, so as not to yield the producers of them the ordinary profits on the capital employed; and they will, accordingly, not be produced as abundantly. A transfer of capital and labour will take place, to a certain extent, from the business of mining to other employments; the worst mines will be neglected; and the capital which will remain invested in mining will be invested under more advantageous circumstances than the capital was heretofore invested. Now that cost of producing any commodity which determines its exchangeable value being always the cost of producing it under the most disadvantageous circumstances in which it is actually produced,—it will, in the instance under consideration, have been lessened. Money will, consequently, have become less valuable; and prices will, of course, have ultimately risen in a certain degree, though in comparatively a *very slight* degree.

The modification just stated, of a proposition previously deduced, may possibly seem to some of my readers to be so very inconsiderable as to render it scarcely worthy of the notice I have bestowed upon it; and my motive for touching here upon it at all has been simply a desire to exhibit my views in as unobjectionable a form as it is in my power to do.

But to proceed: it is obvious that the preceding deduction of the effects resulting from the supposed issue of $100,000 in paper money will hold good, to whatever extent the issue of paper money may have taken place, so long as there is specie procurable for exportation; and specie will be always procurable for exportation, so long as the banks fulfil their promise of paying it for their notes on demand. What will happen if the issue of paper money should go beyond the amount which has been mentioned, will be a subject of future inquiry.

The manner in which the foregoing conclusions must be modified, on account of the expense of the transportation of commodities, is the same, evidently, as was explained in the analogous case of the supply of money having been augmented by an addition to it of specie. I will here only say farther, what is sufficiently manifest, that the inequality which, after the supply of money has been augmented in some one country, may *continue* to subsist between the price of a commodity there and in any other country, will depend, other circumstances being the same, on the distance which those countries are apart from each other;—and consequently, that a given augmentation of the circulating medium will be diffused somewhat more densely, so to speak, in those states or countries which lie contiguous to that where it has occurred, than in those situated more remote.

Had the increase of the circulating medium of Pennsylvania not been equally diffused throughout the state, as was assumed to be the case, it is quite evident that the soundness of the conclusions, to which we have been led, would not be in the least affected. The only difference in the steps of our reasoning would be, that prices will, in the first instance, rise unequally in different places in the state;—all which places may then be regarded in the same light as the whole state was before regarded, viz. as so many distinct sources whence paper money has been issued, and whence money is exported in exchange for other commodities; thus equalising prices (within the limits, of course, prescribed by the expense of transportation) throughout the state of Pennsylvania, as well as every where else.

When paper money is issued in any one part of a country, it is very possible that its credit may be sufficiently good to occasion it to be *exported*, instead of specie, to neighbouring, or even to more distant parts, in exchange for commodities. It is scarcely necessary for me to remark that this case, likewise, will furnish no exception to the correctness of the results to which we have arrived. The paper money, in this manner made to constitute a portion of the circulation in other parts of the country, will have the same effect upon prices, and will induce the same series of changes, as if it had been issued where it circulates.

Again, in what goes before, the banks of Pennsylvania were supposed to add $100,000 in paper to a specie circulation amounting to a million of dollars. I may observe that the possibility of their doing so will depend upon their first procuring from abroad the specie which they will retain in their vaults, and on which their banking operations are to be based. If they have to take this specie from that which at the time is actually circulating, they will have to issue their notes to an amount as much exceeding the $100,000, by which the circulating medium is to be increased, as is equal to that of the specie thus taken. If $50,000 be deposited in the vaults of the banks, they must issue paper to the amount of $150,000, in order that the effect specified may be produced, and that prices may rise in the proportion of ten to eleven.

Another modification to be applied to what has been deduced concerning the effects of paper money is, that the same amounts in specie and in bank notes may not be equally *efficient* in performing the functions of circulation. The efficiency, in this respect, of every kind of money, depends, not only on its quantity, but also on the rapidity, as has been already mentioned, with which it circulates. Now, bank notes will frequently circulate more rapidly than specie, on account of the greater facility of transporting or remitting them from one place to another. An addition, therefore, of $100,000 in paper of that description, to the money of a country, may be more than equivalent, in its effects on present prices, to a like addition to it made in specie. But whether the paper be more or less than equivalent in efficiency to specie, all the conclusions which have been deduced, concerning the distribution of the circulating medium, would still be true, provided only we vary our supposition of $100,000 in bank notes having been added to the circulating medium, by supposing this medium to have been augmented by just such an amount in bank notes *as is equivalent in its effects* to $100,000 of the money originally circulating.

CHAPTER V.

OF THE DIFFERENT CONSTITUENT PORTIONS OF THE CIRCULATING MEDIUM; AND THEIR RELATIVE EFFICIENCY.

Bank notes, whether issued by incorporated companies, or by private bankers, are not the only substitutes for specie; and they are not even the only kind of paper money. The circulating medium must, indeed, be regarded as comprehending every contrivance which performs the office of money, and by means of which, therefore, the use of any other medium of exchange may be partially dispensed with. Such contrivances are of various sorts. Besides the notes of bankers, which are promises for the payment of a certain amount of specie to the bearer on demand, the common promissory notes of individuals, in which they engage to pay a sum of money at a future day for value received by them, may be transferred from one individual to another in payment for commodities purchased, and so may be made use of for the very same purposes as those are employed to accomplish, to which the term money, ordinarily so called, is applied. Bills of exchange, that is orders or drafts for money by creditors upon their debtors residing at a distance, or by merchants or bankers on their correspondents, in favour of third persons, are in the same predicament. Payments may be made by simply removing an *entry* in the books of a banker to the credit of one individual, and entering the amount of it to the credit of some other individual. The bank checks, or orders upon the banker for payment of the moneys deposited with him for safe keeping, may themselves be passed from hand to hand, and thus be made to take the place of money. The same is obviously true concerning every sort of public securities, and every representative whatever of property. Each of the contrivances enumerated constitutes a portion of the circulating medium, the *efficiency* of which is to be estimated, as well in proportion to the comparative rapidity of its circulation, as to its value in exchange. And the effects on prices, as also the farther changes which will be consequent upon those effects, when any one or more of these constituent elements of the circulation are augmented in quantity or in the rapidity with which they perform the office of money, will, of course, be entirely similar to what the effects on prices, and the further changes resulting, have been shown to be in the case of bank notes.

The contrary effects must necessarily take place, if we suppose either of the above contrivances, or species of paper money, to perform the office or functions of money less rapidly than they did before.

It must, next, be apparent to the reader that, if we knew to what extent those various contrivances, including bank notes, supply the place of hard money,—having respect as well to rapidity as to quantity,—we should find no difficulty in estimating what the amount of the circulating medium would be, did it consist exclusively of the precious metals; and in speaking of the amount of the circulation in any one country, as compared with others, or with the world in general, it is such an estimate as this which should always be made.

And it is also easy to perceive what an errour we should fall into, were we to look upon the whole circulation of a country,—more especially of one in as high degree commercial as the United States or Great Britain,—as consisting only of the specie which circulates, and of the bank notes which are made payable to the bearer on demand.

CHAPTER VI.

THE VALUE OF THE ENTIRE CIRCULATING MEDIUM REMAINS ALWAYS UNALTERED—CONSEQUENCES FROM THIS PRINCIPLE.

THE following proposition is an obvious inference from the principles already established,—that, no matter to what extent the circulating medium of a country may at any time have been augmented or diminished, *its value always remains unaltered;* the effect of such augmentation or diminution on the prices of things being to raise them in the one case, and to lower them in the other, in the same proportion.*

Hence too, (notwithstanding the apprehensions which are so frequently expressed among ourselves, even by persons whose opinions generally are entitled to a considerable degree of respect, lest the United States might not possess a circulating medium large enough for the business purposes of the community)—*it is a matter of not the least moment whether this medium be great or small.* Whatever in any country may be the amount of it, if we suppose it to be reduced to the tenth part of that amount, the prices of things, as has been shewn, will likewise become only the tenth of what they are; and an hundred dollars will perform precisely the same functions which are now performed by a thousand. The difficulty of procuring the former sum will, indeed, be quite as great as is at present that of procuring the latter; but these sums of

* There is a reason why the prices of all things will not rise or fall in the *precise* proportion of the augmentation or diminution of the circulating medium; or, at least, why this will be the case only after a certain period shall have elapsed. Some commodities ordinarily fluctuate in value much less than others; and *labour* is such a commodity. A customary rate of wages comes, indeed, to be paid, in every place and in every employment; which, *because it is a customary rate*, is only slowly alterable.

money will, in the two cases, possess the very same exchangeable value, and will, on this account, bestow upon their owner a command *to an equal extent* over the various necessaries and luxuries of life. I need not say that our general conclusion will not be different, though we should suppose the diminution of the circulating medium to occur in any other proportion than that of ten to one.

It is true we may conceive the circulating medium to be so exceedingly reduced in quantity, and a given portion of money, consequently, to become so valuable, that the coins, which are requisite for purchasing the articles most frequently needed, would be inconveniently small. But those coins might also be inconveniently large, if the circulating medium be exceedingly *augmented* in quantity. And it must be obvious that, between these two extreme limits, there is a vast range, in which the quantity or amount of the circulation must be a matter of the greatest indifference.

To avoid being misunderstood, I wish my readers to note particularly that what has just been stated has had no reference to the inconveniences and losses necessarily experienced by creditors whenever the circulating medium is undergoing the process of being augmented or expanded, or to those far greater inconveniences and losses to which debtors are subjected on the occurrence of every diminution or contraction of that medium. These "evils of change" can only be obviated by rendering the change in every case as *gradual* as possible. We may conceive it to take place, however great it may be, so very gradually as to be scarcely perceptible in its effects, even by the parties most interested. And the *ultimate* results are, at all events, such as I have described them to be.

The temporary evils of which mention has been made, it may be proper to say here, will be considered in some detail, when I shall treat of the immediate effects resulting from the expansions and contractions of the paper money issued by the banks.

Now if all bank notes were to cease to circulate, and no other description of paper money were to be issued by the government, or from any other source, to supply their place, —although the quantity of specie, as well as the mercantile paper and other contrivances actually existing in the country, for economising the use of money, would be amply sufficient for performing all the functions of circulation,—there can be no doubt of every contrivance to supply the place of money being made use of to a greater extent than heretofore. While for example, a bill of exchange may be refused, in payment for commodities purchased from an individual who is indebted at the very place on which the bill in question is drawn, and refused because of his preferring to remit the amount of his debt in bank notes,—the bill of exchange, if obtainable at a premium less than the expense of transporting specie, may have a preference given to it when bank notes no longer circulate. Other examples, too, will occur to the reader, of ordinary mercantile paper then finding employment as money, in the room of bank notes.

But such an addition as this to the circulation is of little comparative importance in respect to my present purpose. Even if it were not to occur, it will follow, on the principles already explained, that the diminution which has taken place of the money of the country, by means of the withdrawal of all bank paper, will be distributed, so to speak, throughout the whole commercial world. Hence it is easy to conceive that the actual diminution of the money which circulates, after this distribution shall have been accomplished,—and it will evidently not be slow in being accomplished,—will be considerably less than it was at first. If the circulating medium of the United States be supposed to constitute a tenth part of that of the whole world, and if we, besides, suppose *as much as fifty* millions of dollars to be withdrawn from the circulation, the amount, by which the circulating medium of our country will have been diminished, will be only five millions of dollars.

This, again, is not the ultimate or permanent condition of the circulating medium. On account of its general diminution, prices every where will have fallen, or the exchangeable value of money will have risen. A more active production of the precious metals, consequently, will ensue, until prices return very nearly to their former rates, and the circulating medium very nearly to its former amount.

CHAPTER VII.

THE DIFFERENT KINDS OF BANKS—HOW THE CREDIT OF BANKS OF CIRCULATION IS MAINTAINED.

There are three sorts of banks, viz. banks of deposite, of discount, and of circulation. Any one bank may, however, partake of the character of all of these; as is the case universally throughout the United States.

By a bank of *deposite* is meant an institution which receives the money of individuals on deposite, giving them credit in its books for the money deposited; any portion of which may, at any time, be withdrawn by its owner, or transferred to his creditor without being withdrawn,—the fact of such transfer being duly noted in the books of the bank. The expense of banking may, in this case, be met by exacting a small per centage on the making or the withdrawing of any deposite, or on the transferring of it from one individual to another.

While some of the depositors are withdrawing their money, deposites will be making by others; so that, notwithstanding the liability of the bankers to restore upon demand the money deposited with them, they will, generally speaking, find themselves in the constant possession of a certain sum, which they will be tempted to profit from by lending it out to such persons as may be desirous of borrowing. One of the most convenient modes of doing this is by the discounting of promissory notes; and hence the origin of banks of *discount.* Such discounts, however, may be made, not only with the money of depositors, but with that of individual bankers, or companies of bankers, with a view to the profits to be derived from their respective capitals, as in any other employment.

But a bank, instead of parting with its specie in exchange for the promissory notes of individuals discounted by it, may issue promissory notes of its own, which are made payable to the bearer in specie on demand, and which are capable, on account of their great convenience, as well as the credit attached to them by the public generally, of performing all the functions of money; the bank becoming, in this manner, a bank of *circulation.*

Here I may remark that, when I speak of the *banking system* of the country, I look upon the furnishing of a paper circulation, as a substitute for specie, as constituting its essential feature.

It is evident that no inducement would be offered to a bank for issuing its own paper, had it not the power to issue it to a greater amount than it could do of specie; and the excess of the amount of paper money issued above that which could be issued of specie must be sufficiently great to enable the bankers to pay the augmented expenses of management. From the very nature, then, of such a bank as I am now speaking of, it will put more of its paper in circulation than it has specie in its vaults to redeem it. It promises every day to do what it knows, and what every one at all acquainted with the nature of banking knows, would be impracticable for it to do, if all its notes were to be presented for payment. In this event, nothing would be left for it but to suspend its business. And the question naturally presents itself:—Why is it that the credit of a bank is such that, notwithstanding what has been said, the holders of its notes ordinarily shew no anxiety to exchange them for specie, and that no *run* for specie, in consequence, is made upon the bank?

Before answering the question which has been put, and in order to simplify as much as possible my present subject, I may observe that, whatever may be the capital of bankers, it is only the portion of it consisting of specie held in readiness for the purpose of redeeming their notes, together with the advances necessary in other respects for carrying on banking operations, which in reality constitute the capital employed in banking. All the capital which the bankers may otherwise possess is invested similarly to that of other capitalists who are engaged in the various branches of production. Moreover, it may be here mentioned that I shall, as I proceed, use language implying that the business of banking is conducted altogether by means of the capital owned by the bankers, without the aid of any deposites made by individuals, and liable to be at any time withdrawn by them. My doing so cannot possibly lead to any practical errour in my conclusions, because the possession of a certain average amount of deposites is equivalent simply to so much money borrowed by the bankers; which money they have it in their power to dispose of just as they have it in their power to dispose of every portion of the capital of which they are the owners. The *nature* of the effects produced, on the circulating medium, must necessarily be the same in the one of these cases as in the other.

The reason why the notes of a bank may maintain their full credit, in despite of the fact that the whole value of those notes in circulation is greater than the amount of specie in the possession of the bank, will be quite obvious, if we look for a moment at the credit, as well as the debtor side of its affairs. And to give precision to our ideas, let us suppose a particular case. Let a bank be established,—say in the city of Philadelphia,—with a capital in specie of $100,000. If this bank issue its notes to the amount of $150,000, it will be indebted to the public in an equal amount; and to pay its debts, it holds, in addition to the specie in its vaults, the promissory notes of individuals to an amount somewhat greater than that of its own notes,—greater, that is, by the *discount* upon the former. The payment, too, of the promissory notes which have been discounted by the bank is vouched for, not merely by the promissors, but by *endorsers*, whose ability to pay them, if required to do so, has been pronounced upon by a competent board of *directors*, previously to their having been discounted. And again, the loans made to individuals, on the security of their notes so endorsed, were made for a short period of time only,—generally speaking, for sixty, or at most ninety days. Were those loans, in every instance, made even for the longer of the terms just mentioned, and if we assume as much to be loaned in one day as in another, the bank would have it in its power to call in one-ninetieth of its notes in circulation, or to receive in specie one-ninetieth of their value, every successive day, and thus to provide itself very speedily with the means of meeting its engagements. Besides all this, should the bank be possessed of any property or capital, in addition to its proper banking capital, such property will afford additional means of security to its creditors. It is, then, not at all surprising, that the notes of a bank, when it is managed with a certain degree of prudence, should maintain their full credit, and should be regarded as in fact equivalent to the specie which they profess to represent.

It is very obvious that if, while a bank retains in its vaults the same amount of specie, it extends its circulation more and more, its condition will be continually becoming less secure; until, at length, the specie which it possesses may not be regarded by the public as sufficient to cover the risk of the non-payment of the promissory notes of individuals held by the bank. The notes of the bank will then depreciate in general estimation, and a run upon it for payment of them may ensue. An alarm or panic may indeed be produced to so great an extent, by the supposed inability of the bank to meet its engagements in a short period of time, or at all, as to oblige it to stop payment, and to wind up its affairs in the best manner it can.

CHAPTER VIII.

TENDENCY OF BANK NOTES TO EXPEL SPECIE FROM THE CIRCULATION—MANNER IN WHICH THE NOTES ISSUED BY ONE BANK CHECK THE ISSUES OF ANOTHER.

A LOSS of credit is not the only reason why the specie of a bank may be drawn from it, in exchange for its notes, with more or less rapidity. This will also take place whenever any extraordinary demand shall arise for specie,—say for specie to be exported; and one cause of such a demand arising may be a previous unusual enlargement of the circulation of the bank.

After what has been already delivered on the effects produced upon prices, and on the distribution of the money of the world, by an emission of paper money, the proposition which has just been stated can scarcely require any farther proof. An *illustration* of the changes resulting in the case will, nevertheless, be given, with a view to make them thoroughly familiar to my readers.

Take the instance, already considered, of a bank established in the city of Philadelphia, with a specie capital of $100,000, and which has put forth its notes to the amount of $150,000. Now let it be supposed that prices, and therefore the value of money, have become every where equalised, in the sense in which I use this expression,—so that there is no demand in the community for specie to be exported abroad. I shall suppose the notes of the bank to be then issued more abundantly than before. Let it issue $200,000, instead of $150,000. There will, of course, be a local rise of prices; which will be followed by an exportation of money, and an importation of other commodities, until prices decline to their former level. The specie exported may not be wholly taken from what is actually circulating; it may be drawn in part from the bank, in exchange for its own paper, or by depositors. To the extent in which this is done, the circulation of the bank will, plainly, not be as great as it would otherwise be. On account, however, of the greater convenience, other circumstances being the same, of bank notes than specie, it will be easy for the bank to procure specie for them. So long, indeed, as more specie is in circulation than what is required for payments of a smaller amount than that of the smallest bank notes, and so long as the bank shall be willing to increase its issues, will it be brought to the bank, sooner or later, by the holders of it, in any quantity, and bank notes drawn for it in return. The bank of which I am speaking can, consequently, if it chooses, always retain its original specie capital of $100,000, while it is extending its circulation more and more, and while, by doing so, it is causing the expulsion of the specie circulating within the sphere of its operations. And it will be readily perceived that, if we abstract from any possible loss of credit it may incur by so large an issue of its notes, we may suppose it to go on issuing them, until the whole of the specie originally circulating shall have been sent abroad,—excepting only what is needed for payments which, on account of their comparatively small value, cannot be made with bank notes.

The conclusion which has just been deduced in reference to a bank in Philadelphia, I need not say is equally true in reference to one established any where else, for instance in New York; and it may be added that in every country where a sufficient capital is invested in banking to enable the banks to issue their paper without fear of a loss of credit on their part, and without the fear, on this account, of a run for specie upon them, the *actual* tendency of things will be to an entire substitution of paper money in place of a metallic currency, with the sole exception above mentioned. This is the case in our own country, as every one knows.

After having expelled the specie from circulation, and produced a state of thing in which the specie that may be farther required for exportation can only be obtained from the banks,—should they continue to extend their issues of paper, their stock of specie will be more or less rapidly reduced; and as the profits or *dividends* of the banks will be greater according as they issue a greater amount of paper, they will, in consequence, push their issues to the limits of safety,—safety, not only from their paper becoming in any degree discredited, but likewise from that of having a sudden and extraordinary demand made upon them for specie, which they may not have the means of meeting. Now, still abstracting from all consideration of the former risk, the inquiry occurs, how the proper degree of safety in respect to the latter is to be ascertained. Here nothing more can be said than that experience must be our guide,—a wide experience however, and not one acquired in one set of circumstances only. A stock of specie which might, with propriety, be regarded as amply sufficient in, so to speak, a quiescent state of things, when the affairs of the commercial world have been going on, and are likely to go on, for a considerable period with great uniformity, would, on the other hand, very possibly be pronounced by competent judges to be entirely too small, for the purpose intended, at a time when the relations of commerce, and therefore the demand for money, were liable to frequent and considerable alteration.

If the directors of all the banks in the country were to form the same estimate precisely of the different risks to be guarded against in the management of their affairs, and to be equally prudent,—and if, moreover, the banking capital of the country was every where distributed according to the relative business wants of the community,—the reader will not fail to perceive that the proportion in any one bank of its circulation to the specie it has in its possession would be the same as in every other. In this state of things, let some one bank, violating the dictates of prudence for the sake of greater gain, or, it may be, simply through ignorance of the principles of banking, attempt to enlarge its circulation beyond the usual proportion. What consequences will follow? In the first place, as in the case of every augmentation of the circulating medium, however brought about, this medium will be depreciated in value; that is, the prices of things will rise. Commodities, other than money, will be transported to the place where all this has occurred from other places, and especially from such as are in the vicinity, on account of the comparatively small cost of transportation;—and those commodities will be paid for in money, the motive having been diminished for exporting every thing else. While the money going to remote places will consist, for the most part, of specie, the sphere in which the notes of our bank chiefly circulate will, nevertheless, be extended. Bank notes will, within a certain distance, be preferred to specie. And Philadelphia notes, when unduly increased in amount, may thus, for example, as it were invade the province of New York notes, and interfere with them, provided these have not been increased proportionally.

But the effect described can never be otherwise than temporary. The very fact of Philadelphia bank notes circulating where they did not before, or circulating in greater quantity, and to a greater value, than before, will tend to produce a suspicion that they have been issued unduly and imprudently. This feeling, again, will be apt to check their free circulation, and to cause their value to fall below *par.* They will then find their way gradually back to the source whence they originated, to be exchanged for specie; and the expanded circulation will be contracted eventually to its former limits.

This process may be very much expedited by the action of the banks which have been interfered with. Those of the city of New York, on receiving in payment of the promissory notes discounted by them, or in deposite, an unusual amount of Philadelphia bank notes, can easily send these to the latter city, and draw specie from the banks there in return for them; or the New York banks, if they think proper, might discredit them to a certain extent, and in a certain region, by consenting to receive them only below their nominal or par value, or by refusing to receive them at all.

After what has been said, the reader will understand distinctly how one bank of a country may be a check upon another, and how each bank may be obliged to confine its operations within what may be called its proper sphere.

I may add that the above remarks will apply to the manner in which the several banks established *in the same place* have it in their power to check each other's over-issues of paper money. They will, at least, apply with such slight modifications as will very readily occur to my readers.

CHAPTER IX.

IMPOSSIBILITY OF PERMANENTLY EXPANDING THE CIRCULATING MEDIUM OF A COUNTRY BEYOND THE AMOUNT WHICH IS DETERMINED BY THE COST OF PRODUCING THE PRECIOUS METALS.

The check mutually afforded by the banks of a country to an over-issue by them of paper money may, it is evident, be entirely removed by a combination of them for this purpose. If two or more banks combine together, they will be enabled to act with a comparatively greater efficiency upon the currency, for good, by checking the issues of other banks, or for evil, by unduly extending their own issues of paper money. Their united efficiency too, in these respects, will not differ from that of a single bank with a capital equal to the capitals taken together of all the combined banks.

We must be careful, however, not to form an exaggerated estimate of the power which a bank with a large capital, or a combination of a numoer of banks, can exert over the currency of a country. On account of the checks to the over-issuing of paper money still administered by the independent banks, as well as by the state of the money market abroad, it will be impossible, excepting for a very short period of time, to expand the circulation of any place, or district of country, beyond its usual proportion of the circulation of the whole commercial world.

This proportion, it will be recollected, I before shewed to be necessarily of such an amount, on the average, as would consist with a scale of prices that would repay the cost of producing the precious metals. And the advantages, or disadvantages, of any one mode of regulating the currency over another, all resolve themselves into the comparative extent and frequency of the deviations from perfect uniformity, in the value of a given portion of it, which may be temporarily occasioned.

A proposition which is intimately related to what has just been delivered is, that when the banking capital of a country, *properly so called*, whether there be few banks or many, is extended beyond a certain amount, it will be impossible to circulate, *on the average*, any more bank notes than before. An example will make my meaning perfectly clear. Suppose the circulation of all the banks to have reached the limits of safety; the whole circulating medium being supposed at the same time to consist exclusively of paper money, with the exception of the metallic money wanted for purchases of a small value. Now let a new bank be established; and let us trace the consequences of this institution entering the field of competition with those of like nature already in existence,— consequences, I may observe, which are precisely such as would result from an augmentation to an equal amount of the capital of the latter. Also, let the new bank commence business by discounting the promissory notes of individuals, so as to put into circulation its own notes to the amount of $100,000. It is manifest, from the principles already explained, that the expansion of the currency, thus produced, must soon be followed by a corresponding contraction of it; which contraction all the banks in the same place or region will be equally obliged to make. The new bank will then have obtained a share of the paper circulation at the expense, and only at the expense, of that of the others. Every $100,000 of its paper which it may issue will, of course, be followed by similar effects. And eventually, it will be able to maintain a circulation bearing the same proportion to its specie capital as that which every other bank bears to its specie capital. But our supposition has been that this capital is augmented without the specie, on the basis of which the additional bank conducts its operations, having been taken from the other banks. The inference is obvious, that the proportion *in every bank* of specie to the paper it has put forth will have become greater than before; and it is equally obvious that a like inference will hold good, whatever may be the number of additional banks established, and whatever may be the additions successively made to the capitals of the banks previously existing.

But in the struggle of the different banks to extend their circulations as much as possible, and notwithstanding the checks which they apply to each other's issues, a tendency to a general extension of these will be found, under ordinary circumstances, to take place. The specie of the banks, while this extension is going on, will be drawn from them to be exported abroad, until their stock of it is reduced to the limits of safety. So long, now, as the same average degree of safety shall continue to be aimed at, it will be plainly out of the question for them to extend their circulation any farther. And again, the reduction of the specie of the banks, in the manner which has just been described, is equivalent to a reduction of what is, properly speaking, the capital employed in the business of banking. Hence we may conclude, not only that the share of the circulation of a country obtained by any new bank (when the circulating medium consists already of paper, excepting alone what is required for small change) is obtained at the expense of a diminution to an equal extent of the circulation of all the other banks,—but also that the proper banking capital is at the same time, and under similar circumstances, unsusceptible of being increased. An indefinite amount of banking capital *nominally so called* may, it is true, still be conceived to be created, but which must, in reality, be employed otherwise than in banking. And because it must necessarily be so employed, I may remark that no disadvantage (the reader will bear in mind that I am now concerned with ultimate effects) will accrue to the community simply on account of its increase, no matter how great this increase may be. On the contrary, it will furnish an additional fund for insuring payment by the banks to their creditors on any emergency.

In the exposition which has been made of the theory of banking, I have supposed the notes of a bank to enter into the circulation by means of the discounting of the promissory notes of individuals. This may, however, manifestly occur in more ways than one; in as many ways, indeed, as there are modes of lending money, or of doing what is equivalent to the lending of money; as, for example, the purchase, on the one hand, by the banks of bills of exchange, and the sale by them to individuals, on the other, of their drafts upon each other,—a two-fold business in which the banks of the United States have latterly engaged to a considerable extent. But on whatever occasion, or in whatever manner, bank notes are issued, the reader cannot fail to perceive, on a moment's reflection, that the results which have been deduced, in this and the two preceding chapters, will always be the same.

That after a certain amount of capital has been, *strictly speaking*, invested in banking, no more can be so invested,—that no new bank can then transact any business, excepting at the expense of the business of the banks previously existing,—and that it is absolutely impossible for the banks of a country, under any circumstances, to go on *continually* augmenting the circulating medium, and consequently raising the prices of things,—are propositions of the utmost importance in the theory of banking. They have, nevertheless, been extensively called in question by a class of reasoners who are ever confounding ultimate with temporary effects. It is to ultimate effects alone that these propositions have reference. And the reader, if he will recollect this, will nowhere meet with either fact, or argument, to shake his confidence in their truth.

Were the ultimate effects the only ones produced by an alteration in the value of money, or, which is the same thing, were those effects at once produced, without the intervention of other and temporary changes, the advantages of banks of circulation would scarcely be detracted from by any counterbalancing disadvantages to which they would still be liable. What those advantages are, I shall proceed to state in the following chapter.

The *disadvantageous* action of the banks on the community will be pointed out when I shall exhibit the nature, extent, and frequency of the temporary changes above adverted to.

CHAPTER X.

THE ADVANTAGES, REAL OR SUPPOSED, OF A BANK NOTE CIRCULATION.

The great advantage of a bank note circulation is, that a country is enabled, by means of it, to dispense with the use of the precious metals to an amount equal, or (on account of the quicker circulation, generally speaking, of bank notes) to an amount more than equal to the excess of the whole value of the notes issued over that of the specie retained in the vaults of the banks,—the specie, besides, thus rendered unnecessary, not being parted with gratuitously. My readers will recollect that, when paper money is introduced, there will be a diminished production of gold and silver, until the circulating medium again finds its proper level. And this implies an augmented production of other commodities, which will be an addition to the wealth of the community.

Whether the specie previously circulating was, or was not, procured from sources existing in the country itself, will make no difference here. If the former be the case, it is easy to understand how a diminished production of the precious metals will be followed by an augmented production of every thing else. But if those metals be procured from foreign mines, they could in fact only be procured in exchange for the products of the country; and, like all other imports into it, they may be themselves, therefore, truly considered as the products of its capital and labour. It is manifest that the commodities which were before exchanged for the gold and silver, which are no longer required, are so much clear gain;—not the less so, too, when the labour applied to their production is transferred to the producing of such other commodities as may perhaps be in greater demand.

A country may derive the benefit, just described, from the substitution of a paper currency for a hard money circulation,—at least to a very considerable extent,—without waiting for the transfers of capital and labour to take place; provided it be the only country in which a currency of the kind is introduced. For then the paper money, as it enters into the circulation, will cause the money previously circulating to be exported in payment for such commodities as may be in most demand, until no more than its due share of the *augmented* circulating medium of the world will be retained in the country. That the commodities imported are to be considered as a national gain, follows necessarily from the fact of the circulating medium, notwithstanding a portion of it has been sent abroad, being still adequate to the performance of all the exchanges required, and quite as much so as it was before this exportation occurred.

In proportion, also, to the degree in which paper money is introduced in any country beyond the quantity of it which circulates in others generally, will the immediate benefit be the greater. The *full* benefit can in no case be enjoyed before the amount of gold and silver money shall be reduced to the proper point, by the less active working of the mines.

When this process shall have been completed, if we suppose

fifty millions of dollars to have been excluded from circulating in the United States by the issue of bank paper, the country will thereby have acquired an amount of wealth of equal, or nearly equal value. This addition to its wealth is, however, made once for all. From the nature of things, it can never be renewed. It is, therefore, equivalent to a gain of the annual profits upon a capital of fifty millions; and assuming the ordinary rate of profits to be ten per cent.,—an assumption higher than the facts will justify,—it will amount to the sum of only five millions of dollars per annum, or to about half a dollar for every white inhabitant of the country.

This estimate might even seem to be an exaggerated one, when the reader considers that the whole of the fifty millions in question will not be employed as capital. Indeed, we have no right to suppose that any larger proportion of it will be employed in this manner, or productively, than that which the whole of the capital of the country bears to all the wealth it possesses. But this circumstance is here of no moment. The present value of a certain portion of wealth is precisely the same, whether it is destined to be consumed productively or unproductively; and consequently, no matter in what proportions any given accession to the national wealth may be distributed between capital and what is not capital, it must be regarded as *equivalent* to an accession of a precisely equal amount to the former alone.

All other circumstances being the same, another advantage, which bank notes possess over specie, is their greater convenience to be kept on hand, as well as to be conveyed or remitted from place to place. This convenience is the greater, obviously, where the sums of money are considerable; but that it exists to a certain degree even where these sums are comparatively small, is notorious from the extent in which the coin of the country is excluded from the circulation by the preference every where given to the smallest denominations of notes which are permitted to circulate. For making remittances indeed, from one place to another, we are not reduced to a choice between bank notes and specie. Where the former cannot be procured, recourse may be had to bills of exchange. But, in general, this will not be done, as the reader must be aware, so long as the notes of incorporated and wealthy banking institutions are procurable for the purpose.

Besides the advantages which have been stated to flow from the use of bank paper, many others are very commonly ascribed to it; and banks of circulation have been, not unfrequently, represented as constituting the chief source whence the rapid advances of the United States in wealth and prosperity have originated. It will be proper to examine into the correctness of these opinions, before I attempt to exhibit the disadvantages to the community of which our banking system is productive.

In the first place, bank notes are said to be a cheaper circulating medium than the precious metals. Now, if this opinion has reference to the first cost of the two mediums, its truth might be conceded without dispute. Not so, however, if the maintaining of them in their existing condition, after they have been once procured or established, is the meaning of those who hold the opinion. The *wear* of a specie circulation is quite inconsiderable in amount when compared with the expenses of banking,—including in these expenses the rents (employing this word here in its ordinary acceptation) paid for buildings, together with the salaries bestowed upon presidents, cashiers, tellers, and clerks,—not to mention a multitude of other expenditures, equally necessary. It is, perhaps, not generally known that the wear of the gold or silver money which circulates is as small as it really is. Mr. Jacob, in in his work on the production and consumption of the precious metals, has estimated it so low as one part in four hundred and twenty annually,—that is something less than $120,000 out of fifty millions.

But secondly, a notion, very prevalent even among thinking

men who have not examined our present subject on scientific principles, is, that banks, by the issue of paper money, add to the capital of a country. Here again, as in the instance of the opinion just before considered, there is a sense in which what is maintained will be assented to by every one without hesitation. The substitution of paper money for specie will, as has been frequently repeated, induce an extraordinary importation of commodities other than money,—a certain portion of which commodities cannot fail to be employed productively. This is, however, not the sense in which the notion I am considering is entertained by those who are most forward in putting it forth as an argument in favour of our existing banking system. They imagine something like a *direct* creation of capital to be effected by the instrumentality of the banks. After what has been delivered concerning money in the present treatise, my readers will deem such a creation of capital to be sufficiently incomprehensible, and inconsistent with the principles already established. Irrespective of the additional capital derived from the commodities imported in exchange for the specie, which has been dispensed with in the manner above mentioned, it must be evident that the amount of the capital of the country will have remained altogether unaffected by the circulation of paper money in the place of specie.

Again, there are those who are of opinion that, by extending the system of commercial credit, banks (I speak of banks of circulation) have conferred great benefit on the community; and there are others who, absurdly enough, go so far as to suppose that, but for the existence of such institutions, all credits would cease to be given, and *cash* would have to be paid in the making of every purchase. But the practice of selling upon credit, or of lending the money or capital of one individual to another, is surely in no respect dependent on the issue of paper money by the banks. Though all banks of circulation were to be prohibited, promissory notes could continue to be discounted, and money loaned by chartered institutions or by private individuals, who will perform all the functions of banking, with the exception only of the issuing of their own paper made payable on demand. Indeed, from what goes before, the reader will understand that, should *every species* of banking cease to be transacted, money would still be lent by the possessors of it for the purpose of enabling the borrower to pay the debts he may have incurred, or to be employed by him productively. And there is no reason why a less amount of money should be lent than when the banks were the principal medium for lending it. Since the quantity of money, and of the various substitutes for money, taken as a whole, as well as the motives for desiring to borrow it, are the same in the one case as in the other, the inducements for lending it cannot but also be the very same in both.

I may remark that, besides the obvious inconveniences which would result from abolishing the practice, in every case whatever, of lending, the advantage of the credit system resolves itself into the distribution of the capital of the country, as far it is practicable in the circumstances of society to do so, in such a manner as to be most productively employed. Instead of directly superintending the application of his own means of production, this is now frequently done by the capitalist through the instrumentality of another person who can apply it more skilfully than himself, and who, because he can make a skilful application of it, finds it advantageous to borrow capital, and to pay for it the ordinary profits or interest of money. But whatever portion of the productive power of the country may, agreeably to this view of the advantages of credit, be attributed to it, no absurdity is surely more glaring than that of holding it to be essentially the power which has filled what once was the western wilderness in the United States with flourishing towns, and which has constructed our numerous " internal improvements." It is an absurdity more absurd than the regarding of the banks as so many generators of capital, by means of the simple process of issuing a certain number of paper promises to pay specie to the bearer on demand. The absurdity in question is no other than that of robbing the capital and labour of the country,—capital and labour that would at all events have been employed so as to yield to the producers the ordinary profits,—of their proper functions, and of investing with them the imaginary power of credit.

CHAPTER XI.

DISADVANTAGES OF THE AMERICAN SYSTEM OF BANKING.

I COME now to the *disadvantages* of our banking system.*

The banks have been shewn to possess the power of expanding, and, of course, of contracting, *for a time*, the circulating medium of the district in which they operate; and this power, it is a well known fact, they do actually exert.

When the circulating medium is expanded, a given portion of it, as has been repeatedly mentioned, is depreciated in value. Were all purchases made with ready money, such depreciation would be of no account; for the prices of things would rise universally in the very same proportion; and the various necessaries and luxuries of life would be procurable by every one, with neither more nor less of difficulty than heretofore.† But the case is very different where credit is extensively given to purchasers, and where the practice of borrowing prevails in any considerable degree. If I owe any one a thousand

* Besides its expensiveness, already considered.

† See note to page 150.

dollars, and pay him at a period when an expansion of the circulating medium has taken place to the extent of a tenth of its amount at the time of the incurring of the debt, he will receive a less value than he ought to do. Eleven dollars is now worth just what ten was before,—and a thousand dollars is worth only ten elevenths of a thousand, or not quite $910. The like is manifestly true in respect to every debt, whatever its amount may be. Debtors will be benefited, at the expense of their creditors, throughout the community.

On the contrary, when the circulating medium is unexpectedly contracted, opposite consequences will ensue. Creditors will then derive benefit, at the expense of those who are indebted to them.

Although, in both the cases just considered, the wealth of the country may not have been diminished, since what was one man's loss was another's gain, it will not follow that we should be indifferent to the results produced, or to the causes producing them. It is of great moment to keep the circulating medium as uniform as is practicable on principles of justice, independently of any considerations of expediency. Such considerations, however, dictate to the government, as well as to the citizens by whom the government is influenced, to endeavour to accomplish this object, as they would endeavour, to the extent of their knowledge and ability, to protect in any other way the rights of property.

And notwithstanding there has been here no destruction of property, but only a transfer of it from one individual to another, there can be no question of the sum of human happiness having been diminished. The truth of my present remark will, I think, be apparent to every reader, if he looks at what may be called an average case; one in which the parties concerned are placed in a pecuniary point of view, before the supposed transfer, in similar circumstances. Let two individuals have equal incomes, say $1000 each, per annum. Will there be no diminution of human happiness if, unexpectedly to both, their arrangements for the future be interfered with, by $500 being taken from the one and handed over to the other? Certainly there will be. The distress endured by the family of the one will not be compensated for by any additional luxuries which the other's family will be enabled to consume.

But there is yet another mode in which fluctuations in the amount of the circulation are productive of inconvenience, and, when they are in any degree considerable, of the severest distress. Let the banks refuse to discount as freely as they have been accustomed to do. Money will be rendered less abundant, and therefore more difficult to be procured. The purchase of luxuries may be postponed with comparative ease; and even the necessaries of life may be procured, at least by a portion of the community, upon credit. The money, however, that is requisite, for the fulfilment of existing contracts, cannot be dispensed with. When pay day comes, this must be provided for, or the contracting party suffer the penalty attached to a *failure.* To the merchants especially, of all classes, this penalty is a severe one, in respect both to the pecuniary losses resulting from their being obliged to close their business and adjust their accounts under most disadvantageous circumstances, and to the injurious consequences to their character for judgment or integrity. They will, of course, make every exertion in their power to obtain money, that they may be enabled to meet their engagements. Many of them will succeed in this, by consenting to give to the lenders of money a higher interest than usual,—an interest, too, always so much the higher, as the security for the repayment of the principal borrowed is the less. There will, nevertheless, be many others who, failing to obtain the requisite means for complying with their engagements, will become bankrupt. The persons heretofore dependent upon them for employment will have to seek it elsewhere, at the very time when it will be most difficult to be obtained; and much distress must, on this account, occur. And this is far from giving us a full view of the distress produced. Those individuals who have been relying upon the receipt of the moneys due to them by others, and who have failed to receive such payment, will in their turn, very frequently, be prevented, in consequence, from paying with punctuality what they themselves owe. The distress, of which I am speaking, will thus be extended through the various ramifications of society, and will be every where more or less intensely felt, according to the magnitude of the *disturbance* to which the currency of the country has been subjected.

The class of inconveniences and injuries which has just been shewn to result from a contraction of the circulating medium will, it is manifest, have no existence in the opposite case of an expansion of that medium beyond its ordinary amount. But more than this: not only will no inconvenience of the kind be in any degree experienced, but a scene of prosperity will be every where exhibited. Money being plentiful, the merchants, besides punctually paying their debts when due, will be prompt to make new purchases. Relying too on the continuance of this state of things, they will push their credit farther than they were accustomed to do. If the expansion in question shall go on for a time, they will be enabled, by the corresponding rise of the prices of commodities, to realise large profits; and speculations generally, by whomsoever made, and of whatsoever kind, will eventuate successfully.

All this would be well, provided the course of things were always to proceed in the same direction. A reaction, however, cannot fail to take place, sooner or later; and the probability of its speedily taking place, as also of its being considerable in degree, will depend on the extent of the previous deviation of the currency from its average or usual state. Supposing no other causes to operate which are calculated to produce the effect, the mere augmentation of the circulating medium will, before long, produce it. In consequence of the rise of prices, there will be a larger importation from abroad, and a diminished exportation from home, of commodities other than money, as has been before fully explained,—the *balance* being necessarily paid in money; and not in paper money, but in specie. A demand for specie will be made upon the banks; and they will soon be forced to curtail their discounts and thus diminish the circulating medium,—when the evils before described cannot fail to occur. Moreover, the reader will need no laboured argument for him to perceive that, should any extraordinary demand for specie arise from any other cause than that above mentioned, and arise while the currency is unduly expanded, the contraction of it which succeeds will be liable to take place more suddenly, and at the same time more extensively, as well as be more disastrous in its effects.

The evils of the contraction of the currency, after it has been expanded, are well known very far to overbalance the advantages, or seeming advantages, of its previous expansion. Since, also, every expansion of the currency must necessarily be followed by a corresponding contraction of it, and since the banking system has a tendency to produce, and actually does produce, greater and more frequent fluctuations of it from its average state than would otherwise take place, banks cannot but be pronounced, in this point of view, to be institutions injurious to the public interests.

I must not forget to add to the injurious effects, already mentioned as resulting from every sudden contraction of the currency of a country, the diminished production which must ensue from the great number of persons who, at every period of the kind, are thrown out of employment altogether, or are only partially employed. This is sufficiently known to every one, not to require any illustration.

In my reasonings throughout the present chapter, I have made no allusion to the possibility of the money of a country circulating with more or less rapidity; and it was unnecessary for me to have done so, because it has been shewn that the effect of a more rapid circulation is the same as that produced when the currency has been increased in quantity,—and that the effects of a slower circulation and of a diminished currency are likewise the same. Besides, when the currency of a country is suddenly expanded, the facility of procuring money will, very evidently, cause it to circulate more rapidly than before, thus enhancing the effects produced by the expansion. When a sudden contraction of the currency takes place, a less rapid circulation will, on the contrary, ensue, which will conspire with such contraction to give a greater degree of intensity to the effects produced by it.

CHAPTER XII.

THE SAME SUBJECT CONTINUED.

The evils of the banking system, hitherto exhibited, have been stated to be the results of ignorance or of imprudence on the part of the bank directors, while acting with a view to the interest of the stockholders, or owners of the capital invested. There will be, besides, no small temptation for the directors and their immediate friends to *speculate* successfully upon the rest of the community, through the instrumentality of alternate expansions and contractions of the currency, to be produced by their own agency. It will be always recollected that it is in the power of a bank, or of a number of banks acting in concert, at their pleasure to cause a local rise of prices by enlarging their discounts, and thus temporarily extending their circulation. Let us, then, suppose an exertion of this power to be resolved upon; and we may likewise suppose the resolution adopted to be known only to the bank directors, and to a limited number of individuals to whom they may have communicated it. I need scarcely say that these parties will not be slow to avail themselves of their exclusive information. They will go into the market and purchase commodities, including *stocks* of all kinds, at their existing prices,—selling out again, when, on account of the expansion of the currency, prices have attained to their greatest height. Since now, on account of that contraction of the currency, which will be necessarily consequent upon its previous expansion, the prices of things will, sooner or later, subside to their former level, it is plain that the profits, thus made by the speculators, will be entirely at the expense of the subsequent purchasers. Profits too, made in this manner, cannot be classed with those which may result from *ordinary gaming*: they are precisely of the same nature with the winnings of the gambler, who uses false dice or marked cards, unknown to his victim; and the act of obtaining them is deserving of no milder epithet than that of swindling, or robbery.

On the occurrence, also, of a contraction of the currency, the banks, instead of impartially diminishing their accommodations to all classes of persons with whom they have been accustomed to deal, may grant extraordinary loans to the directors, or other favoured individuals, to enable them to realise a considerable gain at the expense of the rest of the community,—more especially of the mercantile community. *This* will be effected by the lending again of the money, thus obtained from the banks, at a higher rate, and often a much higher rate, of interest, than that to which those institutions are by law restricted.*

* It may be proper for me here to disclaim any personal allusions on my part, in the foregoing remarks concerning the *liability* of the directors of banks, and of

And besides these unrighteous speculations, the system I am considering diffuses throughout the community, by the frequency and extent of alternate expansions and contractions of the currency, a more active *spirit* of speculation. This is an evil; for however useful the commerce of speculation may be shewn to be when restricted within its due bounds, it easily degenerates, if stimulated to excess, into mere gambling; becoming then, more or less, a source of public corruption, although it may be generally conducted according to the ordinary standard of *fairness*. It may be added that an undue amount of speculation implies an unnecessary number of exchanges; and this, again, implies that the circulating medium is, *on the average*, unnecessarily large. By diminishing the business of speculation, our share of the circulating medium of the world will be lessened. Other commodities, in the manner so often stated, will take the place of the money dispensed with; which commodities, whether employed as capital or not, must be regarded as a clear gain to the country. But there can be no doubt of a portion of those commoties being thus employed. It is, consequently, perfectly proper to look upon every augmentation of the speculating spirit as equivalent to the locking up of a certain portion of the national capital, or, in other words, of what would otherwise have been consumed productively.

Though the banks should, however, be conducted with a perfect knowledge of the principles of banking, as well as with the utmost prudence and integrity, there will yet be other mischiefs to tell of, which are incident to their operation on

other dealers in money, to be guilty of improper courses. Their integrity is, without doubt, in general fully on a level with that of the great majority of mankind; and indeed in most instances, as is attested by the confidence reposed in them by their fellow-citizens, it may even be assumed to be above that level. Some of the class of persons of whom I am speaking I am happy to rank among my most esteemed and intimate friends. They must *know* that it is quite impossible that I intend any insinuations to their prejudice.

the currency. Assuming again, as is the case in the United States, the money in circulation to consist of paper, with the exception alone of the metallic money required for purchases of small value, let an extraordinary demand occur for specie, *independently of any action of the banks.* Such a demand may originate in various ways. To mention one of these: Great Britain may engage in a war on the continent of Europe, and may, on this account, have occasion to export thither a considerable amount of specie. An extraordinary demand for money in that country will immediately arise, and the value of it will be there enhanced, or, what is the same thing, prices generally will fall. This state of things will, of course, not be confined to Great Britain alone. British goods will be exported in greater quantity than before; and the importations in return, from all other countries, will be lessened. The balance arising will be paid in specie. What has just been said will apply especially to such other countries as are in the practice of importing British goods most extensively. Our own country is in this predicament, and an extraordinary demand for money may thus occur here very speedily after its occurrence abroad, as well as to an extent which is far from being inconsiderable.

Now, under the circumstances supposed above, let a demand be made for a given amount of specie to be exported from the United States, say $100,000, and, for the sake of illustration, let us suppose the paper of all the banks of the country in circulation to amount to a million of dollars, based upon half a million of specie. The specie demanded will be drawn from the banks; which will then retain in their vaults only $400,000 in hard money. They will, in consequence, not be able to circulate more than $800,000 of their paper,—acting, as I have assumed them for the present to act, with undiminished prudence. Their discounts must therefore be proportionally curtailed, and the circulating medium by this means contracted to four fifths of what it was originally. And if, instead of the banks having a half million of specie in their possession, their stock of it was only $250,000, they would evidently be obliged, when $100,000 was drawn from them, as before, to curtail to double the extent. These examples will suffice to shew that, so long as specie for exportation is procurable from the banks, a contraction of the circulating medium will take place to a much greater extent than the amount of specie actually exported. On the supposition, on the other hand, of there being no other money in circulation besides specie, the exportation of any given amount of this from the country would, it is evident, be followed by no farther reduction of the circulating medium. Hence the reader will perceive another ground of objection to our existing banking system, and one which is altogether independent of the mode, whether proper or improper, in which the banks of the country are managed.

But it may be said that the existence of an exclusive specie circulation is not a supposable case; because other sorts of paper money, such as bills of exchange, the common promissory notes of individuals, &c. will continue to circulate, even though bank notes should cease to do so. This would not *in any degree* invalidate the conclusion just arrived at; provided such paper money would not circulate more abundantly in proportion to the whole amount of the circulating medium, when it does not consist in part of bank notes, than when it does. Where, however, there are no bank notes to serve any longer as a substitute for hard money, the reader will readily perceive that paper money of every other description will be made use of for the purpose to a greater extent than before,—but, on account of its comparative inconvenience, it is evident *not to an extent sufficiently great to compensate for the want of bank notes.*

CHAPTER XIII.

THE SAME SUBJECT CONTINUED.

THE disadvantages of the existing banking system of the United States, which have been stated in the two preceding chapters, are perhaps not susceptible of being estimated with the same degree of accuracy as the advantages of that system before enumerated. It seems to me, nevertheless, that, on a review of those disadvantages, taken in connexion with the very considerable expenses incurred in the management of banks of circulation, the reader, even though he should have come to the perusal of the present treatise with the prevailing prejudices in favour of such institutions, can scarcely fail to experience doubts as to their utility, all things considered; and *some* doubts too concerning the superior advantages, on the the whole, of a bank note over a hard money circulating medium.

But I have not yet done with the disadvantages of our banking system. There is a class of these which attaches to it in its present condition, when the banks are not so numerous, nor the capital actually employed in banking sufficiently large to preclude their dividends from exceeding the ordinary interest of money.

I advert to the means not unfrequently made use of to obtain from our state legislatures a charter for a new bank, or for enlarging the capital of an old one,—to the mode in which the newly created stock is distributed among the parties who are desirous of obtaining it,—to the contrivances, put into execution by many of those who have succeeded in obtaining a considerable portion of it, in order to give to it an artificial and temporary value,—and to the tendency of every enlargement of the banking capital of the country, to induce an expansion, and subsequent contraction to a certain extent, of the circulating medium, and so too to encourage the spirit of speculation and of gambling.

After what has already been delivered concerning money and banking, I need not expatiate at any length on the several *heads* just enumerated. It will be sufficient to say a few words only in relation to each of them.

In the first place, in as much as, under the circumstances supposed, the banks have a monopoly of the power of issuing paper money of a certain description,—a power equivalent also, practically speaking, to that of regulating the currency of the country,—every application to the legislature for an additional banking capital amounts to the applying, on the part of an association of certain individuals, for privileges from the enjoyment of which the great majority of their fellow-citizens are to remain excluded. Just in proportion to the magnitude of those privileges, that is, in the case under consideration, in proportion to the profits expected to be made above the ordinary profits of capital, will be the earnestness with which the legislature will be solicited. All the vices of *special legislation* will ensue in their most aggravated form. Direct and open bribery of the lawgivers may be seldom attempted, and the attempt, when hazarded, may be for the most part repelled; but there are *indirect* modes of corruption which will be found sufficiently unguarded by conscience or a regard to character, to enable those who will venture to employ them to accomplish their object, in many cases without any very persevering or inconvenient resistance. The parties who are chiefly interested in the passage of the proposed law are, quite probably, persons of considerable influence in the community; and a wealthy corporation, on the supposition of the law actually passing, may have it in its power, by the granting of loans or otherwise, to reward the exertions of its friends in its behalf, as well as be much more willing to do so, than the public generally, or the classes whose interests are likely to be injuriously affected, would be to serve in any way those who are active on their side of the question. Expectations, in this state of things, may, it is evident, be easily excited, among certain of the members, and especially among the more prominent members of the legislature, of advantages to be conferred by the corporate body which is asked to be created, or whose privileges it is proposed to enlarge,—without the necessity of making any formal promises, to be fulfilled after the services required shall have been rendered.

One of the modes in which influential men, in and out of the legislature, are apt to profit by the chartering of a new bank, is by the opportunity afforded them of subscribing to, or of early procuring, a portion of its stock; which stock very seldom fails, soon after the original distribution of it, to rise above its par value. But independently of any such improper or vicious procurement of bank stock, the fact of there being, in almost every instance of the kind, a greater demand for bank stock than there is stock to be distributed, will open a scene of intrigue and corruption. Such will, at least, be the case in any of the modes in which its distribution is usually accomplished.

The value of the newly created stock, I have said, seldom fails very soon to rise above par. This is the natural consequence of the dividends of the banks exceeding generally in amount the ordinary interest of money, and of the new bank, before long, obtaining its proportional share of the paper circulation of the country. Besides this, however, an artificial value may be given to the stock for a comparatively short time: and this may be done, not only by the various arts which are every day practised by the gamblers in stocks, and which it is not necessary for me here to specify, but likewise by means of a fictitious demand for the stock before it is distributed,—he who is really desirous of subscribing to a *hundred* shares putting in a claim for a *thousand*, and so on in like proportion. Moreover, it may be mentioned that, when any stock is rising in value,—especially when the rise is a sudden and rapid one,—it will, for this very reason, experience a still farther rise. People generally will be more desirous than they would otherwise have been to obtain it. To purchase it now, and to sell it out after a certain time shall have elapsed, will promise to be a profitable speculation. And an increased stimulus to the corrupt spirit of gambling, as a readier means of acquiring wealth than the regular pursuits of industry, will be thus administered. I need not mention that the greater the rise in value of the bank stock, of which I have been speaking, above its real value, the sooner will it be apt to decline to this value, and the greater will be the losses of the *uninitiated* possessors of it, who have continued to hold on to it rather than sell.

That every enlargement of the banking capital of the country has a tendency to induce an expansion, and subsequent contraction, of the circulating medium, may seem to be a proposition scarcely consistent with the doctrine previously established, that the circulation which is obtained by a new bank is obtained by it at the expense of that of the banks before existing. On a moment's reflection, however, the apparent inconsistency will disappear. As in many other cases in political economy, where our conclusions, legitimately deduced, have the semblance of clashing with each other, the two effects in question relate to different stages in the progress of change; the effect first mentioned being an intermediate or temporary effect; the other being that which is ultimately produced. Where the banking capital of a country is rapidly augmented, there can be no doubt that, in the struggle between the old and the new banks, on the one hand to *retain* as much of their circulation as they can, and on the other to *obtain* as much of it as possible, the whole circulation will in fact become temporarily increased beyond its due or average amount; and the increase may be so great as to be productive, by the contraction of the circulation which subsequently ensues, of all the distress and demoralisation already described as the infallible consequence of every extensive and sudden diminution of the money of the community.

It must now be manifest that the banks of a country may be augmented in number, and its banking capital augmented in amount, until the circulation, which each bank can, ultimately and on the average, possess, will be no more than is adequate, by the gross profits yielded by it to the bank, to enable it to pay the expenses of management. The *whole* of the capital will then yield to its owners merely the ordinary interest of money. And no motive for investing capital in banking, rather than in any other business, will any longer exist.

CHAPTER XIV.

EVILS IMPROPERLY ATTRIBUTED TO BANKS OF CIRCULATION—EFFECTS OF EXACTING A BONUS FROM THE STOCKHOLDERS OF A BANK AS A CONDITION OF ITS BEING INCORPORATED—AND EFFECTS OF THE GOVERNMENT OF A COUNTRY ASSUMING TO ITSELF THE BUSINESS OF BANKING.

There are two evils which those persons who are most opposed to the continuance of our present system of banking are in the habit of attributing to it, and of urging against it perhaps more frequently than any others; which evils are, notwithstanding, in a great measure, if not altogether, unfounded.

The *first* of these is that, by the power which the banks possess and actually do exert of augmenting the quantity of money in the country, they cause a general rise of prices, and thus render it more difficult for the great body of the people, —of the poorer classes of the people especially,—to procure the means of support to which they have been accustomed. That this objection is, as I have said, in a great measure unfounded, results from the impossibility of the banks effecting more, by the issuing of their paper to an unusual amount, than a *temporary* augmentation of the circulating medium,—a proposition which my readers will recognise to have been fully, and I hope, satisfactorily established. But even though such augmentation of the circulating medium were permanent, instead of temporary, it would not follow that any portion of the community would have their command over the necessaries and luxuries of life in any wise diminished. Whatever alterations in this respect might take place while that medium was in process of being augmented, on account of the prices of all things, including the wages of labour, not from the first falling in the same proportion,—eventually, that is when prices shall again have become steady, they will bear very nearly the same relation to each other, in respect to *every* commodity, as they did before the commencement of their fall.

The *second* of the two objections, now adverted to, rests on the opinion that the profits of banking, over and above the ordinary interest of money, is a gain of the bankers, or stockholders of banks, at the expense of all other classes of the people; and it is therefore an objection which is well calculated, wherever entertained, to render our system of banking obnoxious to much popular odium. So far from its being well founded, my readers will probably be prepared, before any farther remarks on my part, to look upon the profits of which I speak as a measure,—or at least an approximate measure,—of the *benefit* conferred on the country by the substitution of a bank note for a specie circulation, that is by the substitution, for the production of the specie dispensed with, of that of commodities of a different description. In as much, indeed, as the amount of the whole circulating medium is not, *on the average*, affected by the action of the banks, neither will the prices of things be in any manner affected thereby, and money will be procurable (also on the average) in the same quantity, as well as on the same terms, as if there were no banks of circulation in existence. As no one, then, is a loser in the case under consideration, the extraordinary gains of the banks must necessarily be a national gain.

Since the due appreciation of this argument is a point of no slight importance, I shall state one or two modifications of which the conclusion come to is susceptible; and the reason will be apparent why I have hinted that the profits in question constitute only an approximate measure of the benefit which is conferred on the country by the *mere* substitution of a circulation of bank notes in place of one composed of the precious metals. I shall make this statement, too, at the hazard of repeating perhaps principles, with which the reader, at this time, may be perfectly familiar, and which he may be able to apply with quite as much facility as the writer.

The bank notes which are put into circulation may not be of exactly the same amount with that of the specie they displace. Because they circulate, on the average, more rapidly than hard money, a less amount of them will be able to perform the same office; which circumstance will render the extraordinary profits of the bankers a *deficient* measure of that portion of the public gain which is now under consideration. Again, the various other sorts of paper money, or contrivances for economising the use of the precious metals, have been stated to be employed somewhat more extensively when no bank notes circulate than when they do. On this account, more bank notes can be permanently retained in circulation than would be of equal value with the specie excluded; and the profits of the banks, beyond the ordinary interest of the specie they possess, will therefore err as a measure of the kind which has been mentioned, and this errour will be *in excess.* And once more, the introduction of a paper money to any extent into the circulation has been shown to render unnecessary the production of the precious metals under circumstances *quite* as disadvantageous as before; thus reducing the cost of producing them, and consequently their value, in a very slight degree. This, in its turn, will establish a *somewhat* augmented circulating medium; which is the same thing as to say that more bank paper will be added to the circulation than there will be specie taken from it; and another errour thus arises, likewise *in excess.*

Should the interest of money at any time differ from its general or average rate, it is plain that the conclusion, into the correctness of which I am now inquiring, will not need to be therefore subjected to the least modification; for the difference between what the borrowers will have to pay to the lenders of money for its use, and the average rate at which money can be procured, will only be so much, more or less, transferred from one set of individuals to another in the same country, and will, consequently, not at all affect the amount of national wealth.

But it may be justly urged that if the extraordinary profits in question be, in truth, a national gain, they ought, instead of going into the private coffers of the bankers, to be made to find their way into the public treasury; and it may be asserted that, for this reason, the present state of things among us enables those who invest any portion of their capital in the business of banking to derive a profit at the expense of the community at large. It is to take from the bankers these undue monopoly gains that our state legislatures have generally, on the incorporation of a bank, exacted, as the price of so doing, a *bonus* from the stockholders. Such bonus may be made to assume the form of a specific sum to be paid into the treasury of the state, on the commencement of its operations by the bank, or at any time or times thereafter,—or it may consist of a certain proportion of the annual profits of the capital to be invested,—or certain loans or other financial services may be stipulated for, as a price for the privileges conferred.

If the expediency of the existence of banks of circulation be conceded, and if no other banks than those on which the legislature has specially conferred the power to do so are permitted to issue paper money,—the objections to the receiving of a bonus by the state, on the incorporation of a new bank, and, of course, also on the enlarging of the capital of one already existing, are twofold: it will be apt to induce the creation of banking capital much more rapidly than would otherwise be the case, for the purpose of thereby supplying a public revenue, which will put it in the power of the legislators to dispense in a certain degree with the ever more or less odious measure of taxation; and it will have a tendency, quite as much as any other circumstance connected with the practical operation of our banking system, to corrupt the integrity of the legislative body,—a tendency which, after what has been delivered in the preceding pages, calls for no illustration here.

All, however, that would be requisite, to guard effectually against the too rapid increase of the number of banks, would be for the legislature to exact in every case a bonus high enough to leave to the stockholders little more than the ordinary interest of their money. Were they, too, to exact a bonus *just so large* as to leave to the stockholders the ordinary interest of money, it is manifest that an effectual check would be applied to the increase of the banking capital of the country, any faster than the general progress of population and wealth.

Another method by which the government can profit directly from the extraordinary gains of banking, is, as has sometimes been done, to assume to itself the business of a banker. The directors of the banks will, in such case, be public officers appointed by the legislature, or by some authority emanating from the legislature; and the net proceeds of those institutions may be appropriated to meet the various demands on the public treasury. This system of banking is especially objectionable because of its exceedingly great liability to the being perverted to party-political, or still worse purposes. Skilfully wielded by those who are in the possession of the chief influence in the state, it cannot fail to be a most efficient engine for the prolongation of their power, considerably beyond the period when they shall have ceased to enjoy the confidence of the people. And this assertion will not appear to be an unfounded one to any of my readers who reflect that, not only in the case supposed, does the government, as has been mentioned, possess the direct patronage resulting from the appointing by it of all the directors of the banks, but that it also exerts indirectly the whole of that patronage which is connected with the power of discounting, or of refusing to discount, the promissory notes of individuals, as the directors of the banks may, in their discretion, choose.

Here I may make the general and quite obvious remark, that in order to prevent the monetary system of a country from being employed by the government, as a political instrument, to enable it to maintain itself against the legitimate opposition of public opinion, it is in a high degree desirable that the system should be as little under its *control* as is practicable, *consistently with the public interests.*

CHAPTER XV.

COMPARATIVE ADVANTAGES AND DISADVANTAGES OF MANY OR OF A FEW BANKS OF CIRCULATION—REMARKS CONCERNING A NATIONAL BANK—AND CONCERNING A FREE TRADE IN THE BUSINESS OF BANKING.

A QUESTION of some moment, in the actual organisation of the American banking system, is,—whether, with a given amount of capital invested in the business of banking, a smaller or a larger number of banks is the preferable arrangement. I reply, that, provided their number be not multiplied to such an extent as to increase unduly the expenses of banking, there seems to me to be the following reasons *in favour* of many banks; *first*, that the *advantages*, whatever these may be, of the system, would then be more equally diffused throughout every portion of the country; *secondly*, that the check to the over-issue of paper money by the *several* banks will be greater than if, on account of the smallness of their number, they had a greater facility of combining together; and *lastly*, the undue influence, political or social, of wealthy monied corporations, would be diminished, or entirely removed. On the other hand, however, we have, to set in opposition with these advantages, the following *disadvantages*. *First*, it is well known to be the general fact, that the directors and officers of the smaller of the incorporated banks have not *generally* the same practical skill in banking, as is possessed by the managers of the more extensive institutions of the kind; and we must therefore infer that, when the number of banks is augmented, and the capital of each of them is, on the average, lessened in amount, the danger of improper management will become proportionally greater. *Secondly*, although the greater the number of independent banks in a community, the more efficiently will they act upon one another to prevent a larger issue of paper money by any one of them than its proportional share of the whole paper circulation of the country, it seems to me that *the general tendency* to an expansion of the currency, to be succeeded of course by a contraction of it, is much more considerable where many than where a few banks are competing with each other to obtain as large a portion of the circulation as they respectively can. And *thirdly*, when banks are very much multiplied, they are apt to be established as well in places where there is little, as where there is much trade; and, in consequence, the farmers, as well as others whose capitals are not *turned* as often as that of the merchants, are tempted, by the facilities afforded them by those institutions, to become indebted to them, thus preparing the way, in the event of a curtailment of bank accommodations being rendered necessary, for embarrassment, and perhaps ruin, to themselves and families. To these disadvantages may be added, in the *fourth* place, the greater probability of bank notes being counterfeited when they are of many different descriptions than when they are of a few.

There are two portions of the community who will be disposed to decide very differently, on a comparison of the advantages and disadvantages which have been enumerated. I mean the friends of a national bank, and the advocates of a *free trade* in banking, that is of permission being given to all individuals, or associations of individuals, to engage in the business of banking, at their pleasure, as they are at present permitted to engage in every branch of mercantile employment. The former class look upon a bank having a large capital, with branches distributed through the different states composing the Union, as not only adequate to regulate the currency, by restraining the circulation of the numerous state banks within their due bounds, but as absolutely indispensable to protect the community from the evils which these would otherwise inflict upon it.

The propriety of a bank of this description being chartered by the general government (on the supposition of the continued existence of our present banking system) will depend on the practicability of constituting it in a manner to be less likely to cause a derangement of the money market, than the institutions are whose unsteady action it is appointed to regulate. And the propriety of the chartering of such a bank will depend, farther, upon the degree in which its action, as a regulator of the currency, renders it of advantage to the country. The advantage, in this respect conferred by it, should, in order to justify its incorporation, be at least considerable enough to overbalance the objection to it which is founded on the probability of the social or political influence which it may, and perhaps cannot but possess, being improperly exercised. This is all that I deem necessary to be said here concerning the *expediency* of incorporating a national bank; and the question of the constitutionality of doing this does not belong to the subject of the present treatise.

With respect to a free trade in banking, it appears to me very evident that all the disadvantages which have been specified, of the multiplication of banks of circulation, would, in consequence of its introduction, be carried to an extreme. Paper money, of even the smallest denominations of value, would be, in every village, and in every neighbourhood, issued profusely, and not by the most *responsible* individuals only. The specie of the country would thus be expelled from the circulation; which, I may say, would necessarily fall into a state of complete anarchy. In so far also as,—on the occurrence of a suspension by the banks of specie payments, and the consequent practical repeal for a time of the laws against the general issuing of paper money,—experience among ourselves of the readiness with which the promissory notes of comparatively irresponsible associations of men, and even of irresponsible individuals, have entered into the circulation, throws light on what would take place in a state of things were every one would be at full liberty to put forth his notes *on the condition of paying them in specie on demand,*—my reasoning will acquire additional force.

In objecting to a free trade in banking, so long as every *banker* is permitted to add to the paper money of the country, I make no account of the evils manifestly resulting from the act, or process, of introducing it. Here, as in almost all the cases which can, by possibility, come under the cognisance of the political economist, the evils, incidental to a transition from one state of things to another, can be almost entirely avoided by simply making the transition sufficiently gradual.

CHAPTER XVI.

LIABILITY OF A CURRENCY TO BE MORE EXPANDED OR CONTRACTED, ACCORDING AS IT CONSISTS IN A GREATER DEGREE OF PAPER MONEY—INFERENCE TO BE DRAWN.

On a review, now, of all that has been stated, in the present book, concerning the relative advantages of a bank note and of a metallic currency, I am not sure that I would not prefer one composed exclusively of the precious metals, if no other choice presented itself excepting a currency like that which exists, or to speak more correctly, like that which existed in the country previous to the late suspension of specie payments, with all its liability to give occasion to such an event.

But our choice is fortunately not confined to so narrow bounds. By prohibiting the circulation of bank notes of the smaller denominations, we would have a *mixed currency;* which we may readily conceive to be preferable to one composed either exclusively of paper money, or exclusively of the precious metals. In proportion as the paper part of the currency is diminished in amount, will the whole of it possess in a less degree the *elasticity* of a medium of exchange that is supplied altogether by the banks. An extraordinary demand for specie to be exported abroad, or for any other purpose, will not require so great a curtailment of bank accommodations. Here, however, it may be said that the supposition of a mixed currency being preferable to one altogether metallic, implies a superiority of paper over hard money, and consequently, whatever this superiority may amount to, that it will be augmented just according as the currency approaches to a purely paper condition. If this view then, of the nature of a mixed currency, be a correct one, we shall be again reduced to the dilemma of choosing between an exclusively metallic and an exclusively paper currency. That it is not a correct one, I shall endeavour to make distinctly appear to the reader.

While the advantages which paper money possesses over hard money in other respects,—granting, for the present, an excess of advantages above disadvantages to exist in the case, —will be proportional to the quantity of paper money in circulation; there is one *disadvantage* necessarily to become of greater account than in proportion to the augmentation of such money. In order to explain the disadvantage to which I am adverting, let us look at an instance or two of an augmentation of it occurring. Let us, first, suppose the specie circulating in a particular country to amount to a million of dollars, and the paper money to be a like sum in bank notes of the higher denominations. If in this state of things, a demand for $100,000 in specie be made, that it may be exported from the country, or for any other purpose, the circulation will be diminished *to a greater extent* than that sum; and although there may be but few of my readers who will not be prepared to assent at once to the correctness of this result,—for the sake of these few, I shall exhibit the steps by which it will be brought about. The sum required will not be wholly taken from the specie in circulation, but a part of it will be drawn from the banks. For were the specie alone which circulated reduced in amount, the consequence will be that an undue amount of the whole circulating medium would consist of bank notes. A demand would be made upon the banks for specie in exchange for a portion of them ; by which means the proper proportions would be again restored between the different kinds of money. But, it is scarcely necessary to remark, from the very moment when the demand of which I first spoke shall have occurred, specie will be drawn from the banks, as well as from the specie actually circulating, to supply it; and the proportion of hard money to paper money will be preserved nearly uniform, during the whole period of the abstraction of the specie demanded. How much of the specie abstracted will be taken from what is in circulation, and how much from the vaults of the banks, will depend on the proportion which the whole of the specie in the possession of the banks bears to the amount of it which circulates. In the case I have supposed, if we assume the specie of the banks to amount in value to one half of the notes they have issued, it will appear, by a very simple calculation, that a third part of the specie required, or $33,333 will be drawn from the banks, —that the paper circulation will be, consequently, $66,666 less than before,—and that the whole circulation will be reduced $133,333.

Now let us examine another instance. Still supposing the specie demanded to amount to $100,000, and the whole circulating medium to two millions of dollars, and supposing also the same proportion as in the preceding instance of the circulation of the banks to the specie on which it is based, namely that of two to one,—let the specie circulating amount to two-fifths of a million, and the paper money to a million and three-fifths of a million of dollars. The like calculation as before will shew us that the $100,000 in question will be taken, one third from the specie circulation, and two-thirds from the specie of the banks, and that the whole sum by which the circulation will be lessened will amount to $166,666.

If we compare together the two instances which have been stated, of the effects produced upon a mixed currency by the occurrence of an extraordinary demand for specie, and note, besides, that the contraction of the currency, if this had consisted only of specie, would have amounted just to $100,000, the following inference will present itself,—that the additional contraction of it, resulting from the substitution of bank notes in the place of specie, is not greater merely in exact proportion to the augmented quantity of the paper money in the currency, but that the *extent* of the contraction increases more rapidly than the quantity of paper money does. The same inference, too, may be deduced from a comparison of any other instances of the kind which may be examined. Conversely, we may, of course, infer that the *expansions* to which a mixed currency is liable, beyond those of one consisting entirely of specie, will augment more rapidly than the bank paper which may be successively substituted for specie in the currency.

The conclusion follows that, however the advantages may otherwise preponderate over the disadvantages of a circulation of bank notes, we have here a reason why the community will be liable to suffer inconveniences, and will therefore from time to time actually suffer them, to an extent more than proportional to the paper money substituted in the circulation for specie. And we are now entitled to consider the proposition as proved,—that, *very possibly*, a currency composed, in certain proportions, of specie, and of paper convertible into specie on demand, may be preferable to one containing either less or more of specie.

This proposition, indeed, would still hold good even though the liability of the currency to extraordinary expansions and contractions, arising out of the substitution of paper money for specie, did not increase any faster than such substitution; and for this reason, that a double contraction of the currency, as every practical banker or man of business knows, is productive of much more than a double amount of inconvenience and distress, among the merchants, and the community at large.

But notwithstanding the *possibility* has been established of a mixed currency, of a paper money issued by the banks and of specie, being of more advantage to a country than one of either of these separately, it would be very difficult to prove, *a priori*, that such is in fact the case. With all our experience, also, on the subject of banking, we find the opinions of the most intelligent men in the community ranging through the whole extent of the interval between an exclusive bank note and an exclusive specie circulation. And, indeed, to determine the peculiar constitution of the most desirable currency, whether composed in part of bank notes or not,—having an especial regard to the rendering a given portion of it, as nearly as possible, always of the same value,—is, at present, truely the great desideratum in our science. It may be added that the difficulty of doing this can only be adequately appreciated by those who have made political economy their particular study. They too, will hesitate to pronounce a positive judgment concerning any course of legislation which may be proposed for the purpose, where the mere zealots of a party will be prompt to dogmatise on the subject.

CHAPTER XVII.

THE MOST DESIRABLE CIRCULATING MEDIUM FOR THE UNITED STATES.

An expression of opinion on the problem of the most desirable circulating medium, more particularly in reference to the United States, will, naturally enough, be expected from a systematic writer on the theories of money and of banking, and in a work published at a period when so large a portion of the public attention is directed to those theories, in their especial bearing, also, on the problem in question. I shall, accordingly, state the result of my reflections on the subject; leaving it to the careful and unprejudiced consideration of my readers.

In view of the difficulties which have been stated of otherwise guarding the community from the disastrous effects of frequent and extraordinary contractions, and expansions to be followed by contractions, of the currency, an opinion has been gradually gaining ground in Great Britain of the expediency of there being but a single issuer of paper money,—of paper money, I mean, exclusive of the ordinary mercantile paper which every where constitutes to a certain degree the medium of exchange. A writer in one of the leading journals of that country has suggested that the single issuer should there be the Bank of England, acting under the inspection of the government; a commissioner appointed by which to have a veto on every additional issue of bank notes that may at any time be proposed by the directors. Such an arrangement amounts very nearly to the conferring of the exclusive power of issuing paper money on the government itself. And I must confess that I see no sufficient reason why this power should not be exercised by it directly, without the intervention of a bank.

When we reflect upon the magnitude of the opposition to a national bank in our own country, even when no peculiar privileges or power were proposed to be conferred upon it than what must necessarily result from the large amount of its capital, the utter impracticability may be assumed of organising among ourselves any institution of the kind in order to constitute it the sole issuer of our paper currency. If a single issuer shall ever exist here, it can only be the government of the Union,—and the government of the Union, too, in its *fiscal* capacity. A national bank under the control of the government, in which the question of lending or not lending to any individual is to be determined by officers appointed by it, I need scarcely say would be more objectionable than a similar institution where this was to be decided at the discretion of men of the highest respectability, appointed for the purpose by the stockholders.

The proposed object can, in my opinion, be accomplished by simply carrying out the scheme of what has been styled the sub-treasury system,—a scheme brought forward, in the first instance, for the purpose of removing for the future the public funds from the keeping of the banks, and from the accidents to which the banks have been shewn by experience to be subject. Let the secretary of the treasury be authorised to issue treasury notes, or drafts upon the treasury, *on which no interest shall be paid*, in payment of the public creditor, whenever they shall be preferred by the latter to specie; and on the other hand, let them be received in payment for taxes, when the tax payer shall prefer making his payments in this manner rather than paying in specie. It will be observed that all the discretion which is here allowed rests with the public creditor or debtor, and in no respect with the government; whose *patronage* cannot thereby be augmented, unless to the extent implied in the appointment of a very few officers in addition to those already employed in the treasury department. This additional patronage, besides, must surely be regarded as altogether insignificant in comparison with that which the government may be conceived to exercise under any supposable connexion of it with a number of *deposite banks.*

Were there no banks of issue in existence, and therefore no such things as bank notes, it is easy to understand how the treasury notes in question would enter into the circulation, and what would determine the extent in which they would do so. Receivable as they would be for taxes, and not bearing any interest, there can be no doubt that, in the absence of bank notes, their superior convenience to specie for remittance to a distance, as well as for making considerable payments, would give them a preference with the merchant, and that, for this reason, they would in certain parts of the country command a premium in the market. So long as this state of things continued, while specie would be flowing into the public treasury, the treasury notes would be passing into the circulation. At length, however, as much of this paper money as was required for the convenience of the merchants will have been issued; when, if more of it be issued, it will only be to be speedily returned by the tax payers.

Next, the limit of the government issues having been reached, as determined by the convenience of the mercantile community, suppose a demand for specie to occur, and let us see what will happen. People generally will choose to pay their taxes in treasury notes rather than in specie; and the creditors of the government will ask for specie instead of treasury notes. The circulation of these last will, in consequence, become contracted; the whole circulating medium being at the same time diminished precisely to the extent of the extraordinary demand for specie. Every thing, also, will take place in a contrary direction, on the supposition of a less demand for specie than usual. We shall then, manifestly, have a circulating medium, susceptible of neither more nor less of expansion and contraction than one that is composed exclusively of the precious metals; and which has this advantage over one so composed, that it is more convenient for making payments of a large amount, and for remitting money to distant places.

For these advantages in our system of paper money, we shall have sacrificed nearly all those which arise from the dispensing altogether with the use of the precious metals as money, to an amount equal to the value represented by the paper substituted instead of them in the circulation. This will be the case because the specie withdrawn is retained in the coffers of the government, and not, as is usually the case on the issue of paper money, diffused throughout the commercial world. The value of the sacrifice thus made may be approximately estimated, as has before been stated, by the *net* profits of the banks of the country above the ordinary interest of money,—a sacrifice which, I am disposed to think, will be regarded by the reader to be of less account just in proportion as he reflects upon the subject.

But it is not at all indispensable that the whole of the specie received by the government should be retained in its possession unemployed. One-half, or one-third, or any other proportion of it, may be employed in purchasing its own obligations, or, when there is no national debt, in purchasing the obligations of the different states of the union. The specie, thus disposed of, will now take the same course with specie which is liberated from the circulation by the issue of bank paper; and the advantage to the country of such a disposition of it will be an accession to the national wealth of an amount of commodities other than money, equal in value with that of the specie whose use has been dispensed with, and which, for this reason, will cease to be reproduced. On the *introduction* of the system in question, it would be expedient to err in having an unnecessary reserve of specie in the public treasury in order to guard effectually against the contingency of the government being obliged to stop specie payments. After it had been for some time in operation, experience would enable us to determine very nearly what should be the minimum amount of specie to be reserved. A circulating medium like *this* would have every advantage which is possessed by any that can be furnished by the banks, and without any counterbalancing disadvantage.

Should the plan of issuing it, as above stated, be objected to on account of the *first* issues being proposed to be made on no specie basis actually provided by the government, the objection could easily be got over by so modifying the plan as to require the procuring, in the first instance, by taxation or loan, of such a specie basis as is desirable, previous to the making of any issues whatever of treasury notes. This objection, however, is in my opinion of no weight. Even if a certain amount of these notes were to be issued before any of the specie to be received in payment of taxes had been actually paid into the public treasury, they would have been issued on the credit of the government; and if the expenditures annually authorised by Congress were invariably limited by the estimated receipts within the year from the different sources of the public revenue, that credit can scarcely be susceptible, under any circumstances, of being impaired.

I have supposed only a certain exact proportion of the specie which may come into the possession of the government to be reserved by it in order to secure itself against a suspension, on any emergency, of specie payments. But if any one prefer the rule to be that the specie reserved should be made to bear a certain exact proportion to the *treasury notes which shall have been issued*, I would cheerfully acquiesce in this modification of my plan. Perhaps, indeed, this may be in a slight degree the preferable arrangement.

To omit any farther mention of objections to it founded on the mistaken notion of its having a tendency to add to the patronage of the executive department of the general government, I know of no others which can be adduced, with any plausibility, against the expediency of its adoption, excepting such as have reference to the introduction of it *in place of* our existing system of a bank note circulation, of the benefits derived from which so many even of our most intelligent citizens entertain the most exaggerated opinions, and which so many are disposed to identify, most absurdly, as I have shewn, with the *credit system,*—and excepting such objections, too, as are founded on its inconsistency with the existence at any time of a *surplus revenue.*

How to pass from our present bank note circulation to the one above described will be a subject of inquiry as we proceed. In respect to the system of credit, it may be observed that, so far from being in the slightest degree impaired by the abolition of banks of issue or of circulation, the greatest obstacle will have been overcome to the removal of all restrictions on the lending of money; and there will then be no reason why every individual in the community, who may think it to be for his interests to do so, might not be permitted to engage in the business of *banking*, with the exception alone of issuing notes payable to the bearer on demand, just as he is now at liberty to engage in any other branch of business without first asking the consent of the government.

Objections, to the scheme of a circulating medium, of the nature described in the present chapter, which are founded on the accumulation of a surplus revenue, and on the consequent mass of specie coming thereby into the possession of the government, and having to be disposed of by it, need not be suffered in the least to disturb us. Not to speak of a disposal to be made of the surplus revenue by the purchase of the different state obligations or stocks, or what amounts to the same thing, by lending to the different states, I may reply that, after the experience we have had of the evils of which, in more ways than one, a surplus revenue is productive,—

although some of these could not again recur if our present banking system were abolished,—there ought to be no question among us of the propriety of reducing the public revenue to the exigencies of the government, and of thus preventing the existence of any surplus in future. And besides this being a sufficient reply to the objections now under consideration,—that the existence of a surplus revenue should be in any degree inconsistent with a fair experiment for supplying a better currency to the country, will be an additional reason with many for being hostile to the accumulation of such a revenue.

CHAPTER XVIII.

MODE OF ABROGATING THE EXISTING BANKING SYSTEM OF THE COUNTRY.

The remark can scarcely be repeated often enough that, however beneficial any proposed change in the policy or government of a country may be, it may not unfrequently be productive of evils, on its too sudden introduction, which will more than compensate the good which it is fitted eventually to confer. It is from a forgetfulness of this important principle that the more zealous, and, at the same time, inconsiderate portion, of the friends of political improvement, are occasionally ready to plunge into all the miseries of a *revolution*, when the object in view could be much more effectually, and more speedily too, attained by the exercise of argument instead of violence. Those friends of improvement to whom I have been adverting are also apt to forget that it is seldom a change of any kind, in the political or social relations of society, can be beneficially carried into execution, before public opinion, or at least that of a majority of the individuals who are chiefly concerned, can be induced to declare decidedly in its favour. And there is, besides, another reason which should always operate, with the intelligent and philanthropic portion of the community, to check every disposition on their part to disturb too rapidly the subsisting condition of things around them;—I mean the very natural tendency of the minds of most men to confound the immediate with the ultimate effects resulting from the action of any cause. By advancing without sufficient caution, even in the right direction, the "evils of change" may, quite possibly, be of such magnitude, and endure so long, as, in consequence of this tendency, to generate a feeling in the community *adverse* to the most desirable alterations in government or policy, and sometimes to constitute a pretext, if not a real ground, for a reaction in a direction opposite to the true one. On the contrary, let any one only appreciate and be guided by the considerations which have been exhibited for not changing rashly the established order of society, and though he should be an extreme "radical" in his political opinions,—if, indeed, this epithet may not be regarded as misapplied to such a person,—he might, notwithstanding, be more of a "conservative" of every thing truly deserving of conservation, than are those rigid conservatives, so called, who exclaim vehemently against every proposed abrogation of abuses, however flagrant these may be, as an act of treason to the public welfare. Such men are often the most efficient revolutionists. They are to be found constantly occupied in revolting the feelings of the people among whom they live, and in thus diffusing a more general spirit of opposition to all existing institutions.

Bearing in mind the observations which have just been made, I observe that it would not be difficult to pass from our existing banking system to a purely metallic currency, or to the monetary system which has been recommended in the preceding chapter.

First, the legislature of each of the states may prohibit, at the outset, the circulation, after a certain date, of all bank notes of the lowest denomination which is actually permitted to circulate. It might then prohibit, after an interval, the circulation of bank notes of the next denomination above the lowest. And so it might go on, until the occupation of the banks, as banks of circulation, was wholly taken from them; the whole proccss being extended through such a period as to prevent the community from being subjected to any extraordinary inconvenience, and to avoid infringing upon any rights which the banks may possess under their existing charters.

Secondly, the legislatures of the states, while they shall refuse to incorporate any new banks, may also refuse to renew the charters, as they expire, of those already existing; or, where they expire in too rapid succession, they might be renewed for a suitable period only, the capital of each bank being, at the same time, reduced in amount. Every precaution, too, should be taken against the over-issues of those banks which shall be the last to exist. For in the process of reduction, the banking capital of the country,—especially if the treasury notes in circulation should be only of the higher denominations, for which, however, there is not the least necessity,—may be so small in comparison to the amount of specie which circulates, as to tempt the banks to issue their notes imprudently, and to incur the hazard of becoming bankrupt. But if the withdrawal of the smaller denominations of bank notes shall be made to keep pace with the diminishing of the capital employed in banking, the probability of any thing of the kind just mentioned taking place will be little greater than it is under ordinary circumstances.

Thirdly, a bonus, say in the form of a per centage on its capital, may be exacted on the incorporation or re-incorporation of every bank; and if the profits of the bankers, over and above the per centage exacted by the government, should be only equal to the ordinary interest of money, no motive would exist for investing any more capital in banking rather than in any other business. Hence, it is evident, the bonus exacted might be so adjusted, that bank after bank should cease its operations, and eventually none should remain. The objection to this mode of *extinguishing* our present banking system is, that, in the latter stage of the process, the temptation to the banks would be very great to issue their notes so extensively as to impair their credit, in order that they might thereby be enabled to realise enough to yield to the stockholders the ordinary returns, after providing for the increased demands of the government. This temptation may, indeed, be met by extraordinary precautions and penalties, to be applied by the legislature. Since, nevertheless, it cannot but be stronger than any temptations to which the banks would be subjected in the mode just before described of getting rid of them, that mode must be regarded as the preferable one of the two.

When the new currency shall have been, thus gradually, substituted for the notes of our present banks, it may be mentioned that the banks (of deposite and of discount) which will remain, and which, on the principles of an unrestricted competition will be multiplied in number according to the wants of the community, will, in addition to the peculiarity of their issuing no paper money of their own, transact the deposite part of their business differently from what is now universally the case in the United States. Owing to the monopoly of privileges enjoyed by the banking institutions of the country, none of them find it necessary, for obtaining the deposites of individuals, to pay them any interest for their money. But under a system of *free trade* in banking,—as banking would *then* be understood,—while the bankers will be charging the market rate of interest for the money which they lend out to others, they will, very naturally, be willing to borrow money from those who may have it to lend, or, what is the same thing, to receive the deposites of individuals, at a *somewhat* lower rate of interest. This is, in fact, the general practice throughout the continent of Europe.

If any of my readers have still doubts concerning the expediency of a free trade in banking, and in money generally, when the banks shall have been deprived of the privilege of issuing promissory notes payable to the *bearer* of them on demand, his doubts, I hope, will be entirely dissipated before he shall have finished the perusal of the present *book.*

I have said that it would not be difficult to pass from our existing banking system to a purely metallic currency, or to one composed in part of the precious metals, and in part of treasury notes or drafts. The difficulty alluded to was of a politico-economical description. *Political* difficulties, however, intervene, of a nature, practically speaking, altogether insuperable without an alteration of the constitution of the United States. No one of the states can be expected to abolish the existing banking system, or even to take many steps in prohibiting the issue of bank notes of the lower denominations, so long as the same measures are not adopted contemporaneously by the other, and especially by the neighbouring states. Though New York, for example, were to act in the manner suggested, the paper money of New Jersey or Connecticut might circulate extensively in the former state, in the place of the bank notes excluded; and the intended effect might, in consequence, only very partially ensue. But this is not all. The profits of banking, beyond the ordinary returns to the capital, properly so called, of the banks which operate within its bounds, will be transferred by the state of New York to those of Connecticut and New Jersey, without any advantage being derived by it in return, —with the *disadvantage*, indeed, of its possessing a less secure currency than it had before;—less secure because such a currency circulates at a more remote distance from the source whence it is issued, and is therefore liable to be issued more abundantly than its specie basis will justify ; and less secure, too, because it will be more subject to being counterfeited than a paper money which is payable nearer home.

The obvious and the only remedy, for the difficulties just considered, lies in an amendment of the constitution, which shall take from the states the power of incorporating banks of circulation,—and which, in my opinion, ought equally to prohibit the issuing, by individuals or companies of individuals, of a paper currency, or, in other words, of promissory notes made payable to the *bearer* in specie on demand.

CHAPTER XIX.

SUSPENSION OF SPECIE PAYMENTS BY THE BANKS.

In discussing the subject of banking, I have supposed the banks to be held strictly to the obligation of paying specie for their notes on demand. But such has not always been the case. As well in Great Britain as in the United States, a suspension of specie payments on their part has occurred, and has continued for a considerable time ;—in the former country, by means of an act of parliament, for so long a period as from 1797 to 1822 ; and in the latter, from 1814 to 1817, without the direct interposition, for the purpose, of the legislature,—which had, indeed, no constitutional authority to loosen the obligations of creditors to their debtors; but yet as a consequence, in a considerable degree, of the measures adopted by it in a time of war.*

* This was written before the suspension of specie payments by our banks in May of the last year.

Before the first occurrence of such a suspension of specie payments, an impression prevailed very generally, even among that portion of the community who might be thought to be the most competent judges of the matter, that the credit of bank notes, if not entirely prostrated by such a measure, would be exceedingly depreciated by it. On the contrary however, the notes of the Bank of England continued for some time to have a market value, when compared with gold and silver, not very different from their former and professed value. An immediate inquiry into the causes of this extraordinary phenomenon very naturally took place; and not only were those causes satisfactorily traced and explained, but the science of money, as of political economy in general, then received a renewed impulse.

Those of my readers who have made themselves masters of the preceding chapters of this book will find no difficulty in comprehending how it is that, when the banks refuse to pay specie for their notes, these may, notwithstanding, continue to circulate, and to perform all the functions of money, without their value being in any remarkable degree, and indeed without their value being in any the slightest degree, injuriously affected. To make this quite apparent, it will suffice for me to *repeat*, that, from the very nature of banking, the *immediate* payment in specie of all the bank notes in circulation, on being presented by their holders for the purpose, would be an impossibility; and that they are, in despite of this circumstance, regarded as equivalent to specie, and as, generally speaking, a more desirable circulating medium than specie. It will be recollected that their credit, in reality, rests on the whole amount of the *property* supposed to be owned by the parties who issue them, as also on the comparative rapidity with which the value of that property can be realised in money, and a speedy redemption of the notes by this means secured. This last condition too, it is evident, may be overlooked, provided the former exist to a sufficient extent, and provided, moreover, there is no exception to the general non-payment, by the banks of a country, of specie for their notes. The superior convenience of bank notes will, in general, secure their continued circulation, without their depreciation in value, until they are issued so abundantly as to expel all the specie previously circulating.

The suspension of specie payments will, however, take from the banks every motive, short of an apprehension of impairing the confidence of the community in their stability, to limit their issues of paper money. The checks too, which are administered by them to one another, will be almost entirely removed,—founded chiefly, as those checks were shewn to be, on the convertibility into specie of the notes of each bank. As a consequence, the country will be flooded, and unequally so, with paper money. And notwithstanding the *possibility*, above exhibited, of bank notes not depreciating after they have ceased to be convertible into specie, they will infallibly, sooner or later, in fact suffer depreciation, unless some other checks to their being unduly issued be applied, in place of those which have ceased to operate.

On account of the existence in Great Britain (through the influence of the government on the Bank of England, and, in its turn, of the bank of England on the country bankers) of other checks to the extravagant issues of paper money, in a degree considerably greater than in the United States,—at the periods of the respective suspensions of specie payments in the two countries,—the depreciation of the bank note currency at no time extended as far in the former country as it, in most instances, did in the latter.

By the depreciation of paper money, it has been intended to denote its depreciation below its nominal value in specie. But here we may be reminded of the possibility of specie, or what amounts to the same thing, of bullion, *appreciating* in value; and that the depreciation of the paper money may therefore be, either wholly, or in part, merely apparent. A case can easily be imagined of a simultaneous change in opposite directions in the value of the inconvertible paper money, and in that of gold and silver. An extraordinary enhancement of the value of these metals may have taken place on the failure of their supply from the more fertile mines, in consequence of the long continuance of civil commotions in the region where these mines are situated, as was the fact in Mexico and in South America, during a considerable period in the present century;—or it may for a certain time be owing, and this in no slight degree, to the breaking out of an extensive war among the principal nations of the world. The effect of its occurrence on an inconvertible paper currency will, of course, be to make that currency depreciate in value when compared with the value of bullion. And should the banks, in this state of things, issue an unusual quantity of their notes, there will also be a real depreciation of them. It must, however, be quite obvious that the possibility of the depreciation being real only in part cannot affect the correctness of the conclusions which have been deduced, as to the tendency of all inconvertible paper money to be issued in excess.

As the banks of a country increase their circulation, will their gains be likewise increased. When, therefore, the check of being obliged to pay specie for their notes is once removed, there will be no desire on their part to have it replaced, and no efforts will be made by them voluntarily to resume specie payments. To bring about this measure, they must be operated upon from without. The only *forces*, too, which can be effectually invoked for this purpose are the force of public opinion and that of the legislature; and the former of these merely on account of its influence on the action of the latter. A remote expectation or apprehension of what the legislature may possibly do to their prejudice will scarcely accomplish more with the banks than to induce them not to carry their expansions beyond a certain amount,—an amount already much too large. In order to *compel* them to contract their issues and to resume specie payments, the legislative bodies, whose creatures they are, will, in most cases of the kind, find it necessary to pass some act imposing a pecuniary penalty upon them, or declaring their charters forfeited, in the event of their not resuming specie payments by a certain day, and of their not thereafter continuing uninterruptedly to make payment of their notes in specie. It is the province, I may add, of our different state legislatures, acting separately or in concert, to control the circulation of the paper money which they have authorised; and it will be time enough for the community to look to the Congress of the United States, rather than to them, for bringing about a return by the banks to a payment of their notes in specie, after payment of their notes has for a while failed to be made, when the states shall have resigned the power they have hitherto exercised of incorporating banks of circulation, and the government of the Union shall have assumed to itself the regulation of the currency of the whole country, agreeably to the spirit and intent of our existing Constitution.

Some individuals who have entertained exaggerated notions of the advantages derived to a community from the substitution of a paper for a metallic currency, and who have been desirous of still farther multiplying those advantages, by dispensing with the necessity of retaining any specie in the banks for the purpose of redeeming their notes, have occasionally proposed various plans for carrying on the business of banking, so as to maintain a bank note circulation professedly not subject to be redeemed with specie. A favourite plan has been to issue notes representing property in *land*, and to limit at the same time the notes issued to a certain amount, when compared with the property represented by them. There are several objections to the execution of every such scheme. The most important one,—one, also, which may be regarded as of itself decisive against it,—is the practical difficulty of maintaining the limit prescribed to the amount of the issues to be made. Should it be argued that laws may be passed, with sufficient penalties annexed to them, to prevent the parties who shall be authorised to issue paper money, from going beyond the prescribed limit, the reply is that the danger to be apprehended exists chiefly in a very different quarter. It is the government, whether of the states or of the whole Union, as the case may be, which is likely to be the great trespasser. Banking privileges, of the kind now under consideration, will be asked of it without end, and inducements for granting them will be held out which it will be scarcely able to resist; and the circulating medium will thus be continually extended, and a given portion of it, therefore, more and more depreciated in value. This will happen, too, almost as fast as if the *government* had exercised the power of emitting bills of credit without any limitation as to quantity.

To what has been mentioned concerning a circulating medium not based on the precious metals, and in no wise representing them, I may add that, if its introduction were practicable, as well as in other respects to be desired, there is one advantage those metals would have over it,—an advantage that would, of course, be partaken of by every currency representing them,—which might, notwithstanding, turn the scale in their favour. Perhaps of all commodities, gold and silver are those whose value is the least subject to variation during comparatively short periods of time, such as a few *years*. This circumstance fits them, in a peculiar manner, to become the measure of value in the case of almost all contracts. And indeed, even though the circulating medium should be constituted wholly of paper money having no direct reference to either gold or silver, it would be expedient, with a view to guard as much as possible against the necessity of discharging the contracts which have been entered into by the payment of a less or of a greater value than that bargained for, to specify particularly that they should be discharged with specie or bullion.

CHAPTER XX.

DEBASEMENT OF THE CURRENCY.

It is not only by their action on the banking system of a country that the rulers of nations have interfered with the medium for exchanging every thing else. They have, not unfrequently, exercised their prerogative of coining money, so as to free themselves from the obligation of discharging the full amount of the debts incurred by them, or by their predecessors in the government, for professedly public or national purposes. The name before applied to a piece of money, containing a certain quantity of gold or silver, has been subsequently applied by them to one containing only a half, a tenth, or even a less proportion of those metals.

That it would be a fraud on the part of the government to pay its creditors, and to enable debtors generally to pay their creditors, in coins which have been debased in the manner described, must be sufficiently obvious to the reader to require no illustration.

Latterly, however, governments have preferred, when pressed by financial difficulties, and when they have not been over-scrupulous to avoid any hazard of violating the rights of the national creditor, to issue *bills of credit*, or, in other words, to pay for the services of the persons in their employ, as well as for the purchases they may require to be made, by promises in writing to pay a certain amount of money *at some future day*. Bills of this description,—call them treasury notes, assignats, or by whatsoever other name, —are necessarily liable to be issued to the same, or even a still greater excess, than is an inconvertible *bank* paper-money. This last must, at least, be the case if the banks be not in a certain degree, or wholly, under the immediate control or management of the government. According as such bills of credit are issued to an extent ever greater and greater, they will become more and more depreciated in value; and although the government of a country may, for a limited time, find in the employment of them extraordinary resources, they will at length be so much depreciated as to render it absolutely necessary to recur to taxation exclusively, in order to provide for the public expenditure. I say to taxation exclusively, because it is manifest that when a government, in the general opinion, is so utterly bankrupt that its promises to pay are regarded as of little or no value, it will certainly be altogether out of its power to procure a loan from any quarter whatever,—at least any but *forced loans,* which is merely another name for a certain unequal species of taxation.

CHAPTER XXI.

ON THE INTEREST OF MONEY.

Besides affecting by their legislation the amount of the circulating medium, governments have passed laws limiting the interest to be received for money to a rate below what it would be, or what it would frequently be, if left to be determined by a free competition between the lenders and the borrowers in the market; and they have even forbidden altogether the lending of money under certain circumstances, as, for example, has been done by the "restraining laws" of the state of New York. After what has been said in the foregoing pages concerning money and capital, I need not undertake to show that every difficulty thrown in the way of their transfer by loan, from one individual to another, must tend to retard the progress of national wealth, by preventing them from being employed as productively as they might otherwise be.

The legal limitation of the interest of money calls for some remark. But it is expedient, in the first place, to understand distinctly what the circumstances are which, independently of the action of the government, determine the rate of interest. I shall, accordingly, now inquire into these.

If money were never borrowed excepting to be employed productively, and if the ordinary profits of capital were the very same in all the various branches of industry, the interest of money would, obviously, be determined by the rate of profits. Were this rate, for example, ten per cent., that of interest could not be, and remain, at nine. A dollar upon every hundred dollars borrowed by any capitalist would, in that case, be acquired by him, as it were gratuitously, beyond the compensation which he is entitled to for his labour of management, or superintendence, of the capital borrowed by him. It is evident that the borrowers of money will then desire to borrow it to a greater extent than before, and that others who hitherto may have abstained from borrowing will compete with them for loans in the money market, until the rate of interest shall have advanced to ten per cent. And had we, on the contrary, set out with supposing the rate of interest to be higher than the ordinary rate of profits, less money will evidently be borrowed than before, till interest and profits are again brought to coincide.

But there is not one rate of profits,—natural rate, of course, is meant,—in all the various applications of capital. Which, then, of the actual rates must be taken as that by which the interest of money is determined? I would say the higher rates; for if, at any time, the lower rates corresponded with the rate of interest, it seems to me there would be no doubt that the capitalists who are receiving the larger profits would offer to borrow money to such an amount as to cause interest to rise. Be this, however, as it may, it is certainly correct to speak, in general terms, of the interest of money being determined by the profits of capital; and on the other hand, when we are told what the interest for money borrowed is, in a particular period or country, we shall have an *approximate* measure, at least, of the general rate of profits.

I need scarcely mention that I have been taking for granted the entire security of property, as well as the non-interference of the government with the right of individuals to dispose of their property, including money, as they may deem to be most conducive to their own advantage. Where these conditions are not fulfilled, where the state of society is so lawless as to subject the possessor of wealth, and especially of *moveable* wealth, to the depredations of his fellow-men, or where the highest interest for the use of money which can be lawfully received is lower than the general rate of profits,—little or no money will be borrowed, on the supposition of money being never borrowed except with a view to reproduction.

Moreover, if all payments of money for commodities purchased were cash payments, the only reason which I can conceive for borrowing would be for the purpose of speculation. When the prices of commodities are expected by the speculators to rise, they will desire to purchase more extensively than usual, and they will make a greater demand for money. On the principles of supply and demand, the interest to be paid for its use will, in consequence, be temporarily enhanced. An opposite effect will ensue from an expectation of a fall of prices. These temporary effects, occurring, as they will do, sometimes in one, and sometimes in another, of two opposite directions, can, very plainly, produce no change in the average or ordinary rate of interest, determined, as this has been shewn to be, by the general rate of profits.

A certain portion only of the payments of the community is, however, made in cash; which portion, too, is commonly less in amount, according as the community has more of a mercantile character, and according to the degree in which punctuality generally, in the discharge of pecuniary obligations, is secured by the laws, or by the influence of public opinion. The demand for money, in order to discharge such obligations, may cause the interest paid for its use to rise, at times, considerably above the ordinary rate; and if the government interfere in any way with the business of lending money,—either by prohibiting altogether the lending of it under certain circumstances, or by the branding of the taking of interest, beyond a specified amount, as *usury*, and annexing to the doing so the legal forfeiture of the loan,—the interest of money may rise occasionally to a very exorbitant height. It must then exceed the interest which would otherwise be paid, by the amount of the insurance required to cover the risk of the entire loss of the principal lent, and must, besides, compensate the lender for the loss of social standing and respectability on account of his having violated the laws of his country and become an usurer. In addition to this, it may be mentioned here that, on the occurrence of a scarcity of money, or on a scarcity of it being apprehended, the interest asked for the use of it will advance more rapidly than would be the case were an entire liberty to be allowed to every one to do what he chose with his own money; and after having, in the course of its advance, reached the limit fixed by law, it will be, obviously, at once enhanced in an extraordinary degree. Hence the policy of a repeal of the usury laws, and of a free trade in money, as in respect of every other commodity.

While, however, avowing myself, in common with every

other political economist, to be hostile to all usury laws, I am not an advocate for their absolute repeal, so long as a limited number only of banking institutions exist in a country, possessing peculiar privileges, and capable of combining together to diminish unexpectedly the quantity of money in circulation. The demand for it, when compared with the supply, will *then*, very probably, be often such as to cause the rate of interest to rise exorbitantly high, and to enable the banks to realise thereby very undue gains, at the expense of the unfortunate borrowers. To avoid *these effects* would indeed be easy, by limiting the rate of interest which the *banks* are permitted to receive. But there is another effect of an injurious character, which, so far from being avoided or diminished in any degree by this measure, will become aggravated in consequence of it. The temptation, I mean, will be greater, on the part of the bank-directors, to borrow money for themselves, or to accommodate their friends with money from the banks, in order to lend it out afterwards to individuals at a higher interest. In this view of the subject, I ought, perhaps, to go farther than to say that I am not in favour of an *entire* repeal of the laws against usury, under our existing system of banking,—and to express my willingness to acquiesce in the continuance of those laws, until the power of regulating the currency of the country, by means of the emission of paper money, shall be taken from the banks, and an unrestricted competition shall also be permitted in the business of lending money.

Where property is insecure, not only will money, as has been stated, be rarely borrowed for the purpose of being employed productively, but, when borrowed (which it may still be to a certain extent) to enable the borrower to fulfil his pecuniary engagements or for purposes of speculation, it is clear that the interest paid for its use will comprehend, as well the insurance against the risk of losing the principal, as the interest properly so called,—in accordance with what was shewn to be the case when the risk of loss arose from the operation of usury laws.

An objection to what has been delivered, concerning the ordinary interest of money, may possibly be founded on the very large profits which are sometimes asserted to be the ordinary profits of the capitalist. While the rate of interest is, in a considerable portion of the United States, so low, on the average, as six per cent. upon the principal loaned, we hear, in the same region, of ten or twelve per cent. profits, and, in some instances of mercantile business, such as that of the apothecary or druggist, of profits even a good deal higher. This discrepance is, however, owing to the occasional, and indeed very general, confounding, under the common designation of profits, of the wages of superintendence and management with the profits of capital properly so called.

I shall conclude what I have to say on the subject of money by noticing an errour, not unfrequently to be met with in respectable quarters. There are those who think that the interest of money depends upon the quantity of it in circulation. If, by thus expressing themselves, they merely meant that, other circumstances being the same, the interest of money would fall temporarily on the quantity of it in circulation being augmented, their meaning would be open to no criticism. Such, however, is not their meaning. They do not refer to any mere temporary changes in the rate of interest, which may be consequent upon a previous alteration in the supply of money. Their notion is that the interest paid for its use,—the ordinary interest,—will be high when the average quantity of money which circulates is comparatively small, and low when that average quantity is comparatively large; and the reason given by them why the interest of money is higher in one country than in another,—in the United States, for instance, than in England, or in England than in Holland, —is that these different countries are not all equally *wealthy;*

which again is the same, with the persons now adverted to, as that money in those countries is not equally abundant. It must be evident to the reader that this reasoning is unsound, as well as inconsistent with the doctrines which have been expounded in the preceding pages. The notion in question, I may add, has probably arisen from an observation of the actual effect of a diminution in the circulating medium in producing a very extraordinary, though temporary rise, in the market rate of interest. And had those who entertain it only been, besides, aware of the fact that just in proportion as the circulating medium is diminished in quantity it will have its value appreciated, and the contrary when its quantity is augmented,—or that it is always, taken as a whole, of the the same precise value,—they would have perceived clearly that the average, ordinary, or as it may be called, agreeably to the analogy of prices, the *natural* interest of money, must necessarily be independent altogether of the quantity of money in circulation.*

* Throughout the discussions in which I have been engaged concerning money and banking, I may remark that I have made no account of one system of managing the currency of a country having any advantage over another in the facilities which it may afford for regulating the domestic or foreign exchanges of a country. And I have not done so, because the best mode of regulating these is for the government, and the institutions created by it, to leave them to be adjusted by the natural and unrestricted competition of the dealers in exchange. The rate of exchange will then be a true index of the state of trade, as well as a correct prognostic of an approaching expansion or contraction of the circulating medium.

BOOK FOURTH.

ON THE PRODUCTIVENESS IN THE SAME DEGREE OF THE DIFFERENT BRANCHES OF INDUSTRY; AND ON THE INTERFERENCE WITH THE NATURAL DISTRIBUTION AMONG THEM OF LABOUR AND CAPITAL.

CHAPTER I.

THE QUESTION OF THE PECULIAR PRODUCTIVENESS OF AGRICULTURE EXAMINED.

The different modes have been mentioned in which governments have interfered, or might be supposed to interfere, with the circulating medium of a country. But this is very far from being the only interference of it with a more natural state of things, which falls under the animadversion of the political economist. Indeed, the great errour of the rulers of mankind has hitherto been, that human happiness is, in a much more considerable degree than it really is, the result of legislative regulation. They have almost entirely overlooked the tendency of society, acted upon continually by the wants and consequent desires of men, to adjust itself naturally in the most advantageous manner; a truth which will be perceived more and more distinctly by the student of political economy, as he advances farther into his subject, and meditates upon it more profoundly.

One of the most remarkable instances,—I might have said *the most* remarkable instance,—of an excessive interference with the order of nature, on the part of governments, is presented to us by their attempts to encourage one branch of industry at the expense of another,—attempts growing out of the notion that the various occupations of men are advantageous to a country in very different degrees, and even, occasionally, that certain occupations, however profitable to the individuals employed, are of no advantage whatever to the community of which they are members. And it will for the most part suffice, for the purpose of shewing the inexpediency of every such encouragement, to exhibit the fallacy of the arguments by which the notion just mentioned has been maintained; for, independently of any *direct* proof of the superior advantages to be derived to a country from the practical establishment of as great a degree of liberty as is possible, in the disposal of the labour and capital of individuals, there is surely no one who will not be ready to acquiesce in the propriety of the natural distribution of these not being disturbed by the interference of government, provided no sufficient reason can be shewn why it *ought* to be thus disturbed.

The first argument whose fallacy I shall here undertake to exhibit is that which attributes to *agriculture* a superiority over every other department of industry, because, as is asserted, agriculture is the only department of industry which is in reality productive. Those who have reasoned in this manner have been, chiefly, the followers of the celebrated Quesnay in France, during the middle and latter portion of the eighteenth century; and they founded upon it the practical recommendation, that the only *tax* imposed, however great might be the pecuniary exigencies of the government, should be a tax upon the land. It was maintained by them, as also by some later advocates of their doctrine, that, while the manufacturer and the merchant were employed in merely *altering* the forms of matter, or in transporting it from one position in space to another, the cultivator of the land was enabled to do something more than this, through the co-operation of the powers of *nature*, which was truly the only producer in the case. After what has been delivered in the foregoing pages of the present work, the absurdity of an exclusive co-operation of nature with man in agriculture will, very probably, be evident to most of my readers. Without any reference, however, to what goes before, the action alone of the expansive force of *steam*, in its numerous applications to the manufacturing arts, as well as to navigation, may be cited as sufficient evidence that nature's bounties are not dispensed to us from so contracted a field. A very little consideration will, indeed, serve to satisfy us that there is no portion of material wealth produced by man without the aid of natural agents extraneous from himself. And this surely could not be imagined to be otherwise, when his very existence would not be for an instant continued, were those agents to become inert or passive around him.

But some of the writers who have held the doctrine of the exclusive productiveness of agriculture have referred for proof of it to the fact that, in this department of industry, not only is the wear and tear of the capital applied continually restored, with the ordinary rate of profits, but a *rent* besides yielded to the landlord; which, it is asserted, is the case neither in manufactures nor commerce. Now if this assertion were true, which it is not universally, it must be obvious to my readers that the doctrine under examination would, nevertheless, not be therefore established. All that we might *possibly* be entitled to conclude is, that the various occupations of men are not *equally* productive of national wealth; and how far *this* may, or may not, be the case, I shall consider directly.

The only mode in which the circumstance of *profits* being yielded to the capitalist in manufactures and commerce, as well as in agriculture, has been attempted to be got over, by those who have attributed an exclusive productiveness to the latter, has been by gratuitously assuming those profits to be so much taken from what should properly be regarded as the compensation for the services of the labourers employed. That there is not the least warrant for this assumption, is sufficiently manifest from the very nature of capital. It being that portion of wealth which is saved from present for future gratification, the motive for such self-denial on the part of the possessors of wealth would be exceedingly enfeebled, and the accumulation of wealth would be effectually checked, were the wages of labour to be at so high a rate as to absorb the whole of what would otherwise be profits. Deprived of the powerful aid of the capitalist, the labourer would then, of course, be left to his own resources; and production could only take place in the rudest manner. The amount of wealth produced would, besides, be comparatively very limited;—which, again, implies that wages would be reduced far below what they are in the existing state of things, when a certain share of what is actually produced is set apart to compensate the possessor of wealth for foregoing the present enjoyment of it, and consenting to employ it productively.

Even though we should grant the correctness of the position that the profits of capital ought to be regarded properly as so much subtracted from the compensation to which the labourer is entitled, it would not follow that manufactures or commerce are wholly unproductive of wealth. Surely the amount of wealth which has been produced is never diminished by being simply transferred from one set of individuals to another. With what consistency, then, can it be maintained that, if the profits of the capitalist were supposed by us, so to speak, to be truly his *legitimate* property, the fact of their existence would be adequate evidence of production having taken place,

—while we must, on the contrary, on the discovery of those profits being the legitimate property of the labourers employed, hold that the occupation in which these very labourers have been engaged is altogether unproductive!

This part of my subject may, however, be now disposed of by remarking that the argument in favour of the exclusive productiveness of agriculture is founded on the supposition of the acceptation of the term *wealth* being restricted to material objects; and of course, it is, *at once and entirely*, set aside by the adoption of the more extended definition of wealth.

There are those who, conceding the productiveness of every department of industry, have yet maintained agriculture to be *more productive* than any other. This notion, too, was founded on the fact, or assumed fact, that the capital applied to the land is the only capital which, besides yielding the ordinary profits to its owner, enables him to pay a rent to the landlord or proprietor of the soil. Now, disregarding the circumstance of rent being occasionally paid in manufactures and commerce, I remark that it would be singular indeed if the existence of rent, which was shewn to be an effect of the ever *diminishing* returns from the land, on the successive application to it of equal portions of capital and labour, could be adduced with propriety as evidence of agriculture being in any especial degree productive. If all the land of a country were suddenly to become equally fertile with that which is at present of the best quality, and be equally favourably situated with respect to a market, no rent would be any where paid for it; while, at the same time, the labour applied to the land would be acknowledged by every one to have become more productive than it was before.

In consequence of rents being paid to a greater extent in agriculture than in either manufactures or commerce,—which rents can only be paid out of the *surplus* remaining, after the ordinary rate of profits has been retained by the capitalist,— it must follow that a greater *value* is, on the whole, actually produced by means of the application of a given capital in the former department of industry than in the other two. This, however, is no reason why a preference should be given, either by individuals or by the legislature, to agriculture; for every additional capital applied to the land will necessarily have to be applied under the most disadvantageous circumstances; and any increase of the rents paid to the landlords which may ensue, on account of more labour and capital being applied to the land than would naturally be the case, will manifestly be so much gained by them at the expense of the producers generally.

It has been shewn that there is no ground for supposing nature to co-operate with man in agriculture alone, thus enabling him to pay a rent to the proprietor of the soil. I now advance a step farther, and assert that no reason can be given why nature should co-operate with man *in a greater degree* in agriculture than in manufactures or commerce. We can, in no case, determine how much of the labour of production is nature's, and how much is man's. Nor is it of any moment that we should; since, if even the determination of the point in question were practicable, and it should be ascertained that the share of the work performed by nature in one case was proportionally more than what it performs in another, the only circumstance which ought to have any influence upon the distribution of the capital and labour of a country,—having a regard to the national welfare, — would be the comparative amount of advantage to be realised by the capitalists individually in different occupations. They will be distributed in the most desirable manner, when this advantage is uniformly the same, that is, when every capitalist is making neither more nor less than the ordinary profits. If a lower rate of profits than this be received in any one branch of industry, it is a manifest indication of a greater amount of production having taken place in it than is required by the comparative wants of the community; and, on the other hand, if more than the ordinary rate of profits be received, it is equally manifest that the wants of the community call for a greater supply of the commodity produced, at the expense of a diminished supply of every thing else.

CHAPTER II.

PRODUCTIVENESS OF COMMERCE—THE COMMERCE OF SPECULATION —DEALERS IN MONEY.

Assuming the productiveness, not only of agriculture, but of every other department of indústry, I have shewn that they are all of them *equally* productive. But some writers,—the Abbé Raynal for instance,—who have attributed the quality of being productive to manufactures as well as to agriculture, have at the same time denied it to commerce, which they defined to be merely the exchange of equivalent commodities. This definition is, evidently, too much restricted. The term commerce is properly applied to the whole series of acts, by means of which the products of the farmer or manufacturer are transported from the places of their production, and distributed among the individuals by whom they are destined to be consumed; and the exchanges which occur of those products are only particular acts in that series. In the actual condition of society, when labour is so much subdivided, these exchanges are absolutely necessary for effecting the distribution, among the consumers, of the wealth produced; but they are certainly not more necessary than are any other acts in the series of which mention has been made. And it is not less absurd to define commerce to consist merely of these exchanges, than it would be to suppose the last, or any other link of a chain, to constitute the whole of the chain, or than it would be, in geometry, to confound any one point of a line with the line itself.

In *direct* proof of the productivenes of commerce, I shall remind my readers that exchangeable value is a criterion of the existence of wealth. Hence we may infer that *every* application of man's labour which contributes to render the exchangeable value, or price,—I mean, of course, natural price,—of any commodity what it actually is, must be necessarily productive of wealth. Now this happens in the case of commerce, just as it happens in that of agriculture, or in that of manufactures. The expense of transporting a commodity from the producers to the consumers of it, and of distributing it among the latter, is quite as much an element of its price, as is any equal expense of producing it while it remains yet in the hands of the former. Besides, on the supposition of commerce being in reality unproductive, no diminished production ought to ensue if all transportation of commodities from place to place were to cease, and all exchanges of them were to be prohibited. But so far from this being the case, it is plain that every individual in the community would be reduced to the necessity of consuming only the identical portion of wealth which he himself produced; and the quantity of it produced would be only a very small fraction of what it now is. The conclusion forces itself upon us, that commerce is a productive department of industry.

But while commerce generally is acknowledged by most persons to be productive of wealth, and as productive of it as is either manufactures or agriculture, we occasionally hear the commerce of *speculation* indiscriminately condemned as a useless application of the labour and capital of the community. This is a mistake. Where no artificial variations are produced by the interference of government, or of the institutions created by it, in the natural rates of the supply and demand of commodities, including money, speculation cannot be carried to excess. In such a state of things, it will serve to *distribute over a certain period* the actual supply of any article in the most advantageous manner, without any counterbalancing public disadvantage. To illustrate my meaning by an example: let the crops of grain in any year have been less abundant than usual. Even though the demand for grain were to continue unaltered, this deficiency in the supply of it will cause its price to rise. But the demand for it will not continue unaltered. As soon as it is surmised that the quantity of grain in the market, or about to be brought into the market, is less than the average supply, an extraordinary demand will be made for it by the speculators. By purchasing at present prices, and selling out, after an interval, at advanced prices, they will expect to make a considerable profit. Some of them will not fail to realise their expectations, by disposing, at the proper season, of the stock of the article which they may have in their possession. Others, however, are frequently losers, instead of gainers, by holding on to it too long. And this is, more especially, apt to be the case where the article in question was purchased a short time after it became notoriously an object of speculation,—on account of the well known tendency of the price of a thing, when it has once from any cause begun to rise, to rise somewhat, and often a good deal, higher than the point at which it will ultimately remain stationary. Now, from this view of the business of speculation, in reference to grain,—and the same is true in reference to any other commodity,—it must be obvious that prices will be rendered higher in the earlier portion of the time during which a diminished supply will necessarily exist, and, of course, lower during the latter portion of it. The *scarcity* will be thus nearly uniformly diffused over the whole time, and will therefore be productive of a less amount of inconvenience.

My readers will easily understand that, if prices were not at once to rise on the occurrence, or expected occurrence, of a considerably diminished supply of any article, and to rise above what they would be but for the interference of the speculators, so much of the article might be consumed, especially if it be a necessary of life, as to cause a very high degree of inconvenience, or even distress, to pervade the community, before the supply could be again renewed.

Just in proportion as the prices of commodities in general are steady, it is plain there will be less room for the occupation of the speculator, and fewer persons will be disposed to embark in it. Where, however, through frequent expansions and contractions of the currency produced by a vicious system of banking, or from any other disturbing cause, the relations which the supply of and the demand for commodities in general bear to the supply of and the demand for money are such as to induce an unnecessary fluctuation of prices, speculation will take place more actively, as well as be carried to a vicious and injurious extent. *Then only* ought it to be condemned and pronounced to be unproductive; exactly as any other branch of business is to be characterised as unproductive only when it is carried on more extensively than the real wants of the community require.

The speculators are not the only class of persons whose occupation has been attempted to be rendered odious, even when they are actually engaged, while promoting their own interests, in conferring upon the community nothing but unmixed good. We occasionally hear the brokers also,—I mean the money brokers,—denounced as a set of men who are enriching themselves at other people's expense. And this is founded on the notion that they contribute, by the additional demand which they make for money, to render it less plentiful than it would otherwise be. That such a notion is at once both superficial and absurd, will appear on the slightest reflection upon the nature of the offices performed by a broker. He is simply a middle-man between the buyers and the sellers. He becomes so, too, on account of the convenience of both these parties being subserved by his intervention. If such were not the case, we may rest assured they would very soon prefer to deal directly with one another.

I may add that the prejudices afloat in society against the dealers in money generally are quite as absurd as those which some people retain against the dealers in flour, or in any other commodity of prime necessity; for money is, indeed, neither more nor less than a commodity of this description.

CHAPTER III.

OF COMMERCE WITH A FOREIGN COUNTRY—DOCTRINE OF THE BALANCE OF TRADE.

Many writers who have gone so far as to admit the general truth of the proposition, that the most advantageous distribution of the capital of a country is when every capitalist is making neither more nor less than the ordinary rate of profits, have denied its application to *foreign* commerce. They argue that one capital only is set in motion or employed in the foreign trade, while there are two employed in the home trade. In the trade, for instance, between New York and New Orleans, one capital is employed in the former, and another in the latter city; but, in that between New York and Liverpool, they maintain that there is only one,—only one *American* capital is of course meant,—that which is employed in Liverpool being an English capital. The fallacy of this objection to foreign commerce will readily appear if we look at the consequences which would follow, were it to be entirely prohibited. Whatever amount of American capital might have been invested in the Liverpool trade will now have to find an investment in the home trade, or in other occupations at home. There will, however, be no creation, but only a transfer, of capital; and the two additional portions of capital which may come to be employed in the home trade will be equal *to only one portion* of what before found employment in the foreign trade. More I need not say in refutation of the argument I am examining.

An argument of considerable plausibility has been urged against the employment of the capital of a country *abroad*,—and, consequently, urged to a certain extent against foreign commerce, and every other occupation having a tendency to induce an exportation of capital,—to wit, that the labour to which the capital employed at home affords occupation is that of the inhabitants of the country, while the labour, on the contrary, to which the capital employed abroad affords occupation, is, generally speaking, of a foreign description. I may remark in reply that, if savings were never made from the wages of labour, there would, obviously, be no sufficient reason, in what has just been said, for any interference with the natural distribution of capital. The *smallest* excess of profits received on that which is employed abroad will furnish the means of a more rapid augmentation of wealth and population, and will thus determine, at a period less or more remote, the actual existence of a greater amount of wealth, and a greater number of inhabitants, than would exist if all the capital of the country had been forcibly directed into domestic channels. Now although savings are in fact, to a certain extent, made from the wages of the labourers, this circumstance is, very probably, more than counterbalanced by the comparatively *high* profits of the portion of capital which is employed in foreign countries. These high profits are not, as some might, at first view, be disposed to think, merely such as, besides an equal return with that to the capital employed at home, is adequate to the greater risk run of the ultimate loss of the capital itself from which they are derived. They will always exceed this amount, because of the great unwillingness which men, in general, feel to separate themselves for any length of time from their property.

But here it may be said that the very circumstance last mentioned affords a strong reason why the employment abroad of a portion of the capital of a country will be apt to have injurious consequences on its prosperity. When a man's property is in another country, and is yielding him a high rate of profit, nothing is more common than, after the lapse of a certain time, to see him take up his residence where it is invested; and the whole amount of his property must then be necessarily regarded as a national loss. On this ground, the interference of the legislature with the disposal of the capital of individuals might perhaps be sometimes justified, were it only sufficiently practicable. To render it practicable, however, nothing short of an entire prohibition of the exportation of commodities from a country to all others would be requisite; for otherwise, in despite of every effort of the government, a man who wishes to transfer his property to another country has only to purchase any one article of commerce, and to export it; or to purchase foreign bills of exchange, the amount of which, when drawn for, can be invested abroad, and, when so invested, may be regarded in the light of a value received for commodities, other than money, previously exported.

In the United States of America, the point which has just been considered is one of no practical moment, in as much as the profits of capital are higher in them than they are almost any where else. Capital is, in consequence, continually flowing to them from other countries; and no inducement is offered, unless under peculiarly advantageous circumstances, to employ it away from home.

I come now to an objection to an unrestrained trade with foreign nations, the discussion of which has occupied no small portion of the attention of the political economists of the last century; and, even at the present day, we hear it occasionally put forth by some among the more zealous advocates of restrictive regulations in respect to commerce. It is this, that only that foreign trade is a beneficial one where the exports exceed the imports in value; occasioning thereby a flow of specie into a country in payment of the excess, or *balance.* Hence the expression "the balance of trade;" this being held to be favourable when the exports are in excess, and unfavourable when the imports are so.

This whole doctrine was founded on the mistaken notion, that the wealth and prosperity of a country depended essentially on the quantity of the precious metals which it possessed; and it, indeed, almost implied the absurdity that those metals alone constituted what should properly be denominated wealth. From this doctrine too, the important consequences were deduced, that government should, in the first place, do every thing in its power to increase the whole amount of exports, and to diminish the whole amount of imports,—and secondly, that it should positively discourage all persons subjected to its control from trading with any foreign country from which a greater value is imported than is exported to it.

If he bear in mind the principles in relation to money which were established in the preceding book, the reader will easily perceive the absurdity of supposing that a country is wealthy because it has a large amount of the precious metals. Those metals constitute only a portion, and by no means the most important portion, of the national wealth; since if the supply of them were to be increased, and the circulating medium proportionally expanded, this could only be effected by the increased exportation, or diminished production, of an equal value of commodities other than gold and silver; while at the same time, as has been fully explained, the value of the circulating medium will continue unaltered, a given portion of it being depreciated in value according as the whole of it has become larger than it was.

But some persons, as I have stated, have not contented themselves with comparing the whole amount of exports with the whole amount of imports, and with inferring the prosperity of a country from an excess, real or supposed, of the former over the latter. Examining the commerce of a country with every other separately, they have pronounced the commerce with that country the exports to which exceed in value the imports from it to be an advantageous commerce, and, on the contrary, the commerce with that the imports from which exceed the value of the commodities exported to it to be a disadvantageous commerce;—and they have, consequently, besides recommending measures calculated to augment the whole amount of exports and at the same time diminish the whole amount of imports (exclusive of money, as the terms exports and imports are commonly used), been disposed, as has also been stated, to discourage all commercial intercourse of the country in question with particular parts of the world. Here there is an *additional* errour implied, viz. that whenever, in the intercourse of one country with another, the exports exceed in value the imports of commodities other than money, specie must necessarily flow from the latter into the former country, for the purpose of paying the *balance*. This position would, indeed, be a correct one on the supposition of the foreign commerce of the two countries being confined entirely to one another, and on this supposition only. In order to make *this* distinctly appear, let us call those countries A and B respectively; and let there be a third C, with which a commerce is carried on by each of the other two. Now it may be conceived that A imports from B more than it exports to it, that B imports from C more than it exports to it, and also that C imports from A more than it exports to it. In this state of the commercial relations of these three countries, A will become indebted to B, B to C, and C to A. To discharge its debt to B, A will, however, not be under a necessity of transmitting specie to that country. The merchants of the country A need only to draw bills of exchange upon their debtors in the country C in favour of their creditors in B; and the equilibrium of their debts and credits may be thus completely restored. It is plain, too, that we may now generalise, and maintain that the circumstance of more commodities, other than money, being imported by one country from another, than are exported by the former to the latter, is no evidence whatever of a *movement* of specie between the two countries. And hence, every objection to the natural course of trade, as that which is the most advantageous to a country, founded on the assumed fact of such a movement of specie, will be perceived to be of no account.

I may observe that, should the trade between A and B be diminished, or be entirely cut off, that of each of them with C, as well as with other countries generally, would, it will be evident, not remain on its former footing; for then, in the case of A, there would be an excess of the whole amount of exports over that of imports, while the contrary of this would take place in that of B. These excesses would only have a temporary existence, and the ordinary relation of exports to imports would soon be re-established by the movement or flow of specie from country to country, as has before been explained.

CHAPTER IV.

THE SUBJECT OF THE BALANCE OF TRADE CONTINUED.

The language in reference to foreign commerce, which has been hitherto employed, has been such as may have appeared to imply an equality, on the average, in the value of the exports from and imports into a country, of commodities other than money. An equality of this nature is certainly possible, but only under a peculiar combination of circumstances. The general law in the case is, that the value of the imports must exceed that of the exports, when both these values are estimated in the country into which the imports, and from which the exports, are made,—and likewise when the value of the former is estimated in the countries whence they are procured, while that of the latter is estimated in the country where they are received.

To shew, in the first place, that such is the general law on the first of the two suppositions which have just been mentioned, I shall set out with assuming all the capital employed in the country to which my remarks shall have relation,—say the United States of America,—to be owned in the country itself; and so, also, in respect to the capital of every description employed in its foreign commerce. Then it will be obvious that the value of the imports must be such as, after replacing that of the exports, will suffice to yield the ordinary profits to all the capital employed in the commerce with foreign countries, including of course, in those profits, the freights, as well as every other expense of transportation. If we, indeed, suppose no more specie to flow from abroad into the country, than from the country in the opposite direction,—a condition of things which is, on the average, very supposable, where the precious metals are, to an adequate extent, the product of the country itself,—the excess of the imports above the exports will evidently be the *measure* of those profits. On the other hand, where the supply of the precious metals is derived in part, or wholly, from abroad, not only bullion, but specie also, will be imported; and the latter in preference to the former, on account of the certificate to its weight and fineness that is impressed upon it. This circumstance may prevent the imports from exceeding the exports as much as they would otherwise do,—exports and imports being here understood in their usual acceptation, as referring to commodities other than money. It may be added that, if a country which derives its supply of gold and silver, in whole or in part, from other countries, should happen to be augmenting more rapidly in population and wealth than the other portions generally of the commercial world, specie would, in consequence, be imported more extensively, and the excess of the ordinary imports above the exports would, on this account too, be lessened.

In the next place, however, let all the capital employed in the country, or in its foreign commerce and navigation, *not* be the property of individuals residing in it. The profits of the capitalists abroad will in this case, of course, have to be exported, or, what amounts to the same thing, an equal value in commodities that would otherwise contribute to swell our imports will be retained abroad, and will again reduce the excess of imports above exports.

Should the capital of a country, tempted by the superior advantages offered for its investment elsewhere, be to a certain extent annually transferred from it to other countries, we would have another reason why the exports will be augmented in value, and why the excess of the imports above them will be still farther diminished, if not made to disappear entirely.

But this, it may be mentioned, is very far from being the

case in the United States. American capital is, no doubt, occasionally, though in a comparatively small amount, employed out of the country: still, speaking in general terms, no one will deny that our capital is continually receiving accessions, and by no means inconsiderable accessions, from the various parts of Europe, and especially from Great Britain. On this account, the excess of our imports above our exports ought to be unusually large.

If the value of the imports be estimated by what they cost in the countries whence they were procured, they will manifestly not so much exceed the value of the exports as when the values of both exports and imports are estimated at home in the same country,—the case already considered. Nevertheless, I think my readers, after the statements above made, can scarcely fail, even here, to assent to the proposition, that the imports will, very generally, exceed the exports in value, in the common acceptation of the terms; and they will, moreover, not be at all surprised to find that such has been the fact in the United States, from the first adoption of the constitution, in 1789, to the present time, when they are told that the value of our imports is estimated by adding 10 or 20 per cent. to their cost in the countries where they are purchased, and when they keep in mind, both the high rate of profits which must be paid from the imports, and the influx of capital which is continually taking place from abroad.

The absurdity of regarding an excess, and sometimes an *impossible* excess, of exports above imports, as the measure of the advantage to be derived by a nation from its foreign commerce, must be too apparent for me to dwell upon it longer. This doctrine indeed, of the balance of trade being favourable to a country when an excess of exports is supposed to exist, however largely it has figured in the writings of the economists, real or pretended, of the last century, may be regarded as at present almost entirely exploded.

CHAPTER V.

ON THE AMOUNT OF THE DUTY UPON A COMMODITY, WHEN IT IS IMPORTED FROM ABROAD, WHICH WILL ADMINISTER ADEQUATE ENCOURAGEMENT TO THE DOMESTIC PRODUCERS.

We now approach the discussion of a subject which has attracted in no small degree the attention of the political philosophers and statesmen of modern times, and which, in our own country, has been the occasion of much excitement and agitation in the community at large. I allude to what is familiarly styled with us "the tariff question,"—or, in other words, to the expediency, or inexpediency, of prohibiting the importation into a country from abroad of certain commodities, with the object in view of establishing the production of the like commodities at home. *Prohibiting* is here the proper word; for although the advocates of this system of interference with the natural order of things have, in most cases, preferred the imposing of a tax or *duty* on the importation of such commodities as are of the same description with those which they are desirous of being produced at home, to the absolute prohibition of importing them from other countries, they have yet insisted upon the duties imposed being sufficiently high to operate prohibitorily. And, according to their notions of expediency, they have done right to insist upon this; as I shall proceed to shew before actually entering on the proposed discussion.

Let us suppose a duty of *ten* per cent. to be imposed upon the value of any article of foreign growth or manufacture, when imported into the United States; and let us also suppose the duty to be paid, in the first instance, by the importing merchant, at the time he receives the article. The quantity of it imported will not be as great as before; since, in that case, in as much as both the supply of, and the demand for it, would remain unaltered, its price would still be what it was previous to the imposition of the duty; and, the merchant would then be obliged to take from his profits,—and, where these were not at a rate high enough to be equal in amount to the duty to be paid, he would be obliged to take from his capital, after having exhausted his profits,—in order to make the payment required. It is evident that a portion of the capital employed in the importation of the article in question will be transferred to other employments; thus diminishing the supply of it in a degree sufficient to cause its price to be ten per cent. higher than it was before, when it will be just sufficient to enable the capital of the merchant to yield him the ordinary profits. If his payment of the duty, and the sale by him of the article imported, be not contemporaneous, but the latter occur at a certain interval after the former, it will be requisite for its price to exceed that just mentioned, by an amount equivalent to the profits, for the intervening time, upon the duty which he advances. Assuming however, for the sake of simplicity, that the payment of the duty on the imported article, and the sale of it, take place at the same time, it will follow that the burthen of the duty is transferred by the merchant who imports it from his shoulders to those of his customers, the retail dealers. And in the very same manner as this transfer of the duty has been shewn to be effected, may it be shewn to be transferred from the retailers to the consumers.

The whole supply of the commodity upon which the duty is levied has been supposed to be still procured from abroad, in despite of the augmentation of its price to the consumers; a supposition, again, implying that it is impossible for it to be produced in the country itself except at a cost greater than that at which it can be procured from abroad, including in the latter cost the amount of the duty.

Suppose now the commodity taxed to be broadcloth of a

particular quality; say cloth which, if allowed to be imported freely, that is without any obstruction on the part of the government, would sell for five dollars the yard. A duty of ten per cent. upon this value will cause it to rise to five and a half dollars; and if the cost of producing the cloth in the country would be six dollars, the supply of it will, it must be manifest, come wholly from other parts of the world. This, too, would be a *continued* state of things, while the duty is increased from ten up to any amount short of *twenty* per cent.

If we suppose the duty to exceed the last mentioned per centage, and to amount say to *thirty* per cent. on the value of the cloth which may be imported, the price of it would rise to six dollars and a half; and as cloth of the same quality is, by hypothesis, produceable at home for six dollars only, the foreign article will be no longer able to compete with the domestic manufacture. While the former will, in consequence, cease to be imported, the latter, by means of the *encouragement* or *protection* afforded to it by the government in the imposition of the duty, will be established as a regular branch of industry. So, of course, if the duty be other than thirty per cent., provided it be more than the rate, viz. twenty per cent., which would cause the domestic and the foreign article to sell at exactly the same price.

But, in the next place, let us inquire what the effect of the duty would be, in the case under consideration, were it to be neither more nor less than just twenty per cent. Here it might perhaps seem, at first view, that one-half of the supply of the article in question would be furnished by the American manufacturer, and the other half by the foreign. On farther reflection however, the reader will perceive that such an equal division is scarcely practicable, and that, if it were so, it could subsist only for a very short period. It is evident that when the duty of twenty per cent. is first imposed, the investments of capital at home and abroad being of a nature to give the foreign producer the possession of the American market, no sufficient motive exists for the transfer of American capital with a view to the production of the article taxed. Any attempt on the part of our capitalists to engage in its production, under these circumstances, must necessarily be followed by an overstocking of the market and consequent lowering of prices,—which lowering of prices must render such an attempt an unprofitable one. On the other hand, should a higher duty than twenty per cent.,—a duty which had been the means of excluding the foreign article, and establishing the manufacture of American broadcloth,—be *reduced* to that amount; the American producer being in possession of the market, no sufficient motive would be presented to capitalists abroad for augmenting their production of broadcloth, and for thus interfering with him.

Speaking generally therefore, we may infer that to insure the production in the country of the article mentioned, and the same is manifestly true of any other article whatever, it will be necessary to impose a duty on the importation of it *greater* than the excess of the cost of producing it at home over the price at which it can be sold on being imported from abroad, that is, as I have said, to impose a duty the proper effect of which is prohibitory.

Notwithstanding, however, the statement which has just been made, if the duty on the imported article does not *much* exceed the excess of the cost of producing it at home over the cost of producing it abroad, it will occasionally happen that it will be profitable to import it; and the domestic producers will not be so protected as absolutely to exclude all foreign competition. This will be owing to the occasional fluctuations in the local value of money; leading, as those fluctuations in value have been shewn to lead, to a variable amount of importations.

I may here remark, it is only in the way just mentioned that a duty, imposed on the importation into a country of any commodity, can operate *alternately* as a means of revenue to the government, and as a means of encouraging its production at home. No duty can, *at one and the same time*, produce both these effects. When it encourages the domestic production of a commodity, it will bring no revenue into the public treasury; and when it brings a revenue into the public treasury, it will not serve to encourage the domestic production of the commodity.*

CHAPTER VI.

DISCUSSION OF THE "TARIFF QUESTION."

THERE are many individuals in our own country who are ready to assent to the general inexpediency of the interference of governments with the natural distribution of capital and labour, and who would strenuously resist any attempt to disturb the perfect freedom of trade as at present subsisting between the different portions of the *Union*, who, nevertheless, entertain the notion, that the commerce between different *nations* cannot be always considered as on the most advantageous footing when it is left wholly unrestricted; and who attempt to justify the imposition of very high duties on the importation of foreign goods by the fact of the rate of wages being lower in Great Britain than among ourselves. They insist upon the propriety of thus protecting the American pro-

* Throughout this chapter, I have supposed the commodities concerned to be produced under circumstances of equal advantage or disadvantage. Should this not be the case, it is very possible that, with a given amount of duty, those which are produced under the more advantageous circumstances in the country itself might exclude from the home market such as are produced abroad under the less disadvantageous circumstances.

ducer from the competition of the *paupers* of Europe. Let us now inquire into the correctness, or incorrectness, of this doctrine.

My readers will perceive that it erroneously implies that mere lowness of wages is the cause of low prices. It will be recollected by them that, in any existing state of the arts, prices will depend as well upon the rate of profits as upon that of wages. If British goods can be imported into the country cheaper than goods of a similar description can be produced in it, this will not be owing simply to the circumstance of wages in Great Britain being lower than in the United States, but to that of wages and profits, *taken together*, being as low as they in reality are in the first mentioned country, and as high as they in reality are in the one last mentioned. Again, I shewed in my first book that, in any existing state of the arts, or, what amounts to the same thing, of the productive power in a nation, if wages were to fall, profits must necessarily rise,—and that, in consequence, such commodities as were the products chiefly of fixed capital, instead of falling in price as wages fall, would have their prices greater than before. Hence too, it follows, —what has been before mentioned,—that, if it were possible at once to *raise* the wages of the English labourer to a level with those of the labourers in America, it might very well happen that the manufacturers of our own country would be at a comparatively greater disadvantage in respect to foreign competition than they are at present.

But waiving all considerations of the kind which has just been stated, I think it will not be difficult to convince the reader that the low rate of wages abroad, *other circumstances remaining every where the same*, is an advantage to us instead of a disadvantage. A low rate of wages will *then* render the cost of producing commodities of all descriptions, and therefore their prices, correspondently low; and a given quantity of them may be procured from abroad in exchange for a less amount of our own products, than when prices were higher. This saving in the expenditure necessary for obtaining the imports into the country is, it is plain, a clear national gain. The imports may very possibly, on account of the increased demand for them at a lower price, be greater than they would otherwise be; but such an effect cannot take place without a similar augmentation of the amount of exports. And a transfer, to a certain extent, of American capital may be required on a fall of wages abroad, in order that it may come to be invested most profitably. Whether, however, such a transfer be large or small, or do not occur at all, the command, on the average, of each individual of the community over the necessaries and luxuries of life will have been evidently enlarged.

Here the advocates for rectrictions upon the foreign commerce of the country offer to us an argument which they sometimes seem to regard as conclusive in their favour. They put the extreme case, that *all things* can be produced cheaper abroad than at home; and they ask if, in such circumstances as these, the friends of a free trade among nations would still insist upon no protection being afforded by the government to the home-producers. I answer for the latter in the affirmative, —on the ground that, although the importation of every species of commodity from abroad cheaper than it can be produced at home is a supposable state of things, it is altogether out of the question to suppose it to have more than a momentary duration. The extraordinary importations, which would flow from every quarter into the country, would have to be paid for exclusively in money; and as the circulating medium is thus diminished in quantity, a given portion of it would be enhanced in value, or prices generally would fall. It is evident, too, that they would continue to fall until no sufficient motive would exist for sending the money of the country abroad. During the fall of prices, first one commodity, and then another, and another, would cease to be imported; while, on the other hand, one commodity after another would begin to be exported.

Moreover, when the value of money was again every where equalised, and it was no longer the subject of exportation, the exports and imports will have the ordinary relation to each other,—a relation explained in a preceding chapter.

The diminution of the circulating medium will have been fully compensated for, by the commodities imported in exchange for the money which has been transmitted to other parts of the world. Indeed, those commodities, as in every other instance of the importation of commodities in exchange for a portion of the medium of circulation, are a clear gain to the country, because of the augmenting in value of a given portion of that medium exactly in proportion as the whole of it is reduced in quantity.

CHAPTER VII.

THE SUBJECT CONTINUED.

My argument against a "protecting tariff" has thus far proceeded on the supposition of the previous existence of an entire freedom of trade among the different nations of the earth; which freedom it is proposed, for the first time, to disturb. I will now take another step in advance, by supposing the condition of free trade to have been already disturbed by some one nation,—Great Britain for example. The question then presenting itself for solution is, whether all other nations would not best consult their interests by countervailing the restrictions which have been imposed upon their commerce, by means of the imposition of similar restrictions on British commerce. Or to bring the manner home to ourselves, the question may be put in the following form:—

should Great Britain refuse to receive into her ports American cotton and tobacco, would it be our true policy to retaliate upon her, by refusing to receive her hardware and woollens?

A reply to this question needs not to be long sought after. For the government of the United States to act on the principle suggested, would be to say to that of Great Britain,—by your legislation you have injured your own country, and you have at the same time injured the people of America; therefore, by way of helping the matter, we resolve upon inflicting a similar injury, absurd and ridiculous as this procedure may seem, upon both you and ourselves.

That the foreign government is guilty of an injury to its own subjects, is sufficiently evident from what has been already delivered in the present book. By refusing to receive our cotton and tobacco, the consumers of these articles will be obliged to pay a higher price for them, than they would otherwise have to do. They will also consume less of them than they formerly did; and at least in reference to the article last-mentioned, which is not a necessary, but a mere luxury of life, many who would have been consumers of it, will not consume it at all. Englishmen, for these reasons, will possess a diminished command over the necessaries and luxuries of life; or, in other words, the wealth of Great Britain will have been diminished. And that a like effect will be produced on the wealth of the United States, will follow from the principle previously established, that the imports into a country, and the exports from it, will always bear to each other a certain proportion, so that the exports cannot undergo a diminution without the imports likewise becoming less than they have hitherto been. Until the imports of British goods are reduced to the proper amount, the excess of them will be paid for in money. Their prices abroad will consequently rise; and they will, moreover, *continue* at a higher rate. Not only *then*, will those of the inhabitants of America, who are not altogether prevented from consuming foreign goods, consume them to a less extent than before, but to consume them will require a greater expenditure on their part. All this, too, is identical with saying that a diminution of American wealth will have taken place.

It is scarcely necessary for me to add that the very same series of effects which I have just traced, as consequent upon a duty imposed in Great Britain on certain of the products of the United States,—effects injurious to both countries,—will occur when a duty is imposed in America on the importation of British goods, only beginning in a different quarter.

But let us, in the next place, suppose the extreme case of all foreign countries refusing to receive any thing from the United States, excepting gold and silver, in exchange for the commodities imported from them. It may be asked, whether it would, notwithstanding, be then proper to import as before from abroad, and to subject our country, in consequence, to being drained of its specie. I observe, in reply, that the foregoing argument will, on reflexion, be perceived by the reader to be applicable to every possible case, without exception. He cannot, too, but be now aware that to suppose a country to part with *all* its specie is an absurdity. According as specie flows from it, in exchange for the commodities imported, the prices of things will be falling; and the imports will diminish in quantity, until, at length, it will become unprofitable to import any thing whatever.

Universally, therefore, the amount of the imports will determine that of the exports; so that no interference of the government will be requisite to protect the country from an entire loss of its specie. And it has been shewn that a *diminution* of its specie is a matter of no permanent moment.

In despite, however, of the above argument,—irrefutable argument I may surely venture to call it,—in favour of the system of free trade as opposed to that of restriction, we hear it continually asserted that, while the former system is an untried one, excepting perhaps in one or two instances on a very limited scale, the latter has every where been accompanied by an amount of prosperity altogether too great to be made the subject of legislative experiment. Here I might reply by a denial of the alleged prosperity; or, what is equivalent to such a denial, I might point the attention of my readers to the great amount of misery hitherto exhibited by every community of individuals, whatever may have been the constitution of government under which they have lived. Even in the most prosperous communities, the wealthy have been few and the poor many. But granting, for the sake of argument, that prosperity to a certain extent has actually accompanied the restrictions which governments have imposed upon commerce, it would be strikingly illogical on the part of any one who is aware of the multitude of causes by whose combined action the condition of mankind is determined to be what it in reality is, to magnify one cause alone in such a degree as to throw every other into the shade. The utmost we would be justified in inferring from the premises, is a *presumption* in favour of things as they are,—a presumption putting the burthen of proof on the party who may at any time propose the introduction of any changes in the policy of a country. This burthen the advocates of free trade have evinced no unwillingness to bear. They have presented, for the consideration and conviction of their opponents, the argument which I have characterised as irrefutable, and to refute which no *direct* attempt has in fact, to my knowledge, ever been made.

The restrictive policy of Great Britain, when viewed in connexion with the degree of prosperity to which she has attained, is what especially has prevented very many individuals from being adequately impressed by the argument in question. But a suspicion, at least, might have crossed their minds that the prosperity just mentioned existed *notwithstanding* the policy pursued in respect to foreign commerce, and not in consequence of it, had they attended to the cases of some other countries distinguished for their comparative prosperity, such as Holland or Switzerland, which afford to us instances of a near approach to the system of free trade.

It may be remarked besides, that, when improvements in any of the arts of life are first promulgated to the world by their inventors, no one whose opinion is entitled to the slightest consideration is found to condemn them *a priori*, on the ground of the danger and inexpediency of interfering with the existing condition of things. Any opposition to their being adopted proceeds invariably on the assumption of their not having as yet been proved to be real improvements. Surely then, no person endowed with the faculty of reason should systematically shut his eyes in the case under examination, to the *demonstrations* of the political economist, and undertake to encounter these simply by the cry of theory! theory! thereby implying that all experience is opposed to them; when the case under examination is one perfectly analogous to that of an improvement in the arts,—in reference, that is, to the effects upon the progress of national wealth,—as the reader will recollect it was stated to be in a previous part of the present work. In both cases alike the labour of the community is rendered more productive than it was before.

CHAPTER VIII.

THE SAME SUBJECT CONTINUED.

Were the restrictionists to content themselves with confounding, in the manner that has been explained, mere casual coincidence in time and place with the relation of cause and effect, it would be tantamount with an acknowledgment on their part of the weakness of the position assumed by them.

But besides being guilty of this not very unusual fallacy in logic, they point triumphantly to the branches of industry which have been actually created, in more than one country, by the fostering hand of government, and to the numbers of the people for whom employment has been thus provided. They forget that it is not in the power of the government of a country, by any legislative act, to command capital into existence. All that can be accomplished by such means, in respect to capital, is to cause its transfer from one employment to another; and if new branches of industry be perceived to spring up, on account of the protection or encouragement afforded them by the imposition of duties on the importation from abroad of goods of a particular description, we may rest assured that the quantity of capital which is employed in all the various branches of industry, taken together, will have remained unaltered. The only point, indeed, really at issue between the advocates of a free trade among nations and their opponents, is whether a certain portion of the capital, and therefore labour, of the country, shall be engaged in producing those commodities which are ordinarily exported in exchange for the commodities imported from other countries, or whether it shall be engaged in directly producing these last; and this necessarily at a greater cost than they could be procured from abroad.

The case of Great Britain, as has already been mentioned, is very frequently referred to, for the purpose of illustrating the beneficial effects of the legislative encouragement of particular branches of industry. For example, in the reign of Edward the Third, the woollen manufacture, which subsequently became so extensive a source of British wealth, was established through the instrumentality of such encouragement. And there is scarcely any other of the staple manufactures of Great Britain which does not owe its origin to the interference of the government in its behalf. Although capital, in all these instances, was merely transferred from one employment to another and less profitable one, yet I am disposed to concede that the encouragement bestowed upon manufactures in a European country some centuries ago, when the community consisted only of the two classes of the nobility and of their retainers or vassals, had, in a certain degree, a beneficial tendency. It contributed, with other causes, to the formation, at that period, of an intelligent middling class, so essential for the attainment by a people of even the smallest degree of political liberty, as well as for maintaining and extending this after it has been once attained. There is more than one country, in our own day too, in which it might perhaps, for similar reasons, be expedient to depart from the course prescribed by the general principles of political economy. In the United States of America, however, the liberal constitution of the government, together with the character of the people generally, furnish certainly not the shadow of a pretence for the adoption of any such measure.

But there are some persons who, while they seem to be aware that the interference of the government, in behalf of a particular branch of industry, merely occasions a different distribution of the capital of a country, nevertheless maintain that what is called the natural distribution of it is the most advantageous one, only on the supposition of the degree of acquired skill in the various arts of life being the same among every people,—a supposition which, I need not say, cannot be admitted, when, in one country, a certain branch of industry has been long established, and at the same time, in another, it has not as yet been introduced. The labourers of the latter country must, in respect to the branch of industry in question, be evidently less productive than the labourers of the former; and capital will, for this reason, not be invested in it. Under these circumstances, the propriety is urged of *temporarily* protecting every commodity from foreign competition which there is good reason to suppose can be produced as cheaply at home as abroad, if only the ordinary degree of skill be once acquired by the workmen of the country. Any sacrifice of national wealth which such a protection as this would imply, during the period of its existence, it is asserted would be more than compensated by the ultimately greater productiveness of labour, in consequence, to ensue.

In opposition to the protection or encouragement here recommended, it may be observed that a practical difficulty will, in most cases, subsist in determining whether or not a commodity can be produced as cheaply at home as abroad; that is, before the experiment is actually made of its production at home under the most favourable circumstances of acquired skill,—and that if the matter be left to the discretion of the legislature, they will be apt, not unfrequently, to discover good reasons, for imposing one duty after another on commodities imported, in the mere urgency of interested and influential individuals, or in other considerations of an equally objectionable character.

That the legislative encouragement of certain branches of industry is very often of advantage *to some particular section of country* will not be denied by the most zealous advocate of the doctrine of free trade. But every local advantage, which may result from the interference of the government with the natural distribution of capital and labour, must necessarily be at the expense of the country at large. Capital will not only be transferred from one employment to another, but likewise from one part of the country to another; or, which is the same thing, it will be invested, in consequence of the action of the government, where it would not have been naturally invested. If, for example, the tariff regulations of the United States have benefited Rhode Island and some other portions of New England, the Union, taken as a whole, has administered the benefit. It would, moreover, have been well had the loss and gain here balanced each other. But since the natural distribution of the capital and labour of the community is the most advantageous distribution of them, it follows that the loss must have been more than equivalent to the gain.

Besides the augmented investments of capital in a particular section of a country, we often hear the increased value of land in it cited as evidence of a creation of wealth, resulting from the restrictions imposed upon foreign commerce; and I mean here, either the increased value of the land on which no additional capital has been applied, or its increase in value beyond what would be determined by the ordinary profits of the additional capital which may have been applied to its cultivation. A rise like this in the value of the land is a consequence of its having become more favourably situated in respect to a market for its produce, by means of the denser population now congregated in its vicinity. In as much, however, as the wealth, and therefore the population of the country, as a whole, will not be as great as it would be on the system of free trade, the rise of value of which I am speaking, will have been accompanied by more than a corresponding fall of value elsewhere.

It has been stated that there is no advocate of a free trade among nations who will not be ready to admit the possibility of a particular section of a country profiting by those very restrictions on the freedom of trade which are injurious to the country, regarded as a whole. Some may, however, be disposed to argue that, because the whole capital of a country is, in such a condition of things, less profitably invested, or, in other words, because the rate of profits is not as great as it would otherwise have been, capital and wealth, and therefore population also, will not increase as rapidly; and a period must sooner or later arrive, when every portion of an extensive country, whatever peculiar adaptations it may possess for the occupations artificially called into existence, will be less wealthy and less populous than it would then be if things had been left to take their natural course, undisturbed by the action of the government. All this is unquestionably true. Nevertheless, those adaptations may, in certain cases, be so extraordinary as to cause the anticipated period to be considerably postponed, and even occasionally postponed to such an extent as to justify us, for all practical purposes, in overlooking its advent altogether. A few localities in the portion of the United States situated north of the Potomac river were placed by our tariff laws, there can be no doubt, in the predicament just described.

But it would be going a great deal too far to maintain, as others have done, that, notwithstanding the disadvantages to which the country, considered as a whole, has been subjected by the action of those laws, the southern states were the only sufferers in the case, and that the North was a *gainer*, although at the expense of the South. And I do not hesitate to say that the reader will, in proportion as he reflects on the subject, and especially on the difficulty of transferring capital from the southern to the northern states, in order thereby to realise a higher profit, be *more and more* satisfied of the latter having been losers by the tariff system as well as the former, though not in an equal degree.

We often hear of the great *resources* of our country, which, it is asserted, require to be developed by means of protective duties. The iron, for example, of Pennsylvania, in so far as it is rendered, so to speak, available by the exclusion of foreign iron, is supposed to become emphatically a source of wealth to the country; while, had the foreign article not been excluded, it would have remained in the bowels of the earth, a voluntary and gratuitous sacrifice of national wealth. I need scarcely observe that all this is inconsistent with the principles which have been already explained. If the iron and other materials of human industry, that are furnished to us by the hand of nature, cannot be wrought into the state required by the consumer at a cost equal to, or less than, that at which the finished article can be imported from abroad, they are in reality of no present value or importance. Is it *then* a matter of no consequence, it may be asked, whether a country is possessed or not of mines or beds of the different metallic ores, or, in general, of what is commonly designated as "natural riches?" I reply that they are, on the supposition made, a desirable possession, in reference to the *future*; and this simply because of the possible exhaustion, in process of time, of the more economical sources of supply,—or because of the possibility of their being rendered in the progress of the arts, on account of the peculiar circumstances under which they are found,—circumstances at present of no importance,—the means of a more economical supply than is furnished to us from other sources.

CHAPTER IX.

THE SAME SUBJECT CONTINUED.

When a protective duty is repealed, the branch of industry which was protected by it can, of course, no longer be carried on advantageously. It will no longer yield the capitalist the ordinary rate of profits; and he will, therefore, transfer his capital to other employments. Though the amount of the duty had been comparatively inconsiderable, his interests will, in most cases, have been affected injuriously by its repeal, owing to the impracticability of transferring his capital from one employment to another and dissimilar one, without sacrificing the more fixed portion of it. Had the duty been a high one, he might even be impoverished by the protection which it afforded him being suddenly withdrawn. And not the capitalist only, but the labourers also, who are in his employ, are necessarily subjected to loss, and frequently to much distress, by a repeal of protective duties. They find at least an equal difficulty in transferring their labour from occupation to occupation, as do their employers in the transfer of their capital; and besides, the transfer of this capital, implying, as it does, the conversion to a certain extent of circulating into fixed capital, cannot fail to deteriorate for a time the condition of the labourers generally, by diminishing the amount of their wages. Again, if extraordinary facilities, by the removal of the duties imposed, be *suddenly* afforded to the importing of commodities from abroad, a flow of specie will take place from the country in question to all others, in the manner previously explained; which, in its turn, will lead to a sudden contraction of the circulating medium, and to all the evils accompanying every such contraction.

On the contrary, when protective duties are first exacted, no corresponding inconvenience or distress is apparent, especially in a country where, as in the United States, most of the commodities exported are produced in very considerable quantities. While the necessity of paying the duties will induce a diminished importation by the merchants of commodities from abroad, the exports, it is true, will also undergo a proportional diminution; but this will not, it must be obvious, take place as suddenly as that of the imports. There will be some time during which the changes before described, as intervening between the diminution of the imports and the consequent diminution of the exports, will occur; which interval of time will have the effect, in only a comparatively slight degree however, of concealing from our view the injurious results. Where, too, the exports diminished are chiefly of such commodities as are extensively produced in the country,—cotton, flour, or tobacco, for example,—the inconvenience incurred will be so diffused as not to be felt as injuriously as it would otherwise be, and, on this account, not to proclaim itself so unequivocally to the observer. Moreover, when the duties under consideration are first exacted, a flow of specie into the country will result from the imports becoming less than before; and the circulating medium will, for a time, be *expanded*, instead of contracted, as it would be if those duties were to be repealed.

There are many individuals, of sufficient sagacity in other respects, who, in place of realising to their full extent the evils of a sudden change in the existing system of things, even though it be in a right direction, and endeavouring to mitigate those evils by passing gradually, instead of suddenly, from the system of restriction to that of free trade, attribute the evils in question to the latter system, and denounce it accordingly, as calculated, more than any other device which its enemies could invent, to be ruinous to the country into which it is introduced. Without doubt, every change of the kind now under consideration should be of a gradual nature, not only that time may be allowed for the transfers of capital and labour to be effected, but likewise, I may add, in order to take away from such individuals as those above alluded to, as well as from some of the mere cavillers against the conclusions of the political economist, the appearance of an argument against them, as being contradicted by practice; however beautiful, or even correct *in theory* they sometimes, very strangely, admit them to be.

Very little needs be said concerning the argument against the abolition of restrictions upon commerce, founded on the the supposed rights of the individuals who have invested their capital and labour in occupations which owe their existence to such restrictions,—or concerning the obligation which the government of a country is under to protect those rights, by maintaining undisturbed all existing investments. If this were to be conceded, we ought, in order to maintain our consistency, also insist upon the interposition of the government, not to encourage the introduction of improvements in the arts, as it is in the habit, in most civilised countries, of doing, by the granting to inventors certain exclusive privileges, but to check, to the full extent of their power, the career of improvement;

for it is plain that nothing of the sort can possibly occur without less or more of injury to some portion of the labour and capital of the community. On this view of the subject too, steamboats should never have been permittted to supersede the various other sorts of craft which in times past used to navigate our rivers; nor should the proprietors of turnpike stock, or of horses and wagons, have been subjected to any inconvenience or loss, by the construction, in so many different directions, of canals and rail roads. It ought always, indeed, to be borne in mind that the removal of all such restrictions on man's liberty, as have heretofore prevented the full exercise of his productive powers, is perfectly analogous in its effects to the inventing of more efficient machinery, or the discovery of new and more advantageous processes in the arts. And the obligations of the government are the same precisely in the one case as in the other.

I must not forget an argument which has, not unfrequently, been urged in favour of the legislative encouragement of different kinds of manufactures in the United States; the argument, to wit, that their introduction into the country gives employment to a considerable number of women and children, who would otherwise be idle,—and that the products of their industry are, on this account, to be regarded as a clear national gain. This argument may be met by once more stating the fact, that, when a government undertakes to encourage any particular branch of industry, it does not create an additional amount of capital, but only causes a certain portion of the capital already existing to be transferred from one employment to another,—as well as by tracing the consequences flowing from this fact. Since the whole amount of capital continues unaltered, and, agreeably to what has been already shewn, is employed less productively than it was before, it is absolutely impossible that the circumstance of a number of the women and children of the country being provided with occupation by the manufacturers should in any way promote the progress of national wealth. We may even pronounce the labour of these women and children to be a positive evil to society, and also to themselves, because the whole labour applied under the system of encouragement is less productive than the whole labour applied before the adoption of that system.

But as the argument, now under examination, has occasionally been very strenuously insisted on by the advocates among us of a high tariff of duties, I will present the refutation of it in another point of view. So long as the same amount of capital exists in the country, so long will the portion of it consisting of wages continue unaltered; that is, if we assume wages in every employment to bear the same proportion to the whole amount of capital. On this supposition, the wages paid to any class of persons, who were heretofore unemployed, will have to be taken from the wages of those who were heretofore the only labourers. Hence, in the case before us, even if we suppose the *men* out of a given population to labour as much as they did, what they receive for their labour will have been diminished by the amount handed over to the women and children. And if a refuge be sought from the consequence just deduced, of the diminution of the wages of men's labour, by gratuitously supposing the men not to work as much as they did before, very little will have been gained in support of the argument urged. Few persons will be disposed to admit the mere substitution, in any degree, of the labour of women and children for that of the adult male population to be productive of a national gain. But the supposition which I have made,—that the wages of labour bear the same proportion in every employment to the whole capital applied,—is incorrect. In some employments this proportion is a very considerable one; in others, the case is the reverse. Since, however, any diversity of the kind furnishes no inducement, as has been proved, why we should prefer any one branch of industry to another, and why the distribution of the capital of a country shall become different from what it was, we may, for our present purposes, manifestly reason as if the supposition made were strictly true.

CHAPTER X.

EFFECTS OF BOUNTIES—MODIFICATIONS OF THE SYSTEM OF FREE TRADE.

HITHERTO I have been treating of the effects of duties imposed on the importation of commodities from abroad, as if such duties were the only means of encouraging the domestic production of the like commodities. But the fact is otherwise. The encouragement required may be administered by the granting of a *bounty* to the domestic producer; that is, by *directly* taxing the community at large for his benefit. In as much as his profits cannot eventually be more than the ordinary profits received in other occupations generally, it is evident that the bounty which is of an amount just sufficient to enable him to realise those profits will be a national loss, without any compensating gain; or, in other words, a bounty of this description will have precisely the same ultimate effect as a duty to an equal amount on the foreign commodity imported.

The nature and operation of a bounty being once properly understood, there is no one who will hesitate to put aside without any farther discussion every objection to the system of free trade, in reference to the United States, which is founded on the supposed expediency of countervailing the effects of a bounty, granted to certain producers by the government of Great Britain, or any other foreign government,

—or who will refuse to apply to the case of the natural distribution of labour and capital being disturbed by the granting of bounties, all that has been delivered in the preceding chapters of the present book concerning the disturbances of the natural order of things by the imposition of duties.

It may be remarked that, notwithstanding the almost obvious analogy just pointed out between bounties and duties, many persons among us, who are not backward in expressing their opposition to a system of bounties for the encouragement of American manufactures, are yet earnest advocates for encouraging them by a high tariff of duties. The national detriment is comparatively easy to be perceived in the former case. In the latter, the effect produced taking place more indirectly, the judgment of the parties adverted to is more apt to be imposed upon by the superficial notions on the subject almost every where to be met with.

Every argument in favour of a protecting tariff which I deem to be unsound, and which at the same time has some appearance of plausibiltiy, has been passed over in review; and I shall now proceed to a statement of some reasons why I conceive a modification of the general principle of free trade is sometimes admissible to a certain extent.

Most of these are founded on the expediency of guarding against the "evils of change,"—an expediency which has been already adverted to. The chief source too, of such evils, is a frequent transition from a state of peace to a state of war, or, vice versâ, from a state of war to a state of peace, and especially the latter. As an illustration, take the case of our own country; and let us look at the effects which ensued in respect to the distribution of capital, on the declaration of war in 1812 against Great Britain, and again on the return of peace in 1815. Previous to the first mentioned event, the legislative encouragement of American manufactures was, as every one knows, comparatively small; and it was found more profitable to procure most manufactured articles from abroad in exchange for the agricultural products of the country, rather than undertake to produce them at home. But the war, by cutting off to a considerable extent the commerce with foreign nations, altered the condition of things very materially. This natural effect too, of a state of war, was aggravated, in the instance under consideration, by the overwhelming power of our enemy on the ocean, as well as by the doubling of the duties on imports, for the purpose of revenue, which then took place. Manufactures, thus powerfully encouraged, sprang into existence in the northern and middle states, where, for various reasons, the most advantageous situations for them existed. Now, on the return of peace, and the consequent repeal of the double duties, there was necessarily a reaction. Much of the capital and labour which had been invested in manufactures was transferred to other, and, at the time, more profitable employments,—a transfer, implying, of course, a considerable abandonment or loss of capital, together with great inconvenience and distress among both the capitalists and the labourers who were thrown out of their employ, and who could not readily adapt themselves to occupations having often little or no analogy with those to which they had been accustomed.

There was another circumstance which, in a very great degree, augmented the sufferings of the community in general, at the period referred to. I mean the sudden enhancement of the value of money resulting from the extraordinary importation of commodities other than money from abroad, unaccompanied by a corresponding augmentation of the amount of exports. Why a change of this description in the value of money should be productive of evil, needs not to be here repeated. It has been sufficiently explained in the preceding book. The only point now calling for remark is the *fact*, that the imports into the country, at the peace, were augmented in a greater proportion than were the exports from it. This was owing, in my opinion, to two distinct causes. First, the ordinary exports from the United States were, perhaps, more indispensable to foreign countries, Great Britain particularly, than our imports from them were to us. It happened, therefore, very naturally, that those countries, on the interruption of their commercial intercourse with us, made new investments of capital, even to a greater extent than was done by ourselves, in order that they might be supplied with what they most wanted : such new investments, also, they were not, by any means, as willing to disturb as we were. And secondly, for several years previous to the commencement of the war, and in a measure during that period, British manufactures had been excluded from the continent of Europe. They accumulated, in consequence, in the hands of the manufacturers at home; who, rather than undergo the inconvenience of transferring their capitals to other employments, continued to manufacture, in anticipation of the *vent* for their products which a peace must sooner or later open to them. Accordingly, when peace at length did return, the accumulated mass was poured into America; every manufacturer and merchant acting as if every other were not doing, or were not likely to do, just what he did; and thus glutting our market, so as, on the one hand, to cause prices to fall ruinously low to the parties concerned, and, on the other, to induce a flow of our specie to Great Britain, greater still than would otherwise have occurred,—and this, too, when the banks of the country had suspended specie payments, and when it was desirable they should make every exertion possible for the purpose of resuming them.

Although some of the circumstances which gave occasion to the pecuniary disasters of 1815 and the immediately succeeding years were of a peculiar nature, and not at all likely to occur again, at least to occur again in any thing like the same degree, it is quite obvious that causes of such disasters will be in action sufficiently, at every conclusion of a war, to furnish an argument to the advocates of a protective tariff. This argument will, besides, gain force exactly according to the probable frequency of the changes from peace to war, and again from war to peace. We might, indeed, suppose these changes to take place so very frequently as to justify the enactment, by our government, of as high a tariff of duties as any which the advocates for the legislative encouragement of domestic manufactures have, at any period of our history, ventured to propose as a means of protection for the branches of industry that have been called into existence during a state of war. And it must be evident that persons, who are perfectly agreed with respect to the general principles of political economy, may yet differ, and perhaps even considerably differ from each other, in the amount of duty which it is expedient to impose for the purpose of giving a greater *stability* to the employments of capital,—according to the different estimates they may form of the probable frequency of the occurrence of the changes in question.

Taking things as they are, and looking at the future prospects of the country, not only by the light of past experience, but also by that which is reflected to us from a survey of the subsisting international relations of the civilised world, there are probably few political economists who would hesitate to give their assent to the imposition of a duty of say *five* per cent. upon the value of a foreign commodity on its being imported into the country; such a duty being adequate to the exclusion of it altogether, and adequate therefore to the effective encouragement of the rival American article. That which before could be procured for twenty dollars will, in this event, require twenty-one dollars to procure it; and if we suppose the whole value previously consumed by us to have been a million of dollars, and suppose farther the *quantity* consumed to continue the same as it was, the entire *additional* cost will amount to $50,000, or rather to something less than this sum, because the duty imposed, that it may be effectual for the purpose intended, should always exceed, as has been shewn, the difference in the cost of the articles, domestic and foreign. On the suppositions which have been made, I need not say that such additional cost would be the measure of the national loss or sacrifice incurred, for obtaining the advantages of a greater degree of stability in the distribution of the capital and labour of the community. One of those suppositions, however, does not correspond with the actual facts of the case, to wit, that the quantity of the article consumed will remain unaltered. When prices rise, which they will do when the cost of production is greater than it was, almost every person will be disposed to consume less than he did before; and some will even cease altogether to consume the articles in question. Hence the national loss has been estimated above at too high a rate. But the proper estimate will not be equivalent simply to five per cent. on the whole value *actually consumed.* It is evident that to this must be added all the inconvenience, or diminution of enjoyment, suffered by that portion of the community who have been induced, by the rise of prices, to dispense with some of the articles which they were heretofore in the habit of buying, and to consume in their stead what, but for this rise of prices, they would not have preferred; so that the loss incurred may, notwithstanding, sometimes *approach* to our first estimate of it.

In respect to many commodities, it is quite possible that political economists might be nearly as unanimous, were the duty proposed one of *ten,* in place of five per cent. ad valorem. When, however, we come to a still higher duty than ten per cent., the *dissentients* among the class of individuals, of whom I am speaking, will soon become exceedingly numerous. And my readers need not to be told that duties of fifty or a hundred per cent,—duties implying a sacrifice of national wealth *in a year or two* equal in value to the entire annual consumption by the community of the commodities taxed,—cannot but be regarded as a legislative absurdity.

CHAPTER XI.

OF THE MOST EXPEDIENT SCALE OF DUTIES—INTERFERENCES WITH THE SYSTEM OF FREE TRADE FARTHER CONSIDERED.

GRANTING, for the present, the expediency, for the reason which has been assigned, of imposing a certain amount of duty on the imports into a country, with a view to the encouragement of particular branches of industry, there is a reason why the same *ad valorem* duty should be imposed on *every* commodity imported from abroad; and this is, impartiality in the system of legislation with respect to individuals, or classes of individuals. If the government act steadily on the plan suggested, its action can scarcely fail to be guided exclusively by a view to the general welfare. However urgent any one class of influential capitalists may be in their applications for farther encouragement, a practical difficulty in the attainment of their object will be presented by the necessity of imposing an additional duty on every thing else imported, as well as on the foreign commodity which comes into competition with the products of their industry. Under these circumstances, the representatives of the people,—wherever the assent of such representatives is a necessary preliminary to taxation,—will be, evidently, much less disposed to comply with the wishes of the applicants, than if *their* case was the only one upon which they were called upon to decide. It may be added that a system of legislation, so simple as that now under consideration, would have moreover this advantage, that it would, perhaps more than any other device which could be imagined, have the effect of preserving the purity of the legislative body. If the motive for bribing, or otherwise corrupting the integrity of the members, would still exist in its usual force, the members will not so readily consent to be corrupted or bribed. The debasing practice too, of certain *interests*, not naturally allied to each other, combining together, in order by their united influence to obtain their private or local ends, at the expense of the people generally,—a practice to which, among ourselves, has been affixed the elegant appellation of *log-rolling*,—would but seldom meet with success, and would therefore fall into comparative desuetude. We would, in short, enjoy all the moral, as well as the physical advantages, of a system of legislation having general and not special purposes in view.

If a uniform ad valorem duty be imposed on every commodity imported from abroad, two consequences must invariably ensue when the existing rate of duty is raised; in the first place, a greater degree of encouragement will be yielded to the domestic producers,—and secondly, the public revenue will be altered in amount. I say altered, and not augmented in amount, because, although in every instance of an extensive addition to the tariff of duties in the United States the revenue has become greater than it was before, we may easily conceive of the duties on foreign goods to be advanced to so high a rate as to constitute a bar to all importation whatever from abroad, and therefore to exhaust altogether the source of revenue. And hence, it is plain, that the public revenue may, under different circumstances, be either augmented or diminished by raising the general rate of duties.

Now let us suppose, what will appear from the foregoing remarks to be quite possible, that, when the rate of duties is rendered just high enough to furnish an adequate revenue, the expedient degree of encouragement or protection is not afforded to the domestic producers,—a state of things, however, not very likely to take place in this country. Here we would be necessarily forced to abandon the ad valorem system of protection, and to impose in certain cases an unequal rate of duty. And the question occurs;—If, for the reason at present assigned, or for any other reason, unequal protective duties are to be imposed, what principle ought to guide us in *proportioning* to each other the different items of the tariff? Or, in other words, why should one commodity be taxed higher, and another lower? I will only reply in general terms, that those branches of industry which are productive of the means of the national defence against foreign aggression, or of the necessaries of life, deserve to receive the aid of the legislature in a greater degree than others, all other circumstances being the same; for the inconveniences suffered by the community in consequence of a deprivation, or partial deprivation, of the articles adverted to, in a period of war, would obviously be greater than would be suffered, were they to be deprived for a season of luxuries merely.

After what has been observed concerning the effects of a transition from a state of peace to a state of war, and the reverse, upon the distribution of the capital and labour of a country, my readers will be disposed to think with me that the greatest obstacle now existing among the civilised nations of the earth, to the general introduction of the system of free trade, is the doctrine, so universally practised upon, that the property belonging to individuals of a nation at war with another may be lawfully captured, and become the property of the latter, or of captors deriving from the government of the latter their authority to rob on the great highway of the ocean. This transfer by a government to *privateers* of its assumed privilege to prey on the property of its enemies is generally considered, and perhaps properly so, to be a more aggravated iniquity than for it to do the same act by the direct exertion of its own power; and on this account it is that the expediency and means of abolishing the practice of privateering has been frequently drawn into discussion among diplomatists, and its abolition even in one or two instances stipulated for by treaty. We may be permitted to hope that with the still farther progress of the nations in the career of civilisation, this detestable system of legalised piracy will cease to be a disgrace to humanity. But the philanthropist ought to aim at something beyond this. Indeed, he ought not to stop short, so long at least as he is not satisfied of the object proposed being a moral impossibility, of the establishment of the same degree of respect for the rights of private property on the ocean as on the land. The preponderating naval power of Great Britain, it must be confessed, renders at the present moment the anticipation of the occurrence of such a state of things almost utopian. It is not be expected that she will consent to yield up voluntarily, as a sacrifice to the general welfare of mankind, any portion of her means of annoying her enemy in war, without some compensating gain. In this point of view, her overgrown navy cannot but be regarded as a nuisance of peculiar magnitude. All other nations should exert themselves, in every just and expedient mode, to abate it. And what would be productive of an approach at least to the result desired, in reference to the matter now before us, they should likewise combine together to obtain the recognition universally, in opposition to the present British doctrines and practice, of the principle that "free ships make free goods," or that "the flag of a neutral covers the property of an enemy," as well as of the principles of "strict blockade."

Transitions from a state of peace to a state of war, and the reverse, are not the only changes giving rise to sudden and frequent transfers of capital and labour from one employment to another. It might occasionally be very desirable to countervail, to a certain extent, the *varying* legislation of other nations, by a corresponding, though *temporary*, modification of our own tariff laws. To illustrate my meaning, let us suppose the government of Great Britain to grant to the producers of cotton goods so large a bounty as to enable them to have the advantage in every description of such goods, over the American producer, in the market of the United States. The effect of this will be to cause, in both countries, a considerable alteration in the distribution of labour and capital. If this state of things were to continue, a benefit will have been bestowed upon us by the British government. We would be gainers by the diminished cost of procuring manufactured cottons. For a time however, while the transfers of labour and capital were going on, much inconvenience, and even distress, would be experienced by both capitalists and labourers. To render those transfers more gradual than they would otherwise occur, and thereby to alleviate the sufferings of the parties injuriously affected, if not to remove them almost entirely, nothing more would be requisite than to grant a like bounty to the American manufacturer as the one granted abroad, or to impose an equivalent duty on the foreign commodity when imported into the country; which bounty or duty could be then diminished at intervals, until it should be entirely repealed. By making in this manner a temporary sacrifice, for the purpose of warding off to a certain extent from a portion of the community the "evils of change," the sum of the public enjoyment or happiness might, all things considered, be rendered greater than it would otherwise be. There is, however, an objection which the advocates of free trade would prefer against the adoption of the suggested course of legislation, and which it is proper should be stated here. In almost every country, the parties of free trade and of restriction are arrayed, more or less formally, against each other; and for the former to yield ground to the latter, even with the intention and understanding of its being resumed, after a short period shall have elapsed, might be deemed by them to be too hazardous a measure. They might find it much easier to impose a duty or bestow a bounty, than to withdraw it when once existing.

Should the government of Great Britain, instead of granting a bounty to the producer in that country of a commodity, with a view to enable him to obtain for it the command of the foreign market, do the contrary of this, that is, should it recall a bounty heretofore granted by it, and which had conferred on the British producer the power of supplying the foreign market, or say, more particularly, the market of the United States,—a power he did not before possess,—a transfer of American capital and labour will take place, as on the previous supposition; but being taken from the capital and labour of the country generally, the temporary inconvenience resulting in any one branch of industry will hardly be perceptible, and no legislation will be necessary to lessen it.

But next, let the British government, after having, in the manner just described, called American manufactures into existence, retrace its steps, and restore the bounty which had been repealed. By so doing, those manufactures may be quite as speedily annihilated as they were at first established. And, if the government of our own country remain all the while a passive spectator of what is going on, it is clear that this twofold process may be continually repeated to the great injury of our people. It is true that neither the British, nor any other government, is likely to act in the contradictory manner above described; since they could not do so without occasioning a similar injury to their own subjects. Nevertheless, were the government of any one country in reality so to act, it would be the imperative obligation of every other government to modify its tariff of duties, or system of bounties, in such a manner as to prevent as much as possible the infliction upon society of the "evils of change."

CHAPTER XII.

THE SAME SUBJECT CONTINUED.

The effects of the imposition or repeal of bounties or protecting duties in any one country upon other countries is, indeed, very far from being generally understood. I will illustrate them farther in the case of a *repeal* of a duty, and the reader will then not be at a loss to understand what will happen in every case where a protecting duty is *imposed*, instead of being repealed.

Suppose that, but for the existence of the British corn laws, corn would be annually exported from the United States to Great Britain to the value of ten millions of dollars. The reader needs not to be told that this supposition is made only for the sake of argument; and that, were those laws to be in fact repealed, it is not at all improbable, from a comparison for a series of years past of the prices of the different kinds of grain in the two countries, that very little of it would ever be exported from this country to the British islands. Ten millions of dollars could not be added to the value of our exports without a corresponding addition being made to our imports, on the principles already explained. If our imports were *not* to increase when our exports were doing so, the balance would have to be paid for in specie; and, if paid for in specie, a general rise of prices must ensue at home, while the contrary will be the case abroad. An additional motive for importing and a diminished motive for exporting commodities, other than money, will then exist. The imports must, of course, go on increasing while the exports will go on diminishing *from their augmented amount;* until at length they will be again in equilibrium with each other, and specie will cease to flow from the one country to the other. When this has taken place, it is evident that no additional amount of commodities can be annually exported without leading to a corresponding addition to our ordinary imports. Hence too, a repeal of the British corn laws, on the supposition above made, would be necessarily followed by a greater consumption in the United States of British goods of a description to come into competition with our own manufactures; and if the repeal be a sudden one, a temporary enhancement of the protecting duties in their behalf would be desirable. This effect of the repeal of restrictions, on our liberty of exporting the products of American industry to other parts of the commercial world, is plainly the reverse of what the advocates of a high tariff suppose it would be. They indeed often, under a conviction that our manufacturers could then sustain themselves without any legislative protection, go so far as to proclaim their willingness to give up their favourite system, provided foreign nations would at the same time admit our products freely into their ports.

The only remaining reasons which seem to me to have any weight to induce a modification of the principles of free trade, in their application, at least, to the circumstances of an agricultural community, and to one continually spreading itself out, as in the United States, over a vast extent of a hitherto uncultivated wilderness, are the two following. *First*, that the introduction of manufactures, even at the national sacrifice implied by the imposition of a duty on imports, or by the enactment of a direct system of bounties, would furnish a greater diversity of occupations, and would, in consequence, be favourable to the development by the people of a greater intellectual, and therefore also ultimately of a greater physical power. Every individual could then more readily find an occupation adapted to him; and inventions in the various arts of life would be likely to be made more rapidly when the opportunity was afforded of comparing together, as would then too be the case, a greater number of the processes actually employed in them. *Secondly,* the population of a country may be diffused over so very wide a surface, when compared with its numbers, as to subject it to a considerable *moral* disadvantage. A greater proportion of the people must then, almost necessarily, remain destitute of the means of education as well as of the services of religion, or must possess them in a diminished extent.

I shall not undertake to estimate with any exactness the degree in which these arguments in support of the system of restriction apply to the circumstances of our own country; and shall here merely oppose to them some considerations which, although only secondary in importance to what has already been adduced to shew that the natural distribution of capital and labour is the one most advantageous to the community at large, ought not to be entirely passed over in silence. The considerations adverted to will, not improbably, be regarded by the reader as constituting an adequate set-off for the above-mentioned *restrictive* arguments.

Although it is unquestionably true that every occupation is equally advantageous, on the average, to both the capitalists and the labourers concerned,—and therefore to the country in general, *in so far as the capitalists and labourers are capable of appreciating the various circumstances of advantage or of disadvantage connected with it,*—it is likewise true that men are in most cases apt to exaggerate the prospects of advantage, and to do the reverse of this in reference to those of disadvantage. This happens more especially to the young, upon their entrance on the profession or career which they have chosen for themselves, or upon their entering on any temporary undertaking. But, at every period of life, we perceive individuals speculating in lotteries, in the stocks, and in property of every description, on the same principle; even with a full knowledge of the chances of success being against them, every one looks with a less or more sanguine expectation to a prosperous result, and, if success does not arrive, experiences something like a feeling of surprise. Consistently too with all this, those occupations which are the most fluctuating in the value of their products will, comparatively speaking, have more capital and labour applied to them than others will have. Those which are productive of the luxuries will be, in this manner, more *crowded* than others which are productive of the necessaries of life; manufactures, consequently, more so than agriculture.

And there is another disadvantage of manufacturing industry, very closely connected with the one just mentioned. The sudden declension to which many branches of them are liable from a sudden diminution of demand,—a diminution of demand that may arise from a change in the fashion of the day,—will frequently throw a large number of labourers out of employment, who will be obliged for a time to content themselves with a reduced rate of living. They will thus have their ideas lowered of what constitutes for them a competent livelihood, and their condition will have a tendency to become permanently degraded. Other circumstances being the same, we have here then a reason of some weight for postponing the period of the introduction of manufactures into a country, and, *a fortiori*, a reason for not forcing them into existence, by the instrumentality of legislative enactments, before the natural period of their introduction shall have arrived.

Again, if the condition of the labourers in any one department of industry be depressed from any cause below the rate at which it would be but for the action of that cause, it will necessarily happen that it will come to be depressed in every other; or, in other words, the wages of labour generally will be lowered.

In a preceding part of the present treatise, it was, moreover, shewn that the command which the mass of the community at any time possess over the necessaries and luxuries of life is determined, other circumstances being the same, by their *moral* condition. To say here, therefore, that the general rate of wages is reduced, is equivalent to saying that the moral condition of the people generally has been depreciated.

There is also an argument against a protecting tariff which I have never seen stated by any other writer on political economy, and which, though not of much comparative moment, deserves, in my opinion, not to be passed over without mention in this place. On the first enactment of such a tariff, or on its being at any time rendered higher than it was, the reader will recollect that specie will flow for a season into the country where this has taken place from all others with which it has intercourse, that is until the due proportion between the exports and imports, which had been *disturbed* by the interference of the government with the pre-existing state of things, is again restored. It is plain that the quantity of specie in the country will be greater according as a greater degree of protection or encouragement has been afforded to the various classes of domestic producers, by means of the imposition of duties on commodities imported from abroad;—and the same conclusion will manifestly hold good if the encouragement be afforded through the instrumentality of a system of bounties, or in any other supposable way. Hence a nation needs only to adopt the restrictive as opposed to the free trade system, and it will secure to itself a permanently augmented specie circulation, and therefore also a permanently augmented circulating medium, in whatever proportions of paper and metallic money this may be composed. But will an augmented circulating medium be an advantage to a country? After what has been delivered concerning money in my third book, I hope there will be none among my readers who will for a moment hesitate to reply in the negative. In that place, it appears to me that I have satisfactorily shewn it to be a matter of great indifference, looking at permanent results, whether the circulating medium be large or small; the value of it, regarded as a whole, being, whether large or small, invariably the same. And so far is the retaining a greater amount of specie in the country an advantage to it, it is a positive disadvantage; for every dollar so retained excludes an equal value of other commodities, which might be procured in exchange for it by exporting it abroad. The whole amount of the specie unnecessarily retained should be therefore regarded as a national *loss.*

The conclusion just arrived at has been deduced on the supposition of the state of free trade having been disturbed by the *first* enactment of a tariff of duties on imports. It is evident that the same conclusion will result if we suppose the existing protecting tariff to be added to by the enactment of other protecting duties. And again, it must be equally evident that there is nothing in my reasoning which is not as applicable when the duties imposed on imports are productive of a revenue to the government, as when they operate prohibitorily; that is when the imposition of such revenue duties is followed by the importation of a diminished value of commodities from abroad; which might not, however, be always the case.

Every condition of society, it may be observed in the next place, is subjected to alteration from the inconstant passions and variable opinions of men; but none is less liable to fluctuation, and especially to great fluctuation, than that which is the most natural, or in other words than that which requires the least amount of legislation to secure its continuance. The laws of nature are as immutable as the will of Him who has ordained them: human laws, on the contrary, only endure for a time, and often, even when least open to well founded objection, for a very short period of time. *That prosperity* therefore, which is the least dependent upon artificial regulation, will be the most stable, and for this reason the most desirable. And here we have another argument in favour of the system of free trade.

I also maintain the expediency of leaning, in every doubtful case, towards a freedom of trade with other nations rather than in the contrary direction, on account of the freedom in question being the most desirable condition of things, if universally introduced; and because the only mode of gradually introducing it is by the more enlightened among the nations of the earth setting the example of advancing in the right direction, whenever an opportunity is offered to them of doing so. Free trade, indeed, should always be looked upon as a goal which all the nations are, in the course of improvement, to strive to arrive at eventually.

And this is not the only point of view in which the cause of free trade is likewise the cause of civilisation. May we not hope that, when, by the gradual removal of the restrictions which at present, almost every where, impede the intercourse of one country with another, this intercourse shall become every where more and more extensive, the extreme inconvenience consequent upon the interruption of it by a sudden change from a state of peace to a state of war, together with the inconveniences which must ensue from the transfers of capital and labour to which the changes from peace to war and from war to peace give occasion, will tend to lessen the frequency as well as the duration of actual warfare, and to substitute the public opinion of mankind in place of the musquet and the sabre as an arbiter of the disputes of nations? But however the reader may respond to the question just put, he will be prepared, with the writer, to look upon the principles of free trade as contributing to the peace of the world, and to the general progress of human civilisation, by their inconsistency with the notion still too prevalent, that what is gained by one nation, by means of its foreign commerce, is gained at the expense of some other,—and by their leading, on the contrary, to a firm conviction of the prosperity of any one country contributing to that of every other, on account of its tendency to render the commerce between them ever more and more extensive,—a commerce which is shewn to be, of necessity, mutually advantageous to all the parties concerned.

CHAPTER XIII.

THE SAME SUBJECT CONTINUED.

Long as I have already dwelt on the subject, of the tariff and free trade, I deem it expedient, before quitting it, to point out a few of the mistakes, in addition to those already adverted to, into which the parties have fallen, by whom it has been agitated in this country. In doing this, some light cannot fail to be shed on the application of the principles which may now be regarded as having been *established.*

At the expiration in 1815 of the war with Great Britain, a tariff of duties was enacted by Congress, intended, on the one hand, to furnish the general government of the Union with an adequate revenue, and, on the other, to administer a certain amount of protection from foreign competition to the American manufacturers. Although this protection might not, at the time, have been judged by many of them to be large enough to secure the accomplishment of the intended object, very few suspected that they would, before any considerable period should have elapsed, become earnest solicitors with the government for the enactment of a scale of duties on foreign imports, which they themselves would not have hesitated to have previously pronounced to be, if not extravagant, at least altogether unnecessary. Whence did this mistake on their part arise? And how was it that, notwithstanding the acquisition of increased skill by the American manufacturers, the tariff of 1816 was followed by that of 1824, and this again by that of 1828, without entirely satisfying the demands of their advocates? The chief reason for all this seems to me to be found in the propensity, before adverted to, of each member of society to act independently of all others, in the disposition of his capital and labour. There is nothing more common than to see people acting in this respect, just as if the very same considerations which have influenced their minds were not likely to influence the mind of every one else. So when, in consequence of the protection or encouragement bestowed upon any particular branch of industry, it has become profitable to invest capital in it rather than in other branches of industry, the capitalists will seldom make due allowance for the competition of one another, and will engage in the protected employment to such an extent as to cause it to yield less than the ordinary rate of profit. It is true that such inequality in the rate of profit would after a time be corrected by the transfer of capital in the opposite direction. But in the meanwhile, before this would take place, the parties concerned in the protected employment would, very naturally, complain that the protection received by them was less than they ought to have, and be clamorous for getting more; and if more be then granted them, the same series of consequences will recur. And we have here an account of what actually ensued upon the successive enactments of the different tariffs above mentioned.

In accordance with these views, we find that some few of the American manufacturers, who, in consequence of superior skill, or superior advantages of situation, were making larger profits than the manufacturers generally, felt no desire for, or were even opposed to the raising of the tariff of duties in 1824 and 1828. They regarded the losses to which they would not fail to be subjected in the first instance as equivalent, or more than equivalent, to the advantages which they might ultimately derive from any measure of the kind.

The mistake of supposing adequate encouragement to have been given by the government to the manufacturers of the country, on the enactment of each of our successive tariffs, I need scarcely mention was common with them to their opponents.

It is not requisite for me to repeat how it invariably happens, on the imposition of a certain amount of duty, that, while the imports into the country are diminished, the exports become also diminished in the same proportion; and also that both exports and imports undergo a diminution to an extent less, and sometimes considerably less, than the value of the formerly imported, but now prohibited articles. I may now take for granted that all this is sufficiently familiar to my readers. That it was very far from being understood at the time adverted to, was of material injury to the *anti-tariff* cause. The prophecies, put forth by its advocates, of the *destructive* consequences to our foreign commerce, to result from an increase of the duties on imports, were, more than once, contradicted by the event, and furnished ground to their opponents of a renewed confidence in their own speculations, as well as of an additional distrust in the conclusions of political economy.

Every duty on a foreign article imported into a country, by having, besides its direct effect of diminishing, or entirely preventing, the importation into it of the article in question, the incidental effect of promoting the importation of other foreign articles in greater abundance than before, cannot but act in a certain degree as a *discouragement* to the domestic producers of similar articles. Hence it is a mistake to suppose that the encouragement afforded in any particular instance is always to be measured by the amount of the imposed duty. Thus, if a duty of thirty per cent. is just sufficient to enable the American manufacturer of a certain article to establish his business, a portion of the thirty per cent. may have become necessary for the purpose of counteracting the opposite tendency of other duties previously imposed. And because of the *fall in the price* of any commodity, when permitted to be imported after the enactment of a protecting tariff of duties, a fall of price necessarily implied, by a greater amount of it being in that case imported than before the imposition of duties upon other articles,—taken in connection with the circumstance of the prices of things having previously fallen abroad on account of the imposition of those duties,—my readers will easily perceive the inaccuracy of saying, as some writers have said, that the sacrifice which a nation makes when it protects the production at home of any article by prohibitory acts, is to be measured by the excess of the cost of producing it at home over the cost of actually procuring it at the time from abroad, were the prohibition of its importation to be removed. The true measure is, plainly, the excess of producing the article at home over that of procuring it from abroad, *if all legislative measures restricting its trade with other nations were to be repealed.*

The circumstance of a duty imposed upon an article of foreign importation operating at the same time as an encouragement to the importation of other articles from abroad, and therefore as a discouragement to the domestic producers generally, will *in part* account for the disappointment experienced by our manufacturers in not being benefited by protective duties to the full extent anticipated by them.

When the tariff of duties is *lowered*, the reader can now also understand how it is that the injurious effects resulting to the domestic producers is mitigated by the partial *encouragement* which the lowering of any one duty administers to them; and consequently, how it may have happened that the compromise act of 1832, by which the duties on imports were gradually reduced, has not been as injurious to the manufacturing interests of the United States as might, at first, have been supposed it would be.

It must now also be apparent that there are two reasons,

independently of the advancing population, and therefore consumption, of the country, why, in despite of the repeatedly augmented protection bestowed, until 1832, on the American manufacturers, the *revenue* derived by the general government from the duties on foreign imports should have been rendered always greater after every augmentation of protection than it was immediately previous ; first, the higher duties exacted on the commodities still imported ; and secondly, *the circumstance of these being imported to a greater amount than heretofore, for the reason above assigned.*

If the tariff of duties may be so raised as to accomplish both the objects, of adding to the revenue of the country, and of giving an increased protection to the manufacturing interests, the contrary must likewise be true, namely, that the tariff may be so reduced as to *diminish* as well the public revenue as the protection enjoyed by the manufacturers. These two propositions are, indeed, so very obviously true that no one will be found to controvert them.

But there are not a few persons who go farther, and look upon it, if not as impossible, yet as a matter of extreme difficulty, to raise or lower the tariff of duties so as to produce, in either case, one of the effects indicated, and not at the same time produce the other. They have puzzled themselves in vain, with an attempt to solve the problem how the revenue might be diminished and a *surplus* in the public treasury got rid of, without removing the protection bestowed on the manufacturers any faster than it is in process of being removed by the operation of our existing laws. In order to attain this end, all that would be necessary would be, in the first place, to reduce the duties on all sorts and qualities of goods which are at present imported from abroad, or on a sufficient number of them. But if this be done, experience in every similar case tells us that the value of the imports will be greater than they were before; and if so, the revenue will not be reduced by a given diminution of the duty as much as might have been at first supposed. Our remedy for the existence of any consequent excess of revenue will, of course, be to lower still farther the rate of duty. That we have it in our power, by going on in this way, to reduce the revenue in any degree we may choose, will hardly be denied by any one; since it is manifest that, by carrying on the process described, the duty may be lowered to nothing, and the revenue wholly annihilated. Let us, then, suppose the public revenue reduced to the desired extent, by the requisite alteration in the revenue duties, without touching those which are of a protective character. I maintain that, for the purpose of administering precisely the same degree of protection as before, those of the last mentioned description will also have to be altered, excepting in the peculiar case of the quantity of the articles imported bearing just such a relation to the diminished value of a given portion of them as to retain the imports, considered as a whole, of the same value as at first. Should *that value* be less than it was, the consequences will be similar to those which were shewn to take place in the case of the imposition, or increased imposition, of prohibitory duties; that is, the value of the *exports* will become gradually less, and specie will for a time flow into the country. When the ordinary proportion between the exports and imports, as well as the equilibrium of the precious metals, shall at length have been attained, the prices of commodities generally will be higher at home, and lower abroad, than before the reduction of the revenue,—a state of things manifestly unfavourable to our manufacturers. Such of them as had been protected by a duty no higher than was just sufficient to exclude their foreign competitors from the American market will find themselves at a disadvantage, and will require additional legislative protection to enable them to stand their ground. It is, moreover, worthy of remark that if, in this state of things, the duties on the protected articles be not raised, it is very conceivable how, notwithstanding the diminution in the value of the imports of those articles which do not come into competition with our own manufactures, the renewed importations of certain articles which do come into competition with them may cause the value of the imports, and therefore of the exports, to equal or exceed what it had been. If the value of the articles heretofore imported be, on the contrary, greater than they were before, and this will very often be the case, opposite consequences to those which have been described will ensue,—that is, an encouragement, and not a discouragement, will be administered to the domestic producer by the reduction of the revenue duties. To maintain the manufacturers on their former footing, it will be requisite to *reduce*, instead of raising, the duties imposed for their benefit on the imports from abroad. I may add that there can scarcely be a doubt of their having derived a benefit, since the passage of the famous compromise act, from the repeal or reduction of revenue duties compensating in part the loss to which they have been subjected by the lowering of the duties which operated prohibitorily on foreign imports. Of this, however, the reader will be enabled to judge for himself by a comparison of the tables of exports and imports, annually published by the government.

CHAPTER XIV.

ON THE TERMS AMERICAN SYSTEM, AND AMERICAN INDUSTRY— REMARKS ON THE DOCTRINE THAT A TAX UPON FOREIGN IMPORTS IS INCIDENT ON THE PRODUCERS OF THE COMMODITIES WHICH ARE EXPORTED IN EXCHANGE FOR THEM.

In the course of the preceding remarks, I have occasionally spoken of the sacrifice made by a nation for the benefit of a particular class, by means of the duties which it imposes on its foreign imports. However convenient such language may be, it is very liable to be misunderstood; and it has in fact been often misunderstood by being taken in too literal a sense. It is, therefore, important to explain it distinctly. If the capital of the favoured class were always applied under similar circumstances of advantage and of disadvantage in respect to *situation*, or, in other words, if no portion of it paid any *rent*, it could in no case yield to its owner more than the ordinary rate of profit. Whatever benefit the class in question may then derive from the duties imposed could only be temporary. The case supposed is, however, not always that of our manufacturers, to which our attention has been latterly so much directed. The situations or sites which they occupy are, in some branches, adapted in very different degrees to the purposes they have in view; so that while some pay little or no rent, others pay a considerable amount of it to the proprietors of the soil. Here it is evident that those manufacturers alone who occupy and possess the situations where a rent is yielded are permanently benefited by the restrictive measures of the government. All others, had the measures of the government not induced them to invest their capitals in manufactures, would have been able to make equivalent profits in some other occupation. They would, indeed, have been able to make more than equivalent profits under a system of free trade; because, under such a system, a greater amount of production would take place, and both profits and wages would have a tendency to be higher than under one of restriction.

What has just been said in reference to the manufacturers, it may be mentioned, will apply to the case of the agriculturists, wherever legislative encouragement has been bestowed upon them; and will apply to them in a still greater degree, because agriculture is that department of industry which presents the most remarkable as well as most numerous illustrations of the payment of rent. There is, however, this difference in many countries,—Great Britain, for example,—between manufactures and agriculture; that while, in the former, the receiver of profits and the receiver of the rent, where rent is paid, is one and the same person, in the latter they are most commonly distinct from each other. It will follow, accordingly, that the landlords, and not the farmers, are benefited by the British corn laws.

To proceed: a *mistake* has, without doubt, been committed by many advocates among ourselves of the system of restriction, in designating it as the *American system*, and in announcing its object to be the protection of *American industry*. Although designing men may have, not seldom, employed these terms with an intention to mislead, being aware of the influence upon their fellow-men of a good or a bad *name* in determining their opinions, even on the most important points, and this sometimes independently of any argument; very many well-meaning persons have honestly believed that the question at issue between the tariff and free trade parties was whether the *industry* of their countrymen or that of foreigners should have a preference given to it by our own citizens, and by our own government. Operated upon by the names American system and American industry, they were, in some instances, led to look upon their adversaries very much in the light of traitors to their country, and as deserving, in consequence, of the public odium and indignation. All this has, however, passed away; and we might now almost imagine that it had never been. Yet it is possible that the discussion which gave rise to it may at some future time be again renewed. Partly for this reason, and partly on account of the singular illustration the subject presents of the misapplication of terms in the discussions of political economy, I have noticed it in this place. To repeat what has already been mentioned, the true question at issue between the advocates of free trade and the advocates of restriction is, whether the natural distribution of capital, or another distribution of it, the result of legislative regulation, is most advantageous to a country. The same amount of capital is employed in both cases alike; the only difference being that, in the one, a certain portion of capital is applied to the production in the country itself of commodities, which are procured, in the other, by the application of the very same capital to the production of other commodities, which are destined to be exchanged for them when they are introduced into the country from abroad. These too, because they are always procured in exchange for the products of our own citizens, are to all intents and purposes entitled to be likewise considered as the products of American industry. And the system of free trade is, therefore, quite as much entitled to be denominated the American system as is the system of restriction. I have said *quite as much entitled:* it would have been strictly proper, on the principles already, I hope, successfully established, to have said *more entitled* to be denominated the American system; for the free and uncontrolled distribution of capital and labour is the *most productive* distribution of them, and is consequently that which is calculated to give to both capitalists and labourers the largest command over the necessaries and luxuries of life.

Much more space might be occupied in noticing the errours of our writers and speakers on the subject now under examination; but I will content myself with one more only. I mean the remarkable doctrine, which was first broached by a southern statesman of high standing, that the duties imposed on foreign imports are eventually paid, not by the consumers, as is generally supposed, but by the producers of the commodities exported in exchange for those imports. It followed from this doctrine that the cotton growers of the United States were sufferers from the operation of our tariff laws to a degree altogether extraordinary; and that, while the country north of the Potomac experienced from them all the benefits they bestowed, the country to the south of that river experienced from them nothing but unmitigated evil. All this was very well fitted to aggravate the hostility of a considerable portion of our citizens to the protective system, as it existed among us previous to its modification and gradual repeal by the act of 1833; to which act it may have in a certain degree happily contributed. My readers nevertheless, if they have adopted the principles which I have attempted to establish in the present treatise, will not hesitate to reject the doctrine in question as an illegitimate support of the liberty of commerce. The duty on any article, although levied in the first instance on the importing merchant, has been shewn to be ultimately incident on the consumer. This has, at least, been shewn to be so when the article taxed still continues to be imported; and that it is so when, in consequence of the duty operating prohibitorily on foreign imports, the article consumed is a domestic one, is an obvious inference from the cost of procuring it, and therefore its price, having been enhanced, as has also been previously shewn, by the amount of the duty imposed; provided, of course, the duty imposed be just equal to the difference in the cost of procuring the article from abroad and producing it at home. To establish the production of it, however, at home, it will be recollected that a duty *somewhat* greater than this will be requisite. I may observe that it is often much greater; in other words, it is greater than what is necessary for the object in view. If a duty of ten per cent. will exclude the foreign article, it must be a matter of entire indifference with the home producer, as well as with the community whether the duty imposed shall be one of ten or a hundred per cent. Any larger duty than ten per cent. is, under such circumstances, merely nominal.

But while the duty will, in every instance, fall upon the consumers, and not upon the producers of the articles heretofore exported, the latter will not fail to suffer a certain degree of inconvenience and loss. The imports into the country cannot be diminished, without the exports also becoming less than they were before. A partial transfer must take place of the capital of the producers adverted to; and such a transfer implies that a loss has been incurred by the capitalists,—a loss, moreover, which is the greater according to the difficulty of effecting the transfer. Now that the difficulty of transferring the capital of the *cotton growers* to most other employments is extremely great, cannot be denied. There are, however, two considerations to be adduced, of a nature to satisfy the reader that the amount of the injury, notwithstanding this, inflicted on them, instead of being greater than might at first have been supposed, was after all comparatively small: in the first place, I shewed that the whole amount of imports, and consequently the whole amount of exports, was always reduced by a less amount than that of the articles whose importation has been prohibited; and secondly, a home market for raw cotton was generated by our tariff laws, as a substitute, to a considerable extent, for the loss in part, by the growers, of the foreign market.

It may be added that whatever temporary benefit may have been conferred on the cause of free trade by the propounding of the doctrine just refuted, it is calculated like every other doctrine founded in errour, to do an eventual injury to the cause it is adduced to support. The sooner, too, so bad an argument is discarded the better. Should the contest between liberty and restriction, in relation to commerce, be again revived in our country, we may, accordingly, hope that no individual of high political standing will be disposed to employ it. And after the investigations to which the student of political economy may have been introduced by the remarks which have been made in the present book, I feel confident that he will be ready to express his conviction that good arguments in a sufficient number, and of sufficient force, are to be found in support of free trade, to render unnecessary the use of any bad argument for this purpose, even though such an argument could in reality serve to promote it.

BOOK FIFTH.

ON THE INTERFERENCE OF INDIVIDUALS AND OF GOVERNMENTS WITH THE NATURAL ORDER OF THINGS, FOUNDED ON OTHER GROUNDS THAN THE UNEQUAL PRODUCTIVENESS OF THE DIFFERENT BRANCHES OF INDUSTRY.

CHAPTER I.

ANALOGY IN THE EFFECTS PRODUCED BY THE INTERFERENCES OF INDIVIDUALS AND OF GOVERNMENTS WITH THE NATURAL DISTRIBUTION OF CAPITAL AND LABOUR—THE QUESTION EXAMINED, AS TO WHAT PROPORTION OF A PERSON'S INCOME IT WOULD MOST CONTRIBUTE TO THE NATIONAL WELFARE FOR HIM TO SAVE.

THE expediency of an interference, by government, with the natural distribution of the capital and labour of a country, has been maintained, in all the instances of such interference already considered, on the ground of the various branches of industry, in the actual circumstances of society, not being equally productive of wealth. Other interferences however, of a different character, still remain to be made the subject of discussion.

And besides these, my present book will embrace an inquiry into the effects of certain changes in the condition or circumstances of individuals, or of associations of individuals, which might very possibly become, where they have not yet become, the ground of legislative action.

In the preceding book, as the reader will have observed, I omitted to make any mention of the conduct to be adopted by the several members of a community, in consequence of the opinions they may have formed respecting the comparative productiveness of the different branches of industry; having then confined myself to the course which it has been thought expedient for the community regarded as a whole, or, which is the same thing, for the government, acting in behalf and with a view to the welfare of the whole community, to pursue. There was, indeed, no necessity for me to have done otherwise than I did; since the very same arguments, which were adduced to shew why the government should or should not act in a particular manner, are equally applicable, as must be manifest to my readers, to shew the propriety of individuals acting, or abstaining to act, in a similar manner. But another reason for saying nothing in reference to the action of individuals, was the fact that very few persons have ever deemed it to be worth while for them to concern themselves in their private relations with the public welfare. Very few persons, for example, even among the most zealous advocates of a high tariff of duties for the purpose of administering adequate encouragement to the American manufacturer, have hesitated, where in their opinion adequate encouragement was not administered to him, to purchase and to consume the foreign article in preference to the corresponding domestic one, if the former were procurable at a price in the smallest degree lower than the latter.

The inconsistency of their so acting falls rather under the animadversion of the moralist than of the political philosopher. Yet I may be permitted to remark here, that there can be no escape on their part, from the charge of being inconsistent with themselves, in the inconsiderable amount of the effect it is in their power individually to produce. It seems to me that a man might as well refuse to pay a just debt to his creditor, in a season of general pecuniary distress, on the plea that, because so many other debtors had been unable to fulfil their engagements to the creditor, he also was not in conscience bound to pay him his debt,—as that a "tariff man" should refuse to encourage the manufactures of his countrymen, by clothing himself in them at a higher price than he would have to pay for foreign goods, on the plea that the government, or the country at large, would not agree, by raising the price artificially of those foreign goods, to force, so to speak, a preference universally for domestic manufactures.

Instances will occur in the discussions that are to follow, in which, unlike those above adverted to, it may be nearly or quite as important to trace the course most expedient to be pursued by an individual as by the government of a nation; and although that course is in the one case perfectly analogous to what it is in the other, it may be more convenient to consider a subject in the first place, sometimes with a bearing on the individual, and sometimes with a bearing on the government.

I may observe that the order in which the subjects of the present book are to be treated is of comparatively little moment. The *principles* to be applied to them have now been fully explained; and, although more or less intimately related, they admit of being discussed without any immediate reference to one another.

A beginning will be made by considering, or I should rather say, reconsidering the case of the different dispositions which may take place of a person's income.

It will be recollected that there are only two ways in which he can dispose of it. He may either appropriate it to his immediate, or to his future gratification; that is, he may consume it unproductively, or save and employ it as capital. The question now presents itself:—How much of income is it desirable should, on the average, be thus saved? To prepare ourselves for giving any thing like an approximate answer to this question, if even *such* an answer to it be possible, we ought to bear in mind the effect previously deduced of the accumulation of savings, or, in other words, of the increase of capital, as contrasted with the effect of every unproductive expenditure, on the progress of population and wealth; to wit, to cause them to increase in the same proportion. Many political economists, in their attempts to find an answer to the proposed question, have looked at the effect just stated alone, disregarding every other circumstance. They have thus persuaded themselves that the man who saved a considerable portion of his income deserved to be ranked in the class of public benefactors; while he who spent, on the contrary, the whole, or the greater portion of his income, ought to be looked upon somewhat in the light of one who, by wantonly destroying a public edifice, or any other product of the labour and capital of the community, was directly instrumental in retarding the progress of national wealth.

And in all this they would not have been far wrong, if for a nation to advance in wealth and population were synonymous with its augmenting in prosperity or happiness. But such is by no means a matter of course. An increase of numbers, even when accompanied by a corresponding increase of national wealth, can scarcely be desired, should it at the same time imply a deteriorating of the general condition of a people. This will, in fact, be the case when the increase of wealth has resulted from an excessive degree of saving. For then the *style* of living among those classes of the community who can best afford, and who are therefore expected, to expend the most for the consumption of themselves and families, will be lowered; and with it that standard of enjoyment must also be lowered, to attain which will be the constant aim of the poorer classes. They will in consequence, on the principles established in my second book, accustom themselves gradually to a diminished command over the necessaries and luxuries of life.

But it may be said that, in the part of the present treatise now referred to, the acquisition by the poorer classes of habits of saving has been as earnestly inculcated upon them as the acquisition of a more extended desire for necessaries and luxuries. Would not, then, the *example* of the wealthy when they save, be quite as beneficial to the poor as when they expend, their incomes? It seems to me that it would not be; because the amount which is, in the actual condition of things, saved by the poor, bears no comparison with the amount expended by them; and because, under the most favourable circumstances, their savings cannot be expected to be otherwise than inconsiderable.

Experience informs us, however, that a large expenditure by the rich, upon their own unproductive consumption, is by no means always contemporary with an elevated rate of living, or what is very nearly the same thing, with the receipt of a high rate of wages, by the labourers generally. So far from it, that we find, not unfrequently, the great body of a people to be *most degraded* where a class possessed of overgrown wealth exist in the midst of them, spending their means profusely on all manner of extravagances and luxuries. I am disposed to think, that any example, in respect to expenditure, which may be set to the poorer classes of the community by those whom Providence has placed in easier circumstances, will be calculated to have little or no beneficial effect, unless the latter class of persons be *not* a great deal more wealthy than the former, and be moreover sufficiently numerous to be found in every neighbourhood. And, perhaps, it would not be incorrect to attribute even an injurious influence to great wealth, expended in the manner above described; since, by the total improbability of competing with it on the part of the great body of the people, it will have a tendency to check, rather than to stimulate, their efforts to better their condition.

On a comparison of what has been said concerning the effects of saving a greater or a less portion of the incomes of individuals, I think it would be extremely difficult, and I may say impossible, for the political economist to form any definite opinion as to how much of his income a man ought to spend, and how much of it he ought to save, *in reference to the public welfare*. The conduct of each person must be regulated, in the matter, by the same prudential considerations which determine his course of action in the affairs of every day life.

Having come to the conclusion that every individual of society is quite as good a judge of the most expedient mode of distributing his income between his productive and his unproductive consumption (regard being had as well to the public as to his own welfare) as the political economist can be for him,—it is almost tautology to add, that he is, in general, better fitted to judge for himself, of the most expedient mode of distributing his income, than the government, or any *statesman*, can possibly be. In my opinion, all that the government should here undertake to do, is to remove, wherever any may exist, every artificial cause of the accumulation of large fortunes in particular families; such as laws of primogeniture, and laws for preventing the alienation of landed estates. When this shall have been accomplished, it may safely leave things to their natural course; perfectly satisfied that, where man's wisdom is at a stand, an adequate provision will have been made by nature, or to speak more accurately, by the Author of nature, for the attainment of the greatest amount of human happiness, which, under the circumstances, is attainable.

CHAPTER II.

MODE IN WHICH GOVERNMENTS HAVE INTERFERED WITH THE UNPRODUCTIVE EXPENDITURE OF INDIVIDUALS — MISTAKEN NOTIONS BY WHICH THE ACTION OF GOVERNMENTS HAVE BEEN SOMETIMES INFLUENCED—APPLICATION OF THE PRINCIPLES OF POLITICAL ECONOMY TO THE "TEMPERANCE QUESTION;" AND TO THE BESTOWING OF MONEY FOR RELIGIOUS AND PHILANTHROPIC PURPOSES.

For the government of a country *directly* to interfere with the natural distribution of the wealth produced, by dictating to the individuals under its control how much they are to expend productively, and how much unproductively, would have been altogether too obvious an infringement of the rights of property, to be ventured upon with impunity, in an improved state of society. The same thing in effect has been, however, attempted in more ways than one *indirectly*.

Sumptuary laws have, for instance, been enacted, for the purpose of checking the advances of luxury. To consume certain articles, has been pronounced by legislative authority to have a tendency to corrupt or enervate the character of a people; and their consumption has, accordingly, been either entirely prohibited, or rendered expensive by taxing them more or less heavily. Even though the proceeds of this taxation were needed for supplying the necessary expenditure of the government, and were, for this reason, a transfer of the unproductive consumption of individuals, to become the productive consumption of the government, the measures adopted would not be therefore rendered proper. The public treasury could be supplied, to the requisite amount, without disturbing the natural distribution of labour and capital, and without the inequality and injustice of taxing one class of the consumers only.

I may here observe that governments have not been always *so enlightened* in their views, concerning the wealth of nations, as is implied by the taxation of unproductive in preference to productive consumption. They have sometimes proclaimed, as a principle of action, the doctrine that it was a matter of no moment whatever how the incomes of individuals, and their own incomes too, were spent; but that what was really important was, that those incomes should indeed be spent, and not saved. The public expenditure was seriously maintained to be so much of the people's property, which, after having been taken from them, was again returned to them, undiminished in amount by its being for a time out of their possession. And the practice of the governments alluded to was, very naturally, not seldom in entire conformity with this theory. Taxation was occasionally pushed by them to the limits of endurance,—limits removed to a remoter distance by the military force which was kept in readiness to suppress the incipient efforts of popular insurrection.

In the mean time, however, political science has been advancing, and has found its way, to a certain extent, from the writings of the philosopher into the cabinet of the statesman. Governments now a days, accordingly, do not put forth opinions so utterly absurd and ruinous, as those I have been animadverting upon. There are very few persons, too, who now venture, in the intercourse of society, to express any such opinions in relation to the action of government; although, it is true, we still frequently hear them maintained in reference to the action of individuals. Most of my readers will probably remember, more particularly, having at some time or other heard the remark adduced, in palliation, if not in justification, of an apparent extravagance of individual expenditure, *that the money expended was thus made to circulate,* and for this reason, to benefit the community; while, in other respects, no disadvantage was incurred by them, because what was one man's loss, in consequence of the expenditure in question, was another's gain.

The student of political economy, who has read and understood the preceding part of the present treatise, I hope will need no farther aid from me in this place, to enable him at once to refute the errours above mentioned; and I shall, therefore, without delay proceed to another topic.

There are some articles, to consume which, or to consume which to the extent in which they are actually consumed, has an injurious effect upon society. Hence, a sentence of condemnation, either wholly or partially, as the case may be, has been passed upon them by the moralist. And the philanthrophist and the christian have latterly exerted themselves in the instance of unquestionably the most injurious of these, viz. spirituous liquors, to diminish their consumption as much as is practicable. Success of no ordinary magnitude has already rewarded those exertions. A still greater degree of it, also, may be eventually expected. The question now occurs:—Can the political economist add any arguments of his own to those which present themselves to the mind of every reflecting man, and which have been repeatedly and impressively urged upon the community to enlist them in the cause of temperance? Or, in other words, can he contribute any thing to render the victory over *intemperance* more speedy, and more decisive? This is an important question; and the answer to it deserves to be well considered.

Here, as in a case previously before us, I hold that the moralist can derive no additional light from the science of political economy, to exhibit more clearly the evils of intemperance, as well as the tendency of the use in any degree of spirituous liquors to become an *abuse* of the worst possible description, than any unprejudiced man of good sense is capable of doing. The arguments against their use which have been advanced on the ground of the extraordinary expenditure incurred, and consequently of the extraordinary amount of the labour and capital employed, in procuring them,—which labour and capital might far better have been employed to procure the means of promoting, in various ways, the cause of religion, of morals, or of education,—are applicable, to a greater or less extent, to shew the propriety of the reduction, on the part of most of the members of a community, of their unproductive consumption generally. Without doubt, if a man would consent to appropriate the value of the spirituous liquors he is in the habit of consuming to philanthrophic purposes, he would be doing a very laudable act. But the same thing may be said of him who, for a like purpose, foregoes the personal gratification derived from any other portion of his unproductive expenditure,—from what, for example, is expended by him on tobacco,—in entertaining his friends,—or even on his own food and clothing. Politico-economically speaking, all these, being objects of men's desire, are to be regarded as useful objects; and their utility to any individual, in the circumstances in which he is actually placed, must be estimated by the labour, or the products of labour, which he is willing to give in exchange for them, rather than be without them. And the argument against the use of spirituous liquors, in so far as it applies with greater force to those liquors than to any other article of consumption, is altogether a moral one, and is, besides, not in any degree on this account the weaker.

Now and then we hear of a *grocer* becoming a convert to the "temperance cause," and not only coming under an obligation to abstain altogether from consuming spirituous liquors, but likewise, from a sense of duty, pouring out upon the ground the stock of that article which he may happen to have in his possession, in order to prevent its consumption by any one else. By acting thus, he gives the strongest evidence the case admits of the sincerity of his conversion, as well as produces the greatest possible moral impression on the minds of other men. To produce this impression is plainly a very important object, and it may be highly desirable that instances of the kind described should occasionally, or even frequently, occur. Nay, I may go so far as to say that it may be difficult to conceive how a dealer in spirituous liquors, professing to be a sudden convert to the *sin* of consuming them, could be sincere and yet act otherwise. Nevertheless, it is proper that the *politico-economical* effect produced in the case should be rightly understood, although to understand it rightly might *seem* to weaken the motive for well-doing; and this on the incontrovertible principle that whatever apparent inconveniences may be connected with the substitution of truth for errour, the ultimate consequences to ensue must of necessity be salutary. The effect adverted to is very easily to be traced. When the stock of spirituous liquors in any market is diminished, their price must rise, and they will be produced in greater quantity, until the supply is once more accommodated to the demand. But to suppose the spirituous liquors destroyed to be in any degree replaced by an increased production of the same article, is manifestly equivalent to supposing that the production of other commodities generally will take place to a less extent than before. It follows, therefore, that *every constituent element* of the national wealth will be proportionally diminished. And so long as the desires of men continue unchanged, any attempt to lessen the consumption of spirituous liquors, by destroying a portion of the existing stock of them, will have the desired effect in no greater degree than the destruction of an equal value in houses, furniture, clothing, or any other description of property would have; for the above reasoning is general, and not applicable to spirituous liquors alone. Let the reader apply it to the case say of a *theatre*, or of a *church*, and he will satisfy himself of the correctness of what I say.

In this age of extended christian and philanthrophic effort, considerable sums of money are, from time to time, collected and disposed of, with the direct object in view of meliorating the moral or physical condition of our fellow-men. Such an expenditure as this has been objected to by some, who have supposed themselves to be arguing on the principles of the political economist, when they maintain it to be so much taken from the sum of the national wealth and expended without any return. Their errour is a two-fold one. They do not perceive, *in the first place,* that their argument is applicable to every instance of expenditure for the purpose of ministering to the unproductive consumption of individuals; and that they might, therefore, quite as well object to a man's wearing two coats or two hats, where he could get along with only one, as object to a partial appropriation of a man's income for benevolent purposes,—even though it were in this case to be consumed unproductively. But *secondly,* what is thus appropriated is not, by any means, consumed unproductively; since, in consequence of its consumption, much wealth, —sometimes material, and sometimes immaterial,—is produced. The reader will recollect the sense in which the terms employed here have been defined.

More than once I have heard the fact of a liberal donation for some religious object, by some poor *widow,* or other person in comparatively narrow pecuniary circumstances, stated in a manner to imply that the party was guilty of an absurdity, if not of a crime, in what had been done. It was assumed as a manifest truth that it would be much better for all such persons to devote their means to the present or future support of themselves and families; and to leave the field of christian benevolence to be occupied exclusively by the more wealthy portion of the religious community. So far from this opinion being sanctioned by the conclusions of political economy, any more than they are by the precepts of the gospel, I cannot but look, consistently with those conclusions as deduced in the preceding part of this work, upon a state of things in which considerable sums are contributed voluntarily by the poorer classes for religious and other philanthropic purposes, as indicative of their having attained to a considerable elevation of character, and *therefore* to a more than ordinary command over the necessaries and luxuries of life. Shew me a people who estimate highly the advantages of religion, of morals, and of education, and, as I have in substance more than once observed, I will shew you a people among whom wages are high.

Where the money which has been collected, and of which I am speaking, is sent out of the country, as in the case of the sums appropriated to the support of foreign missions for the propagation of christianity, the parties referred to have been particularly loud in their objections,—from the circumstance of the money expended having the appearance more unequivocally of being without a return. Looking at the moral effects on the minds of the donors, as well as at those which may be ultimately anticipated to take place in every country from the more general diffusion of the blessings of our religion, we may confidently deny that the money expended is expended without a return. But though this were in reality the case, the loss to the country would be neither more nor less than what results from every unproductive expenditure of equal value; and, to be consistent with themselves, the objectors ought therefore to declare war against every unproductive expenditure, excepting only what is required for procuring the necessary means to sustain our bodily existence. And after what has been delivered on the subject of money, I need not surely here waste a moment of my readers' time in again proving to them that to send *money* abroad, rather than commodities of a different description, is a matter of not the least consequence in its bearing on the progress of national wealth.

CHAPTER III.

OUGHT A PREFERENCE TO BE GIVEN TO ONE BRANCH OF INDUSTRY OVER ANOTHER, BECAUSE OF THE GREATER NUMBER OF LABOURERS EMPLOYED BY A GIVEN AMOUNT OF CAPITAL?—WHETHER ROADS AND CANALS SHOULD BE CONSTRUCTED BY GOVERNMENTS, OR BY INDIVIDUALS?

THE rates of profits and of wages, when left to regulate themselves, will tend to become equalised in all the various branches of industry. Political economists are, for this reason, agreed in regarding all of these as equally advantageous to a country. But is not the circumstance of one branch of industry having a larger proportion than another of fixed, when compared to circulating capital, a sufficient reason for making a distinction between them, in reference to the public welfare,—because the number of labourers to whom employment is afforded by a given capital is always determined in a greater degree by the circulating portion of it? And ought not the government to disturb the natural distribution of capital, by causing a greater amount of it to be invested in the employments where the circulating portion of it predominates over the fixed portion? I remark in reply, that, if no savings were ever made from the wages of labour, the interests of the capitalists need alone be regarded in determining the most advantageous distribution of capital; and I need not here repeat the reasons why the natural distribution of it is that which is best fitted to promote those interests, by establishing the highest possible rate of profit. A very small difference in this rate, in favour of the capitalist, will, on the supposition now made, give rise to a more rapid accumulation of capital, and therefore a more rapid increase of wealth and population than would otherwise take place; and will determine, at a period more or less distant, the existence in any country of a greater number of inhabitants than would then exist were the natural order of things to be disturbed in the manner suggested.

Savings are, however, in fact made by the labourers; especially by those labourers who receive a high rate of wages. Now even taking this circumstance into consideration, I hold to the expediency of not interfering with the natural course of things, for the following reasons. *First,* fixed and circulating, as applied to capital, are merely relative terms, and the degree of fixedness is so very various as to render any equitable interference, of the kind now under consideration, with the different branches of industry, extremely difficult on the part of the government,—and it is evident that it is the government only that can interfere in the matter to any effectual purpose. *Secondly,* any interference by the government in the present instance necessarily implies a very inquisitorial and annoying system of intermeddling with the concerns of individuals. *Thirdly,* the government could not interfere in favour of employments in which the capital invested is chiefly circulating, without setting itself in opposition to the progress of human invention, and endeavouring to check the progress of improvement in the arts; a policy on which no government has hitherto acted, and which no one will be found to justify, however hostile he may be to the principles of free trade. I have said that the adoption of such a course by the government of a country is for it to endeavour to check the progress of improvement, because that progress is always accompanied by the substitution of fixed for circulating capital. Indeed if *this* were otherwise, man's labour could not become more and more productive, and there would be no room for improvements to take place. And *lastly,* according as fixed is substituted for circulating capital, the processes of production will become continually more and more complicated, and the number of labourers who receive a comparatively higher rate of wages will, in consequence, be augmented; and as the savings which are made from wages are in a far greater degree made from the wages of those labourers who receive the higher than from the wages of those who receive the lower rates, this circumstance alone may be regarded as sufficient to counterbalance the disadvantage of fixed capital giving employment to a less number of labourers.

Of all the branches of *material* industry there is none which has been regarded as calling, in so great a degree, for the interference of the government, as that of constructing the means of communication, and of transportation, from one district or region of a country to another. That any private individual should be empowered to make a road or canal, at his pleasure, through his neighbour's property, even though he should pay him the full value of the ground taken from him for the purpose, has been every where put out of the question as a moral absurdity. And the public, as well as the political economists, are divided in opinion into two classes, as to the most expedient instrumentality by means of which roads and canals should be constructed; the one class maintaining the expediency of their being constructed by agents appointed by the government, and directly accountable to it, and the other the expediency of their being constructed by individuals or companies of individuals, simply acting under its authority,—the net proceeds of the tolls exacted going in the former case into the public treasury, and in the latter into the coffers of the individuals or companies concerned.

It has been maintained, on the one hand, that there can be no better criterion of the expediency of constructing a new road, between two different points of a country, than the willingness of individuals to invest their capital in its construction, on the condition of the finished road becoming their exclusive property; of which criterion the country will be deprived by the government undertaking to be the sole or the principal constructor and proprietor of its roads. The chief argument, however, against the *direct* interference of the government in the business of road-making, is the greater costliness of whatever is produced by it through the instrumentality of its agents, when compared with the cost of production where the agents employed are either themselves personally interested, or are closely superintended by those who are personally interested, in the work to be performed being accomplished in the most economical manner.

Those who prefer the immediate action of the government in the case object strongly, on the other hand, to the creation of large incorporations, for road-making as for any other purpose, at least where the *necessity* of their existence cannot be distinctly exhibited; and this objection they are especially urgent in pressing when, as not unfrequently happens, it is proposed to confer on the company incorporated the monopoly, for a long term of years, of conveying passengers and goods from one place to another. Such a monopoly, it is true, is seldom or never formally conferred. But it may, in effect, result from an obligation which the legislature may choose to impose upon itself, not to permit the construction of any similar line of communication between the extremities, or within a certain distance, of the one the construction of which it may at the time authorise; or the parties, in whose behalf the legislature has been pleased to act, may have the exclusive privilege granted to them of conveying passengers or goods along their route in a particular manner,—this manner being the most expeditious and most desirable manner. Even, however, should the company incorporated possess no privileges of the kind just mentioned, it will possess the power, in an extraordinary degree, which is incident to the application of a large capital directed by a single individual, or combination of individuals, to any employment, of whatever nature it may be. It will find it practicable to prevent the competition, to a certain extent, of all other parties who, in the natural course of things, might be disposed to compete with it, by the circumstance of its being in possession of the field of action. Another road will not be constructed along side of an existing one, unless there be a fair prospect of deriving from it the ordinary rate of profits; and this cannot happen unless the new road be a considerable improvement on the other, or the profits received by the proprietors of the other considerably exceed the ordinary rate. If at any time, too, the opinion should become prevalent that the proprietors of a road are making extraordinary profits on the capital invested by them in its construction, and other capitalists should, in consequence, begin to discuss the project of a new road, the former could often postpone, or even prevent altogether, the execution of it, by *temporarily* lowering the rate of toll exacted by them from the passenger or the merchant.

Again, apart from the objection I have been considering, founded upon the inequality of the privileges enjoyed by the different classes of capitalists, it is argued that, if a road or canal is to be a profitable speculation, it is proper that the people in general should have the benefit of it, through the government, which is their agent acting in their behalf, *in order to be relieved to a certain extent from taxation;* while, on the contrary, if the speculation is to be an unprofitable one, neither the government nor any other party should embark in it. In other words, if the work referred to is worth doing at all, it ought to be performed by the government.

Perhaps the proper conclusion, on comparing both sides of the question under consideration, as they have just been stated, is for all roads and canals to be constructed by individuals or companies of individuals, acting under a legislative authority,—on condition of their being permitted to enjoy, *for a term of years only*, all the profits resulting from the tolls to be exacted, *these tolls being at the same time forbidden by the law to exceed a certain rate.* There is room for the exercise of much judgment in determining the length of this term of years, as well as in fixing the rate of toll which is not to be exceeded. Every effort should be made so to adjust these as, on the one hand, not to raise up any undue obstacle to the progress of improvement, and, on the other, to secure to the country the benefit of an interested agency in the superintendence of that progress, without making too great a sacrifice to the grasping spirit of monopoly. At the expiration of the period during which the parties of whom I have been speaking are permitted by the law to enjoy the property of the works constructed by them, these may become the property of the public at a price equivalent to their original cost, or at any other stipulated price.

In what has just been stated the necessity is implied for legislation in reference to the construction of roads. All laws on the subject should, however, be as general as possible, in order to secure the greatest degree of impartiality towards every individual and every district of a country, both as to the benefit rendered, and the damage to property which cannot fail to be to a certain extent incurred. Provision, it seems to me, might be made by a single law for every case that may present itself. A tribunal, for example, might be constituted, or rather the mode pointed out of constituting a tribunal, to decide on the roads or canals proposed to be constructed, and to decide concerning their expediency or inexpediency, upon principles established by the legislature; principles having for their object to determine how far the public good, viewed on the most extensive scale, justifies an interference with private property without the consent of the owner being first obtained, as well as to protect the holders of real estate from having a road at any time cut through their property by persons who are actuated by motives of hostility to them, or by other improper motives.

CHAPTER IV.

ENCOURAGEMENT OF INTELLECTUAL PRODUCTS.

We come now to a class of producers who are very generally acknowledged to have peculiar claims to encouragement, as well from the more enlightened portion of the community, as from the government. I mean that class whose products are of an intellectual or immaterial character.

The grounds of a distinction here are, *first*, that while almost every individual may be looked upon as estimating, with sufficient accuracy, the relative advantages which the different descriptions of material wealth are capable of affording him, such is far from being the fact in respect to intellectual products. No recondite knowledge of human nature is requisite to satisfy any reflecting mind that, without the species of encouragement now adverted to, the great body of the people, even in countries where civilisation exists in the highest degree to which it has yet attained, would advance very slowly, if at all, in the career of improvement. Indeed, to me it is apparent that, but for the efforts which have been made, and which will continue to be made, by the more enlightened portion of society, to diffuse the blessings of education, of morals, and of religion, as extensively as possible among their fellow-men, and made irrespective too of any previously existing *demand* among the latter for those blessings, mankind would degenerate into a state of hopeless barbarism.

The *second* ground of distinction in the present case, in favour of the intellectual products which have been mentioned, is, that every individual of a nation, or of the great community of mankind, is interested in their being diffused, and, to speak technically, consumed, to the greatest practicable extent. In a country like our own especially, where the right of *suffrage* is enjoyed by almost every adult male citizen, and is exercised at comparatively short intervals, where too, in consequence, the government is under the direct control of the people, the importance of their being an educated, a moral, and a religious people, cannot be too strongly felt, and acted upon.

I have before stated that what it was the duty of an individual to do in reference to the national welfare, it was, generally speaking, the duty of the government of a country likewise to do. An exception to this is presented to us in the case of religion; at least in the opinion of every American. *We* are unanimous in thinking that the cause of religion is injured, instead of benefited, by an alliance with men in power, and that an entire equality of civil privileges on the part of the different religious sects is better adapted than any other condition of things to turn them from vain speculations, and fruitless controversies with each other, to the exercise of a practical piety. To give the reasons for this our opinion, would hardly be in place in a treatise of political economy; and it is the less necessary here, because, if the opinion were a wrong one, the general doctrine which I am now maintaining would not be thereby in the slightest degree invalidated.

How far it would be expedient for the government of a country to adopt measures with a view to the promotion of the public morals, is a question of some complexity, and one which has some connexion with that concerning the interference of the government with the religion of the people. I shall leave my readers to decide it for themselves; and it is not improbable that their decision of it will be very various in its application to the different cases of public morals as they occur.

To the propriety of a legislative appropriation of the public money to the support of common schools, in which every child in the community may have an opportunity of acquiring the elements of an education, and be prepared by it to become a useful citizen when he shall have arrived at manhood, very few educated men will be any where found to object. Some people, however, have a notion that the public money granted for purposes of education should be appropriated *exclusively* for the support of common schools. Academies of a higher order, colleges, and universities, they say are places of education for the sons of the rich, and ought to be left to be supported by the rich. Fortunately, however, the interests of the rich and of the poor are not by any means so often in opposition to each other as many persons are apt to suppose; and they are certainly not in opposition to each other in the instances just mentioned. While the common schools are, on the one hand, open to the rich and poor alike; the colleges and universities, on the other, are institutions where, in consequence of the endowments bestowed upon them, by wealthy individuals or by the state, the children of persons in moderate pecuniary circumstances, as well as of the rich, can receive an education of a higher order. If the children of persons in still more moderate circumstances are practically excluded from the benefits of a college or university education, all that needs to be said is that the remedy for the evil is to be found, not in exciting the prejudices of the "democracy" of the country against all seminaries of a higher order, by promulgating the doctrine which I am occupied in refuting, but in maintaining the expediency of a still larger appropriation of the public resources to such seminaries, in order to enable them to educate their pupils at a comparatively small expense, or even to educate a number of them gratuitously, who may be selected for their capacity and merit from among the children in the common schools, or on any other principle that may be preferred.

But the poorer classes, besides being interested in the legislative bounty bestowed on universities and colleges, as opening to their children in a certain degree the doors of those institutions, receive benefit from them, when fostered by the state, in a different mode. Other circumstances being the same, the people generally will be benefited by the existence in a country of a greater number of highly educated men, than would exist in it were education of the higher order to be left to be taken care of by the wealthier portion of the community merely. A taste for knowledge will then be more surely, as well as more rapidly, diffused through the successive gradations of society, down to the most ignorant; and the consequence cannot fail to be to elevate the character of the labourer, and thereby to augment his command over the necessaries and luxuries of life. This last effect, moreover, will result from the influence of an augmented degree of knowledge in accelerating the progress of improvement in the various arts.

Encouragements administered in general to science or literature, and to the fine arts, are evidently to be regarded as proper, for the same reasons precisely as those which have been adduced to evince the propriety of the legislative encouragement of the higher seminaries of learning.

The useful arts,—improperly so called, because the *fine arts* are equally *useful* with them,—have been assumed above to be worthy of especial encouragement. The reason why, the reader can supply for himself.

All regulations which have a tendency to prevent persons, not properly qualified, from belonging to any of the learned professions, or from engaging in any other employment, are justifiable, in so far as they are justifiable, on the principles on which the interference of individuals, or of governments, has been justified in the cases already considered in the present chapter,—the principles that can alone justify the interfering in any case whatever with the liberty of our fellow-men to act according to their pleasure,—to wit, that it is the duty of the lawgiver to protect society from the injurious action of any of its members, and likewise to promote the general welfare as far as lies in its power. The regulations in question proceed on the supposition that a considerable portion of the community are not sufficiently well informed to be able to form a proper judgment concerning the qualifications of the professional man, or other *labourer*, for whose services he may be disposed to apply. Under these circumstances, the government, or persons deriving authority for the purpose from the government, undertake to judge for them. It is evident that the expediency of all measures of the kind will be lessened, according as knowledge is more generally diffused; and that first one, and then another of them, can be removed or repealed with advantage to the public.

There is another class of interferences with man's liberty of action, respecting which little needs here be said. I refer to the subjecting of certain articles of merchandise, before they are permitted to be sold, to the *inspection* of officers appointed for the purpose of testing their quality; and to the prohibition, often existing, of buying or selling certain articles, excepting at particular times and places. Such interferences as these are often exceedingly annoying to both buyer and seller, and unaccompanied by any compensating advantages. They are, indeed, at times so very absurd as to serve no other purpose than to furnish the occasion of creating a number of offices, to be filled by partisans or creatures of the administration of the government for the time being.

CHAPTER V.

EFFECTS OF A DIVISION OF THE PROPERTY OF THE RICH AMONG THE POOR; AND OF INTERFERENCES IN GENERAL WITH THE PROPERTY OF THE RICH FOR THE BENEFIT OF THE POOR—OF TRADES' UNIONS.

HAVING, in the preceding chapter, touched upon one of the cases in which the interests of the rich and the poor have been, although wrongfully, supposed to clash, it will be in order for me to proceed with the discussion of the various modes of improving the condition of the latter of these classes at the expense of the former. The converse of this, how the rich may profit at the expense of the poor, I shall not be expected to treat as a separate question. At any rate, after the argument in behalf of the poor shall have been exhibited and animadverted upon, the reader will be able to supply for himself, if he chooses, that in behalf of the rich.

Let us begin with the case in which, of all others, the poor would be *apparently* most benefited. Let an equal division be made of the national wealth. What will be the consequences to ensue?

In the *first* place, a blow will have been struck at the rights of property. What has once occurred may occur again. In the hope, and even expectation, of its doing so, the industrious will relax his industry, and the indolent will become more indolent still. Production will therefore be lessened. A greater proportion, too, of what is in fact produced will be consumed unproductively; for when a man's savings may be taken from him, the motive for saving any part of his income cannot be as great as it would be under a system of entire security to property; and capital will, of course, not be in reality accumulated *as rapidly as before.* To say, however, only this, is doing injustice to the importance of ever preserving the rights of property inviolate. The more my readers will ponder upon the effects which must necessarily result from every violation of those rights by the hand of power, whether that power reside in a monarch or a mob, the more extensive and disastrous, in my opinion, will the effects described appear to them to be. Now if the accumulation of capital proceed at a much diminished rate, two consequences, on the principles previously established in the present work, must ensue; the population of the country will not by any means increase as fast as it did; and the wages of labour will be considerably lowered. Again, a community, where such a measure could by possibility be adopted as that whose effects are now the subject of examination, must be an immoral, irreligious, and degraded community; one consequently, also on the principles previously explained, which, whatever temporary advantages it may succeed in obtaining by dishonest means, will unavoidably have its command over the necessaries and luxuries of life ultimately reduced to a comparatively small range of enjoyment.

But this, although sufficient, and more than sufficient for our purpose, is not all. For *secondly,* where all the members of a community are comparatively poor, as they would be notwithstanding the division among them of the property of the rich, it would be much more difficult than at present to bring together, and wield efficiently, a large amount of capital. The divisions of labour could not, in consequence, take place to the extent required by the existing state of the arts; and production would, on this account, take place more rudely, and less abundantly.

Thirdly, on the supposition which has been made, of the division of the property of the rich among the poor, every man would be, nevertheless, so poor that he would have to be engaged in some bodily or manual occupation; the few instances only excepted where extraordinary natural or acquired capabilities qualified their possessor, in the opinion of his fellow-citizens, for the superintendence or management of combined capital. The great body of the people would, it is obvious, be placed in the most unpropitious circumstances for the development of the powers of human invention. So far, it seems to me, from improvements of any moment being then introduced in the arts, thus augmenting the productive powers of man, the arts would gradually deteriorate, and many of them, as happened in earlier times, would eventually pass away and be forgotten.

And *lastly*, even though the progress of improvement and and the accumulation of capital were to go on as before, the command of the several members of the community over the necessaries and luxuries of life would gradually become contracted. The desires and habits of the people remaining the same, the possession by them of larger means of expenditure would have the effect of giving a corresponding stimulus to population; and eventually, the population would be augmented, at the very time when, on account of the diminishing returns from the land, the *rate* of production would be diminished, so as to reduce the whole community to a state of poverty. But because the temporary enjoyment of a greater amount of necessaries and luxuries, than the mass of the community had been previously accustomed to, would have a tendency to improve their habits, and enlarge their desires for enjoyment, some modification, it is true, may be proper of the conclusion just arrived at. Not, however, to any great extent; as the reader cannot fail to perceive on a moment's reflection.

Now putting together all the considerations which have been stated, to exhibit the inexpediency of a division of the property of the rich among the poor, it is impossible not to conclude that, while the temporary advantages, to be derived by the latter from so violent and so dishonest a measure, would be much less in amount than might on a superficial view be expected, the whole community would before long be reduced to a state of almost irretrievable wretchedness and barbarism.

The inexpediency of dictating to an individual how much he shall consume of his income on his immediate gratification, and how much he shall save or consume productively as capital, has been shewn in a foregoing chapter. And every other contrivance or scheme which can be imagined for taking in any degree from the enjoyments or property of the rich without their consent, in order to give to the poorer classes of labourers, is liable to precisely the same objections as is the proposition to make an equal division of the wealth of a nation among all the individuals composing it. If it shall be said that, where a *little* only is taken to be disposed of in the manner suggested, the consequent evils will be comparatively small, I would remark that the temporary advantages, bestowed upon the mass of the community, will likewise be proportionally diminished; and the argument above presented will retain its full force.

At the present period, in our own country as well as elsewhere, there is no expedient oftener tried to effect a rise of wages than combinations among the labourers engaged in a particular occupation, or among the labourers engaged in more occupations than one, to compel their employers to pay them at a higher rate by means of a *strike,* that is of a refusal on their part to work until their desires are complied with. These *trades' unions,* besides, seldom stop at this point. Not content with a voluntary enlistment of the workmen in their number, they attempt to act, and often succeed in acting compulsorily upon those who are disinclined to unite with them in their measures. While they contribute, in a certain degree, to the support of a workman and his family who have nothing laid up in store against the emergency of being without occupation, they cease to have any intercourse whatever with him, or persecute him in a still harsher manner, if, rather than comply with their wishes or commands, he prefers to work at the wages which the employers or capitalists are willing to pay.

No one will deny that the existence in a community of all combinations of the nature of the trades' unions is an evil, of no little magnitude, not only on account of the inconveniences to which the capitalists and labourers are subjected on the occasion of every strike, but also on account of those experienced by the consumers of the articles produced, in consequence of the necessary interruption, resulting from a strike, of the ordinary rate of supply. Perhaps a greater evil still is their tendency to propagate the notion that, so far from the the natural course of things being on the whole, as political economists maintain it to be, the most conducive to the interests of both rich and poor, a constant struggle of the poor against the rich is imperatively required to prevent the former from being reduced by the latter to the necessity of contenting themselves with a bare subsistence merely. To justify the infliction upon society of the evils which have been mentioned, I need scarcely say that some great good should be unequivocally shewn to be likely to result. A permanent rise to a certain extent in the ordinary rates of wages would be such a good; since, as has been before stated, the prosperity of a people depends more upon the circumstance of wages being high than upon any other cause. I shall, however, proceed to shew that no permanent augmentation of the ordinary rates of wages can possibly be accomplished through the instrumentality of trades' unions; and that all such institutions are productive only of unmixed evil. My argument will probably not reach the parties who are more immediately engaged in them, and who are the principal sufferers of the evils they inflict; but I may assume it to be not altogether improbable that it may meet the eye of some who have hastily given encouragement to them, supposing themselves, when so doing, to be contributing to "the greatest good of the greatest number," and may induce in them a conviction of their having been in errour.

CHAPTER VI.

THE SUBJECT OF TRADES' UNIONS CONTINUED.

I HAVE said that I would proceed to shew that no advantage can be derived, by the receivers of wages, from the trades' unions. But this I have, in fact, already done, when treating generally of the effects resulting from a compulsory transfer of a portion of the property of the rich to the poor. It matters not whether such a transfer be accomplished by taking from the rich in one way or in another, excepting only that, in as much as there is no *dishonest* taking where higher wages are exacted, the degradation of character ensuing cannot be at all as marked as it must be in the case of a more palpable violation of the rights of property; and consequently, wages will not be lowered to such an extent as it was before shewn they would be.

The subject is, however, one of so much practical importance, at the period and in the country in which we live, that it will not be superfluous to state the argument in question in direct reference to the particular case now under consideration.

First, let a certain class of workmen, in some one place, succeed in getting their wages raised, by means of combining together in the manner which has been described. For example, let the class who have thus attained their object be the journeymen carpenters, and the place where they have attained it the city of Philadelphia. It is obvious that this state of things can only be of a very temporary duration. A motive will now exist for the removal to this city of workmen of the kind specified from other, and especially from neighbouring places; and an influx of them into the city will actually occur, with more or less rapidity, according to the degree in which wages have risen. The rate of wages here will fall, but will rise elsewhere, until the rate in one place will again bear to the rate in every other the same proportion which it had before; when wages throughout the country will be evidently only *somewhat* higher than they formerly were.

In the above reasoning, no account has been taken of the efforts of a trades' union to prevent any of the *trade* from working at lower wages than what they insist upon receiving. Such efforts will not be likely to produce an effect by any means as great upon strangers coming from abroad, as upon those workmen who have been in the habit of association and companionship with the members of the union; and according to the extent in which the effect is actually produced, will the expenditure incurred by the members of the union, in contributing to the support of every workman who is thrown out of employment in consequence of their acts, be augmented, and become the sooner an obstacle to the successful prosecution of the warfare undertaken by them against their employers.

Now suppose the parties in question to succeed, by help of the various modes of annoyance or persecution in their power, in excluding all competition with them for work from other parts of the country; or, what amounts to the same thing in reference to our present topic, let the journeymen carpenters, every where else in the country as well as in Philadelphia, strike for higher wages, and thus actually obtain them. The series of changes will not yet have been traced to its ultimate term. The carpenters will, before long, be deprived of their advantages, if the other trades do not likewise follow in their footsteps, and strike for wages. So long as they are receiving more than the ordinary rate of wages, labour will be transferred from other occupations to theirs, and the rising generation will prefer their occupation to every other. But here again, let the trades' unions of every description throughout the whole country follow their example, and let there be therefore a general rise in the wages of labour. Such a rise of wages, the productive power of the country remaining unaltered, will imply, as my readers will recollect, a corresponding fall of profits; and as the amount of savings made from wages is in general less than from an equal portion of profits, and the amount saved besides, when other circumstances are the same, being always greater or less according as the rate of profits is greater or less, the conclusion may be drawn that the accumulation of capital will be very much retarded by the successful operation of the trades' unions. And my readers need not be again told that every retardation of the rate in which capital accumulates will be accompanied by the two effects of a less rapid increase of population, and of a diminished rate of wages. Moreover, but for the enjoyment *for a time* by the labouring classes of a higher rate of wages, which will render them less disposed to content themselves with the wages they were before accustomed to, the diminution of wages will proceed until they are reduced once more to their former rate. The tendency of them, however, to be for this reason at a somewhat higher rate than formerly would in all probability be more than counteracted by the sum total of production, when compared with the augmented population, having, from the necessity of applying capital and labour to the land under more disadvantageous circumstances than before, become diminished; a condition of things, it will be recollected, implying a rise of rents, and a fall of profits and *wages*.

Although too, as I have said, the action of the trades' unions can hardly be stigmatized as of a *dishonest* character, since what they propose to take from their employers, in addition to the rate of wages which would be determined on the principles of free competition between the employers and the employed, is no doubt regarded by themselves as a remuneration for their labour to which they are justly entitled,—such action is, nevertheless, a violation to a certain extent of the rights of property. And if these rights may be once violated by the trades' unions, they may be again and again violated by them; and the apprehension of this taking place would constitute a check to the accumulation of capital with its usual rapidity; inducing, in consequence, a fall of wages below the usual rate.

But here it may be said that, provided the rate of wages could be raised by the compulsory action of the trades' unions upon both the capitalists and the labourers whom they employ, the present generation of men, and especially the members of the unions, need not concern themselves with what is to happen when they shall have passed from the stage of life. The good sense, the patriotism, and the enlarged philanthropy of the reader, will, however, I trust, repel the proposition thus hypothetically stated. We are all of us bound in duty to act, during the period of our abode on this earth, not with reference to ourselves and our contemporaries only, but also in a certain degree in reference to those who are to come after us. But even if this were not the case, the compulsory rise of wages in question can be shewn to be productive of little or no advantage to the labourer.

From the very moment a rise of wages takes place, the rate of profits will be reduced, and capital will accumulate less rapidly, and wages therefore commence falling.

Again, until the increased demand which the higher *pecuniary* wages of the labourers enable them to make for certain commodities shall have induced the transfers of capital requisite for supplying that demand, their *real* wages cannot be much greater than they were before. The same quantity of those commodities will have to be distributed among the same number of persons, and distributed among them in nearly the same proportion.

For both the reasons which have just been stated, it will happen, on a sudden rise of the wages of the labourers, that they will, on the one hand, find it more difficult to get employment, and, on the other, be obliged to purchase the necessaries and luxuries consumed by them at a higher price; especially the necessaries, for which a more extensive demand is made by the classes receiving wages than is made by them for luxuries. So that even at first, the advantages derived by the labourers from a compulsory rise of their pecuniary wages, produced by means of trades' unions,—and the same may be said when the rise is produced in any other manner, —are far less than they are commonly led to anticipate.

If now from these advantages, whatever they may be, we subtract the expenditure necessarily incurred by the members of the unions, and likewise duly estimate the other inconveniences and even distresses suffered from time to time by them and their families, in consequence of their system of combining against their employers,—*even setting aside wholly the permanently injurious effects to result,*—I think that an unprejudiced person can scarcely avoid concluding against every system of the kind; not only in respect to the interests of the community regarded as a whole, but also in respect to those of the very parties to benefit whom is the object proposed.

CHAPTER VII.

EFFECTS OF A LEGISLATIVE REGULATION OF THE HOURS OF LABOUR.

An attempt has sometimes been made to improve the condition of the labourers by diminishing the number of hours in the day during which they are required to work. The reader will easily perceive that this is equivalent to an attempt to raise the wages of labour. Whether an individual receive the same compensation for working ten which he received previously for working twelve hours of the twenty-four, or whether, the time of his work remaining unaltered, his wages are augmented in the proportion of five to six, must be a matter of indifference to the capitalist who employs him. The motives most commonly urged for a diminution of the hours of labour are these two; first, the physical deterioration of the individual from being overworked; and secondly, his want of leisure, from the same cause, for improving his intellectual and moral nature. I will make a word or two of remark on each of these heads.

It is not owing alone to too much of his time being devoted to labour that the physical or bodily constitution of the workman is affected injuriously. The medical statistics of different countries teach us that the mortality, out of a given number of persons, is always less among the comparatively rich than among the comparatively poor; and that, from the upper extremity of this scale to the lower, a progressively augmenting physical deterioration is thus indicated. At least, the only exception to this general remark is presented by the *very rich*, who live in idleness, and who are in consequence apt to seek a refuge from the miseries of the ennui which it generates in the pleasures and the vices of dissipation. In proportion, then, as *the wages of labour* are lowered, will the physical condition of a people be deteriorated. Now the wages of the labourer are lowered,—his real wages I, of course, mean,—when his command over the necessaries and luxuries of life is diminished; and this again can take place, either by his being unable to obtain, in exchange for a given portion of his labour, as great an amount of those necessaries and luxuries as before, or by his being obliged to labour during a longer time that he may procure the same amount of them. As great a gratification surely may be enjoyed by being relieved from oppressive labour, as can be furnished by the commodities produced by it. The tendency accordingly, in the progress of society, will be for the daily wages of the labourer to be augmented, while the hours during which he works in the day are less numerous than they were; and, on the contrary, diminished, while the hours of work are greater in number than they were before. And the analogy having been pointed out between the two cases I have been comparing together, it will follow that every argument which will apply to evince the propriety of diminishing the hours of labour, will apply with equal propriety, so far as the physical deterioration of a people is concerned, to evince the propriety of augmenting the rate of wages generally.

Let us, in the next place, trace the consequences which will result from abbreviating the hours of labour, *without at the same time making any alteration in the amount of daily wages to be paid.* This, as has been explained, being in fact an augmented rate of wages, must be accompanied by a fall in that of profits. Population, on account of the first of these effects, will advance with unusual rapidity; while capital, on account of the other, will be accumulated more slowly. For both these reasons, my readers will now understand, without any explanation on my part, that wages will gradually fall to nearly their former rate,—so nearly to their former rate, as to render the additional wages received by the labourers no sufficient compensation to society for the violation of the rights of property implied in every compulsory raising of the rate of wages. Or, in other words, since every violation of those rights has a tendency, by checking the accumulation of capital, to cause wages to fall, more will, in consequence, be eventually lost to the labourers than the little advantage which they may derive in the manner and for the reason above stated.

In the remarks made by me in this and the two preceding chapters, my language may, perhaps, have been somewhat too unqualified when I spoke of every taking from the rich for the benefit of the poor being a violation of the rights of property. There can be no doubt of the correctness of this assertion where the poor are the only parties to be benefited. Where, however, any transfer of property, of the kind mentioned, can be shewn to be ultimately advantageous to the rich themselves, to an extent more than equivalent to the loss incurred by them in the first instance, it may become the duty of the government of a country to cause it to be accomplished. It is, indeed, on this ground alone that the interference of the government with the property of individuals of whatever class, by taxation, or in any other way, can be at all justified.

We have here a test of the expediency of taking from the capitalists and giving to the labourers employed by them, which, however it may fail in the case of a full-grown man, may possibly yield us a different result if applied to the children who find employment in factories and elsewhere. By restricting in their case the hours of labour, time would be found for educating them; and when those children shall have arrived at manhood, the condition of the labouring community will not fail on this account to be essentially changed for the better in a moral point of view. It is scarcely necessary to say how desirable such a result would be in reference to the best interests of a country, and in reference too to the interests properly understood of the richer as well as of the poorer classes. Any attempt to improve the condition of the uneducated *adult* labourer, by a positive interference on the part of the government to relieve him from some of the hours of labour, would in my opinion be productive of very little corresponding benefit. It is not improbable that the leisure time provided for him, and to which he has been hitherto unaccustomed, may contribute to deteriorate instead of improving his condition, by being spent as often in dissipation and vice, as in the business of acquiring knowledge or exercising his mental faculties.

CHAPTER VIII.

THE SYSTEM OF PRISON LABOUR CONSIDERED.

Some two or three years since, a considerable clamour was raised by the mechanics in the state, and especially in the city of New York, on account of the system adopted of setting the state-prisoners at Sing Sing and Auburn to work, and then disposing of the articles produced by them, with a view to provide either wholly or partially for the expense of supporting and guarding them. They (the mechanics) complained that an indignity was put upon them, and their rank in the community lowered, by the prisoners being employed exclusively in mechanical occupations; and that it was not only injurious to their interests, but likewise unjust, to subject their *honest* industry to a competition in the market with that of persons convicted of crime.

To inquire into the validity of the former of these complaints does not properly lie within the scope of our science; and I shall, therefore, content myself here with an acknowledgment of my inability to perceive any ground for it in the circumstance of the convict being employed in mechanical and not in other occupations, or, in other words, being employed in the production of material and not of immaterial wealth. Such must of necessity be for the most part the case, if they are to be employed at all in the business of production. Moreover, it should also be recollected that the employment in question is not assigned as a degrading punishment. The true objects of it,—whether in this way best attained or not, is here a matter of no moment,—besides that of relieving the community from a certain amount of taxation, which would otherwise be necessary for meeting the expenditure required for the support of the prisons, is the reform of the criminal, by the useful occupation of the time at his disposal, and the furnishing him at the period of his discharge, where he did not already possess it, with an honest and therefore honourable means of gaining a livelihood.

Whether the mechanics, because of the competition of convict labour, will make less profits than they would otherwise do, is a question which I shall first examine on the supposition of the products of the labour of the convicts being disposed of at their market price, that is, at a price neither cheaper nor dearer than that at which the like commodities are ordinarily sold. Here, it is plain, the competition will be precisely of the same nature with what would ensue upon the investment of an additional amount of the labour and capital of any portion of the community in the business or employment of the mechanics concerned. The prices of the commodities produced will fall, and the profits of the producers be reduced below their usual rate. Capital will then, of course, be transferred to other employments, until prices and profits be restored to their former level. But when capital is transferred from any one employment to another, the fund from which wages are paid in the former will be necessarily diminished; and a transfer of labour must therefore also take place. During these transfers, much inconvenience will be suffered by both capitalists and labourers. As soon, however, as they shall have been completed, the ordinary rates of profits and wages will be received in every branch of industry alike. And those mechanics, be they masters or journeymen, who continue to be engaged in the branch of industry interfered with by the system of convict labour, being as well off as the mechanics generally,—nothing besides having occurred to *diminish* in any degree the whole amount of production,—will have no reason for just complaint.

Most of the complainants adverted to would, indeed, readily assent to the conclusion just arrived at. They do not so much object to the competition of convict labour in general, as to all such competition when the commodities produced are thrown into the market at a reduced price; and it is when the regular mechanic is thus undersold, that he has loudly invoked the legislature of his state to interfere in his behalf. Let us examine if, in so acting, he has had reason on his side, or if he has been deceived by appearances only.

Let us suppose the products of convict labour to amount to a tenth part of those of the regular mechanic which were purchased and consumed in a given time, and in a given market; and moreover, that the former products are sold at half the price they will usually command. It is manifest that the persons who have obtained the commodity in question at half-price will be disposed to consume it more abundantly than if they had had to pay the full value for it. The demand for it will, in other words, become greater than it was; and the consequence will be, that the supply of it will not be required to be diminished to the same extent as it would be if the price of what is produced by the convicts were left to be determined by the freest competition among all the parties. This again is tantamount to saying that a less amount of labour will have to be transferred, and that the present inconvenience suffered by the mechanics will not be as great. When those transfers shall have been effected, all classes of the mechanics will receive the ordinary profits and wages; and no room will exist for just complaint on the part even of those who have been undergoing a temporary inconvenience.

There is nothing in the above argument limiting its applicability to the case when the products of the convicts' labour are sold at half the usual market price. The conclusions just arrived at will be the same at whatever deduction from their market price those products are sold, excepting only that, in proportion as their price is lowered, the inconvenience temporarily undergone will be lessened; and this will be the least when their price is lowered to the greatest possible extent, that is when they are given away gratuitously.

It must be apparent to the reader that if the employments of the prisoners be sufficiently diversified, so that only a few of them shall be set to work to produce the same kind of commodities, the temporary inconveniences of which mention has been made may be rendered so very trifling as to be wholly unworthy of notice, when compared to the relief of the public from a certain amount of taxation, and the attainment of the other advantages proposed by the system of prison labour.

The clamour against the system, however, occurred not on its *introduction* as a measure of state policy, when the temporary inconveniences were yet to be suffered by the mechanics whose labour was about to be interfered with for the purpose of promoting the general welfare; but when all those inconveniences had passed away, and the transfers of labour and capital were accomplished which had been rendered desirable. It was the abolition of what already existed that was aimed at; which abolition of it, so far from being an act of justice to the parties who were engaged in the branches of industry which had been interfered with,—unless where they were the very same individuals who had been engaged in them at the time the system I am speaking of was introduced,—would have increased their profits and wages beyond the ordinary rates, and have given them an undue, although temporary advantage, above their fellow-citizens.

What has been delivered, concerning the effects of prison labour, will apply to the labour of persons employed in houses of industry, and in the workhouses of the poor; and will apply with equal force.

CHAPTER IX.

OF ABSENTEEISM.

A COUNTRY has been sometimes thought to be injured in an extraordinary degree, and the condition particularly of the labouring classes depressed, by the absence abroad of a considerable number of its men of property; whose incomes in consequence, instead of being expended at home, are employed in the purchase of foreign necessaries and luxuries. It is in reference to the *absentees from Ireland* that this opinion has been oftenest put forth; and against them, accordingly, no slight amount of odium has been occasionally excited in the breasts of certain philanthropic and patriotic individuals of the British Empire. Independently, however, of its connexion with a country which, for various reasons, is now attracting so considerable a portion of the attention of the political philosopher, the subject is one of sufficient general interest not to be passed over, in the present treatise, in silence.

That the emigration of *capital* is a national loss, has been sufficiently established in my second book. But the question under examination has no relation to capital. When the annual incomes of the absentees from Ireland are exported or remitted to them, they are in almost every instance destined to be consumed unproductively. The true question indeed at issue is, whether a certain unproductive consumption shall take place in one country or in another. Some writers have pronounced this to be, from the very nature of the case, a matter of the most entire indifference, and the outcry against absenteeism to be therefore altogether absurd.

In my opinion, the analysis of the subject is not pushed as far as it ought to be, when all unproductive consumptions, of equal value, are assumed to have *precisely* the same effect on the wealth and prosperity of a people. There are two reasons, founded on the principles of political economy, why a certain value consumed unproductively at home should be more advantageous to a country than an equal value when so consumed abroad. The possessor of the wealth consumed is assisted in consuming it by his family, as well as by the domestics and other persons who may be *in any way* employed by him; and counting all these in the number of absentees, the diminution in the population of the country, whence they have absented themselves, will not appear to be by any means insignificant. And again, had all these staid at home, there can be no doubt, however unproductively the head of each family might consume his income, that a certain amount would be added to the wealth, and, as a consequence, to the population of the country, by means of the *savings* of the persons whom he employs. All these effects are, nevertheless, inconsiderable when compared with those which have been supposed to result from the practice of absenteeism.

To avoid the possibility of my meaning being misapprehended, as well as to obviate any seeming inconsistency with my own definitions in what has just been delivered, I shall here remind the reader that, in speaking of the consumption of an individual as being at any time wholly unproductive, I do so, in accordance to the usage of political economists generally, on the ground of all the wealth, material or immaterial, which is *produced* for himself and family by the persons whom he employs for the purpose, being consumed by him unproductively, and therefore without constituting any permanent addition to the national wealth.

It may be proper, too, to meet an objection that may perhaps be made to the full force of one of the reasons assigned above for absenteeism being, to a certain extent, an evil. The absentee, it may be said, when he goes abroad, does not necessarily take with him the persons whom he means to employ in his service. When, for example, an Irish nobleman changes his residence from Dublin to Paris, his servants, and others who minister in any way to his desires, will for the most part be Frenchmen, and not Irishmen. This circumstance is, notwithstanding, a matter of no consequence here. If the means for supporting a given population be increased or diminished, population will, on the principles in relation to it which have been explained in a previous part of this work, be sooner or later increased or diminished proportionally, or nearly so. And whether or not all the persons to be employed in furnishing the services or commodities which shall be actually consumed by the absentee and his family are brought from Ireland to France, the result, in so far as we are at present concerned, will be the same. In both cases alike, there will be eventually a less number of Irishmen, and a greater number of Frenchmen, in existence, than there would otherwise be.

Now when we have succeeded in shewing that the progress of wealth and population in a country is repressed or retarded by any measure, the inference may be drawn that the measure in question has also a tendency to deteriorate the general condition of the people. Hence absenteeism has an injurious effect, to a certain extent, upon the condition of the people of Ireland.

The circumstance of the incomes of the absentees being received by them in the form of money will neither add to nor take from the strength of the argument above stated. As money is abstracted from a country in one direction, it must necessarily flow into it from some or many others, on account of the tendency to a general fall of prices consequent upon such abstraction of it. Indeed, in almost every instance of the remitting of income from one country to another, it will not be money, but commodities other than money, that will be remitted; the money actually received by the parties being in reality the proceeds of the sale of those commodities, —which proceeds are thus received by them through the instrumentality of bills of exchange.

I may here add that, in stating the disadvantages resulting to a country from the absence of some of its inhabitants, I have also stated the advantages to be derived by a country from foreigners who travel, or temporarily reside, in it: for *in relation to our immediate subject,* what is one country's loss is another's gain.

Concerning the effects of an *emigration* of a portion of the inhabitants of one country to another, I have already treated in my second book.

CHAPTER X.

OF PAUPERISM.

Having examined in succession the different modes in which the condition of the labourers of a community may be improved, or in which that condition has been erroneously supposed to be susceptible of improvement, I now come to the very important and difficult subject of pauperism. What are we to do with the able bodied poor who are unable to find employment? And what with the sick, the aged, and the young, who are unable to work?

For a considerable period of time, the injunctions of the Bible, and the example of Christ, were so interpreted as not only to justify, but even to sanction, the *indiscriminate* giving of alms to the poor. It was thought that nothing could be more acceptable to our Maker than to establish hospitals and other institutions of charity, in which the parties gratuitously provided for enjoyed more comforts, in sickness and in health, than those of the same class, who, or whose relatives and friends for them, preferred to get along, under all circumstances, without any extraneous aid. A premium was thus administered to idleness and improvidence; and it is no wonder that industry, independently of the co-operation of other causes, should have lain comparatively dormant, and pauperism should have rapidly propagated itself.

At length, the appearance of the celebrated "Essay on Population," by Mr. Malthus, opened the eyes of the political economist to the evils of this system; and, for a time, led some of them almost to revert to that indifference of feeling, concerning the poor and the wretched, which pervaded the heathen world before the light of christianity dawned upon it. Here a state of things was presented in which religion and science seemed to be in direct opposition to each other. Many good people were disposed to escape from this difficulty by simply denouncing the speculations of political economy, as *metaphysical* and obscure, and as even pregnant with dangerous errour; while, on the other hand, not a few of those who professed to be guided in their practice by the principles of this science sought to reconcile them with the precepts of the Gospel, as well as with their own kindly feelings, by making a marked distinction between public and private charity, and by maintaining the propriety of administering the latter only, and of administering it too only in extreme cases; so as to affect injuriously in the slightest possible degree the habits of independence and forethought of the labouring poor.

With the progress of investigation, the differing parties have, however, been brought much nearer to each other; until now the subject of pauperism admits of being expounded in entire conformity both to scientific principles and christian precept. Political economy has thus, like geology, furnished us with a remarkable instance of a science which, at a certain stage of its advancement, seemed to lead to results incompatible with the certainty of our previous knowledge; but which, on its farther advancement, may be cited as a striking illustration of the consistency of truth. And from this, I may be permitted to add, we derive the important lesson,—a lesson which I would inculcate upon all those individuals who find it easier to utter vituperations of the science of political economy than to refute its conclusions by reasoning,—that the only effectual method to be adopted by any class of men to persuade the rest of the world to be of their opinion, if their opinion be a correct one, is not to sneer at, and repress by every means in their power the cultivation of any branch of human knowledge which may seem to oppose that opinion, but, on the contrary, to do every thing they can to promote its increased cultivation. The consistency of the great system of truth is a proposition which constitutes the main argument for the unity of God, and which is indeed the foundation of natural theology; and it cannot be too strongly impressed on the mind of every reasoner, or the *impiety* too firmly realised by him of undervaluing, or affecting to undervalue, the investigations of science, in whatever channel they may be directed.

But to proceed with our subject. I shall first examine the case of the able-bodied poor. That of the infirm and the sick will then present to us no difficulty. And let us begin with the administration of *private* charity.

Suppose in the actual condition of things in the city of Philadelphia, whatever this may be, the wealthy to appropriate a certain portion of their incomes, to the value say of $100,000, for the relief of the poor who are able and willing to work, but who find themselves unable to obtain employment. What will be the series of changes which will ensue? And what, more especially, will be the ultimate effect produced?

Here however, before attempting an answer to the foregoing questions, I feel the importance of stating distinctly what is meant when we speak of the poor, or the labouring classes generally, being unable to obtain employment. The expression, I shall remark, is one having reference to *time*. Whatever may be the number of workmen who happen at any period to be without employment, when compared with the number who continue to be employed, they will be *eventually* provided for by a fall of wages. The wages, actually paid, will come to be divided among all the workmen. This would at least be the case, were not one set of workmen thrown out of employment as another is in the act of obtaining it. If the unemployed labourers, then, could only wait long enough, they would in no event become the objects of charity. Here we have the difficulty, and the whole difficulty, in respect to them. But many of them will be utterly unable to wait long enough, and will earnestly appeal to the sympathies of their fellow-citizens for aid while they are in a state of transition from employment to employment, or from the service of one employer to that of another. And it is to meet this appeal, that the distribution among them of the $100,000 above mentioned is supposed to be made.

Let this sum be distributed among them, in the first place, gratuitously. I need scarcely say what a premium would thus be bestowed on improvidence and idleness. The expectation of being supported, in part or wholly, when unprovided with employment, will render the workmen generally less anxious to obtain it, or, having obtained it, less careful, by a diligent performance of the work assigned them, to secure to themselves a continuance of it. It will, in consequence, necessarily happen, independently too of any influx of paupers from neighbouring districts in which an equally extensive charity may not have been exercised, that the claimants for gratuitous aid will be multiplying from year to year; and where $100,000 was deemed to be an amount sufficiently ample to administer all the aid required, double the amount will, before long, be inadequate for this purpose. Indeed, no limit will be assignable to the increase of pauperism and of the funds requisite for its relief. The process described, if only continued long enough, would not stop until all the property of the rich was divided among the poor,—a state of things which, as I have before explained, could not fail to be yet farther deteriorated, so that at length one scene of pauperism and wretchedness would pervade the community.

In what has just been stated, I have taken no notice of the particular source whence the funds which have been charitably applied were derived. They may have constituted a portion of the wealth that was destined by its possessors to a productive consumption; or a portion of the wealth that was destined by them to an unproductive one. To the extent in which the former, rather than the latter of these two suppositions, may have corresponded with the facts of the case, an additional reason would be presented, wholly superfluous as it is, why the most injurious consequences should ensue from the administration of charity in the manner which has been described. Capital will have been transferred from the support of the employed poor to the support of the unemployed poor; in many cases, from the support of the industrious workman to that of the idle and worthless portion of society. The effects before pointed out cannot fail, on this account, to be aggravated, and to be brought on with a greater rapidity.

Next, let us suppose the $100,000 in question, instead of being bestowed gratuitously, to be employed in setting the unemployed poor to work in the business of production. It will then, of course, constitute a portion of the capital of the country; and its effects on the condition of the poor will be the same as those of any other equal portion of capital. When once invested, it will however, no more than any other, furnish employment to the workmen who may happen to be unemployed. These will have to be provided for in the time to come, that is if their number continue to be on the average the same, by a like subtraction as before from the incomes of individuals. But their number cannot fail to be augmented, in consequence of the habits of improvidence which the greater probability of obtaining employment, when from any cause they have been deprived of it, must necessarily generate; and a larger and a yet larger sum will, therefore, be requisite, in order to afford the same degree of relief from year to year. Although, very probably, a certain portion of the wealth which would otherwise have been consumed unproductively will have been applied to the reproduction of wealth, and for this reason will have had a favourable influence on the condition of the community generally, there seems to be no reason for doubting that, not only will the disposable property of the rich, by the process now under consideration, be in time exhausted, but also that the poorer as well as the richer classes will, however slowly, be ultimately reduced to the same degree of wretchedness, as it was shewn would be the case under our former supposition of the *charity* administered being administered gratuitously.

Not content with setting *a certain number* of the unemployed poor to work at the ordinary rate of wages, the benevolent feelings of some of the inhabitants of our smaller towns have sometimes induced them to associate together, with a view to provide work at that rate of wages for *every one* who might happen at any time to be unemployed. The promise, thus held out by the society, was soon met by applications so numerous as to render it necessary on their part to solicit donations, in all manner of ways from their fellow-citizens, in order to augment the means at their disposal. But the more they got, the more also they found they were called upon to expend; until at length, they found themselves *overwhelmed* by the rapid extension of the pauperism belonging to the place, and by the influx into it of that belonging to other and neighbouring places. An utter discouragement then seized upon the society, which either dissolved itself, or sank into a state of inactivity. And just such consequences as these must ensue from every attempt to benefit the poor which is founded on the absurd notion that the funds for employing them, without compensating them at a lower rate of wages than the ordinary rate, are inexhaustible.

CHAPTER XI.

THE SUBJECT OF PAUPERISM CONTINUED.

The two cases have been examined in the preceding chapter of the administration of charity to the able-bodied and unemployed poor, first gratuitously, and in the second place, if charity it can then with propriety be called, by setting them to work at the usual rate of wages. I shall now proceed to the consideration of the case of the poor who apply for aid being *underpaid* for their work, or, in other words being paid less wages than at the ordinary rate.

Such a proceeding as this has been sometimes stigmatised as a piece of injustice to the parties whom those denominated charitable profess to relieve; and the latter have, in consequence of its adoption by them, been charged, in no very elegant form of speech, with "grinding the poor." Nevertheless, since every other method of dealing with the unemployed portion of the poorer classes has been shewn to be productive of evils of the greatest magnitude, we naturally turn to this as our only resource. If it should also be found not to be available for our purpose, we shall, indeed, be obliged to give up the cause of the poor in despair, excepting perhaps only in case of the last extremity; or assenting to the doctrine,—I had almost called it the unreasonable doctrine,—of the possibility of the conclusions of science being inconsistent with the precepts of religion, declare hostility against political economy for bringing us into a position where our reasoning powers are rendered altogether so unavailing. Fortunately, however, we are not reduced to a choice thus inconsistent with the analogy of our knowledge in general. The method of dealing with the poor which I am now considering will be acknowledged by the reader, when properly understood, and properly carried into execution, to be that which will reconcile every difficulty of the kind just stated; and to be likewise the only one by means of which the poor of the present generation can be relieved, when thrown out of employment, without entailing a still greater degree of poverty and misery on the generation that is to follow.

If a poor man, when without employment from the regular employers of labour, knew where to apply for work to be paid for at a lower rate than the ordinary wages, it is clear that he would very often make application for it, rather than be without work; and having obtained the work for which he applied, it is equally clear that he and his friends would diligently occupy themselves in endeavouring to procure for him regular employment in his trade or vocation. His interests will be promoted by passing as soon as he possibly can from the receipt of a reduced to that of the ordinary rate of wages. He will, consequently, only be a temporary object of relief. As the same remark can be made, too, in reference to every person who may apply for work at a reduced rate of wages,—while one set of labourers are thrown out of employment, and are disposed to become the objects of relief in the way now supposed, another set will cease to be the objects of relief, and will be passing into the service of the regular employers or capitalists. And were the system I am now considering to be for a time in operation, experience would teach us how to adjust the *wages of relief* in such a manner that the number of applicants to obtain them should be no greater than that of those who were declining to receive them any longer.

Here then we have an important advantage of this system of managing the unemployed poor over those systems concerning which I have already inquired, to wit, that it is practicable to limit the number of objects to be relieved; provided, that is, there be nothing in the system itself, all things being taken into account, which is calculated to deteriorate the general condition of the community,—a position I shall now endeavour to make good.

I shall admit, in the outset, that the confidence of being relieved in a season of difficulty, no matter how that relief may be administered, will of necessity have a tendency to impair the habits of foresight of every individual; and all that can in this respect be said, concerning the workmen who are placed in the circumstances I have supposed, is that, consistently with being relieved, their habits of foresight and independence could scarcely be impaired in a less degree.

But the condition of a people, or to express myself in other words, the command which they possess over the necessaries and luxuries of life, depends quite as much upon the comparative extent of their desires for enjoyment as upon their habits in respect to foresight. In accordance with this view of the subject, it would in my opinion be found, on comparing together two different countries, in one of which the wages of labour were double what they were in the other, or the same country at two different periods, in the one of which periods the wages paid were double what they were in the other period, that twice as much would not be saved from the double rate of wages. Political economists seem to me, indeed, in general to estimate too highly the amount which the labouring poor can be expected to save, in preference to consuming it on their immediate gratification. It is to be feared that, even when their condition shall have become improved to the fullest extent in which we can reasonably expect it to be, by far the greater portion of their incomes will be consumed in the last-mentioned manner, or, in other words, without leaving any trace of it behind.

Now the effect, other circumstances being the same, of their being enabled at all times to get employment at reduced wages, will be to prevent their desires for luxuries from being contracted as much as they would otherwise be; or what here obviously amounts to the same thing, to enlarge those desires.

To satisfy ourselves of this, we need only reflect on the misery to which the poorer classes of the labouring community are liable to be occasionally subjected, where no provision has been made by the wealthier portion of society, or by the public, for assisting them on the occurrence of any emergency,—a misery to suffer which cannot but tend to render the parties less desirous than they were to obtain the range of enjoyment they were accustomed to, and permanently to degrade, to a certain extent, their condition.

A due consideration of what has been said above appears to me to be in itself quite sufficient to induce us to hesitate in giving our assent to the doctrine, that a provision for the otherwise unemployed poor, of the nature supposed, must necessarily be productive of more evil than good. When, however, this provision is accompanied in its administration, as it ever ought to be, by every practicable effort to better the *moral* condition of the subjects of our charity, there can no longer be any doubt on my mind of the expediency of adopting it, and of complying by so doing with the unequivocal injunctions of the religion which we profess, as well as with the promptings of our benevolent feelings. Just in proportion as we shall succeed in diffusing among the paupers, whose bodily wants we contribute to relieve, the blessings of religion and of sound morals, and shall see that their children receive the benefit of even the lowest order of education, will we the more effectually guard against the evils adverted to, by the tendency of religion, of morals and of education, as has been repeatedly mentioned, to enlarge the command of a people over the necessaries and luxuries of life. And *in this way only* it is, in my opinion, possible to be the instrument of much immediate good to the poor and the wretched, without incurring the hazard of eventual detriment to the community.

The confidence which I have in the influence of the *moral appliances* of which I have been speaking, in extending the *physical* enjoyments of a people, is so great, that I have no fears of injurious consequences of any description to ensue from the widest exercise of private charity that is at all probable. In my view, let an individual, instead of indiscriminately relieving every applicant for his bounty at his door, from a mistaken notion of duty, or that he may speedily rid himself of the annoyance to his feelings resulting from the presence of so unwelcome a class of visiters, resolve in no case, unless where the distress suffered is manifestly extreme as well as real, to administer any relief whatever to the poor, without first making sufficient inquiry to protect himself and the community from the effects of imposture, and also without first visiting the abodes of misery, or it may be of vice, and supplying the moral as well as physical wants of their inmates;—let him do this, and he may have the satisfaction of knowing that the good which he is doing, whatever evil *tendencies* may be in operation, will be pure and unmixed good. But most persons will say that they have not the leisure to spare from their regular occupations, which is required by this mode of dealing with the pauperism of their vicinities; or that they are otherwise disqualified. I reply that they should be careful not to mistake their indisposition to undergo that trouble, without which no charity can be beneficially exercised, for a want of leisure, or for inability on their part. If, however, this be in reality the case, the only proper proceeding for them to have recourse to is to appoint others to be their almoners with the poor, who have more adaptation and leisure for the purpose than themselves, or who are actuated in a greater degree by the spirit of a Howard or a Fry.

A question of great importance, and one on which political economists are not yet agreed, is now presented for our consideration. Shall the relief of pauperism be left entirely to the benevolence of private individuals, or is it a proper subject for legislative enactment? With some, the abuses of the poor-laws in England, together with the abuses in the public administration of charity which it is notorious have not unfrequently occurred in our own country, have induced an opinion altogether hostile to any legislation concerning pauperism. There are others, on the other hand, who mistrust the adequacy of private charity, or of charity administered by voluntary associations of individuals, to provide for all the cases of pauperism which may occur, of a nature to render it desirable that they should become the subjects of relief.

Such a system of poor-laws as is based on the principle of setting the able-bodied pauper to work, at wages lower than the ordinary rate, has the advantage, over a condition of things in which he is left, in the time of his utmost need, exclusively to the tender mercies of his fellow-man, in the greater certainty of finding the assistance he requires, and at the time too when he most requires it, as well as in the greater uniformity of the assistance rendered under similar circumstances of distress;—a certainty and a uniformity, as I have shewn, not at all productive of injurious consequences to society; but on the contrary desirable, on the system of pauper relief in favour of which I have expressed myself, because of their beneficial effect, in preventing the labourers, who are from time to time thrown out of employment, from being, in consequence, depressed in their condition as much as they would otherwise be.

The great difficulty of an efficient poor-law lies in its practical execution. It is to be hoped that, with the diffusion among the community of more enlightened views of political economy, and especially of the principles which should regulate our practice in relation to alms-giving or pauper relief, properly qualified overseers of the poor will be more readily procurable than they have hitherto been. And I am, at least, not yet prepared, without farther evidence from experience, to embrace the opinion of the impracticability of every attempt, by the action of the legislature, to relieve the destitute portion of the community, so as at the same time not to affect the public welfare injuriously by the encouragement of habits of improvidence and dependence among the labourers generally.

One advantage of a public provision based on proper principles, for the labouring poor when thrown out of employment, seems to me to be sometimes entirely overlooked. I allude to the consequent greater willingness of the poorer classes generally to acquiesce in the inequalities of fortune which unavoidably result from the maintenance of the rights of property; rights so important, in reference to the interests of both rich and poor, to be always inviolably maintained.

After what has been delivered concerning the destitute poor who are able and willing to work, I need not dwell on the case of the infirm, the aged, and the young, who are unable to do so. Few or none who refuse to extend a helping hand to the former class would refuse it to the latter; and a large proportion of those who earnestly object to every public provision for the able-bodied poor concede, notwithstanding, the expediency of such a provision for all others. Moreover, if my readers shall have assented to the general correctness of the views which I have laid before him in this and the preceding chapter, I may safely leave him to apply those views for himself to the elucidation of the case now before us.

I shall now conclude what I have to say on the subject of pauperism by once more stating the main principles on which every systematic effort for relieving it should be based. These are, *first*, that the party relieved should never be rendered as comfortable as the independent labourer, and, for every piece of work done by him, that he should be underpaid; and *secondly*, that relief administered to the physical wants of a pauper should, as far as practicable, be accompanied by an attempt to improve him religiously and morally. It is by a disregard, or forgetfulness, of these principles, that pauperism has been so often multiplied by the very means which were destined to eradicate it; thus furnishing one of the most remarkable instances of the injury which benevolence, unenlightened by knowledge, is capable of inflicting.

CHAPTER XII.

OF TAXATION.

The only subjects remaining to be discussed in the present treatise are those which relate to the revenue of the government, and the sources whence it is to be derived. These sources may be classed under the two general heads of *taxation* and *public loans.*

In reference, first, to taxation, it will be most convenient to inquire into the operation of particular taxes, with an especial view to ascertain the parties on whom they are ultimately incident, before deducing the general principles by which the legislature of a country ought to be guided in the enactment of a system of taxation. It is in fact, only by adopting this arrangement that those principles can be exhibited to the student in an unobjectionable form.

I shall begin with supposing a tax to be imposed upon rent, wherever this may be paid, be it in agriculture, manufactures, or commerce; or I may say simply a tax upon the rent of *land;* considering the land, as was done in a preceding book, as the representative of all the situations or sites in which there is a return of rent to the proprietor, over and above the ordinary profits of the capital invested by him. Such a tax is merely a supposable one. From the impossibility of drawing the line practically between what is rent and what profits, the actual imposition of it may be regarded as out of the question. Still it will not be uninteresting or unimportant to trace its operation and ultimate incidence. By so doing, we shall, indeed, be throwing light on the effects of some very customary modes of taxing a people.

Whether the government exact the tax of which I am speaking from the landlord or proprietor of the land, or exact it from the farmer to whom he may have leased the land, and who pays him rent, it will be ultimately incident upon the landlord alone. If the first be the case, the landlord will not on this account, on the renewal of the lease, be able to get any additional rent from his tenant; for there is no reason why the supply of or demand for land to be leased should be altered in the slightest degree. He got as much as he could for the use of his land before the tax was imposed; and he can do no more than this now. Should he be so unwise as to insist upon receiving a higher rent,—and rent, it will be recollected, is the excess of the net produce of the land over the ordinary amount of agricultural profits,—the farmer would, obviously, not be able to realise those profits, and would consequently refuse to take the lease. So, too, would every other farmer; and the result would be that the landlord would have to cultivate his own land, and to continue therefore to pay the tax.

On the other hand, if we suppose the tax to be imposed in the first place on the farmer, there is no immediate remedy to which recourse can be had by him. At the expiration of his lease only, will he have it in his power to throw the burthen of the tax from off his shoulders on those of his landlord. Then, however, he will most certainly do it in the manner above described.

From the ultimate incidence on the proprietor of the land of every tax imposed upon rents, it follows that the whole rental, *strictly so called,* of the land of a country, could it be distinctly separated from the profits of the capital invested upon the land, might be considered as constituting a fund for taxation, which could be diminished by it to any extent, and even entirely exhausted, without the community,—the landlords alone excepted, — being subjected to the payment of the minutest portion of it.

Rent has been shewn to be property of a description differing from every other, in the very remarkable circumstance of its being conferred *gratuitously* on the owners of the land; and, whatever may be its amount at any particular period of time, its owners may, almost always, calculate upon deriving from it a revenue which will be continually augmenting in every succeeding period of the advancement of the country in wealth and population, and, all the while, without any sacrifice on their part. Now granting the extreme importance to the welfare of society of preserving inviolate the rights of property, and of studying to make the burthen of taxation press as equally as practicable on all the classes composing it, might it not be asked, with some plausible expectation at least of the inquiry being answered in the affirmative:—Whether, under the circumstances which have been mentioned, it would not be just, as well as expedient, to raise the whole of the public revenue by a tax upon the rent of land, and if more revenue were needed than all the rents of the country would amount to, not to resort to other taxes until those rents had been first exhausted? There could be no hesitation, it seems to me, to give an affirmative answer, if such a method of taxation had been practised in the country from its original settlement. Every person then, who at any time became possessed of land, would be aware that it would never yield him a greater revenue than the ordinary profits of the capital invested by him upon it, and that it would never be worth more than the value of such capital;—that is, provided the government were always to take for itself *the whole* of the rent. And in case it only took a part, the land, when sold, would be transferred from the seller to the buyer, subject to the whole of the rent being taken at the pleasure of the government. This condition of the sale would have its full effect on the value of the land, and could manifestly be pleaded by the government in justification of its taking afterwards as much of the rent as it pleased. But, in the actual state of things, the case is very different. The possession of the lands of a country has been passing, it may be for many centuries, with more or less frequency, from individual to individual; every new purchaser having as entire a reliance on the secure enjoyment of the produce, or advantages generally to be derived from it, as he could possibly have in the possession of any other kind of property. Hence it is that it would be quite as unjust, and therefore inexpedient, to tax exclusively or in an extraordinary degree the owners of the soil, as it would be to tax exclusively or in an extraordinary degree any other class of the community.

It will be impossible to take from the incomes of the landlords, or of any other class of men, without disadvantage to the community at large; since the whole amount of savings will consequently be lessened,—or, in other words, the rate of the accumulation of capital will be retarded. Hence some of my readers may, perhaps, think it inaccurate to speak of the *ultimate* incidence of a tax on one class of the community alone. And so it would be, did not the political economist neglect for the time all consideration of any disadvantage so arising; or which is the same thing, assuming it to arise, did he not limit his attention in the case to the greater degree in which it affected one class rather than another.

Others among my readers may regard the remarks just made to be altogether superfluous, and the impossibility of taking from the incomes of certain classes of the community without disadvantage to every other to have been too hastily asserted. They may maintain that, if what is taken is destined to a necessary, and therefore a productive expenditure or consumption, the national wealth could not be thereby diminished, nor the rate at which capital is accumulating be, in consequence, in any degree retarded. But while this is undeniably true, I shall remark that, in what has been above stated, and when the question is argued of the ultimate incidence of any tax imposed, all taxation is regarded as a *sacrifice* of a certain portion of the national wealth, which, however desirable or necessary it may be, is nevertheless an evil to be deprecated.

CHAPTER XIII.

THE SUBJECT OF TAXATION CONTINUED.

Let us now trace the consequences of imposing a tax on the profits of capital, and on the profits of capital in all employments alike.

Such a tax, *where it has not the effect of altering the exchangeable values of things*, will, obviously, not have the least influence on the amount of *rents* paid. The proportions in which the community will choose to consume the various necessaries and luxuries of life will continue the same; and these will, therefore, be produced in the same proportions as before. No transfers of capital will take place; and the share of the whole produce of the land, and of the whole produce too of the labour and capital of the country, which is distributed to the landlords, will remain unaffected. But, so long as we suppose wages to suffer no diminution, the rate of profits will have been lowered. Now, when the rate of profits is lowered, it has been shewn that the prices of all such commodities as are, in a greater degree than usual, the products of fixed rather than of circulating capitals will fall, when compared with the prices of such as are in a greater degree the products of circulating than of fixed capitals. In so far, consequently, as agricultural products may, on this account, have a higher or a lower exchangeable value, will it be possible for rents to be affected by a tax imposed, in the first instance, on the profits of capital.

Wages, however, will not be maintained at their former rate, if that of profits be lowered. In whatever degree the capitalists may be disposed to economise their expenditure,—their unproductive expenditure I mean,—it is not to be supposed that they will economise it to such an extent, as to enable themselves to save as much out of their incomes as before. Hence capital will accumulate less rapidly than it would have done but for the imposition of the tax under consideration. The consequence of this on wages, I shewed, when treating of population, to be to reduce them to a lower level. This, again, implies that profits will not fall quite as much as they would otherwise have done; so that the tax, instead of being incident exclusively on profits, will come to be divided between profits and wages.

The effect of a fall of wages on the relative prices of commodities being the opposite of that resulting from a fall in the rate of profits, viz. to cause the exchangeable values of those which are the products chiefly of fixed capitals to rise, when compared with those which are the products chiefly of circulating capitals, it is very possible that the fall of both profits and wages, just deduced, might so neutralise each other's influence, as to prevent any alteration whatever from occurring in the exchangeable value of agricultural products; and therefore in the rent of land, excepting such as may *continue* to result from the general retarding of the rate of the accumulation of capital. It will *then* be correct to say that no portion of the tax originally imposed on the profits of capital will be incident upon the landlords.

To what extent a tax on the profits of capital is incident

upon wages, will depend, other circumstances being the same, on the rate of profits. Where profits are high, the motive to save will be greater, as has before been mentioned, than it will be where they are low; and the same proportional tax upon them may, consequently, cause very different values, in the two cases, to be abstracted by the capitalist from his productive expenditure. In other words, the degree in which the labourer may be affected disadvantageously will be according to that in which the rate of profits was previously reduced.

By diminishing the capital of a country, or, what amounts to the same thing, by retarding its increase, a tax on the proceeds of capital operates, very plainly, in the same manner as if it were a tax on capital itself. If the government indeed, instead of ten per cent. upon profits,—profits being say at the rate of ten per cent. on the capital invested,—were to tax capital one per cent., the sum to be paid would be the same in both cases; and the productive would, in all probability, bear very much the same proportion to the unproductive consumption of the capitalist in the one case as in the other, were it not for the impression on the imaginations of men of the *names* given to the two taxes respectively. To a certain extent it will for this reason be true that, when an individual has a portion of his capital taken from him, he will more readily acquiesce in the loss he has sustained, and will be disposed to make somewhat less of a sacrifice of present gratification for the purpose of replacing it, than if the same amount were taken from his income. The extent of this difference is however, not unfrequently, very much exaggerated.

Here, as in the case of a tax on rents, it may be observed, that, on account of the impossibility of distinguishing in practice between rents and profits in those employments where rents are paid, especially in agriculture, a tax on profits is merely a hypothetical tax. And the same may also be observed in reference to a tax on capital; since we can in no instance form any definite estimate of the amount of capital which has been expended, or would require to be expended, to bring a portion of the soil of a country into its present condition.

Let us, next, look at the nature of a tax on wages. Such a tax, it may be surmised, cannot be as dissimilar in its mode of operation from that of a tax on capital, as some have supposed; for it will be recollected that wages constitute one of the elements of capital. I say surmised, since things which go by the same name, on account of their agreement in certain particulars, may yet, in other respects, be possessed of very different attributes. I shall proceed, then, to compare together the series of changes which will ensue on the imposition of a tax upon the wages of labour, and of an equal tax on capital in general.

First, it is evident that, if the government shall exact from the *employer of labour* a sum proportional to the amount of wages paid by him, he will regard it precisely in the same light that he would an equal tax on the whole of his capital; because, in the existing state of the arts, he will of course find it for his interest to apportion his capital between wages and the other descriptions of it just as he did before. A tax on wages is thus far, therefore, necessarily identical with a tax on capital.

Now let the *labourer* be taxed, and a certain per centage, suppose ten per cent., be subtracted from his wages by the government. The question is:—Will he be subjected to more deprivations than if the same value had, in the first instance, been taken from the capital of his employer? Will the fall of wages, in fact, be greater in the former case than in the latter? It seems to me that, in reference to the *immediate* results produced, no reason can be conceived for thinking that the fall would be greater in the slightest degree. As this is a point of some importance, I would not only request of the reader to consider it well before he advances farther, but likewise to look carefully at what would happen if the contrary from the imposition of a tax were to occur; for, by this means, the point itself under consideration cannot fail to be more clearly understood. In place of supposing a tenth of his income to be taken from the labourer, or an equal sum from the capitalist who employs him,—let an amount equivalent to the tenth part of his income be *added to it,* by the repeal of a tax previously imposed or in any other conceivable way, or let an equal value be added to the existing capital of the country. The reader cannot fail to perceive, on a moment's reflection, that such an augmentation of this capital can in reality only occur, by the capitalists being enabled to pay wages exceeding in amount the wages before paid by the value which has been added to capital; and that the immediate effects resulting from the two additions which have been supposed must be precisely the same.

And if the immediate effects in the two cases be the same, I need scarcely add that the *ultimate ones* must likewise be the same.

But even though the labourer should be affected in the first instance in a greater degree when a tax is imposed upon his wages, than when it is imposed upon the capital of his employer, it will not follow that his wages in the two cases will be ultimately different. On the contrary, through the more or less active operation of the principle of population, the reader cannot but perceive that very much the same rate of wages will come to be paid eventually in the one case as in the other.

If a tax be imposed on the profits of capital, on capital, or on wages, in one branch of industry only, or in a greater degree in any one branch of industry than in others generally, the effect will plainly be to cause a different distribution of the capital and labour of the country; these being transferred from where, in consequence of the supposed unequal taxation, they are now applied at diminished rates of profits and wages, to where these rates are comparatively higher. This new distribution too, of capital and labour, will be accompanied by a diminished production of wealth; since the community will be obliged to consume to a certain extent what, but for the tax imposed, they would not have preferred to consume.

CHAPTER XIV.

THE SAME SUBJECT CONTINUED.

A TAX on *property* differs from one on capital, *first,* in being a tax on the landlords as well as on the capitalists. The land possessed by the former class will have a certain value; and it is on this value that the tax in question is imposed. But two pieces of land, or other portions of real estate, of the same exchangeable value, may yield very different returns to their proprietor. Supposing them to be worth each $10,000, the one may, for example, yield him $600, and the other $300. Hence it may possibly be argued, that a tax on property would here be a very unequal one. Not so, however; because the only reason why the land which yields only $300 is worth as much as that yielding $600 is that it is expected to compensate for a present deficiency by a larger future return. Accordingly, as the period for this approaches, the value of the land will be continually augmenting. And its value at the end of a year will be $300 more than it is now. Its proprietor has, therefore, no reason to complain of the rate at which he is taxed. Independently too of this reasoning, the mere fact of this property being of equal exchangeable value with that of the other piece of land might be assumed as a sufficient ground for such taxation; for this circumstance alone is satisfactory evidence of equal advantages, all things considered, being derived in the two cases which are compared together.

But *secondly*, a tax on property will equally affect the wealth which is consumed unproductively and that which is consumed productively; and from this view of the nature of such a tax, its effects will very nearly correspond with those that have been shewn to be consequent upon a tax on the profits of capital.

On a review of what has thus far been delivered on the subject of taxation, I cannot doubt that my readers will be led to assent to the general equity of a tax on property. There are two considerations only which, in my opinion, may perhaps induce some of them to pause for a moment before assenting to it,—that many persons having large incomes have, nevertheless, comparatively very little property,—and that it may be difficult to form a proper scale of taxation for the rich and the poor.

In respect to the first of these, it will be recollected that, when capital is taxed, the effects are very nearly the same as they are when an equal tax is imposed on the *profits* of capital, and again that a tax on profits will operate very much in the same manner as one upon wages. And in respect to the second consideration just mentioned, I would make the scale of taxation a very simple one. I would tax every man's property, as far as practicable, in the very same proportion. To adopt this as a principle of action would be a refinement on the doctrines of free trade. It would be proclaiming to the world that government is in no case instituted for the purpose of discriminating between the different classes of society, according as they are rich or as they are poor; and that when the public good requires a certain amount of the wealth produced to be taken by the government, every portion of it should be affected exactly in the same way as if the productiveness of labour were proportionally diminished. By such a system of taxation inflexibly pursued, much of the jealousy, less or more every where existing, of the poor towards the rich, would be as effectually removed as by any means which could be imagined. Both classes, also, would be more likely to feel that their interests are identified; seeing that, in so far as all contributions for the general welfare are concerned, the one cannot be called upon to make a sacrifice, without the other being at the same time called upon to make a proportionate one. Indeed, the advantages of the system in question, in the view now taken of it, seem to my mind to be so very important, that I am almost disposed to maintain that governments have no right of acting on any other.

Should it, however, be still urged by any one that a man owning property to the value of $100 is less able to bear the loss of a dollar than another worth $100,000 is able to bear the loss of $1000, and that to tax them proportionally is therefore in fact to do injustice to the former,—I shall remind him of the manner in which a tax on property, however imposed, diffuses itself eventually among the different classes of the community, and shall express my conviction that the temporary inconveniences of a uniform rate of taxation are far overbalanced by the advantages which have been mentioned.

And let me not be charged, in consequence of any thing I have said, with being more disposed than political economists in general are to make the burthen of taxation press upon the poor. By shewing that the rich cannot be taxed without the poor at the same time suffering almost as much as if they themselves had been directly taxed, I have, on the contrary, not only furnished an additional instance of the manner in which the interests of the different classes of society are bound up together, but I have also furnished an argument against all taxation, of the rich as of the poor, excepting for purposes of unequivocal necessity or utility.

Next to an uniform tax on property, I would prefer such a tax on *incomes* of every description.

The former of these taxes is the preferable one of the two, first, because the incomes of individuals are not as susceptible of being estimated with as near an approach to accuracy as is their property, or the amount of what they are at any time worth. This is sufficiently evident in the cases of those whose incomes are derived from profits or wages, and still more so in that of the landlords, whose incomes, as this term is commonly understood, are often a very deceptive indication of their increase in wealth. Such increase, it has been before mentioned, may frequently exhibit itself by the increased value of the lands which belong to them.

Another reason for preferring a tax on property to a tax on incomes is the greater degree in which the poor will be taxed in the latter case than in the former; although the disadvantage to them will be in a great measure only apparent. Why so, I need not explain to the reader.

CHAPTER XV.

THE SAME SUBJECT CONTINUED.

The difficulty of estimating with accuracy the property or the incomes of individuals, together with the desire on the part of governments to disguise as much as possible from the different members of society the precise amount of the taxes which each of them is called upon to pay, have led to a very general reliance, for supplying in a considerable degree the wants of the public treasury, on certain *indirect* modes of taxation; to which I shall now direct the attention of my readers. I allude to the taxes which are imposed on *commodities* when produced at home, or when they are imported from abroad. In the former case they are denominated an *excise*, and in the the latter they are spoken of as *customs* or *duties*.

When the excise is paid by the producer, as must necessarily be the case in the first instance, it is plain that it can be of no importance in respect to the ultimate incidence of the tax, whether he shall be obliged to advance it immediately after he shall have completed the entire act of production,—or at some previous stage of that act, as will commonly be the case when, instead of the commodity produced, the processes or instruments of producing it are the subjects of taxation. At whatever period payment may have been exacted from him by the government, he will expect it to be refunded to him by the purchaser of his products; for then only will he be able to make the ordinary profits; and unless those profits are made by him he will transfer his capital to other employments. The purchaser again, if his business be to retail those products, will, for a like reason, expect his advances to be, in their turn, refunded; and so on, until the tax imposed fall wholly on the consumer. It is, moreover, worthy of note, that the consumer will not only have to pay a price for what he buys, greater by the amount of the tax than he would otherwise have had to pay for it, but that price will be yet farther enhanced by the profits which would have been yielded to the sum paid as a tax, had this been invested productively at the time of payment.

These conclusions will likewise all hold good in reference to the duties imposed on importations from foreign countries, as was fully explained in the preceding book. The merchants cannot continue their business without receiving the ordinary profits; and their capitals will be accordingly transferred to other employments, until profits are again equalised.

It will not appear singular that the importers of commodities from abroad should be *here* on the same footing with the producers at home, if we recollect in what the business of production really consists, and that the merchant is a producer in the very same sense in which the farmer or manufacturer is entitled to be so designated. They are all of them occupied in adding utility to matter, not by any act of creation,—this is the prerogative of Omnipotence alone,—but by simply removing it from one position in space to another.

I have noticed in another place the singular doctrine which has been maintained by some individuals of the highest political standing in our own country, that, instead of a duty imposed on foreign commodities imported being ultimately incident on the consumers of those imports, it is in reality incident on the producers of the commodities exported in exchange for them. At present, it may be proper to repeat that the only modes in which the producers or capitalists of a country can be ultimately affected by any tax whatever upon the consumption of the community,—and the parties, who hold to the ultimate incidence on the producers of a tax upon imports, do not deny the *prior* incidence of it upon the consumers,—are, first, by the difficulty of making those transfers of capital and labour which might be rendered necessary in the course of the changes resulting from the imposition of the tax, and secondly, by any fall in the rate of profits which might ensue.

Political economists adopt as a principle that an excise should be levied as late as possible in the production from first to last of a commodity, or, what is the same thing, on the finished product, rather than on the raw materials, and the materials in different stages of preparation, from which it is produced. By proceeding in this manner, the advances required to be made by the capitalist will not be needlessly augmented, Where a commodity too, on which a tax has been paid, becomes successively, when subjected to change, the materials of farther production, not one only, but several needless advances may be required. This last remark is, plainly, applicable in an equal degree to commodities imported from abroad, as to those produced at home. In all these cases, indeed, it is no doubt true that the advances made will be fully reimbursed, and reimbursed with the due amount of profits. Nevertheless, to be obliged to carry on one's business, as may not unfrequently be the case, with a larger amount of capital than, but for such a tax as I am now speaking of, would be required to carry it on with advantage, is a *disadvantage*, especially to the smaller capitalists.

Where an excise is levied on particular processes or instruments of production in the arts, the employment of all other processes or instruments is apt to be regarded as illegal, and to be proscribed accordingly. A check to improvement will thus be most improperly and most injudiciously applied by the government itself; one of whose chief objects should, on the contrary, ever be to give every encouragement in its power to the progress of improvement.

Another evil, connected with every system of excise, is the inquisitorial character of the manner of collecting the tax imposed. The tax-gatherer must necessarily be clothed with an authority very susceptible of being abused, and therefore in fact very often abused; and his undesirable visits to the manufactory or workshop will of itself be an annoyance. And this evil, like every other to which the producers of wealth are subjected by taxation, will not be confined to themselves. They will, in truth, receive full compensation for it in an augmented rate of profits, of course brought about by the transfer of capital to other employments, and the consequent enhancement of the prices of the commodities which they produce; that is, every vexation or annoyance inflicted will be paid for by the consumers.

Here it may be observed that care should always be taken, in the enacting either of a system of excise or of a tariff of duties,—and this is true whether these last be intended as revenue or protecting duties,—that the tax imposed shall be comparatively lighter according to the facility with which it admits of being evaded. If this consideration be neglected, or if the taxation of any article be exorbitantly high, the consequence will inevitably be a disposition, more or less generally extended among the community, to evade the law, and by dishonest artifices avoid the payment of the tax,—not to speak of the more aggravated offences of the *smuggler*.

Besides the inconveniences, already mentioned, which are connected with the taxes we are now occcupied in considering, their collection costs more, generally speaking, than that of an equal amount of taxes directly imposed would probably do. And indeed, as was stated in the beginning of the present chapter, the principal, if not the only reason, why governments have so often preferred them to all others, is the possibility, on account of their comparatively imperceptible operation, of extracting from the people in this way a greater revenue than in any other.

I need scarcely in this place remind the reader that, in speaking of the ultimate incidence of a tax on the consumer, and not at all on the producer, it is not intended to deny that the latter will be affected by the diminution of the national wealth which may be consequent upon the unproductive expenditure of the tax. Such expenditure of it must have precisely the same effects as if labour had become less productive. It will therefore tend to produce a fall of profits. What the government actually receives is, however, never equivalent to the loss incurred by the tax-payers. Even if we omit the expenses of collection, this will not be the case when the tax imposed is a partial one. To illustrate my meaning by an example: let the only commodity taxed be *tea* on its importation into the country. Its price, as has been shewn, will rise. Many persons, especially if the duty upon it be considerable, will cease to consume it; while those who continue to consume it will consume it in less quantity than they were accustomed to do. Now the gratification foregone by the consumption of other things instead of tea, which, but for the tax upon it, would have had the preference, is an item, and it may be a considerable one, that is manifestly a sacrifice made by the parties concerned, without any accession to the public revenue; a sacrifice tending, also, to render the fall in the general rate of profits greater than it is necessary that it should be. It becomes important to diminish all sacrifices of the kind as much as is practicable, by distributing the taxation imposed among the various articles of consumption. And we may *conceive* the distribution to be so adjusted as not to interfere in any degree with the proportions in which those articles are consumed.

It may be added that the unequal taxation of the various articles of consumption will induce the same transfers of capital and labour, as are consequent upon the unequal taxation of the capital employed in the different branches of industry.

CHAPTER XVI.

THE SAME SUBJECT CONTINUED.

After having inquired into the effects of taxing rents, the profits of capital, capital itself, and the wages of labour, I proceeded to consider those resulting from the system of indirect taxation, on which, in modern times, so much reliance has been placed for supplying the wants of the public treasury. I shall, next, examine in succession the operation and ultimate incidence of certain taxes chiefly of a direct nature, most of which have been often imposed as collateral means for the same purpose.

To begin, let a tax be imposed upon the land of a country; and say on all land alike, whether cultivated or uncultivated, —whether employed for any useful purpose or not. In what respects will the effects be different from what they were shewn to be in the case of a tax on the *rent* of land? I observe, in the first place, that if the value of land were determined exclusively by the present income derived from it, the portion of it which is in a state of nature, being suffered to remain in that state simply because it cannot yield the ordinary profits to the capital applied to cultivate it, would have no value whatever. When the tax is imposed upon it, its ownership will for this reason be abandoned to the government; to which it can be of no more service than it was to its former owner. Indeed, there is no reason why the owner, even before the imposition of the tax, should not have been quite as willing to abandon all claim to the land, as to hold it. But the present value of land is determined, in a degree, by what its value at a *future* period is expected to be. Very possibly, therefore, it might bear to have a tax imposed upon it of a certain amount, though it be not sufficiently fertile or favourably situated with respect to a market to admit of its being profitably cultivated. Such a tax as this will evidently be paid at first by the proprietor of the land: and it must be also ultimately paid by him, because there is no one to whom he will be able to transfer it.

The rent of land, employing the word rent as men commonly do, may be the subject of taxation. This kind of rent consists of two elements, to wit, rent properly or technically so called, and the profits of the capital invested on the land by its owner. If the tax imposed be less than or equal to the former of these two elements, it will in fact be a tax on that element alone: if the tax be greater, it will, in part, become a tax on the profits of the capital invested; and the consequences will be a transfer of this capital as far as it admits of being transferred, together with the abandonment of the land as in the case just before considered.

Similar consequences will result when the gross, instead of the net produce, of the land, is taxed, as in the case of *tithes*,—and will result, indeed, from every supposable tax on the land.

A repeal of the taxes, of which I have been treating in the present chapter, will, of course, be followed by consequences the opposite to those which ensued when the taxes were originally imposed. To give only a single illustration, suppose the tithes paid in Great Britain for the support of the established church to be abolished. So long as the existing leases continue, the profits of the farmers or tenants will be above the ordinary rate; and so long will they enjoy the whole benefit conferred by the abolition of the tithes. But when their leases shall have expired, that benefit will necessarily pass from them to the landlords; it being always in the power of the latter to exact from the farmers, in every instance, as much rent as will leave them the ordinary rate of agricultural profits, and no more. The whole benefit would, at least, be thus transferred to the landlords, were it not that a certain portion of land can now be cultivated with advantage, which was before incapable of yielding the ordinary profits to the capital invested upon it, and was incapable of doing so on account of the necessity of paying tithe. The cultivation of additional land will prevent rents from rising as much as they would otherwise do; as they did not fall (on account of the necessity just mentioned) as much as they would otherwise have done, when the same land was obliged, by the imposition upon it of tithe, to be thrown out of cultivation. And the diminution of the exchangeable value of agricultural products which will have taken place,—a diminution of value, without the occurrence of which rents would, indeed, have risen to the full extent at first mentioned,—will confer an advantage to a certain amount upon the community, at the expense, if the expression may be here used, of the landlords. Besides this advantage, which is no doubt smaller, and, very probably, much smaller, than that derived by the landlords from the augmentation of their rents, a peculiar advantage would result, from the repeal of tithes, to the parties by whom it is in the first instance paid, in their being relieved from the vexations unavoidably connected with the collecting of it; aggravated, moreover, as those vexations are, by an impression of tithes being paid, as well ultimately, as in the first instance, by those from whom it is levied by the government. The extraordinary expenses, too, of collecting so vexatious and therefore so obnoxious a tax, which have often to be incurred, would be saved to the public by its repeal. And I may add that we shall find an additional reason for its repeal, in the injury inflicted on the cause of religion itself by rendering the clergy, through whose instrumentality and for whose especial benefit, the tax in question was imposed, in a certain degree the objects of dislike or aversion to the poorer classes of the people;—not to mention the purely political considerations that ought to prompt to the adoption of such a measure.

The question as to the most expedient mode of providing for the clergy is, however, foreign from the subject of the present treatise; and I am, therefore, not called upon to give my reasons why, in common with the universally expressed opinion in the United States, I hold to the *voluntary* system. Men may differ *toto cœlo* concerning this matter, as they may do concerning the form of government best fitted for a particular nation, and yet be ready to subscribe to all the essential doctrines of political economy.

But whether, on the abolition of tithes, other taxes of an equivalent amount shall, or shall not, be substituted for them in order to provide for the clergy, it will be proper to impose such a tax on the land as may, in its effect upon rents, counteract that rise of them which would otherwise ensue. Unless something of this kind be done, a considerable part of what was before the support of the clergy will have been taken from them, and simply handed over to the proprietors of the land. Should the diminished wants of the government not require the revenue which is to be derived from the suggested tax, it might, notwithstanding, be the most expedient course to impose this; at the same time repealing one or more others.

CHAPTER XVII.

THE SAME SUBJECT CONTINUED.

I NEED not dwell at any length on the several modes of taxation which are yet to be mentioned, as they must necessarily partake more or less of those already considered. They may be mentioned, also, in almost any order.

Let a tax be imposed upon the sale of property, or upon contracts for the transfer of property from one individual to another at a future day. These taxes have this disadvantage, that they prevent in a certain degree the most profitable distribution of the national wealth. If we suppose the price of a certain article to be at such a rate as to induce its possessor to offer it for sale, but that a tax of the kind just mentioned is imposed before any sale shall have been actually effected, the inference is plain that the article in question would be withdrawn from the market, unless it can be sold at an advance above its former price equal to the amount of the tax. Now the individual who might have been willing to purchase it before, being thus obliged, in the event of his becoming a purchaser, to refund the tax exacted from the seller by the government, may very well refuse to purchase. And the article will have to remain in the possession of its present owner; although, if transferred to some other individual, it might, very probably, have been employed more productively, that is with a greater profit, and, of course, more advantageously to the whole community. Should the tax be exacted from the purchaser, the conclusion to be drawn is obviously the same.

The customary mode of deriving a revenue from the transfers of property,—a method recommended by the facility and very inconsiderable expense of collection,—is by requiring the evidences of all contracts and sales to be recorded on stamped paper, issued by authority of the government, and having a different value according to the amount of property to be transferred.

A tax bearing some analogy to the foregoing, because the circulation of commodities is impeded by it, is one imposed on their transportation from place to place. Such, for example, are the tolls which are levied upon carriages on roads, and upon boats on canals. They can be shewn to be ultimately incident, like every other tax upon the producers, on those who consume the commodities transported, and are therefore no more liable to objection than are the taxes in general that are paid by the consumers.

Travelling, as well as the transportation of commodities from one part of a country to another, is a subject of taxation; and a moment's reflection will suffice to satisfy the reader that, whether imposed in the first instance on the traveller, or on the proprietor of the stage-coach or other conveyance in which he performs his journey, the whole burthen of the tax will, in fact, be borne by the former. The advantage gained, or gratification received by him, will evidently, in this case as in every other, have to be paid for by the consumer.

Both the descriptions of tax which have been last considered are recommended by the facility of collecting them; and there would be no ground for objecting to them under any circumstances, so long as they were not higher than a fair equivalent for the use of the *communication* by land or water along which passengers or goods are conveyed. This is a self-evident proposition. The only difficulty here is,—as to what is to be regarded as a fair equivalent for the benefit conferred. It may, indeed, be stated to be such a tax or toll as, after paying for keeping the road, or whatever the communication may be, in repair, will enable the government to make the ordinary profits on the capital expended in its construction. But how is this point to be determined? If the business of road making were open to every member of the community to engage in it, there would be no need for us to concern ourselves on the subject. Competition would not fail to keep the rates of toll at their proper level, on the roads constructed by the government as on every other. A state of things like this exists in no country, and it may be regarded as one altogether out of the question. The making of roads, and of canals too, being every where monopolised,—I use this word in no bad sense,—by the government, or by parties authorised for the purpose by the government, more than the proper rate of toll may, it is plain, be exacted. Of every such payment beyond the value received there would be good reason to complain, unless other taxes were at the same time imposed, bearing more particularly upon the classes of society not affected by the tolls of which I have been speaking. In a country however, like our own, where the commodities consumed have to be conveyed to very unequal distances, and where those who travel are of almost all descriptions of persons, it would be not a little difficult to discover any such *compensatory* taxes. This difficulty, together with the acknowledged principle of avoiding as much as is practicable the taxing of particular classes of the community, is, in general, a sufficient security against the *excess* of taxation of which mention has been made.

Remarks similar to the above may be made in reference to the postage of letters. The government of a country should never look to the post office for a revenue. It ought to rest satisfied if the expenses of the institution are borne by those who are directly benefited. I might, perhaps, with propriety, go even farther, and maintain the expediency, in so far as newspapers and periodicals are concerned, of making some *sacrifice* to promote by their circulation the diffusion of knowledge, political and literary, among the great body of a people.

Governments have not always contented themselves with taxing the transfer of property from one to another among the living, but have sometimes interfered between the living and the dead, by the imposition of a tax upon legacies, or upon the property generally of those who die. A tax of this kind, there can scarcely be a doubt, is, of all possible taxes, that which is paid with the least reluctance. The deceased owner of what is taken was permitted to keep quiet possession of it to the last moment of his life: and the heir or legatee will more readily pardon the act of the government in appropriating to its own use a part of his predecessor's wealth, at the time when the remainder is transferred to himself than at any subsequent period. The disadvantage which may be imputed to this manner of raising a revenue is, that the productive consumption of the country is affected by it in a greater degree than the unproductive. We may infer this from the circumstance of what is received from another at a period not previously determined, but depending for its occurrence on a contingency, being regarded by the recipient as so much clear gain. He will be indisposed to economise his unproductive consumption in order farther to augment his capital; and the result will be a greater retardation of a nation's advance in wealth than if a tax had been avowedly imposed on the profits of capital, or even on capital itself.

A tax was, a few years ago, imposed in Pennsylvania on collateral inheritances; that is, on the property of those persons who die without leaving any children behind them. One advantage of such a tax is, obviously, the same in kind, though somewhat enhanced in degree, with that which was stated to subsist in the preceding case. The property inherited from more remote relations will have been regarded, before the possession of it is actually obtained, less in the light of property belonging to the heir, the enjoyment of which is only postponed for a time, than if it had descended from his immediate ancestor. He will, on this account, acquiesce still more readily in a part being taken from him for public purposes, at the time of his becoming possessed of it. There is also another advantage which may be ascribed to a tax on collateral inheritances when compared with one upon inheritances descending from parent to child, to wit, that the children who, having had their own parents to provide for them, have besides had property left to them of the former description, will be relatively better able to sustain the weight of taxation. I need scarcely say that the *disadvantages* of taxing the different kinds of inheritances will correspond very much with their comparative advantages. If, indeed, the notion of some of the advocates of the tax under consideration had any foundation to rest upon,—the notion, I mean, that it would operate as an encouragement to matrimony, and thus tend to increase the population of the country,—it would be accompanied by a disadvantage of a peculiar nature. To contribute to such a result by the very measure adopted to take from the national wealth, or, what is the same thing, from the means of support of the community, would be altogether preposterous. It would be the decreeing the degradation to a certain extent, in place of the improvement, of the condition of the people. But I have no idea of any one having been stimulated, by the collateral inheritance bill of Pennsylvania, to marry, with the purpose in view of evading, *on his death*, the payment of the tax imposed; and the bill, in my opinion, was therefore, in this respect, perfectly harmless. Nor do I think it probable that, amounting as it did to only a small per centage on the value of the inheritance taxed, the imposition of the tax in question has led to many removals of unmarried persons from the state. Such removals from it, implying too the withdrawal of capital, would have been necessarily injurious to it. The tax may be *conceived* to be so high as in fact to produce a considerable amount of injury.

And I may be permitted to remark here that, after what

has been delivered in the second book of this treatise on the principle of population and the consequences flowing from it, the reader must perceive the absurdity of every measure, financial or otherwise, having for its object to increase the number of marriages. The governments by whom they have been enacted have been deplorably ignorant of the subject on which they undertook to legislate; and they were, especially, unaware that the difficulty was not to multiply the numbers of a people, but to provide for them adequate means of support.

CHAPTER XVIII.

THE SAME SUBJECT CONTINUED.

To tax judicial proceedings is, obviously, to render the administration of justice unnecessarily expensive: and worse than this; because in proportion as the administration of justice is rendered more expensive to litigants, it is converted into the administration of injustice to the poorer classes of society. When injured in their property or otherwise, if the expense of a law suit be so great that they cannot afford to incur it, there is nothing left for them but to submit, as quietly as they may, to the injury inflicted.

A poll tax, or tax, to an equal amount, upon every member of a community, or upon every member of it who has arrived at a certain age, is liable, in the same or a greater degree, to the objection which has been made to a tax on wages, namely, that more in proportion is taken by it from the incomes of the poor than from those of the rich.

But it would be needless for me to notice all the varieties

of possible taxation. The principles which have been explained, and the details already given, will enable the intelligent reader to trace for himself the advantages or disadvantages connected with any case that may be presented to him. I shall, accordingly, specify only two cases more,—a tax on *exports* to foreign countries, and a tax on *dwelling-houses*, or say on the *rent* of dwelling-houses.

The former tax might, perhaps, have been treated most appropriately immediately after that upon imports from abroad; but it is not easy to arrange in a manner wholly unexceptionable the discussion of the different topics embraced in so comprehensive a subject as taxation; and I shall be content if my arrangement shall have been such as is consistent with a perspicuous and logical exposition of my opinions. To proceed however, I remark that the merchants, who must necessarily pay the tax upon exports in the first instance, will no longer ship to foreign countries the same quantity of the articles taxed; and their prices abroad will, in consequence, rise. This rise will continue until prices shall become high enough to enable the merchants to repay themselves the amount of the taxes advanced by them; when they will once more make the ordinary profits on their respective capitals. In this state of things, the tax will be incident on the foreign consumers. The articles taxed will not be consumed abroad as extensively as before; and the quantity of them produced at home will therefore be also diminished. A transfer of capital must on this account ensue, bearing a close analogy to that which was shewn to take place when the exports of a country are diminished by the imposition of duties on imported commodities. Exports may be taxed so highly as very much to reduce the quantity of them consumed, or even to prevent their consumption altogether; just as the tax upon imports may be so high as to produce the like effects. While in the latter case the price of an article may have risen so much that a similar article may be produced *at home* at the same or a less price, or people may, rather than purchase it at the present rate, contrive to do without it; in the former case, the price of an article may have risen so much that either a similar article may be produced *abroad* at the same or a less price, or people may contrive to dispense with the use of it altogether. The analogy between the two cases is, in short, complete, excepting only the circumstance of the tax imposed being, in the one, paid by the foreign, and, in the other, by the domestic consumers.

Recourse has been very seldom had to taxes upon exports; and, in the United States, there is a provision in the constitution of the general government, prohibitory of the imposition of any such taxes. Why has this been the case, and why this prohibition? For if a tax upon exports is ultimately incident upon the consumers abroad, and a tax upon imports upon the consumers at home,—while the effects moreover, which are produced by the two taxes respectively, are in other respects so analogous as has been stated,—it would seem that the action of governments in the matter has been entirely wrong, and that they ought clearly to give a preference to a tax upon exports over one of imports. In our own country, too, the collection of the tax upon exports would, all other circumstances being the same, be more easy and more certain, from the more uniform nature of the commodities sent abroad, when compared with those received in return for them, as well as from the greater value in a given bulk they possess, generally speaking, and by possessing which they cannot so readily evade the payment of the tax imposed.

The most influential reason which can be assigned, why the exports of a country have been protected so extensively from taxation, is unquestionably to be found in the erroneous notions that have been less or more extensively prevalent with respect to the true nature of national wealth. When it was supposed that a country was wealthy and prosperous exactly according to the quantity of money in circulation, and when the possibility of maintaining always a permanent excess of exports above imports was every where adopted as a maxim, which excess was, besides, to be invariably paid for in the precious metals, it is not to be wondered at that the imposition by any government of a tax upon exports, unless for some very peculiar reason, should have been regarded by its subjects, as well as by itself, as an absurdity, or even worse, —as a sort of treason against the state.

Another reason for not taxing exports, rather than imports, has been, that the parties who are the immediate sufferers would, in all probability, complain much more in the former case than in the latter; partly, perhaps, because a commodity which is to be exported, being in the actual possession of its owner, and capable of being disposed of by him in the country itself where he lives without the payment into the public treasury of any portion of what he receives for it, seems to his imagination to be more emphatically his property than is another commodity which is imported from abroad, and which can scarcely be said to have come into his possession, or to be his, until the duty upon the importation of it shall first have been paid;—but especially, because the different classes of producers whose interests are affected disadvantageously, and who will be obliged to transfer their capitals from their existing employments to others, are more distinctly traceable in the case of a tax upon exports, than they are in that of a tax upon imports.

But the question may be asked,—whether, consistently with the principles of political economy, as they have been deduced in the present treatise, it would not be preferable to impose duties upon commodities exported rather than upon those which are imported? Whether, in other words, it would not be better to levy a tax upon the foreign, than upon the domestic consumer? The answer is plain, that it would be so, provided only that other countries would submit to such a state of things without retaliating; and which it may be taken for granted that they are not at all likely to do. If every government were to derive its revenue from the taxing of exports, and these were taxed everywhere in a similar proportion to their value, no advantage could possibly result to a country at the expense of any other. And if the system of taxation was not thus uniform, it appears to me that it would, far more frequently even than the existing tariff systems, tend to generate hostile feelings among nations, and to embroil them with each other. Where, indeed, any one nation was found to be obstinately adhering to the antiquated notions concerning the balance of exports and imports, or, to use the more technical language of former statesmen, of the balance of trade, they would *deserve* to be punished for shutting their eyes to the progress of knowledge which is going on all around them, by being obliged, in consequence of the imposition by other nations of a tax on exports, to pay tribute to them for whatever foreign products they consume.

In relation to a tax on dwelling-houses, which is the only tax I propose yet to remark upon, I may mention that it is precisely of the same nature, however it may be imposed, with some of the taxes already considered. When imposed upon the rent, as this term is commonly understood, paid by the tenants to the landlords, it is analogous in its effects and ultimate incidence to a tax imposed on the *gross* product of the land. It may not, however, be superfluous to trace those effects here as they successively occur, on the amount required being exacted in the first instance from the *landlords;* furnishing, as in this case they do, a striking illustration of a transfer of the burthen of taxation from one class of persons to another.

Let a tax, then, of ten per cent. be imposed on *house-rent.* It must, in the first place, be evident that, during the whole period of every existing lease of a house, the landlord can find no remedy for what he has thus to pay. If his rent was before $400, it will now be equivalent, in so far as he is concerned, to the sum of only \$360. But when the period for renewing the contract between landlord and tenant shall again come round, will the former be able to get rid of the tax by in any way inducing the latter to pay him a higher rent,—to pay him \$440 instead of \$400. Certainly not, so long as the supply of houses and the demand for them shall remain the same. The landlord got as much rent from his tenant before as he could; and there is no reason why he should now get more. He will, however, be making less than the ordinary profits upon his capital: a check will thus be given to the building of new houses; the supply of houses will be gradually diminished, while the demand for them continues unaltered; and house-rent will consequently be on the rise. Families which before occupied houses of a certain description will be content with those that are inferior: others which already lived in the smaller or inferior sort will be obliged to rest satisfied with merely occupying apartments in a house. This deterioration of the condition of the tenants will only cease when the ordinary profits are once more received by the landlords; that is, when the whole of the tax imposed has become incident upon the tenants. Building will, of course, be then resumed, and the supply, in this case as in every other, be accommodated to the demand.

CHAPTER XIX.

THE GENERAL PRINCIPLES OF TAXATION.

What, now, are the general principles which should serve as a guide to governments in the enactment of a system of taxation?

I answer, first, that the amount of taxation should be as small as is possible, consistent with a due regard to the interests for the protection and promotion of which governments are instituted. This remark may seem to be a very obvious and common-place one, even to those persons who are the least versed in political economy. My object, in nevertheless formally stating it, is to impress upon the reader's mind, as forcibly as I can, what is a productive and what an unproductive public expenditure; agreeably to the meaning annexed to these terms in the present treatise. The writers who adopt the distinction between the productive and the unproductive *labourers* are led by it to designate all the individuals employed and paid by the government, in the different departments of the administration, executive, judicial, military, &c., as well as the government itself, as unproductive,—and the whole of the public expenditure likewise, without exception, as unproductive. It will be recollected, on the other hand, that the various classes just referred to are considered by the author as all and equally entitled to be styled productive; and that, in his view, no portion of their labour or services ought at any time to be regarded as unproductive, unless where more persons are employed than are necessary for accomplishing the object proposed, or where that object is an improper one. The salaries or wages too, which the government pays for the labour thus styled productive, if they be no more than a fair compensation for it, are necessarily a productive expenditure; as is manifestly the case with every other expenditure on the part of the government for some legitimate object. Hence the greater portion of the public expenditure, and even the whole of it, may be *conceived* to be of a productive kind. If the last were in fact the case, so far from taxation having any tendency to diminish the existing wealth of a country, or to retard the progress of national wealth, its effects will be exactly the reverse, in as much as what it takes from the people would, had it been left with them, have scarcely been at all productively consumed. And the inference cannot be resisted that, with an economical administration of the government,—economical, I mean, in relation to the proper wants and duties of government,—taxation is no evil. I will add, in order to guard against any possible misapprehension of my meaning on a point of so much importance and delicacy as this, that, when taxation is asserted under the circumstances supposed to be no evil, it is taken for granted that there is nothing in the manner of its apportionment among the community calculated to cause any unnecessary vexation, or to press unequally upon particular classes, especially if these be the poorer classes. Let it be observed, moreover, that I have not asserted the *probability* of a government being administered with the strictest attention to economy. This has, indeed, been very seldom the case. Generally speaking, a government is tempted to expend profusely and unnecessarily, exactly in proportion to its ability of extracting the means for so doing from the pockets of its subjects.

To illustrate my meaning of the distinction between a productive and an unproductive public expenditure by the example of a standing army, I shall assume that, under the circumstances in which the United States are placed in respect to the nations with which they are likely to come into collision, and in respect to the Indian tribes on their frontiers or within their borders, an army of 20,000 men is adequate for providing against any emergency that may occur in the midst of peace, or for forming the nucleus of a still larger army in time of war. Now to maintain such an army would be a productive expenditure; on the supposition, however, of this expenditure not being at an extravagant *rate*. And for the government to insist on maintaining an army of only 10,000 men, or to undertake to maintain one of 40,000, would be, in both cases alike, to cause the national wealth to be consumed less productively than it ought to be. The *capital* which might have been applied to the maintenance of the 20,000 men with the proper returns, will not yield proportional advantages if it be either diminished one half, or if it be doubled in amount. A diminution of *wealth* would result, of a nature precisely analogous to the loss of wealth that would be incurred, were the government of a country to regulate the investments of capital in such a manner as to cause to be produced twice as many or half as many hats and shoes, as would be produced should the hatters and shoemakers be guided by no other consideration than the relative wants of the community.

It is no argument to prove the *unproductive* character of the soldiers of an army to say that if the men composing it were discharged they could and would be engaged in some productive employment, and that the same wages which maintained them before could still be applied to their maintenance while thus productively employed. I say this is no argument, because the like may be asserted in reference to every other class of the communiy; the criterion of the unproductiveness or productiveness of the labour employed being always the same, to wit,—is there, or is there not, more labour employed in any occupation than the interests of the community require?

If the expenditure of the government was always regulated with a single eye to the real interests of the governed, I may observe that all that part of my reasoning in the foregoing chapters which was founded on the implied supposition of the national wealth being diminished, or its progress retarded by taxation, would have no foundation to rest on; and the consequences deduced would be of no effect. Their effect too, in reality, will always be proportional to the unproductive expenditure of the government.

The next general principle in reference to the subject of taxation I shall mention is, that, other circumstances being the same, it is desirable the taxes imposed should be so distributed as to give occasion to as few transfers of capital as possible. This principle has been frequently referred to in what precedes; and it is, therefore, already familiar to the reader. I shall, accordingly, merely remind him that, when no transfers of capital shall ensue on account of taxation, the various products of industry will be consumed in the very same proportions as before, and the community will not, besides the proper evils of taxation, suffer any of those collateral evils which result from the individuals composing it being obliged to consume what, but for the taxes imposed, they would not have chosen to consume.

Another principle, closely connected with the preceding, is, *cæteris paribus*, that an old tax is preferable to a new one. To substitute the latter in place of the former is at the same time enacting that, on the one hand, more than the ordinary profits, and, on the other, less than the ordinary profits shall be made by the capitalists respectively employed in producing the commodities taxed. Although here, at first, what is one man's loss is another man's gain, yet there can be no doubt, as I have before explained, that the loss is uncompensated by the gain, if we estimate all the circumstances of advantage or of disadvantage concerned. In taking from one man and giving to another, the inconvenience or distress which the former suffers is never, in the scale of national happiness, or what is the same thing as wealth has been defined, in the scale of national wealth, equivalent merely to the augmented command possessed by the latter over the necessaries and luxuries of life. But again, in the transfers of capital consequent upon the loss of which I speak, a certain portion of capital is always abandoned; and although, by the abandoning of this, no *additional* loss is incurred, but rather (as I before mentioned in an analogous case) prevented, yet some idea of the actual loss, the reader will not fail to perceive, may be formed from it.

A tax which will have the effect of lowering the profits received in a branch of industry where the circulating predominates over the fixed portion of the capital invested, is preferable to one which will diminish the profits of capital where this is in a greater degree fixed than circulating. The truth of this proposition follows necessarily from the greater facility, generally speaking, of transferring circulating than fixed capital.

Taxes should be imposed rather upon a commodity which is prepared for *final* consumption than upon one which is in any degree the material on which labour is still farther exerted; rather also upon such objects as cannot easily, on account of their possessing a great value in proportion to their bulk, or for any other reason, be subtracted from the operation of the taxes; and they should be imposed with a view to readiness and economy of collection. After what has been stated, in the preceding chapters concerning taxation, the reader will not need any proof of these several propositions.

I need not here repeat my reasons for not imposing a greater tax on one species of income than on another, or for preferring a direct tax on property to any other tax.

Nor is it necessary for me to say any thing farther concerning the inexpediency and injustice of governments undertaking to travel out of their proper province, and to violate the rights of property, as they do when they sit in judgment on the *distribution* of the national wealth, determining at their pleasure how much of it shall belong to the rich, and how much to the poor; for this is what is in reality done by them when they take from the former, by means of taxation, any more than their proportional share.

In opposition to the opinions, which, so far as I know, are universally prevalent, concerning the peculiar respect due by a government to the capital of a country, and concerning the propriety therefore, in every system of taxation, of taxing in preference the unproductive, rather than the productive consumption of the community, I shall remark that, in my view, governments ought never to meddle, in any manner whatever, with the proportions in which the wealth produced is destined by its owners to constitute their present or their future consumption; and that they ought to endeavour so to distribute the taxes imposed by them as not to interfere with the existing habits of the community as regards saving or spending. Indeed, if governments are entitled to interfere with those habits when legislating for the purpose of raising a revenue, why should they not interfere directly with those habits by the enactment of sumptuary laws, now every where condemned as an improper invasion of the rights of individuals?

To avoid all possible misconception of my meaning when laying down general rules for the imposing of taxes, I may state what is sufficiently obvious to every reflecting mind, —that those rules will often in practice be found to be inconsistent with each other. As an illustration of this, I may adduce the instance of the same *ad valorem* duty on the importation from abroad of tea and coffee, and of jewelry, being out of the question, unless when the duty is a very low one; on account of the last article possessing comparatively a great value in a given bulk, and being, in consequence of this, easily made to evade the payment of the duty, or, in other words, being easily smuggled into the country. We may also conclude, if the rate of taxation be high, against taxing the importation of tea and coffee *in a less degree* than the importation of jewelry, although the former articles, in the actual condition of society, partake largely of the character of a necessary of life, while the latter is manifestly a mere luxury. Other illustrations cannot fail to present themselves to the reader on a little reflection. And in the case of taxation, as in every other where the rules of action deduced are found occasionally to clash with each other, all that can be done is to endeavour to reconcile them in practice as far as we can possibly contrive to do so.

Before leaving the subject of taxation, it may be proper for me to mention,—what is, indeed, implied in the statements which have been already made,—that, just in proportion as a greater amount of the whole produce of labour is taken to itself by the government, will the general cost of production be enhanced. The effect will be the same as if labour had become less productive. Wealth and population will increase less rapidly than before; or they may even be made to decrease. And the cost of producing a particular commodity, and consequently its price, may have been so much enhanced, as to diminish exceedingly the quantity of it consumed, and therefore produced. This remark, too, leads me to make another of considerable practical importance, to wit, that nothing is more common than for the government to miscalculate egregiously the amount to be yielded by a new tax, or by the augmenting of an old one, especially where the article taxed is a luxury, and not a necessary of life, with the great body of the people. By doubling the tax imposed, the public treasury, instead of receiving twice as much, is not unfrequently a loser, on account of the diminution of consumption which results. The loss, however, is often in part only apparent; since the parties who cease to consume, or who consume in less quantity than before, the article on which the tax has been augmented, will necessarily consume a greater quantity of other articles, and in all probability a greater quantity of some of those which are the subjects of taxation; and the revenue consequently, derived from these, will be larger than it was heretofore.

When taxes, again, are lowered, it sometimes occurs that the public revenue is not only undiminished, but even becomes augmented in amount; the more extended consumption of the articles on which they had been imposed, and from which they have been partially removed, more than compensating for the less amount paid by a given quantity of what is consumed, and for the loss which the treasury suffers by the contemporaneous consumption of other articles which pay taxes having undergone a diminution.

And I shall conclude the present chapter with the general remark that the changes which are consequent upon a repeal of taxes are precisely the contrary to those which ensue from the imposing of them, and that, after what has already been said concerning taxation, the reader may be safely left to trace them for himself. I proceed, accordingly, to the next topic in the natural order of discussion; that, namely, of the effects resulting from the incurring, and the paying, of a national debt.

CHAPTER XX.

OF A NATIONAL DEBT.

Men are so much the creatures of habit, that while they are often content to pay a high amount of taxation which they have from year to year continually paid, they are apt to complain loudly of every new tax which is imposed upon them, as in a peculiar degree oppressive. Hence it has been the policy of governments to add only gradually to the taxes of a country. To enable them to do so, they have sometimes had recourse to the accumulation of a treasure in a time of peace, as a provision against the exigencies of a state of war. That this provision should seldom have been found adequate for the purpose intended is not to be wondered at, when we bear in mind the warlike propensities of mankind, and the very slight pretexts which, from the earliest to the present day, have afforded occasion for national hostilities. In modern times, governments have resorted, in consequence of this, to public loans; more particularly in countries where the government, from the manner in which it is constituted, is possessed of a certain degree of credit. The facility of borrowing has however, as in the case of a surplus treasure, almost invariably led to an extravagant expenditure of the public money, and to the engaging in useless and even frivolous wars with other countries; which, in their turn, have led to the continual extension of the borrowing or *funding* system; the United States of North America furnishing a singular instance of the entire payment of a considerable national debt.

At first view, it might perhaps appear to be hardly consistent with established principles that a nation, which, instead of paying its debts, goes on for a considerable period augmenting them, and augmenting them too until they amount to a sum so enormous as to take from the most sanguine minds almost, or altogether, all hope of their ever being paid, should notwithstanding maintain its credit, and continue, whenever it has occasion for so doing, to borrow yet more on reasonable terms. Yet such has been the fact in Great Britain, and that in despite of the most sinister predictions of her enemies, as well as of the more desponding of her own people, uttered repeatedly at different stages of the progress of her debt. And why this should have been so, is not a matter of very difficult explanation. There are in every country a number of individuals who, if they were assured of the continued and punctual payment of the interest on the money loaned by them, would never be disposed to call for payment of their principal, or to complain of its being withheld from them. As the debt is, besides, made transferable from one individual to another, the national creditor needs be at no loss to realise any portion of it which he may hold, by the transfer or sale of it to some one else. The government, again, may not content itself with regularly paying the interest on the debt out of the funds generally received into the public treasury: it may pledge, for this purpose, the proceeds of certain taxes already imposed; or rather, on the contracting of any new loan, it may impose additional taxes, the proceeds of which are to be thus appropriated. It may do yet more than this. At the same time that a provision is made for paying the interest of the national debt in perpetuity, if this should be required, the means may be procured, by another addition to the taxes imposed, for gradually extinguishing the debt itself. The process of extinction, however slow, is evidently a sure one, whatever may be the amount of the debt incurred; that is, provided the government does not go on borrowing at the very time that it is paying off what it already owes, and borrowing too, as was for a series of years the case in Great Britain, to a greater amount than it paid. Notwithstanding this, the British government was able to maintain its credit, so as to borrow continually on comparatively advantageous terms, on account of the punctual payment of the interest contracted for; and of the confidence produced in the public mind, by the system of simultaneously augmenting the taxes to an amount more than adequate to meet such payment, that the country had not as yet attained to the limit of its resources, and that a national bankruptcy was therefore wholly out of the question, unless the institutions of the country should be all recklessly swept away by a revolution, in the worst sense of this term.

But I have expressed myself rather too strongly. The

circumstances just mentioned were not the only ones which enabled the government of Great Britain to maintain the public credit unimpaired. There was an illusion extènsively, and indeed universally, diffused concerning the nature and operation of the *sinking fund*, or sum annually set apart for the extinguishment of the debt, which contributed to that result. I allude to the notion that the fund in question was really operating to produce the effects for which it was created; although, more money being annually borrowed than was paid to the existing creditors, the national debt was all the time rapidly increasing. In such a state of things, the sinking fund, however nominally the product of taxation, was in truth altogether a loan; and its management consisted in the simple and very superfluous occupation of borrowing with one hand in order to pay with the other.

In what respects is a national debt an evil? In replying to to this question, there has been quite as much vague and unmeaning declamation as perhaps respecting any other point of interest in our science; and the evil is often very much exaggerated, while it is sometimes entirely misconceived, and supposed to be of a very different nature from what it is in reality. The evil will be perceived by any one of my readers, who has made himself acquainted with the principles which have been explained in the first book of this treatise, to be dependent for its amount on the degree in which the money borrowed has been unproductively expended. So far as it was necessarily or properly expended, its expenditure was a national good, and not a national loss. And the *debt*, instead of having been an evil, was a blessing; just as a debt of an individual is to be regarded in that light which is productive to him of a gain, greater in amount than the inconvenience suffered by him from the necessity of paying the interest of the money borrowed.

The circumstance, it is true, of a government being able to borrow the means of going to war on any emergency, or of engaging in any expensive undertaking, has repeatedly led to a lavish and useless expenditure of those means. In so far as this last may have taken place in any country, the debt will have been any thing but a blessing.

But to look upon the whole of a debt as indicative of an unproductive consumption of an equal value having been incurred, is an errour of no ordinary magnitude; an errour, too, not to be sustained by assuming the ground that, if what was borrowed by the government had not been expended in providing for the national defence, or for other purposes of public utility, but had been left in the possession of the people to be by them productively expended, population and wealth would have advanced more rapidly. The very same thing might, indeed, be said in reference to any other productive expenditure. For example, were the human species so constituted as to require no food for the sustaining of life, how much more rapidly would not wealth of every other description, and therefore population, admit of being augmented in a given time!

To make payment of a national debt will not remedy the expenditure unproductively of any portion of the money borrowed. If the public creditors or fund-holders reside within the country itself, such payment will be equivalent simply to a transfer of the amount of the debt from the pockets of the community in general to those of the creditors; the community, on the other hand, being relieved, in time to come, from the payment of the interest. But to possess a given portion of wealth and to pay the interest upon it, is here manifestly the same thing in reference to the country regarded as a whole, as to part with that wealth and to be relieved from paying the interest.

In the next place, let the debt be due to parties residing in foreign countries. Then if the rate of the interest to be paid be equal to the ordinary rate of the interest of money in the country itself, it is plain that the payment of the debt would amount to a sacrifice by the debtor-country of all the advantages to be derived from the possession of the wealth thus parted with, beyond the ordinary profits it is capable of yielding. I say beyond the ordinary profits it is capable of yielding; because, even though all the wealth in question be not employed as capital, a given portion of what is so employed is of no more exchangeable value, and therefore of no more advantage to the country, than is an equal portion of it that is consumed unproductively. And if the interest of the debt be *less* than the ordinary rate of interest or of profits in the country itself, as it in all probability will be when the national creditors are resident abroad, my readers will easily understand how the payment of the debt might be, to a certain extent, a public loss instead of a public gain.

But by the payment of the principal of a national debt, the community will, under any circumstances, be saved the expense of collecting the taxes which are requisite for providing for the interest; and be saved all the other inconveniences or annoyances less or more connected with the collection of those taxes. In addition to these savings, I know of no other advantages which can be derived from the paying off of a national debt, excepting only the *moral* effect of such payment in confirming the public credit, and in the impression it is adapted to produce on other nations of the magnitude of the national resources.

CONCLUSION.

In bringing the present treatise to a close, it may be proper for me to make a few remarks on some of the most important principles which I have aimed at establishing.

I shall begin with once more calling the attention of the reader to my application of the term capital as well to immaterial as to material products. Of the practicability of such an application of it, I may now assume that he can have no doubt. As to its expediency, I cannot but think that, if he will recur to the numerous discussions which occupy the preceding pages, he will perceive the analogy between material and immaterial products to be so very striking, that there is scarcely any important conclusion to which I have arrived respecting the one of these classes, which cannot be equally predicated respecting the other. To enable himself to perceive this analogy in the clearest manner, all that is necessary is for him to re-examine any portion of what I have written, and which he may consider to be vitiated in any degree by immaterial wealth having been comprehended in the definition of capital,—and while he re-examines it, to do so on the supposition of capital having a reference to matter alone. He will discover how very rarely it will be necessary to alter a single word, in order to render the language employed consistent with itself. In my opinion too, he cannot fail to look upon the generalisation of the term in question, which I have ventured to propose, as perfectly justifiable; and not merely as perfectly justifiable, but also, like every other successful generalisation in science, as in a high degree expedient.

To repeat a remark which was made by me before, the definitions of wealth and of capital should always be in *keeping* with each other. If the former have a reference only to matter, it will be proper to confine the latter likewise to matter only: if the former be made to comprehend immaterial as well as material products, so should the latter. Moreover, by adopting the more comprehensive definitions of these terms, we are enabled to rid ourselves of the distinction, so liable to a wrongful application, between productive and unproductive labour; no labour being then to be *stigmatised* as unproductive, excepting when a greater amount of it is employed in producing a commodity, than is required by the natural relation in respect to it of supply and demand. I may add that in applying the term wealth to the products of the intellect, we shall be enlarging the province of political economy, from a concern with our mere bodily wants, to the consideration of all the various circumstances which are capable of contributing to our prosperity or happiness; and be thus conferring upon it a dignity which it would be otherwise far from possessing.

In the next place, I may request of the reader to call to mind the frequent, and indeed continual use, that I have made of the theories of rent and of population, in the discussion of the most interesting practical problems which our science presents to us for solution. I hope too that, in doing this, he will agree with me in the opinion that to deny the truth of those theories, or even to give to them a secondary place among the doctrines of political economy, is to throw the science into utter confusion, and indeed to take from it all pretensions to the rank of a science.

A proper understanding, too, of the *principle* of population discloses to us the *moral relations* of political economy; relations which confer upon it a peculiar dignity, and, I do not hesitate to say, elevate it to the highest rank among the branches of human knowledge. The great truth has thus been impressed upon us in the clearest manner, that the command of the great body of every community over the necessaries and luxuries of life is determined in a much greater degree by moral than by physical causes; and that its enlargement depends, therefore, in a much greater degree on the general diffusion of education, of morals, and of religion, among the people, than upon the particular system of legislation that may be adopted by the government.

Political economy is, nevertheless, very far from leading us to conclude that the form of government or system of legislation to be adopted is a matter of only slight importance. While, on the one hand, it checks the presumption of the statesman in substituting his own views, and not seldom his own very superficial views of expediency, for the wisdom of nature, it points out to him distinctly the cases where he can interfere with things as they are with advantage to his fellow-men, and how rapidly he shall do so. Hence it is calculated, when its doctrines shall be more generally diffused than they are at present, to become the most *efficient* reformer of existing abuses; for, where every step that is taken in the progress of improvement is taken in the right direction and at the proper time, no *reactions* will have to be apprehended. Hence too, the general diffusion of the doctrines of political economy will co-operate powerfully with the necessary effect of the continually extending influence of christianity, in restraining, on the one hand, the tendencies to *revolutionary* measures, which are in our own day so widely prevalent among the more civilised nations of the earth; and inducing, on the other, a reverence for the laws, and a readier acquiescence in their dominion. Such will be the results produced on the minds alike of all classes of the community. The more privileged and wealthy classes, instead of being disposed, on the principles of an *absurd* and *rigid* conservatism, to resist, at the outset, every proposal for a reform in the existing state of things, will become anxious for reforms to be introduced, fast enough to prevent any supposed necessity or pretext for revolutionary action on the part of the multitude. And the people in general, now made aware that violent measures will often, by the reactions to which they are liable, retard the attainment by them of the objects which they have in view, will more readily consent to bear the evils of which they complain for a somewhat longer period, rather than plunge themselves, as well as every other class of the community, at once into all the miseries, or even horrors, of a revolution.

But it is not only by their tendency to operate on the minds of men in the manner which has just been described, that a diffusion of the doctrines of political economy is an object in the highest degree desirable, and that the revolutionary temper of the times can be allayed. By inculcating upon the rich and the poor that their interests, properly understood, are not in opposition to each other, as these parties, and especially the latter, are now so apt to imagine, and that to preserve the rights of property inviolate, never taking from the rich for the mere purpose of giving to the poor, is the most effectual means of permanently benefiting both, the political economist contributes effectually to remove the grounds of controversy between them, and to secure the internal tranquillity of society. And again, he contributes to secure this tranquillity, by pointing out distinctly how much of the good and of the evil, which is the lot of mankind, flows from causes wholly independent of the constitution of the government under which they live, or of the manner in which it is administered. They are led, in consequence, not to attribute *every* evil endured by them, and not readily traceable to other causes, to the misconduct of their rulers, or to that constitution of government; nor to expect any *sudden and extraordinary* advantage to result from mere political change.

And while the science of political economy is adapted to shed a kindly and a peaceful influence *at home* upon the mutual relations of the different classes of society, it is equally adapted to exercise a beneficial influence on the mutual relations of the different countries of the civilised world. It does this by putting the seal of its condemnation upon various barbarous practices, which are still tolerated by the law or the forbearance of nations; but especially by its promulgation in unequivocal terms of the great truth, that the prosperity of any one country is conducive to that of every other with which it has intercourse; and of this other great truth, that an entire and uninterrupted freedom from restrictions of every description would be the most desirable state of things, in respect to commerce, among all the nations of the earth,—a state of things in which each nation would be able to derive the fullest advantage from the advances in wealth and prosperity of every other, and in which the advantageous division of labour could be carried to the greatest extent.

Finally, I may observe that the whole spirit of political economy, like that of christianity itself, is a spirit of peace and good-will to all mankind; and if civil contentions, or foreign warfare, shall hereafter occur less frequently than they have hitherto done, or, when occurring, shall be carried on with a greater degree of respect to the rights of individuals in their persons and property, all this will be owing, next to the wider diffusion of christian principles and practice, to the more general acknowledgment of the truths of our science.

With the observations before him which have just been made in this "conclusion" of the present treatise, may the author not hope that his readers will agree with him in the opinion, that political economy is not only entitled to a place, as he has already said, in the highest rank among the various branches of human knowledge, but that it is in fact the master science of the age in which we live? And will they not therefore pronounce him to be in no wise extravagant, when he urges the study of it upon every individual in the community having leisure for the purpose, and especially upon every individual who aspires to the attainment of a liberal education?

ADDENDA.

1. In my second book, when I adduced the extensive use in Ireland of the potato as an illustration of the disadvantage of cheap food and dear luxuries, when compared with a state of things in which food was dear and luxuries cheap, I did not intend to imply that I was stating the only mode in which the use of that root by the people of Ireland has tended to deteriorate their condition. The other modes in which it has this tendency are stated by Mr. M'Culloch in the following manner. I quote from the valuable notes in his edition of the "Wealth of Nations."

"In the *first* place: owing to the impossibility, as to all practical purposes at least, of preserving potatoes, the surplus produce of a luxuriant crop cannot be stored up or reserved as a stock to meet any subsequent scarcity. The whole crop must necessarily be exhausted in a single year; so that when the inhabitants have the misfortune to be overtaken by a scarcity, its pressure cannot be alleviated, as is almost uniformly the case in corn-feeding countries, by bringing the reserves of former harvests into the market. Every year is thus left to provide sustenance for itself. When, on the one hand, the crop is luxuriant, the surplus is comparatively of little use, and is wasted unprofitably; and when, on the other hand, it is deficient, famine and disease necessarily prevail."

"In the *second* place: The general opinion seems to be, that the variations in the quantities of produce, obtained from land planted with potatoes, are decidedly greater than the variations in the quantities of produce obtained from land in which wheat or any other species of grain is raised."

"And *lastly*: Owing to the great bulk and weight of potatoes, and the difficulty of preserving them on ship-board, the expense of conveying them from one country to another is so very great, that a scarcity can never be materially relieved by importing them from abroad. In consequence, those who chiefly depend on potatoes are practically excluded from participating in the benevolent provision made by nature for equalising the variations in the harvests of particular countries by means of commerce, and are thrown almost wholly on their own resources."

"For these reasons," continues Mr. M'Culloch, "it seems as if the rapid extension of the potato cultivation was one of the most serious evils with which this and most other European countries are now threatened."

It is evident, I may add, that it is by frequently depressing for a time the condition of a people the circumstances above enumerated have a tendency *permanently* to depress their condition.

2. When treating of paper-money and banking, the reader will recollect that my language, in general, had no reference to the deposites made with the banks by individuals, and which they were at liberty to withdraw again at their discretion; and that the reason for this was the entire similarity in the nature of the business of a bank of circulation, whether it discounted the notes of individuals and issued its own notes on a capital of its own exclusively, or on an equal capital composed in part of that which was properly its own, and in part of the average amount of deposites in its possession.

The reader will also recollect that I have all along estimated the efficiency of the different component portions of the circulating medium, as well by the comparative rapidity with which they circulate, as by their quantity. Having done all this, I supposed that it was unnecessary for me to state explicitly any opinion as to whether the bank deposites were, or were not, a constituent portion of the circulating medium. Upon farther consideration, however, I have become somewhat apprehensive lest my opinion on this point should, after all, be misunderstood. Accordingly, I now state that those deposites compose, I think, as much a portion of that medium, as if they were in the *immediate* possession of their owners. Indeed, they compose a more efficient portion of it; because, while they are held by the banks, they give occasion to the discharge of debts by means of bank checks, or of transfers on the books of the banks of an entry to the credit of one individual to the credit of another; and because they furnish a basis on which a certain portion of the circulation of the banks is made to rest.

To illustrate the last remark, and at the same time to guard against any mistake being made by the reader concerning another point in respect to which I may possibly not have expressed myself with sufficient distinctness, I may mention that, on the occurrence of an extraordinary demand for specie, this will be drawn from the banks, not merely in exchange for their notes, but also by the withdrawal of the deposites made with them. The consequence will manifestly be that the banks will curtail their discounts, and diminish the amount of their paper in circulation, as well on one of these accounts as on the other; or failing to curtail sufficiently, will on both those accounts be obliged to suspend specie payments.

3. Since that part of my treatise relating to money and banking was written, a great variety of suggestions have been made for the purpose of correcting the evils of our existing

system of banking. It would be scarcely worth while for me now to go at any length into a discussion of these; and I shall content myself with a short notice of one or two among them that are of a nature to require it most.

It has been proposed that the stock of every new bank should be always sold, in the first instance, at public auction to the highest bidder; the excess of the proceeds of the sale, above the par or nominal value of the stock, to go into the treasury of the state. This would be a very convenient mode of transferring from the bankers to the public the extraordinary profits which they might otherwise receive, and of placing them on a level with all other capitalists. But, in itself, it would be evidently altogether unavailing to accomplish the great and desirable object of preventing the alternate expansions and contractions of the circulating medium, which are attributable to our American system of banking. Neither the holders of bank stock, nor the directors who are their agents, will be the less anxious to make large profits, or, which is the same thing, to receive large dividends, because they had originally to make purchase of the stock at a higher price.

The measure accordingly, which has at the same time been proposed for checking the undue expansions, and consequent contractions of their circulation, by the banks, is to limit by law the amount of their dividends, by rendering it obligatory on them, where their annual profits exceed a certain per centage on their respective capitals, to pay over the excess into the public treasury; which excess is then to be at the disposal of the legislature for any purposes to which the other portions of the money of which it disposes are applied. I have no hesitation in saying that, if we are much longer to have our present system of banking in any *form*, this would be a desirable modification of it. It is, however, not by any means free from objection.

In the first place, while the advocates for it declare themselves to be opposed to the receiving hereafter by the state of a *bonus* as the price of incorporating a bank, the state will in reality be receiving such a compensation for doing this, and in two different ways; by the excess of the price of the stock, when sold at public auction, over its par value; and by the amount which may occasionally be paid into the public treasury, in consequence of more profits having been realised by the bank than is allowed by the act incorporating it. That this last will sometimes occur, will follow from the anxiety which the directors of the banks will naturally entertain to divide as much among their constituents, the stockholders, as the law allows them to do: to extend the circulation of their notes beyond what is necessary to accomplish this object, will be looked upon by them as erring *on the safe side.* Now I may ask if there be not some danger of the reception of such a bonus as this having the effect of disturbing the regular and impartial action of the legislature, when the question shall be brought before them of the re-incorporation of a bank? Will not, quite probably, one bank have its charter renewed, and another be refused a renewal of its charter, on the ground that the one had been more liberal than the other in the tribute paid by it into the public treasury? And again, will not all this take place to an extent sufficiently great to diminish materially the advantages anticipated from the proposed restriction upon the business of banking?

But there will be an extraordinary inducement for the legislature to multiply the number of banks, in the amount to be received by the state from the sale of their stock in the manner before described. And although, as was before shewn, after a certain amount of capital has been already invested in banking, no new bank can obtain any share of the circulation excepting at the expense of that of the banks previously existing, and every incorporation of a new bank will therefore be interfering with the profits of these banks, and will be reducing them more and more below the ordinary profits upon the value which was originally paid by the stockholders, there can be no doubt of the multiplication of the banks going on until at length no bank shall be able to make more than the ordinary rate of profit upon the *par value* of its stock; when, too, no one would be disposed to invest his capital in the business of banking, rather than in any other branch of industry. At this point in the series of changes ensuing from the adoption of the measures under examination, and indeed long before it, it is plain that the restriction of the dividends or profits of the banks to a certain per centage would be wholly nugatory. I may add, what some of those who have proposed those measures are scarcely aware of, that the state of things, thus shewn to be the ultimate consequence of their adoption, is very similar to that which would take place with a free trade in banking, comprehending, under the term banking, the issuing of a paper currency. This similarity in the two cases, my readers, after all that I have delivered on the subject of banking in my third book, will be able to perceive distinctly without any farther explanation on my part.

I have said that the measures into the téndency of which I have been inquiring would be a desirable modification of our American system of banking, because they would without doubt *for a time* have the effect to alleviate the evils of the system; and not because of their being likely to lead the way to the ultimate adoption of a free trade in the business of banking. By reducing, too, the profits of the capital invested in banking to the ordinary rate of profits, they would, quite probably, abate the zeal of the holders of bank stock for the existing state of things, and prepare the way for the introduction, in place of a bank note circulation, of a circulation of treasury notes issued by the government, and constituted in some such manner as that described in the present treatise,—the only paper money which, in my opinion, combines all the advantages of bank notes, and which is at the same time not more susceptible of alternate expansions and contractions than specie itself.

THE END.